THE
LIVING LIGHT
DIALOGUE

Volume 2

THE
LIVING LIGHT
DIALOGUE

Volume 2

❧

Through the mediumship of
Richard P. Goodwin

Living Light Books

This volume of wisdom is dedicated to the principle of care, as demonstrated by the angels of the Living Light philosophy who guide us and encourage us in their humble way to serve God and the light of reason.

CONTENTS

ACKNOWLEDGMENT

Grateful acknowledgement is made to the many friends and associates for invaluable aid in compiling this book, for their helpful suggestions, for their loyal interest and encouragement.

Special acknowledgement is due to those who painstakingly and selflessly transcribed and proofread the text.

PREFACE

It was through the mediumship of the Serenity Association founder, Mr. Richard P. Goodwin, that a philosophy known as the Living Light was given in more than 700 classes over a twenty-five-year period.

To be specific, the philosophy was imparted through Mr. Goodwin by a magistrate who had lived on Earth some 8,000 years ago. The former magistrate is known to Living Light students as "the Wise One," and he narrated the journey of his soul on the other side of life, the experiences—especially the difficulties—he encountered in having to face himself, as well as the teachings he earned to help himself through the realms in which he traveled. It was his decision to share the teachings with souls on both sides of "the curtain."

Prior to the advent of the Wise One, Mr. Goodwin had prayed for a teacher from the realms of light. Mr. Goodwin, since age fourteen, had been the instrument through which spirit was able to communicate with those seeking help. But he saw that his mediumship brought only temporary solace, because the people he was trying to help soon became fascinated with the phenomena and ignored the help that spirit was imparting. He prayed for someone who would bring forth teachings that would benefit any soul seeking a path to a greater awareness of himself and of God.

His prayers were answered in 1964 when the Wise One came through for the first time. Mr. Goodwin, at first apprehensive about what this new teacher would impart, was taken into deep trance and not able to control what was being revealed through him. Upon hearing the recorded classes afterward, however, he became convinced of the goodness of the teacher and of the value of the simple, beautiful teachings he had to impart. This, then, was the beginning of the Living Light philosophy given to Earth through the mediumship of Richard P. Goodwin.

In carrying out the request of the Wise One and Mr. Goodwin, students of the Serenity Association transcribed from audiotape the classes that had been brought through. Because most are in the form of teacher-student interaction, the classes became known as *The Living Light Dialogue*; and the students were instructed to publish the classes as a multi-volume set of the Living Light philosophy. *Volume 1* was published in the autumn of 2007.

The present book, *Volume 2*, continues with two semesters of spiritual awareness classes, from CC (Consciousness Class) 22 through CC 44, covering the time period of September 6, 1973, through March 21, 1974.

These particular classes were given to a relatively large group of students who were organized into small circles and sat facing one another. Classes began with one student reading a discourse from *The Living Light*, the first book of teachings published by Mr. Goodwin and Serenity in 1972 and often referred to as "the textbook." After the reading, the class spoke in unison the "Total Consideration" affirmation (located in the appendix), which was followed by a short meditation period on peace. Then the class began.

The foundation of the classes—the foundation of the Living Light philosophy itself—is the Law of Personal Responsibility which states, in part, that we are responsible for all our experiences, and that our experiences are the return of the laws that we have established with our thoughts, acts, and deeds. Through greater awareness of our thoughts and by exercising our divine right of choice, we may choose to establish laws of greater harmony and goodness.

The Living Light Dialogue teaches that we have come to Earth to learn the lessons that are necessary to free us from the dictates and limits of our own thoughts and judgments, the mental patterns that we follow through our own lack of awareness and are so very potent, forceful, and limiting. This book guides us in making the necessary changes in our thinking in order to free ourselves from those patterns and to express our soul consciousness.

The choice of guiding the direction of our life, as stated by the Wise One when he speaks of being with a person, place, or thing, is, in essence, of being in this world and not a part of this world. He further explains that no matter what experiences we encounter, no matter what we do or do not do, we—our spirit—may view the experience in objectivity from a soul level of consciousness where peace reigns supreme.

The teachings of this volume help us to restore harmony or balance in our life by flooding the consciousness with spiritual affirmations and prayers, which can be found in the appendix. When reason is restored, by balancing our sense functions with our soul faculties, we will consciously experience peace. Without annihilating our ego or our sense functions, we will find a pathway of expression for our soul. Where there was once disturbance, now there is acceptance. Where there was disease, now there is poise. And where there was hopelessness and despair, now there is reason, divine neutrality; and peace shows the way.

If you make the effort to apply these laws, such as, "If man is a law unto himself, what are you doing with the law that you are?", and demonstrate the wisdom of patience, the truth of this philosophy will be your living demonstration.

As the Teacher states in CC 130, "My journey of many centuries and much experience has brought me here to Earth to share with you these simple teachings that have come as the effect of a long, long, long journey. Let not *your* journey be so long in the realms of illusion. For it is not necessary for you. For in your evolution, you have earned an awakening. But it is up to you to do something that is constructive and worthwhile."

CONSCIOUSNESS CLASSES

Now we have come to our time for our questions and answers. And those who have questions concerning the teachings of the discourse that was just read [Discourse 40] or anything of a spiritual nature, kindly feel free to raise your hand. When called upon, kindly rise to speak forth your question. We'll try to get to the first question from each one first and, time permitting, we'll go on to other questions that you may have. So you may feel free at this time to raise your hand. Yes.

It has been stated in our text, "As a Light can never shine without its so-called opposite of darkness [Discourse 40]." This so-called opposite of darkness, is that the destructive nature within ourselves? Can we deal with this destructive nature in a meaningful way, since it does seem to create chaos and yet it's a very inherent part of ourselves? Is it also our subconscious self?

Thank you very much. In answer to your question, Is the statement the so-called opposite or darkness, which is a lesser light, the destructive, and if it is destructive, how best may one cope with it—is that basically your question?

Yes!

And is it the animal nature or part of the subconscious within oneself? Of course, we realize that nothing that is under the guiding hand and discipline of the soul faculty of reason is, in truth, destructive. It is the imbalance of any particular vibration, a vibration that is out of control of the soul faculty of reason, that becomes what we call destructive. For example, arsenic taken in a certain dosage is not detrimental to a person's life; in other words, they're not going to pass out of the physical form from a minute dosage. And so it is in reference to what is destructive. Now, some people may think in a certain level of awareness that the limitations that are placed upon us today by society are destructive to the free expression of one's feeling and one's thought. However, without those controls and disciplines the society, as it is, could not long exist. And so it is that which seems to be destructive is simply not under the control and the discipline of reason. Does that help with your question?

Yes, it does. Thank you.

Thank you. Someone else have a question?

There was a reference to speaking out the sound, and I thought of prayer. Is it necessary to speak a prayer aloud or is thought sufficient or does it need the physical sound?

Yes, that's a very good question on prayer. Is it necessary to give prayer the spoken word, the life-giving energy of the spoken word, or is it sufficient to just give it the thought? Well, now, that is a very individual thing in the sense that many people are able to pray simply in thought because they put their heart into their prayer and they put their feelings into their prayer. Now, as is stated in *The Living Light*, the original sense is the sense of feeling, the sense of touch. And when you put feeling into something, you put your heart into it, you put your soul into it, so to speak. It is not necessary, to my understanding and experience, in order to be receptive to the Intelligence that answers what we call prayer, to give it the life-giving energy of the spoken word. What is necessary is that we give it our heart and our soul, because those are the levels that touch the Divine Intelligence. It's when we put ourselves into it and we demonstrate the faith that it is already accomplished.

Now, so many people think that their experiences are circumstances and conditions outside of themselves; this is entirely contradictory to the demonstrable teachings and science of Spirituality. All experiences are the direct effect of energy directed by the individual through the vehicle of thought. One of the many purposes of these classes is to awaken us so that we not only will realize and will not only recognize, but we will become the living demonstration of the control, through discipline of our thought; because thought is the vehicle through which the Divine energy expresses itself.

Whatever you give thought to in your mind, you give power over you. If something disturbs you, that disturbance is controlling you and you're experiencing a lack of peace. And so it is with prayer. When a person prays to whatever they care to call the Divine Intelligence—they call it God; it has many names— when a person truly prays, that is a soul aspiration, that is a communion direct with the Divine Intelligence. When they do that, they don't ask for things, they don't ask for peace: they become the thing itself. So remember, we cannot experience what we do not entertain in thought. We cannot experience what we do not become, and what we become is through the vehicle of thought.

In the third paragraph, there is a statement, "We are working each day in every way to remove from your lives the obstacles on the path. Be not concerned and misunderstand the removal of them for they have become attachments [Discourse 40]." Isn't this judgmental?

I wouldn't say so. Read the paragraph again. "We are working every day in every way . . ."

"To remove from your lives the obstacles on the path."

What is it that you interpret is working?

What is—I'm sorry. I didn't hear.

What is it that you interpret is working every day in every way to remove the obstacles from your path?

I don't know.

The Divine Spirit within oneself.

I see. So the "we" is really collective. Thank you.

The Spirit within us is constantly at work to remove the obstacles and the obstructions from our path, which, of course, become our attachments. Now, a person may say, and usually does, "Well, this is a very distasteful experience to me. What do you mean that I'm attached to it?" Well, the attachment is a living demonstration. That that entertains our thought— you understand?—reveals our attachment. If we are entertained in thought, constantly, with a certain obstruction, then we must accept the demonstrable truth that we are attached to that obstruction or we would not continue to entertain it in thought.

It's like the person that says, "It's so difficult for me because I don't understand." And they continue to say, "I don't understand." Well, as long as we entertain in thought that we don't understand something, we direct the Divine Intelligence to the obstruction and we will never understand it. So the simple thing is to direct the energy through the mind, the mental body, to what you want to become, to what you want to attain and never waiver from the direction. Now, what does it take to keep one's thought single, to keep one's eye single? What does it take, when all around and about us, creation is revealing to our mind the opposite? It simply takes, my good friends, a little bit of faith. Yes.

That's very confusing to me. Where I get confused is that I don't know whether I'm willing myself in a certain direction. Sometimes I find that where I think I need to go in a single-eyed way, is not where I really need to go.

Yes.

I get confused in that.

That's most understandable, my good friend, because consciously we think we're willing ourselves to go in a certain direction—that is your basic statement, is it?

Yes.

And then there is a confusion within because we feel we should be going in a different direction, is that not correct? That is known as what they call dual decision or indecision. That is, the conscious mind is willing and trying to direct us along a certain path and the subconscious mind keeps impressing us to go on an opposite path. Is that what you're referring to? Yes. Now, as the good Bible has spoken, Man, know thyself and ye shall know the truth and the truth shall set you free. We cannot expect, of course, to know ourselves unless we're willing to make the effort. We can't know truth and we can't be free, until we know the minds that our soul is expressing through, would you not agree? So the thing is to become aware of this other self, the so-called subconscious mind, this magnetic field that attracts all experiences into our life. And when we become aware of what it's truly doing to us, then we will be able to retape it, to reprogram it, and experience the true joy and wonder of life herself. Does that help with your question?

Yes, thank you.

It's a matter of becoming aware of oneself. Now, how does one become aware of oneself unless one makes the effort constantly to know what thoughts one is entertaining? So that's the first step.

In Discourse 40 of The Living Light, *it states, "Continue on with the raising of your vibrations."*

Yes.

I'm not sure I understand what that means.

All right. Well, I'll be happy to share my understanding with you. In the statement, "Continue on with the raising of your vibrations," we understand that thoughts in the mind constitute our basic attitude; that our attitude of mind is our rate of vibration. And in the statement that you just read, "Continue on with the raising of your vibrations," it is basically saying continue on with your efforts to entertain thoughts of good.

You see, he who sees the good can only experience the good. Now a person, of course, will say, "Well, I think good all the time and yet I see all these things happening in the world." Well, the moment that we see them happening, we have lowered our state of consciousness (our level of awareness) to where we can see that that is the opposite, or bad, you see. Now, if there are experiences outside of us that are distasteful, we change the level of awareness within ourselves. Now, that we have power over. We can do that. And when we do that and we have that faith, we reach a point, in time, and usually very soon, when those experiences start to change. Because what has happened to most of us in this lifetime is we've given away—we've sold—our soul. We've sold our soul to things and to circumstances and to the world at large and to conditions, when we, in truth, have the right to be the master of our ship and the captain of our destiny. So we are trying, in our way, to share with you the many paths that lead to the freedom of the soul's expression here and now.

In this day and age and with the things that are happening around us, how can we learn to improve on disassociation so that we won't get ourselves emotionally involved? You know what I mean?

Yes. It takes constant effort. It takes constant effort. When we stop and we think, how frequently we are brainwashed in the world—we read the newspaper, we read the magazines, we listen to the radio, to the television, and there's a constant emanation of negative vibrations going out into the world. But we have a power within us that is greater than those emanations and those vibrations. It's up to us to reach a decision within ourselves to say, "That has no power over me." See, nothing can have power over us—and I do mean nothing—unless *we* give power to it in our mind. All experiences, my good friends, take place within the mind. The mind says, "Well, it's taking place in New York or London or someplace else," you understand. No, the experience takes place within our own aura, within our own mental body. Now we have the power to control that mind, or mental body, in which our soul is expressing, but if we choose to give that power to another human being or something outside of ourselves, that, too, of course, is our right. It takes spiritual discipline to be free while yet in form.

You just mentioned spiritual discipline, which brings up the thought, to me, of concentration and meditation. When we concentrate on peace, do we give our peace out to wherever a person might be who is not peaceful? Does that spoken word go out into the universe and help? When we become quiet in meditation, does that magnetic force come back to us and make us peaceful? I mean, can we do selfless service by willing this peace to go out into the universe?

No! No. That is one of the seeming failings of many teachings dealing with spirituality. If you want to share the divine peace that you experience with another human soul, you use the process of concentration and visualization and release. Number one, you become that peace that you wish to share. I mean, after all, a person wouldn't want to share something with someone that they had not, in and of themselves, proven to themselves. So you become that peace that passeth all understanding. And when you become that, you visualize the person you wish to share that peace with. You visualize them in the perfection and the peace that you yourself are experiencing at the moment of concentration.

Now the hardest step, it appears to be for many, is to release the image that they have garnered up within. The moment that you release it, and we call it the RTD—you release it to the Divine—that created image of perfection and peace that you have within your aura, you release it to the Divine Intelligence. Now, that image reaches its kind; it finds that person. It reaches it by this Divine Intelligence. It superimposes upon their mental body, if they are receptive to it. The laws are not mocked. If they are receptive to it, then they will experience that great peace that comes, of course, from God. We are only the channels through which it is expressing itself. And so it is when you send your mind out, you know, like, "Mary Jane is in peace and perfect health," etc., you're working on a mental level; you're working on a thought realm and that is not going to be sustained. If you work on a spiritual, soul level when you go into your peace, then you may share with whom you choose to share. Now, if the person that—you have released this to the Divine in so-and-so's name—if they are not receptive to that vibratory wave, that will return unto you. Yes, in that way. You see, he who helps another, in truth, has helped himself.

I would like you to explain to me about intuition compared with premonition. And I got the feeling in reading this discourse that we have to feel in order to have intuition. How do we explain suddenly having an intuition about something without having felt about it prior to that?

Yes, thank you very much. The question is in reference to intuition and premonition and how does a person have intuition, when it is not preceded by feeling. The truth of the matter is that it is preceded by feeling, though we may not be consciously aware of the feeling at the time. Now I'm sure you all realize, or many of you realize, that there are eighty-one levels of awareness. There are eighty-one states of consciousness right here and now inside of us. We are expressing on these various levels of awareness and sometimes, of course, we are on the same level as another human soul, or many human souls, and we can feel certain things. Now, intuition is preceded by a feeling, though we may not be consciously aware of the feeling at the moment we're having the intuition.

Premonition is something on an entirely different level. A person has a premonition that a certain disaster is going to take place. That may or may not be coming from a psychic level of awareness. It may be coming from a mental and emotional level of awareness. For example, I think it was a year or two ago there was so much thought and premonitions and predictions and prophecies, so-called, concerning the San Francisco earthquake, which did not take place. All right, now what happens is this: a person gets a little publicity concerning a certain premonition—and it's usually one of disaster. That excites the emotions of people. And then, sensitive people start picking that up. That doesn't mean that that's going to come to pass. It does mean that they are on a level of awareness which is receptive to that particular vibration or thought force going out into the atmosphere.

Now intuition comes from within the soul itself. A person has an intuition—an inner knowing, that's what it *really* is. And when you have that inner knowing, that intuition, regardless of what anyone tells you, you will stick to that inner knowing because it just permeates your whole being. You know regardless of what your senses are dictating. You know regardless of what your eyes see. You know regardless of what your ears hear. You know! That inner knowing is your spirit impressing your soul and, consequently, that feeling comes to the fore, sometimes with a thought, but not always. Does that help with your question?

Yes. Thank you.

Yes.

I believe you just stated that we have this feeling or this sense that we may not be consciously aware of at the time. And I believe it also states in the discourse, we understand that this original sense or feeling and awareness or intuition are one and the same. Could you explain a bit about the difference between awareness in principle and conscious awareness?

I will be happy to share with you our understanding. And the question is, What is the difference between conscious awareness and the principle of feeling or intuition? Is that your basic question?

Well, it states in the discourse that awareness is the same as feeling or intuition.

It is. And you want to know the difference between that awareness and conscious awareness?

Yes.

All right. Now conscious awareness—for example, we are consciously aware of sitting in this particular log cabin at this time with so many people around and about us. We are consciously aware of that. We are, within our being, intuitively aware and can feel many other dimensions. The simple difference is that we have not trained ourselves, yet, to become consciously aware of these other levels of awareness or these other dimensions.

Now many people are sitting here this evening and especially during—and I'm going to give this for an example—during the meditation time. I happen to know because I saw different people from the worlds of spirit and I happen to know that some of the people present in this classroom knew beyond a shadow of any doubt that those people were with them. Now, they knew that. They knew that not with their conscious awareness. They knew it with another type of awareness: their intuitive knowing, which sifted through to their conscious mind. When man practices daily meditation and spiritual discipline, he will become more aware of his intuition, more aware of the awareness of his spiritual knowing and feeling. The basic difference is that man has yet to train his conscious mind. That's the basic difference.

I have two questions. One is that you mentioned there are eighty-one levels of consciousness. And I'd like to know more about that.

The eighty-one levels of consciousness? You want to know more about—

May I say my second question, also, at the same time?

Yes, certainly. You go right ahead.

The other one is you keep mentioning the term "spiritual discipline." And I would like to know more about what you mean by that.

I'll be more than happy to share with you my understanding of those two questions and we'll begin with the last one, which is on spiritual discipline. By "spiritual discipline," I mean a daily effort of organization: to organize and to supervise one's own inner being to a set time, every day, seven days a week, year in and year out, of silence and meditation. Also, to make the constant effort to become consciously aware of where our thoughts are coming from.

Most of us are controlled, and our whole lives are guided, as I said earlier, by influences and we are not aware of their true source. For example, on many of the eighty-one levels of conscious awareness we are receptive to thoughts of other people in the flesh and out of the flesh. Now, when a person makes the effort daily to ask themselves the question, "From whence cometh this thought?"—for not all thoughts originate within the human being. If a person is receptive to a certain level, then they're receptive to certain thoughts that are passing through the atmosphere. For example, you might be in your day-to-day activities in your work and, all of a sudden, you get a feeling that you want to do this or you want to do that. That may be your intuition; ofttimes it is not. You have become receptive to the desires of another human being. This is what we're talking about: to become aware of the source of one's thoughts, because those are the things that are guiding and controlling one's life. That's the discipline of which we are speaking.

Now in reference to the eighty-one levels of awareness, we all here are aware of our conscious mind at this moment. A few of us, perhaps, are aware of our subconscious mind at this moment. And perhaps even a lesser amount are aware of our superconscious, which is the path to our Divine Spirit within ourselves. Now, to start off with the levels with which we are familiar—this is what the course starts off with. It starts off with the mind: how the thoughts work; how to control one's thoughts; how to reprogram one's subconscious. For example, imagine you're walking down the street. Perhaps you're passing by a store and you see a red dress in the window. Now consciously you're aware of seeing the red dress, but you're not aware of the Law of Association that has been set into motion. If ten years ago you had a certain experience that was distasteful to you with a person in a red dress, the subconscious mind starts to play that tape. We are trying to help the students to become aware of what really takes place, because the moment the tapes of the subconscious start playing in a particular level, our life starts going through those experiences.

The moment of which we are conscious is our only eternity. When we entertain thoughts that are of yesterday, we come under the influence and the control of those particular tapes or recordings that are in our memory par excellence and in our own subconscious. This is the only moment that is our eternity, that is, the conscious moment. So this is the moment that we work with. That does not mean that we never give thought to a person who has crossed the veil or to an experience of the past, but in giving thought to it we become objective. In other words, we do not become emotionally involved, because if we become emotionally involved with an experience that has already passed, then we become controlled by it. Do you understand?

So spiritual discipline is a conscious effort and a constant effort of becoming aware of oneself. You see, there's a simple statement that says, "Life is ever as we make it and she's just the way we take it." So let us become aware of how to make it, you see. Now, say that a person wants to be a doctor or wants to be a lawyer or whatever they want to be and they're having a great struggle in becoming what they desire to be. Why is that individual having such a great struggle? They've got to become aware of all patterns connected with what they want to be, because those patterns are controlling their life. And that's what we want to help all of you with: to get through an understanding of the mental world, so that you can move on here and now to the spiritual world, where you can be free from what the youth of today call hang-ups. Does that help with your question?

Yes. Thank you.

You're welcome. Yes.

This is a six-part question on healing. I had asked something previously, but I wonder if we might have a little more technical discussion. Is the healing energy exactly the same as the prana *or is it different? And would you follow the circuit of the energy in the healer's body to what actually happens when it reaches the aura of the person that he is working with? And how do the spirit doctors, then, make use of this healing energy emanated by the healer? Do they direct it to the vital body or what do they actually do with that? I assume that they are channels, but simply on a higher level than we are. And how is the faculty of faith really used by the healer? It's a thought-directed energy, but what part does it play in this?*

Thank you very much. I'll take your question, point by point, in reference to spiritual healing and are the healing energies also known as prana? Well, what they call the prana is the intelligent energy flowing through all forms, whether it is a tree or a dog or a human being. And that *is* the healing energy. It *is* the energy. Now in reference to healing, this energy is concentrated by the healer and it is also concentrated by their guides and helpers and doctors from the world of spirit. And it enters the vital body through what is commonly referred to as the pineal gland. Now, these healing energies—some people seem to be more receptive to spiritual healing than other people. Then, some days, a person is receptive to healing, spiritual healing, and the next day, they're really not.

Now, what does faith, the faculty of faith—which is faith, poise, and humility—have to do with spiritual healing, especially on the part of the spiritual healer? Well, my good friends, if the spiritual healer or the person who is attempting to be a channel for God's work to be accomplished, if that person does not have the faith within themselves that they are receptive to the divine healing energies, then they will have an obstruction to the healing power, because they will be entertaining thoughts of limitation—do you understand?—within themselves. And therefore, it will be more difficult to direct the healing energies into the recipient.

Now, everyone and everything in form has what is known as prana or the Divine Light or energy, which is the healing power. What happens is simply this: in our mental bodies we become disturbed, and when we become disturbed we dissipate this energy. And when this happens—this is why we ask in our church services to kindly remove thoughts of a controversial nature. That doesn't mean don't be a skeptic, because one should be skeptical of things that one has not proven to oneself, you understand. But to be receptive, to be at peace within oneself, because so-called poor health simply is disease or discord.

Now there's much talk nowadays, for example, about cancer and the use of meditation in healing of cancer, etc. Well, everybody knows that we all have what they call cancerous cells in our body. It isn't something, you know, that flew in from Asia. We all have it. The thing is that the so-called good cells, or the opposite ones, have been winning the battle and we don't experience what they call that particular disease. Now, fortunately, according to *Psychic Magazine*'s article here this month, a doctor at Travis Air Force Base has been very successful in the healing of cancer through proper meditation and visualization. And he's had his patients literally visualize the cancerous cells, visualize the good ones winning the battle and has had excellent results. Well, it simply goes to prove, my good friends, that the physical body is merely an effect of the inner mind; not your conscious mind, but your subconscious. Now, if your subconscious is peaceful, then there is a harmonious flow of this energy throughout your entire body.

Now we all know, or many of us know, that each part of the body emanates a certain color according to the organ which is emanating it. When it is healthy, it emanates a certain brilliance that it doesn't when it is not healthy. Well, what the difference is in the density of the light is very simple: there's less energy going to that particular part of the body and we call that disease or discord. But, my good friends, it is all in the mind, and the body reacts or is the effect of it.

Now I'm not saying that a person says, "Oh, I'm thinking that I'm going to have cancer and cancer I have." I'm not talking about that. I'm saying simply this: that when peace reigns supreme within your conscious and your subconscious being, you will express what is known as perfect health. Now, the subconscious is a very delicate mechanism and it's been studied by many great men and continues to be studied. If a person has a certain condition and that condition brings them attention, which their mind decides that they need, then you may be rest assured whenever the person has what they think is a need for attention, that so-called disease or disturbance will express itself. But that is something that's been set into motion in the inner mind. That's the great importance of knowing about our mind and how it truly works.

Now, most people who come to a healing service have spent some time and a great deal of energy directed to the condition that they think that they have. One of the first jobs of the healer and the counselor is to get the individual to direct that thought, which is their energy, to something else. It doesn't matter if it's playing cards or going to the races. Just get the energy directed someplace else and give the Divine Intelligence an opportunity to help bring balance into the person's universe, you see.

Man who sees the obstruction can never see the way. So when something bothers you, don't put your attention upon it, and before you know it, through the principle of to ignore, it will disappear from your universe. You see, the subconscious is the great magnet: it just pulls things magnetically right into our lives. It's not an easy thing to say to oneself, "I am where I am because I am who I am." You understand? But when man decides to say that to himself, he will start on the path of freedom and he will really know himself. And when we know ourselves, we know the universes. Does that help with your question?

Yes, it does. May I ask about animals?

Yes, certainly.

Do these same principles hold true: that their subconscious mind is not at peace or out of balance?

Absolutely and positively. And it holds true with the tree and the plant and all of form. You see, my friends, there is an Intelligence in all form—it doesn't matter whether it's the rock or human being. The Divine Intelligence is only limited by the form through which the Divine Intelligence is expressing at any given moment. The Divine Intelligence that causes us to think—you understand?—causes the dog to walk. It is identically the same Intelligence. There are not two gods. There is one God. And the Intelligence that garners up the various atoms, electrons, and molecules and makes a form, a rock, or a plant, it's the same Intelligence in the human being. There is no difference. There is no difference between ant and angel. The seeming difference is in our thought. Thank you.

In the very first part of Discourse 40, we read about the Law of Responsibility. And I would like to know, if possible, who are we responsible to? I mean, responsible to whom and to what? Thank you.

Thank you. In reference to the question, To whom or what are we responsible? Man is responsible unto himself, the true self: the Divine Spirit that is expressing through this form. Now, some people call that God. Well, we're responsible for this particular incarnation. We're responsible for being here. You see, friends, we didn't come here by chance, I mean, to

Earth. We came here along the evolutionary path of the soul's incarnation through form and forms unlimited. This is not the first time that the Divine Intelligence has expressed itself and, of course, it's not going to be the last time. For if God is God, then God has always been. And having always been, of course, God will always be. And so it is that the soul expresses through the form that it has merited on its evolutionary path of incarnation.

In other words, some souls come into poverty, some come into wealth, some come into perfect health, etc. Well, that is what the soul and its multitude of experiences through incarnation, of course, has merited. And we are responsible to that Spirit and to that soul, which is our true self. First, we are responsible to that Spirit, or God within us. Then, of course, we're responsible to the children we have created; and by that, I mean all of the circumstances and conditions we brought into our life. We are, then, responsible to that. I don't mean just the human children we may have given birth to.

In the answer to the preceding question, you said something that I've been struggling with for a long time. I don't understand about turning loose of—or how you turn loose of something that's bothering you.

Yes.

So it will dissipate.

That is correct.

What I've learned in my work with people is that, say, in their childhood they experience some difficulty that has set up a pattern in their lives so that when they grow into adulthood they behave in a certain way without even realizing it.

That is true, yes.

When they go to bring it to awareness, there's a tremendous amount of emotion that's tied up with it.

Most understandable.

*As I am understanding you, if you bring people to pay atten-
tion to it, to begin to become aware, then they can just turn loose
of the emotion. But my experience is that people have to go through
the emotion and experience it. And I'm puzzled about that.*

Yes, I can understand. Now are you talking in reference to
psychology as it's practiced today and psychiatry? Because that
is usually the system that psychiatry, at the present time, is
using.

I'm actually talking about my own work with people.

Yes.

And I don't practice in a traditional, analytical model.

I see. Well, now, what happens is simply this: we all recognize and realize that we have various tapes or experiences in the
depths of our inner mind or our subconscious, right?

Yes.

All right. Now, to place thought, which is energy, upon them,
to go through the various emotional traumas that are connected
with them, does not dissipate them. What it does do is it simply brings it to conscious awareness: that the conscious mind
becomes aware that that tape exists in the tape banks.

We teach, in Serenity, a better way. It is not necessary, you
understand, to review every single tape that is in the computer
of the subconscious. There is a way of programming new tapes
for new experiences, do you understand? Now, whatever man
places his attention upon—and thought is attention—he has
a tendency to become. So of what benefit is it to man to constantly review certain programs of the past that have caused
him a traumatic emotional disturbance? It simply brings it to
the conscious awareness so he can thrash it out and what he
says then is, "Well, that no longer has any power over me," so he
programs a new tape. Why not start this moment and program
new tapes? Does that help with your question?

Now, how does that work with a little child? Well, it works
very simply with a little child. If you take a little child and

whenever they meet a certain person, they have an emotional traumatic experience, would you agree? That happens with some children.

Some children, yes.

All right, fine. Now, which is the wisest way to handle that particular child in that situation: to talk to the child, to hash it over, to keep his attention upon that trauma, upon that emotionalism, or to introduce a new tape bank at the time he's meeting that person? Perhaps when he meets that person you give him an ice cream cone, so through the Law of Association he starts to play a new tape out of the subconscious. Isn't that a much better and simpler way?

Same thing, you know, works with a dog. Very same thing. Or with animals. All of God's creation. It works so simply. It really and truly does. But we've got to make the effort to work at it, you see.

Now, what happens in meditation, as we go through our concentration and meditation—it is true, some philosophies say that they go through a process of ventilating. And they call it all types of names, you know. Well, what it is, my friends, we're trying to get to our spirit and it's so cluttered with all those different tapes that we sometimes find it difficult. But we don't entertain the thought of difficulty. We sail serene right straight through it, because we make the effort and we direct our will, you see?

Now some people can say, "Well, you know, it's nice to say it's a beautiful world, when it isn't." Well, see, they don't yet have that new tape "It's a beautiful world" fully programmed, that's all. Now we can say it's a beautiful world and if we keep saying that and feeling that and thinking it, well, that's all we experience anymore. Do you understand?

Yes.

Now, the truth of the situation is—look at the world, and just take a look at ourselves. It's known as the robotical level, the robotical vibration. We are robots and we are programmed certain ways. So if we're governed by all this programming, let's choose the tapes we want to play. Wouldn't that be the wisest thing?

I'd like it. I'd prefer it.

Yes. I do myself, I know. So it's just a matter of making that effort, you see. Now, take maybe five or ten people, and if you can get them to think what the world calls positive—but you have to *feel* it, you understand, and you can really *feel* that way—see, that's a magnetic field and like attracts like and becomes the Law of Attachment. So if you can really get them to feel that way and to think that way, that's the only thing that they can attract out of the universe. They can't attract anything else, because like attracts like. A man who is great is one who not only thinks great, but feels great: that's a great man. Not one who says they are or just thinks they are, but one who truly feels that greatness. Because that greatness is the greatness of God, of the Divine Intelligence inside our soul, which is in our heart.

In order to increase your powers of concentration, of sense, of touch, etc., can you tell me the proper way of meditating in order to accomplish this?

Yes, I'll be happy to share with you the understanding we have for our classes for our students. It's a very simple process; not to exceed twenty minutes in any given day. Our students usually meditate in the morning hours, the first thing they do. Most people get up in the morning and the first thing they do is brush their teeth. Well, I always have tried to feel in my heart that God is more important than my teeth and so I try to put my meditation first. But, of course, that's up to the individual. So when they get up in the morning, they sit in a straight chair and try to keep the spine erect, but comfortable—because this energy comes up from the base of the spine and up through the spinal column, and when it finally gets to the forehead here and activates the pineal gland, then that opens what is commonly referred to as clairvoyance.

Now, the first five minutes should be dedicated to concentration. And we teach a concentration upon peace. And when one is truly concentrated on peace, they're no longer thinking the word *peace*. They don't see a quiet lake anymore. They've gone beyond that level. They become the peace itself; they actually become that peace. Then, after they have become that peace, they meditate for about five minutes and that means that the mind is a total blank, you see. Just totally blank. After that five minutes of meditation, they spend about ten minutes of contemplation or manifestation and experience, yes.

You see, friends, all that we could possibly desire, we have already been given. But we have to become consciously aware of that in our own mind; then we will experience it. See, there's nothing outside of us that can bring us joy. Everything, every blessing, every goodness that we could possibly experience is waiting for us to rise to the level of awareness where it exists, you see. Why chase the rainbow up there, when the rainbow's in here, you see? That's where it is: it's in our hearts.

I was waiting for you to make a reference to that energy that goes up the spine, commonly known as kundalini.

Yes?

Do you teach management of that very strong force?

I most certainly do not, for the simple reason that it is not recommended to place the attention upon it. You see, there are many books that have been written on the kundalini. There are many books that have been written on how to raise it, etc. I have found—I am aware of how it works—but I have found in my years of experience that one should not place the mental energies upon what is known as the kundalini.

If one's thoughts are on God, on peace, and one is making an effort to apply the laws that govern the universe, this universe, then one need not have fear of these experiences involved in the rising of the kundalini.

Now, as I said, there are many books written upon the subject and for some people it becomes uncontrollable, or, at least, they think that it does. Now, you stop and think. When this energy rises, it's going to express through the level that a person has gravitated to in their consciousness. No higher and no lower. Consequently, if a person has a little hostility within—and we all do on a certain level, you understand—but that's the level that that person is on, that hostility becomes magnified a thousand times a thousand. That is not the thing to concentrate upon. It is not the thing to be concerned about, because, "Seek ye first the kingdom of heaven and all these things I shall add unto you." All of the clairvoyance or the psychic or clairaudience or com-munication, all of those things of the kingdom will be added unto us, if we first seek the kingdom itself. So the thing that we look for and the thing that we strive for is the peace that passeth all understanding. Then those things will fall into place.

Is it not true, in a technical sense, that the kundalini must rise to the pineal gland or to the seventh chakra?

At least to some degree of it.

Right. In order to transcend. But I have found this energy, basically, in its initial stages, a lot like the electrical current that comes in this building. It is raw, brute current and over a period of time it must be refined, like a radio refines energy when it comes into accord.

That's refined through the purity of one's heart.

Right.

Through working on one's own thoughts, yes.

And, like you said, for every thought you have, good or bad, it magnifies it a thousand times.

Indeed, it does.

I was meditating two hours a day, working with this kunda-lini. Some days I could take care of it and some days it took care of me.

Yes, that is one of the many reasons that we do not recommend a meditation period to exceed twenty minutes in any twenty-four hours, you see. Twenty minutes is more than long enough for any soul. Because, what happens, they come under the control of these influences which they are not yet familiar with and then, you know, it's like turning on the water faucet. They can't turn it off, you see. Now, once the energies have risen to a certain level, you understand, they will always rise to that level, until one makes a great effort to purify their thoughts by purifying their own heart.

Would you discuss confidence, self-confidence, and overconfidence and how this relates to faith?

Yes, in reference to self-confidence, overconfidence, and how it relates to faith: Well, if one is expressing true self-confidence, then they are expressing the confidence of the Divine within themselves. In other words, they're on a level of awareness of humility. There is a humbleness that they are aware of in their confidence, do you understand? That humbleness is a recognition that they are not the doer: it is the Divine that moves them. That is a self-confidence. That is a faith that never fails.

Now, when man experiences what he calls overconfidence, that is when that same type of thinking enters what is known as the ego, or the brain. Then man denies the source of what's happening and he says, "Lord, look at what I have done." That's when he starts on the pathway down because—why does he start on the path down? Because he has denied his own Divinity, the Divinity being the God within us that does the work. You see, we're just the vehicle that gets moved. Now we do have a choice and we think, "I'll move north" or "I'll move south," but we're not the mover. We're the moved, you see. That's the difference between my understanding of self-confidence and overconfidence.

We have had quite a bit of discussion tonight on directing one's attention: directing your attention to the obstruction, directing your attention to the kundalini, directing your attention in general. It would seem that most of the time when we direct our attention, we usually end up building an obstruction, rather than achieving what, perhaps, we may be consciously setting out to do.

It depends from what level we are directing the attention.

I know that releasing it to the Divine, the RTD, does work because I've had it demonstrated to me. Is there a way that we may guide this attention constructively, so that in directing attention we can become more consciously aware as we're building these obstructions or as we're building avenues to what we truly wish to achieve?

Yes, thank you very much. In the directing of the energies, if one will be consciously aware in their directing of the energies and they're making the effort not to be concerned to any extent with the effect of the directed energy—now, for example, it is one thing to direct some energy and to say, "Now I release it to the Divine." That's fine, if one truly does that. Then, there is another thing: that one does what they feel is right. Now what happens is this: a person takes great effort in directing energy to do what they feel in their being is right. All right. Now, if they're doing what they really feel is right and that's from their own soul level, they have no concern about what's going to come out of that directed energy. Do you understand? They have no feeling whatsoever. They're doing it because they feel in their heart that it's right for them to do it. They're not concerned whether it works this way or that way, whether it's going to happen tomorrow or it's going to happen next year. Do you understand? Now when they do it that way, what they really do is, they become receptive, to the degree that they are able to do that, to an Infinite Intelligence that goes to work and it brings about, according to the laws that man has set into motion, what is right for them.

Now ofttimes what is right for us is not what we're willing to accept when it appears, you know. That's the problem. It may be right for—you know, it's just like here. We just started a twelve-week course again. From one of my levels I could say, "Whoops, twelve more Thursdays." You know, and maybe be happy or not happy. That's a ridiculous type of thinking. The truth of the whole matter is, if we are doing what's right, we're not concerned whether or not the effect is coming tomorrow or next week. And we're not concerned what kind of an effect it's going to be and, consequently, we are not controlled any longer by the effects. In other words, our emotional body, our mental body remains in balance and we're free. We are truly free. We're free in thought and we're free in life itself.

But that is a matter of retraining the mind, because the mind steps in the way and it says, "Well, 2 and 2 makes 4." Well, 2 and 2 makes 4 to the one who believes it makes 4, and that's all it makes 4 to! It doesn't make 4 to the person who believes that 3 and 2 are 4. And some people, of course, they can believe that way. You see, that's all educated stuff. That's all it is. You know what I mean. And then, they say, well, the physicist and the scientist, they've convinced us that 5 and 5 is 10.

As you believeth in your heart, so you becometh. Again and again the prophets have taught: you are where you are because you are what you are. If you want to change where you are, just simply change what you are. It's really that simple. But it's not that simple unless you're willing to accept that. If you're willing to accept that and give it a try, then you'll find it's really that simple. But if you are completely controlled by the opinions already established within the mind, then for you, of course, it's going to be what one may call difficult. But if you're willing to give yourself half a try—enjoy this world. That's why it's been put here. It hasn't been put here for man to suffer. It hasn't been put here for man to struggle. It hasn't been put here for man to live in what the Spirit calls *lulu* vibrations of lack and limitation. See, God didn't do that to us. My friends, we keep doing it to ourselves. Let's be free from that type of insanity. We're here to live and to enjoy what the Divine has brought into being. And we cannot enjoy it and we cannot live the wonder of life as long as we insist upon telling the Divine Intelligence how to run the universe. Let's be free—and let's go have some refreshments. Thank you all very much.

SEPTEMBER 6, 1973

CONSCIOUSNESS CLASS 23 ❧

Good evening, students. Now last week we had a discussion, a little bit, about the mind and how it works and about the great importance of becoming aware of your thoughts.

Would you kindly stand and read Discourse 39? And will the other students turn to Discourse 39, please.

[At this point in the class, Discourse 39 is read aloud by a student.]

Following the affirmation, we will go into our concentration upon peace. Now when you concentrate upon something, you are directing your thought, which is your energy, to the thing concentrated upon. So you are moving in point of time to this peace that is within the self. When you're concentrating, your mind is pointedly and fixedly upon the object of your choice; no other thought entertains your mind. And when you unite, this evening, in your concentration upon peace for a few moments (approximately three to five minutes) and you follow that with the total stillness of the mind—that's an absence of all thought—then you will experience your own spirit inside of yourself. So you want to move from the thought of that word of *peace* to the feeling and to the experience.

[The "Total Consideration" affirmation is spoken in unison by the class. A short period of meditation follows.]

The process of teaching these courses is to give you the opportunity to ask whatever questions that you have of a spiritual nature and, to the best of my ability, I will be happy to share with you the understanding of the Living Light. Now you're free to raise your hands to ask whatever questions that you may have of a spiritual nature. And when you do ask your question, would you kindly rise? So those who have questions this evening, please feel free to raise your hands.

[No hands are raised. After a short silence, the Teacher continues.] Of course, you know, if you don't have any questions, then I won't have to work. We'll have a short class and we can go have refreshments.

I noticed in the reading the descriptions of the various parts of the anatomy, in reference to color, etc. Why does the solar plexus reflect illumination?

Yes. The question has been asked by the gentleman in reference to the teachings explained in *The Living Light.* "Why does the solar plexus reflect"—in his words—"illumination?" The solar plexus is the part of the anatomy which is the center, the nuclei, the sun, or the solar of our universe, and it is also the psychic seat, or psychic center. It is where all the nerves of the body—all transmissions are centered in the solar plexus. And it is stated in the teachings that it is yellow; yellow is the color, in our understanding, of divine wisdom and illumination. Does that help with your question?

Partially. I thought the color yellow would be the third eye or pineal gland or the Christ consciousness.

The pineal glad is also colored yellow.

I find that unusual, or at least interesting. It seems to me, from what I understand, that the solar plexus is attached to ego, or self.

Yes, of course. I believe, from what you're expressing, that you are sharing an understanding of certain teachings that you have studied. Is that correct?

Right.

Yes. You will find, my good students, many people read a multitude of different books and studies and you will find varying teachings, of course, from various teachers. But the teachings of our study course and of our understanding is that the solar plexus is the nerve center, the psychic seat; that it is the expression of divine wisdom. It is colored yellow and so, also, is the pineal gland, which is directly connected to the solar plexus. Yes?

Is this also the famous sun-moon relationship, the plus and minus?

Yes, it is.

The so-called kundalini action, where you have a mystical marriage of the two meeting?

It's known as the celestial marriage.

Right.

Yes, it is.

I believe it's taught, in this particular understanding, what is termed evolutionary incarnation, as opposed to reincarnation, and to my recollection, we have never gotten into a discussion of that. I would appreciate very much a rough outline of that particular understanding.

In reference to the teachings in the Living Light philosophy of the evolutionary incarnation of the soul, it is our basic understanding and teachings that the soul evolves through the universes and that whatever form that it enters, it has merited that on its evolutionary unfolding path. Now that does not mean to imply that these teachings are referring to a transmigration on this Earth planet of evolving from, perhaps, a blade of grass to a human. I believe we spoke in our last class in reference to there is no difference, in truth, between an ant and an angel, because it is the same Divine Intelligence that expresses through both forms. There is no separation, you see, in truth.

However, I believe you wanted some explanation or expansion upon that basic teaching of evolutionary incarnation, and in reference to what is commonly referred to in the world of return or reincarnation. Now the basic difference is that we do not teach that the soul leaves the physical body and then waits in some limbo or some other state of consciousness to return into an earth body in a specified number of years. We do teach that the souls that have entered this earth realm have entered this earth realm on their evolutionary path; that this is the fifth planet in the solar system; that the souls that have entered this planet have entered this planet to learn to demonstrate what is commonly referred to as faith.

Now, I feel at this time that that, perhaps, will be sufficient for all of the new students we have here. I do realize, of course, that a more detailed explanation of—well, where did we come from and, having come from that, then, of course, where are we going. When man becomes aware of where he truly is, he will not only become aware of where he has been, but he will become aware of where he truly is going. And so the first step is the step of seeking a full awareness of what we truly are this moment, here and now. And through that awareness, my friends, we will not only become aware of past and future—the reason we become aware of things past or things future is because we become aware of the eternal now. So that is what we want to strive to become aware of: this instant, this moment, this eternity. Thank you very much.

On the question about, Why are the elbows conscience? I just never pictured that the elbows would be your conscience [Discourse 39]. I thought it would be a more integral part of the anatomy,

*other than an elbow. I have a sore elbow and I was just wonder-
ing if my conscience has been bothering me or something?*

That is a very interesting question and we must go to the
cause that has prompted the question. And it appears that
the cause that prompted the question is the possibility that
whereas the elbows represent in the physical anatomy what is
known as conscience, then it is the conscience that is prompted
to ask the question. Because if you did not ask the question,
then you would not have been prompted by the discussion that
you were just making on conscience. If there is an effect in any
part of the body, it is directly attributed to a state of consciousness that exists in the mind. Now if a person stubs their toe, for
example, that does reveal that there's a certain attitude of mind
that was being entertained and that is simply the effect.

Now, these teachings do not accept what is commonly referred
to as accidents. We do teach that everything that happens to us
is caused by us; that it is not something you must blindly follow
or believe, because it is revealed to you. It is demonstrable that
man is a law unto himself. We do not stub our toe by accident.
We do not bruise our elbow by accident. And we do not pinch our
finger by accident. We set a law into motion and the bruising of
the elbow or any other part of our anatomy is an effect. And so
in reference to your question, it doesn't necessarily mean that
the student's conscience is bothering them, but it does reveal
that it is wise to consider the conscience if one's elbow is being
bruised.

Now the conscience is a spiritual sensibility with a dual
capacity that knows right from wrong; it does not have to be
told. So in reference to your question, you see, you don't need—
nor does anyone need—anyone to tell them what's the matter
with the conscience, because the conscience knows; it doesn't
have to be told. Does that help with your question?

In a way, yes.

It will be clearer. Remember, friends, when we see the obstructions, we cannot find the way. And so what we do in thought is to be at peace and the way is revealed, you see.

The mind works this way: it stubs its toe and this is what it says: "Well, the toes represent indecision." Then it says, "Well, I wasn't indecisive about anything at the time I stubbed my toe." Well, who said that they were indecisive at that exact moment, you see? The stubbing of the toe or anything else is simply an effect of a law that man has set into motion. Well, one stubs their toe, which deals with decision—and why did they stub their toe? Because they didn't see where they were going. And what is it that causes us to see? What does seeing represent? Awareness. And so when we're having difficulty with decisions and we're filled with indecision, it is really self-evident and demonstrable that we have, perhaps, what might be termed a little problem with what is known as awareness. And so it is with all parts of the anatomy.

Yes, in classes prior to this one, you had made mention of the nine minds.

Yes.

There are nine minds?

That is our understanding.

There was a great deal of discussion on the conscious, the subconscious, and the superconscious.

In the last course, that is correct.

I believe at that time I had asked a question in regards to the nine minds and possibly you felt that I was not able to receive that at that time.

Perhaps you might consider that whereas man is a law unto himself, that man may not have merited the particular answer which they felt they might desire at the particular time, don't you see. I am not trying to say that I didn't feel or did feel that you should have the answer. I'm simply trying to reveal that whatever experience that we encounter in life, my good students, is simply an effect of laws that are established within ourselves. But now you would like to know about those minds, would you?

Yes, thank you.

Well, I would be more than happy to share with you a bit of understanding. It is our teachings that we have a conscious, a subconscious, and a superconscious mind. It is also the teachings that each mind has three levels; that three is the number of manifestation. Now, for example, the conscious mind may be controlled and expressing from the superconscious or the subconscious or the conscious. And so, my friends, those are the three levels of the conscious mind. Now you have the key for all of the others. Thank you very much. Now does someone else have a question?

Would you go back to what we were discussing about accidents? Would you clarify how this is applied to negligence on someone else's part of you having an accident?

I'll be more than happy to. You see, friends, like attracts like and becomes the Law of Attachment. And so it is that if we're crossing the street and we have merited the experience of an accident, caused by a person who is negligent, you see, like a magnet, we have pulled that person out of the atmosphere and we have crossed that street at that particular moment, on that particular day, at that particular time. So the individual that was negligent merited the experience and so did the recipient of the experience.

You see, man is not alone. There is no separation, in truth. Everything is united. Whether we want to believe it or not is immaterial. The law is demonstrable and it can be proven to the satisfaction of the truth seeker.

So, you know, sometimes a person asks a question and they receive an answer that is most satisfactory to the mind. And then another person asks a question and it's not satisfactory at all; it seems as though the answer didn't even come. Well, each person has established the law unto themselves and each one, of course, is responsible to themselves.

I don't understand what you mean when you say that man is a law unto himself.

Thank you. I'll be happy to share that with you. Please bear with us, because we not only have new students in these courses, but we do have many review students.

Man is a law unto himself. In other words, whatever man thinks returns to him totally impartially. Whatever man entertains in thought, he experiences. Man is that law. Do you understand? Man himself. In other words, our teaching is not that God has put you into a certain circumstance or that God will take you out of that circumstance. Our understanding of God is a divine Infinite Intelligence; a divine neutral Power that sustains all things in all places, that has no beginning, has no ending. If man chooses to use this Law, this Divine Intelligence, for his awakening, for his joy, for his wonder of living, he may do so. Another man may choose to limit that Divine Intelligence—and perhaps it will help you on a discussion of what people call love, because most people are interested, to some extent, in that word called love. Either they love another human or they love a plant or a dog or a cat or money or something. And so perhaps by a little discussion on the word *love,* we may gain a greater understanding.

When man experiences things that are in harmony with his attitudes of mind, he—by man, I mean humanity—feels and experiences what he terms is love. Now if a girl gets married to a fellow and he does basically what she wants, though she's not consciously necessarily aware of this, then they say that they are in love. What they are really saying is that they are in harmony or in rapport with the basic taped patterns of their own subconscious. Consequently, they have that experience for a *limited* time. Now the reason that it's usually a limited time is because people are introducing new tapes into their subconscious. Well, if their husbands or wives don't introduce similar tapes, then there's no longer any rapport and, consequently, they no longer experience this energy, this intelligence, divine intelligence, that they term love. Man limits himself; God doesn't.

If a person says, "Well, I would like to have a true friend," well, of course, it's very simple: we cannot have what we aren't. If we accept that we don't have a true friend, then we certainly cannot experience one. So, my friends, what we've got to do is to become the thing that we desire. And when we become the thing that we desire, then we experience it, for it's magnetically pulled to us according to the law that like attracts like and becomes the Law of Attachment. So, you see, if there's anything that you're hoping for and if there's anything that you are desiring, become the thing you desire. Then you will experience it. You cannot experience something that you are seeking until you become it. Does that help with your question?

And many more. Thank you.

You're more than welcome.

This came up last week, about the subconscious, and I remember you saying that kindness is the bridge between the electric and the magnetic field. I was very interested in speaking kindly to the subconscious and I tried it and it worked. Would you give me a little more on how it is the bridge?

Yes. The lady is referring to last Thursday's course in reference to kindness is the bridge between the electrical (the conscious mind) and the magnetic (the subconscious). It is the bridge between the two minds. And she has asked the question of how does this work or why is it that bridge. Because it does work. Of course it works. Once man tries the laws and he puts his soul into his effort, he sees that it works.

What is kindness? What is kindness? Ask yourself the question, my friends. Kindness is consideration. And consideration is flow. And when you have total consideration, you have divine flow. So kindness is the bridge between your conscious aware-ness and your subconscious awareness. And you move mentally across that bridge that's known as kindness. You see, you treat it kindly, as you would want to be treated. And therefore, what you want to put into it is accepted on the bridge of kindness. Otherwise, it is rejected by the tapes that are predominant.

I was wondering about the contemporary theory of reincar-nation. You build up so much karma and you come back on the wheel of life, one reincarnation after another to the earth plane, until you finally either work off your karma or fall under the law of grace and burn up your karma. Could you enlighten me on that?

Yes, I'll be happy to share with you our understanding, because you are expressing an understanding of the Eastern philosophies. As the gentleman has already expressed that understanding of divine grace and karma, we do not teach that divine grace is able to go around what you call karma, etc. In fact, that is not our basic terminology, but we will do our best to share with you in reference to this so-called wheel of delusion or karmic expression or the soul's return or reincarnation. We do not teach that the soul gains experience here in the earth realm or that the earth is the only realm in all the universes. Therefore, we do not teach that for a person to grow through the grades of school that they must return to an earthly form.

You see, my friends, if reincarnation is a fact—that means, the karmic wheel of constant return—then that means there has to be a moment when a soul entered brand new. Would you not agree? If the teachings of karma, in the Eastern philoso-phies, is a demonstrable truth, then it means that somewhere along the path, someplace, a soul entered the earth realm com-pletely uncontaminated. Would you not agree? Well, now that soul would be whole, complete, and perfect, having come direct from the Divine, right? Or seemingly so, right? Therefore, my friends, we must look around at the world about us and ask ourselves, how many messiahs and how many truly perfected souls are in our earth realm, right? Because that would mean that there are times when there are multitudes of new souls expressing on the earth realm.

That is not our teachings. We teach that the soul enters this form and it enters this form that it has merited according to the laws that it, and it alone, has established in its prior lives and in its prior incarnations. Does that help with your question?

Now, in reference to what is termed *divine grace*, or not to be affected by a law that man has established, it's quite simple: it's known in this terminology as the divine bank account. There is no selfless thought or deed or act that is not recorded. When you do something right because in your heart you know it's right to do right, and when you selflessly entertain a thought or do a deed or an act, you literally deposit that energy into what is known as a spiritual bank account. In times of need, this energy may be withdrawn, as you go to the bank and draw out X amount of dollars, depending on how much you've put in. It may be withdrawn from that bank account and used, so that a person will not experience the full impact of a seeming transgression. Do you understand?

Now, how does this really work? Well, it's very, very simple. Everything that takes place is the effect, the effect of energy. Say, for example, that a man has transgressed the laws governing material supply and he finds that he's very short in that area. In fact, it does seem in this world that most people do entertain that type of thinking, unfortunately for them. And he has a great need for material supply. Well, material supply, like anything else, is the effect, you see, only the effect of directed energy. So, according to what he has in his spiritual bank account, he may withdraw so much energy and, through direction, experience the effect or what is known as material supply. Does that help with your question?

Somewhat.

Somewhat.

Right. It sounds familiar and I'm balancing it against all the books I've read on the traditional Eastern philosophies. It fits in, but it's kind of hard to make it all kind of glue together into one cohesive theory.

When the mind seeks to find a way to the path of peace and understanding and freedom, it entertains the possibility that not only is each day, but each moment, a new beginning. And I just wanted to share with you that if you, as students, will entertain the possibility—for it is a truth—that this moment is a new beginning for you, that this day is a new beginning, what has already been learned is well recorded in your memory par excellence, and if you will give yourself a chance to try what you're presently seeking to try, I know that you will find your way.

Otherwise, what simply happens within the mind is dual decision. Dual decision is entertaining that teaching while at the same time absorbing this teaching. Then what happens, there's a comparison that takes place. That comparison starts to set into motion the Law of Contradiction. The Law of Contradiction guides the soul to the realms of confusion, and the realms of confusion guarantee for that soul the pits of regret. What I am trying to share with you, friends, is at least give yourself a chance to try something new beyond the depths of the intellect, where duality exists. Let it touch your soul. Give it that short twelve weeks and if you will do that, you will be able to see a bit more clearly. Thank you very much.

I wasn't arguing with you, I was just—

I don't accept things in an argumentative level because, you see, it only wastes energy.

Right.

But I did want to share with you, friends, if you compare one teaching with another and you go on to the wheel—you see, there's a little statement in our *Pages To Ponder* that says very clearly, "When of thy mind thou seekest to know the truth, on the wheel of delusion thou shall traverse." Now why does man traverse the wheel of delusion when he seeks truth with his mind and intellect? It's very simple, friends: that's not where truth is. This thing is designed to compute facts and logic, not truth or reason. This is why you have such a multitude of philosophies in the world. Thank you very much. Someone else has a question. Yes.

An explanation of this saying would be appreciated: "You are ever testing yourselves and ever tempted to leave the Light; and the greater your soul expansion, the greater the temptation from the worlds of creation. There is but one responsibility and that is the responsibility to the Light, for that is the only thing that is eternal and the only thing that merits responsibility to it. Be not deceived by the creations of mind [Discourse 39]." How are we testing ourselves? Is this a law unto ourselves?

Yes. Man is a law unto himself and it seems that there is a part of the mind—and I'm sure that many psychologists will agree—there is the part of the mind that has an insatiable desire to suffer, and it finds a multitude of ways to entertain and enjoy that suffering. Now, some people, it seems, like to entertain the thought that everything to them seems to be confusing; that it's a terrible world in which we're living; that the politics and the government are all miserable. And they literally suffer through all those experiences mentally within their mind. Now we must ask ourselves the honest question, "What is it inside of us that has such an insatiable desire to suffer?" You know, sometimes a man and a woman, they get married and they have their little family and everything and it just seems they love to experience that suffering of not getting along. Well, now, of course, as long as we enjoy that disturbance and all of that suffering, of course, that's as long as we're going to have it. A very simple statement, you know, our problems, they are our companions as long as we love them. Why do we continue to suffer? My friends, it is our way of gaining attention.

You see, everything needs to be loved. It needs to receive and experience what is known as energy, because that's all love is. And so it is that the mind has devised a multitude of ways of gaining this attention, because, remember now, that energy follows attention. And so, stop and think what we do to ourselves to get a little bit of attention. Think about that for just a few moments, what we're doing to ourselves in order that we may experience this energy or divine love.

Now, the reason that we have this need for this attention or energy or divine love is very simple. The reason that we have the need for it is because we have limited the expression of God's love. We have told our old tapes (our subconscious) "When I do such and such, I feel exhilarated. I just feel wonderful, when I'm able to have this or I'm able to do that." And we have limited the influx of God's divine love because we have denied our own divinity. We have denied that we can feel wonderful by walking down the street and looking at a star in the sky or passing by a tree. You see, it's all been done up here. We have accepted the mass programming that if we get on that rat race to make a million dollars, we're going to feel wonderful. And as we start making it, of course, we start feeling wonderful. But don't you see, that's all that we've taped our minds to. Now we could tape our minds that we could look at the moon for two minutes and we could feel the same way.

I'm trying to share with you, my friends, it only exists in our head; that's the only place it exists. Now a person meets a person and they say, "Oh, I like that person. Why, I just feel great." Well, that's what fits into their computer. Then, they meet another person and they say, "I feel miserable around that person." Well, that's what fits into their tape.

But there is a dimension of mind that is beyond that foolishness. And in that dimension, when you rise your soul to that point, then you will see God everywhere in everything. Because if you lose God anyplace, you're going to lose God everyplace, sooner or later. So let's give a little more consideration, perhaps, to the thought that not only is God one, but everyone is God, and everything *is* God because that's the truth about the whole matter, so that we can feel better and not go through all of these, what is known as, attention-getters, you see.

I ought to know a little bit about something like that. I spent five years of deprivation and foolishness, and I set that law into motion. I wish I had had those teachings in that day, but, you see, I didn't. So I'm very grateful for them.

I have two questions.

Yes.

Could you tell us, please, what the function or purpose of the three subconscious minds would be?

I'll be more than happy to share that with you. We'll take one question at a time, if you would like. You want to know, What is the purpose or the function of the three minds?

We have the conscious mind so that we may be consciously aware of what is known as the conscious dimensions. Then, we have the subconscious mind, which records everything: every experience and every thought that we have ever had. And then, we have what is known as the neutral, the odic, or the superconscious, which is just exactly what it says: it is neutral.

Now, if a person is moving in this dimension and controlled by their subconscious mind, where, you understand, reason is not expressed—the subconscious is the memory bank, the computer that records all experiences from the moment, my friends, of conception. From the moment of conception. The potential of the mind exists in the cells, you understand. Because each cell has a mind, you see; it has intelligence, yes. So the subconscious is in the process, you understand, of formation from the moment of conception.

Now, at that moment, the thoughts, the feelings, the emotions, the attitudes of mind that are entertained by these two people, you understand, govern and control the cells that make up that forthcoming child. And this is why a virgin birth is one that is conceived in pure, divine love. There are no thoughts of lust. There are no thoughts of the gratification and the satisfaction of the senses. Therefore, you have the purest possible sense, you understand, combining to bring about the new birth or child.

Now, if you did not have a conscious mind, you would not be able to express what is known as the soul faculty of reason, for it is the conscious mind that is receptive to the soul faculties. It is the subconscious mind that is the computer that records all of the experiences. Now, the conscious mind is a doer and the subconscious mind is a reactor. Does that help with your question?

Thank you.

Do you have another question?

I'm sorry, that really wasn't my question. My question dealt with the three levels—maybe I should put it that way—of the subconscious.

Then, that's a different question. It was my understanding that you had asked about the three minds, but your question now is in reference to the three levels of each mind. Is that your question?

Yes.

I believe we discussed a bit earlier about the three levels of the conscious mind, and I am sure if you will recall in your mind there was some discussion and perhaps that will help with your question. Yes. Because I believe that it was stated "the three levels of the conscious mind" and it was also stated that you now have the key to open the door.

Thank you.

Yes, thank you very much.

If we feel that there is understanding from the moment of conception—and I believe, and I'd like to know if our teachings believe, that there is a soul—if a person has merited coming to the earth plane under a certain circumstance and then someone decides to end this before birth, had they already merited this?

Absolutely and positively. They have merited entering the earth realm for perhaps two months.

They knew this, though?

They merited that, yes. You see, prior to all incarnation, the soul reviews all experiences yet to come for that entire earth span. Once it leaves this earth realm, it goes into review of every thought and experience that it had and the books are balanced. You understand? Now, you see, there is no God outside of us that does that judging, my friends; that is done inside of us, you see. "Well, I flunked out here, but I made it there. And I flunked out there." And then, you see, then there is a review. After those reviews, there's another review and that review directs them into the next expression.

By the same token, how does our teaching feel about suicide?

Now, for example, the soul that has entered a form that is going to commit suicide, they already know that. They know that before they entered that form. Now what has happened, the soul entered the form that it had merited with the experiences necessary for its own growth. That does not mean that Serenity teaches pro or con on these various issues, because, you see, that's all a mental judgment by people. The soul itself has merited its experience and has the divine right to its expression. Yes, does that help with your question?

Yes.

Yes.

May I ask for a definition of the words study *and* investigation?

Yes, now you're reading that out of context. Would you kindly read the sentence, please?

Yes. "Be patient in your study and investigation. You are coming along well, but do not be tempted to put the cart before the horse." And it says, "Therefore we ask your patience, your continuity of investigation [Discourse 39]."

Yes. Now I would like to ask you a question and perhaps help clarify what the words "study" and "investigation" mean to the reader. What does the word "study" mean to you in comparison to the word "investigation"? Does a man study mathematics? Or does a man investigate mathematics? That is the question. Does a man study spirituality or does a man investigate spirituality?

He studies.

He studies.

To me.

Yes?

Study, to me, is more encompassing than investigating is.

Yes.

Study—I mean, investigation can be very impersonal, but if one studies, it is much more personal.

What is the difference in the motive, if any, of the course of study and the course of investigation?

I'm so glad I asked this question. I would have to think about it.

Let me answer your question this way. Man chooses to study many things and investigates very few. Think about that. Man chooses to study many things, but investigates very, very few.

Thank you.

One deals with the principle of a teaching and another deals with the effect of a teaching.

In your answer to the question about the soul's knowing of its suicide in advance to its incarnation—

It knows all experiences.

Right. It sounded like predestination. Once the soul is impulsed into form, the form has a mind. And man is a law unto himself and has the right to change this course of events.

That is within his merit system.

Is there not that 10 percent?

Oh, yes, that 10 percent is in all merit systems.

OK. Thank you.

Now, friends, it's kind of like you're going to go to New York, but you have a choice: you can take the train, you can fly, you can drive, or you can take the boat. You see, the Divine does not leave us without this 10 percent so-called free will. But once the law is set into motion—now, for example, I know what you want to ask. You want to ask, "Well, if I have this 10 percent free will, then I not only merit the entire incarnation, but I'm also aware of everything involved in it." Why that awareness, my good friend, includes all your 10 percent free will and whether or not you exercised it. Do you understand? But that's not on this level. No, that is not on this level of mind. Because, you see, if it were, what's the sense, my friends, in going to school—life is a school—and taking any test? Because you already have all the answers. There's no growth involved. See, you already have the answers to the test before you take the test.

Regarding study and investigation, the word in tells me that you go within to investigate. To study a thing, maybe, means something that has already been set up. To investigate might be to look into new things?

What does the word *in-ves-ti-gate* mean?

Well, to invest *is "to put into."*

Thank you very much. That answers the question. Just give it some thought now, friends. Does someone else have a question?

I would appreciate more of a clarification on the word growth.

On the word *growth?*

Yes. It was stated, If we knew all the answers, what would be the purpose of going to school? There would be no growth.

That's very true.

I must ask, then, what is growth?

Growth or *growing* is progressing; it's changing.

Is it the soul that is progressing and growing?

The soul is unfolding. The forms are progressing. Now the soul—and we best clarify that for our new students. We understand that the soul is not the divine, formless Spirit: it is the covering or the individualization of the Spirit in order that it enter form. And so it is that form, all forms—soul forms, astral forms, spiritual forms, mental forms, physical forms—all forms are in a constant process of change, progression, or growth. Yes. Does that help with your question?

Yes, thank you.

Now, friends, I know the question is arising in the mind, "Well, if all this has been reviewed before I got here, well, now why can't I just touch that and become aware?" Well, as the Good Book says, Ye shall be permitted to prophesize in part, as ye are permitted to know in part. What does that really mean? That God is limiting us? Of course, it doesn't mean that at all. It means that we're more than one form in this form, and it means that each form has its limitation, see? So what you're able to know with one form has a limit, and you can't go beyond that limit until you grow, until you expand in consciousness and rise up into the higher forms. And then we expand, we know a little bit more. Then, we move on up that ladder of eternal progression and we know, yea, even more.

And then the day comes, from the formless we came; to the formless shall we return. Because the truth of the whole matter is that we're formless and free; that we are the fuel that runs the car. That's what we really are. We're not the car itself. The car goes back to where it came from and so do the forms, don't you see? But we need not worry about being formless and without identification, because we cannot expand to universal consciousness until we start to demonstrate it in our thought.

So we have no fear or concern of something like that, at least, my good friends, in my short life I have no fear of it.

May I ask, regarding our future incarnations, are they also revealed beforehand or must we first experience, as we are now, this birth experience?

The entrance prior to all forms is revealed.

Pardon me?

It is revealed prior to the soul's incarnation into any form at any time. The experiences, yes, are revealed.

Before the incarnations?

That is correct. Before the soul—

Of all forms?

That is correct.

I see.

Yes. You see, the truth of the matter is, friends, we really do know where we're going, because we really do know where we're at. We just have to become consciously aware of it.

If that is true—I'm not doubting it—

Please do so, because that is the expression of your divine birthright.

Is it possible to ever skip a certain expression? Or must you just take it like a number, like 1, 2, 3, 4?

I know of no way of escaping a law that is set into motion. If you're referring to soul incarnation?

Yes.

Well, if it merits the second realm, it goes to the second. It doesn't skip to the fourth, no. I know of no way that it does that. Now that may be possible—of course, to God all things are possible—but I am not aware of any way of escaping. Sometimes I used to entertain the thought that there must be a way. In fact, I even accused them that they made an error in the divine computer when they sent me down here, but, then, of course, you know, those are just those levels of self. Yes, I know of no way of escaping acts and laws we've set into motion. Thank you very much.

I believe you said each cell has a mind.

That's right, it has. The Divine Intelligence expresses in every cell.

Thank you.

Yes, absolutely and positively. Now the question is, "Well, if each cell has a mind, does it know it is a cell? Does man know that he's a being?" Why, of course. Absolutely. The plant knows that it's a plant. And the plant has emotion and it has feeling. Some people it likes and some people it doesn't like. I mean, after all, this is being demonstrated, thank God, finally. You know, after a hundred years of understanding of it. "Well, now, how does the plant know," we say to ourselves, "that a person—why does the plant shudder, literally shudder emotionally when someone comes near it with a pair of scissors?" Well, it's very simple: the plant has recorded from experience that they're going to snip off some of its leaves or maybe cut it down completely. So that experience is recorded. Well, now it takes a mind to record anything; so in that sense, of course, the plant has a mind. It has intelligence. It most certainly does. Absolutely.

Now, then they say, "Well, you say the rock has a mind." Well, of course the rock has a mind. Those atoms, electrons, and molecules are held together intelligently, you know. I mean, there's just not some power outside that says, "Whoops, that's a rock," and this is forcing it to be held together. It's the intelligence within it that holds it together, friends. It's the intelligence within us, you understand, that moves our body and causes us to speak.

When a rock goes through its normal cycle of forming a solid form and then gradually decaying and returning back again to the grains from which it was formed, is this the evolutionary growth of rock?

The evolution of the form, certainly. Remember, friends, man has a great responsibility. The Bible prophets taught us that in so many, many ways. Man is responsible unto himself and to all his creations.

Now, for example, when you sit down and you eat your dinner, what do you think about? What do you think about when you stop to eat? Do you not realize that we are, supposedly, the highest-evolved intelligence in form on this Earth planet? And here we're taking in food all of the time and what kinds of thoughts are we entertaining? Because, you see, the thoughts that we are entertaining is our attitude of mind. Our attitude of mind is our rate of vibration, and our rate of vibration—hear me now—is affecting the food that we are digesting. Then that returns back to the earth realm and it comes up again. You see, our bodies are composed of all of the elements of this earth realm, all of them, without exception, in varying degree. So when you partake of food and you don't have a little feeling of a blessing or joy or something—you have a direct responsibility to help the intelligence that is passing through your being on its evolutionary path upward. Think about that.

Now man's thoughts—when man is disturbed and there are wars and things of that nature, all of Nature herself reacts. She reacts with her earthquakes. She reacts with her hurricanes. She reacts with her tornadoes. You see, there isn't some God out in the universe that I've ever found that says, "Let's see, today is September such and such. Oh, well, we'll have a tornado today." This is an effect of vibration, and vibrations, my friends, are affected by people and their thoughts.

All of nature responds to kindness, all of nature, including man himself. All of nature responds to kindness and to love. And so it is that you are a vehicle that refines whatever enters it. You have that opportunity to be that. That's what we are designed for, you see: to help this evolution of the form. The purpose of the soul's incarnation into form is to raise the vibratory waves of form that, in time, in eternity, they will know their divine Source.

That means, my friends, you won't have to listen to anyone to find truth. That is not what these classes are about. These classes are designed to help you to think, to truly think. Not to have information fed into your mind. You already have plenty of that fed into it, just by the so-called education system. But to learn to think, to go to deeper levels of consciousness inside of yourself where truth waits humbly and patiently for you to experience it. You see, it isn't outside. The truth of the matter is it never was. It's inside. Learn to still the mind. And when the mind is still, your soul, your God will speak in a very soft voice within yourself. And when that voice speaks inside of your being in that stillness, you will know. You will not have to be told and you won't have to ask anyone whether or not it was the Divinity inside yourself, because you will know that.

I feel that if everyone on this earth plane believed in our teachings and what we talked about tonight, and the example you gave of someone crossing the street and getting hit by a car— this was merited—if everyone felt this way, then we wouldn't have all this bitterness as a result of something like this. And we wouldn't have lawsuits.

That is so true. We would be free.

If a neighbor were nasty to us some morning, we would say we merited this and forget it, rather than hold a grudge against her. So in other words, this would be an ideal place.

It is true because, you see, forgiveness is God's greatest blessing. What does it mean to forgive? To forgive is to free. If we're married to someone and we're experiencing great problems, be at peace, my friends, because we have established laws that have guaranteed that. But having established those laws, we have the divine right to establish new laws.

And in reference to that, I would like to bring up the spiritual understanding of this Association in reference to what is commonly referred to as capital punishment, a law of society. When man awakens to the great truth that he escapes nothing and that these dimensions are around and about him, these invisible dimensions—that it isn't a blind so-called faith or belief that life is continuous—but man opens his eyes and sees that life truly is continuous and sees that if we are filled with hatred and animosity this moment and we lose our physical body, we are still expressing hatred and animosity, then man and society will not close the light, so to speak, and send these criminals and these murderers into so-called invisible dimensions, where they hover in earth-bound realms to impress sensitive souls to commit like crime.

I want to share that with you, my good friends, because there was just a change here in our California legislature. We're not dealing with politics; we're dealing with some type of understanding that life is eternal and that no matter who we are or what we are here and now, if our physical life is taken from us, we are still the same way. And if we are in those dark realms, so to speak, of error and ignorance, then we continue to influence the people of this earth realm. And this is why the spirit has repeatedly recommended to consider, as the rest of the world has considered and is demonstrating, to work with these souls where you can establish contact with them here and now in this physical world, to program new tapes or what they call to reeducate, don't you see? Yes. I wanted to share that with the class this evening because when—and we're living in an age where the eyes of the world are opening and where more and more people are becoming, or, let us say, better expressing a view into these invisible dimensions.

And so it is, my good friends, communication, in truth, sustains and supports all religious philosophies, because they're all paths to one God. If our minds may think they're detours, that's our right to think that they're detours, but it does sustain and support all paths that lead to the Divine. Now we have time for one or two more questions.

Is there anything that we can do to soften the emotional shock if we should have to prune a plant?

Absolutely and positively. Now remember, Divine love is different than conjugal love. Conjugal love has want, need, and desire. Divine love loves for the sake of love. It loves a plant with the same emotion and feeling that it loves a human being; there is no difference in divine love, its expression. If you emanate from your being and in your thought that divine love—divine love is the language of the soul. You see, the plant, of course, has a soul, naturally. All form has soul, definitely and positively, the soul of the thing in which it is encased. But, you see, man has got it computed that he's the only one that's got a soul. It's kind of a strange thing, in truth, because we have also computed that we're the only intelligence in all of the universe.

You know, it has to take a pretty fair-sized ego, I would think, to have to think that we're the only intelligence in God's kingdoms. Now, your soul and that soul, you understand, will respond, you see? It has the soul of a plant. If it didn't have a soul, then you would not see, physically, a form that's called a plant. You couldn't see it. It wouldn't exist, you see. Perhaps that's too new of a thought for most people, but anyway, give it some consideration. Yes.

Could you consider, when pruning, if you were to take just a branch and not destroy the tree itself?

Absolutely. You see, I am aware that there are some philosophies, particularly in India, where they won't even step on an insect. Well, that's their right to that feeling and to that expression, you see. But balance is the keynote in all things. You see, the truth of the matter is that the plant will not have this emotional reaction if you are emanating that feeling at that time.

Now a person may say, "Well, why should I bother?" Remember, friends, what we grant to another we have, in truth, granted to ourselves. And what we deny another—when I say another, you know, I'm talking about all God's expression—and what we deny to another, that is what we, in truth, deny to ourselves, you see. When a person says, "Well, you know the way I'm treated, etc." Well, we have set that law into motion. We've done that.

See, we can change—this is the key, my friends—we can change ourselves, but we cannot transgress the divine law and change somebody else. The brain might like to think that we changed someone, but we never did. We were simply expressing our levels and that person was simply receptive to it, and they went within themselves and made a change. Nobody, in truth, changes anyone. It's a delusion and illusion to think that we do so. Just ask some parents. They say, "That's not the way I've trained them. They're nothing like I was at all, totally turned out entirely different." Well, if a person can change another person, how come they didn't mold their child as a carbon copy? See? No, you can't do that. It transgresses the Law of Individualization.

We have time for one more question only.

When we were in Mexico, there was a headline about the earthquake, and it stated that God has punished us. It's something that we wouldn't find in our local papers here.

No, I don't think we would find that in our local papers. Remember, friends, in finishing, that man's God is ever equal to his understanding. So if our God is a little god, if that's our understanding, if our understanding is that long, that big, that's how big our God is. So as we expand our understanding, our God becomes bigger. That's what it's really all about. So let's broaden our horizons.

Now our time has passed. Let's go have refreshments. Thank you very much, friends.

SEPTEMBER 13, 1973

CONSCIOUSNESS CLASS 24 ❧

Good evening, students.

"He who does what is to be done without thought or interest in results is ever free to do the work of the Divine [Discourse 56]." And so it states very clearly that man is free when he is not bound by what is called the fruits of action. When he does what he knows in his heart is right to do, he's not concerned with the results, he's not concerned with what effects he possibly may be garnering or losing, then he is free to do the work of the Divine.

Now you are free, friends, to ask whatever questions you have of a spiritual nature.

In meditation, is there a time in our meditation where we reach a perfect balance in our spirit or a perfect balance with the faculties?

Yes. The question is asked by the student, Is there a time in our meditation when we reach a state of perfect balance? Of course, my friends, that is entirely dependent upon the students and what laws they're setting into motion. Meditation, in and of itself, does not guarantee or bring perfect balance to anyone. It does not do that. Now, if you mean by perfect balance, a balancing of the soul faculties and the sense functions in our day-to-day thoughts and activities, if that is what you mean by a perfect balance, then meditation, in and of itself, does not guarantee that. However, there are moments in meditation where you may free your consciousness, so to speak, from levels of disturbance and you may experience this peace that passeth all understanding, but that is not a guarantee of a balance of one's own being.

Could you speak on the difference between concern and consideration?

Yes, I'll be happy to share with you our understanding. The question is, Would we speak on the difference between concern and consideration? We understand that concern is a sense function that is stimulated by what is commonly referred to as the brain or ego and that consideration is a soul faculty that considers all things. And in considering all things, recognizes, realizes, and accepts the divine law and the divine merit system: that whatever happens to us is caused by us. And by an understanding of that law, we also understand that whatever happens to anyone else is also caused by them. With consideration there is an understanding and, therefore, that understanding guides the individual into a policy of noninterference. Now, a person may say that someone is walking across the street and they're about to be hit by a car, and would that be considered interference to move the individual out of the way so they do not experience that so-called accident? That is entirely dependent upon the promptings of one's own conscience, because the conscience within us knows whether or not we are expressing consideration or concern. In other words, concern is a mind function and consideration is a soul faculty.

Thank you.

You're more than welcome.

What is the definition of instinct?

Instinct?

And I was also wondering, on what level or realm does the person lose their conscious thought on passing?

Well, in reference—we'll take your last question first. And in reference to your question, does the soul or does a person lose conscious awareness at the moment of passing? Is that your last question?

At what level do they lose that?

Well, you see, friends, the loss, seeming loss of conscious awareness on one level is not the loss of conscious awareness on all levels. For example, a person who passes out of the physical body may or may not lose conscious awareness of the physical surroundings, do you understand? Because they may still be in that conscious awareness. Now the thing is, I'm sure you've heard of earth-bound spirits or earth-bound entities; it simply means, friends, that you do not need a physical body to have a conscious awareness of this dimension. This physical dimension is the effect or the result of the astral dimension and the mental dimension. So when we leave the physical body, we take with us an astral body and a mental body. Now our conscious awareness could be functioning through either the astral body or the mental body, do you understand? Therefore, we could not only at the moment of transition, but even for some time thereafter, if we stay in that level of awareness known as the astral world, we continue to be aware of this dimension, yes.

That's your last question, I believe. Your first question was that you would like us to share some understanding on the word *instinct*. Is that correct?

Yes.

Yes. Now are you referring to the instinct that the four-legged creatures are commonly referred to as having or are you referring to the instinct of the human being, which is the two-legged animal? Which instinct are you referring to? Because there is a difference.

I was thinking in reference to both being the same, such as the instinct of an animal and the instinct of a human being the same.

They have different expressions.

I really don't know.

Yes. Well, in reference to instinct, one may realize—one may, perhaps, give some thought that an individual has a basic instinct to consume food when it experiences what is termed as hunger. Now this is a basic instinct. This is not what is known as a soul faculty, but that is self-preservation, a preservation of the form in which the soul is expressing at any given time. So the desire to eat or to drink is the effect of the basic instinct for survival.

Would instinct be considered a feeling?

Well, some people, when they experience what is known as instinct, may experience it as a feeling, yes. And then, of course, it prompts a thought and the thought is to get something to eat. Yes.

Am I to understand that the instinct of an animal is much different from that of a human animal?

It's differently expressed. For example, if an animal is hungry, the animal will take whatever food he can get, whether it belongs to another individual or not, all right? Now, usually. Not all animals will. Not all animals will do that; most animals will. And so it is that that basic instinct also exists in the two-legged animal. However, we find few people that would just go, when they're hungry, if they didn't have any food, and just go take somebody else's. The simple reason they wouldn't do that is because the laws of society have made it in such a way that it is not beneficial to the individual to do that. You see, instinct in the four-legged animal is more freely expressed than it is in the two-legged animal, do you understand? Now man has brought about some degree of self-control in some areas for the preservation of what he calls society. But that is a very strong, potent force, what is known as instinct, you see, and it's energy. And if the energy is not directed, then the form goes through quite a traumatic experience. With that, I think we were discussing last class, in reference to love, in reference to energy, because, you see, that's all energy.

The teaching is not to suppress desire, not to suppress those things, but to educate them or fulfill them. Don't suppress energy. That's where all the problems begin, you know. All these frustrations, etc., are because you hold back and suppress these rampant desires that cannot be fulfilled, that is, what one's mind won't permit them to fulfill for naturally varying reasons. Yes, thank you very much.

Could you tell me about the light that is within us? Does that particular light shine on each and every one of us in a different way?

Yes, thank you very much. In reference to the light within us: the light that they're referring to in *The Living Light* is the Light of the Divine or the Light of God or whatever you care to call it, this Light of this Infinite Divine Intelligence. Now the Light exists, of course, in all forms, all people, in everything, because that Infinite Intelligence exists in all things. The Light is the same Light. It varies in its luminosity, according to how much obstruction there is in the form, but the Light is one and the same Light. There is no separation, in truth, and the Light is the Truth. And there is the One and it is in everyone. Yes, does that help with your question?

I believe so.

In Discourse 56 it says, "We have come to serve and in serving have we indeed gained." Is there a hierarchy that sends us to serve from the realms of the Light? From the teachers on high down through to us? I don't understand, "We have come to serve." Who sends us to serve? Some of us serve and some of us do not. How does this come about?

Thank you very much. In reference to the statement, "Some of us serve and some of us do not." We must remember, friends, that everything serves, but it serves different levels of awareness. But there is nothing in the universe that is wasted, in truth, because everything is serving a purpose, humans and all forms. Now the question is in the statement, "We have come to serve." Well, who sent us? The truth of the matter is, of course, when we go to serve, friends, we send ourselves. You see, it's our own being, our own soul, that sends us to serve wherever we go. Now there are schools and philosophies in these other dimensions that are very interested in the awakening of what is known as this, the fifth planet in our solar system, this Earth planet. And so it is that teachers from different schools and different organizations in the world of spirit, as part of their work of service, have merited to come to this earth realm to help share their understanding of the purpose of life. But when a person comes to serve, we must remember that they have established that law and placed themselves in the position where they have been sent. Does that help with your question?

Yes, indeed. Thank you.

You're more than welcome.

In Discourse 56 it says, "The purpose of teaching, my good students, is not to tell you the way to grow but to reveal unto you a way that you may find of awakening the light within you." In book after book I have read of awakening the light within you.

The light within never sleeps. It is the awakening of the mind in order that it may experience the divine light, yes.

To me, they're talking about the recognition of your ability to comprehend the kundalini, right?

No, it's something greater than that. Kundalini is an expression within the form, and God is the formless and greater than the kundalini. That's only a part, that's only the energy channeled through the spine, but the Divine Intelligence is not just in that particular form. No.

Why is it that when the kundalini goes through the chakras unobstructed and, let's say when it gets to the throat chakra, it burns incessantly?

Well, that's most understandable, when you understand what that part of the anatomy represents.

Resentment.

That is correct.

So it's burning through the etheric garbage?

That's right.

I have several questions. As a general rule, society believes that a child develops reason at the age of seven. I want to know how we feel about this because, I think, last week you mentioned that the soul begins to think from conception. If we, in our thinking, create illness, would this explain why a newborn child can be born with a horrible, in our vision, what appears as a horrible disease, because they are able to think from the moment of conception?

Thank you very much. In reference to your questions—number one: the soul enters the form at the moment of conception. And reason is a faculty of the soul. So the soul brings with it in its incarnation reason and the varying soul faculties. Now, in reference to your statement concerning present understanding, society's understanding, that a child begins to reason at the age of seven, this, my good friends, although it is rare, is certainly revealed that a child prior to the age of seven can express a great deal of reason, because there have been such things in society known as child geniuses.

All right. So we have to ask ourselves the question if—and it has been demonstrated that a child can be a genius at the age of five and society claims that reason doesn't begin to function until the age of seven; this is certainly contradictory—so we must ask ourselves, what is it that permits the soul to express its reason at the age of five? Well, it is the form that the soul has incarnated into. Now, when the thinking of the masses begins to evolve to the greater possibilities that exist within the human being and no longer limit the expressions of the soul faculties, whether it's in a two-year-old or it's in a twenty-year-old, then those souls will be able, you understand, to express more fully in a younger child.

Now, why do some souls enter bodies that we consider to be defective or diseased, etc.? Well, that is also according to what that particular soul, in its evolving incarnations, of course, has merited. Now, who set that law into motion? Number one: The individual soul entering the form set it into motion that it would enter that type of form for the experiences necessary for its own unfoldment and soul expansion. Number two: The parents who

conceived that physical form and mental form also merited that
type of an experience for their own soul growth and expansion. Now Nature, in and of herself, does not, if left alone, have
what we call defects. Defects are created by the intervention
in nature's divine natural laws. And so it is, friends, that man
experiences—whether it's the air we're breathing or the forms
that we're in—we are constantly experiencing the effects of the
laws that we're setting into motion and the laws that we have
transgressed, nature's natural laws. We experience earthquakes
because we interfere with the natural laws that govern this particular planet. Does that help with your questions?

Yes.

Because it is possible for any soul, if the form, you understand, is not obstructing it, for the soul faculty known as reason
to express itself. Absolutely and positively. Remember, in that
nine-month time the mind records all experiences that the parents have, especially the mother. Every experience, every emotion, every thought, every act, and every deed for those basic
nine months is being recorded in the embryo of that little child,
yes. And so the mothers and parents bear a great responsibility
when they have children. Now someone else had a question?

*If disease is the imbalance of the soul faculties and the bodily
functions, how is this energy directed to cause chemical changes
in the physical body or deficiencies or neurological deficiencies?*

Thank you very much. Some of the parts of the physical
anatomy have been given in *The Living Light*. More have been
given, of course, in the classes. For example, when harmonious,
peaceful thoughts are entertained in the mind, there is a chemical change that takes place within the physical body and the
person will experience what is known as good health. Now each
attitude of mind, which is a combination of thoughts entertained
by an individual—and I'm not saying that a person says, "Well, I
have a backache," and consequently they have a backache. Now,

we're not discussing that: we're discussing something else. We are discussing the emotions especially.

Now what happens when a person has desire and the desire is not fulfilled? There is no release of this energy. A certain amount of it gets released during a sleep state and that's called their dreaming, but unfortunately, not a sufficient amount, considering the number of desires that a human being has in the course of a day and the number of desires that they do not express or fulfill. Now that energy gets bottled up, so to speak, in the mind, in the subconscious. Now something's going to happen to that energy: it is going to find a release somehow, someway. This energy starts to bring about an imbalance in the physical body, and that imbalance, you understand, releases energy. Just ask a person that's sick and ask them how energetic they feel. It releases this energy. And so it is again we mention and stress the great importance of not suppressing desire, you see.

Now most of us are so used to suppression of desire that we're hardly even consciously aware that we're doing it, moment by moment, you see. We've become addicted to the suppression, instead of working with it. And so it is that our bodies become imbalanced, because our thoughts, you understand, are imbalanced. How many minutes in the course of a day does a person really think thoughts that are peaceful and joyous and harmonious? How many times in a day, how many minutes in a day do we really think, you know? It's kind of like, here we are a machine and we go and we do this according to the system that we have established for ourselves. How many times do we really stop to think about—really think about—anything? It's very rare that the average person spends any time to think about anything, unless it's how difficult life is. That seems to be a common thought with many people.

If you have an excessive amount of energy, then how can you constructively alleviate any illness? By right thought?

Definitely and positively. Now, for example, if a person has a great deal of resentment, you know, they're going to have problems in that area of their anatomy. It just isn't a cure-all to release the energy. It is most beneficial to bring the chemical balance into the body, but we cannot entertain thoughts of resentment, you understand, and be free from the effects that are going to take place in that part of our anatomy, you see. And we cannot suppress our conscience, which is a spiritual faculty with a dual capacity, knows right from wrong, doesn't have to be told, without having some problems in that part of our anatomy. And we cannot continue to beat our head against the wall in misunderstanding and not have problems with that part of our anatomy.

I was thinking more if a person is aware that they have an excessive amount.

Oh yes. Some people have an overabundance of energy. Well, the truth of the matter is they're that receptive, you understand, to the divine flow, which is everywhere. And some people, they seem to have about this much energy.

Right. So the people—

· Of course, energy follows attention, you know. You get their attention, you'll see they have just as much energy as everybody else. But you have to first get their attention, then you'll see how much energy they have. The people that seem to have this overabundance of energy, of course, they are the ones that have the greater potential for problems and difficulty, because they are not balanced. They are not expressing as much of that energy as is bottled up inside of them. And so they should go deep inside of themselves and seek something within themselves that they really would like to do, you know.

Now, there's another factor involved, too, with people who seemingly have an overabundance of energy: they must have feedback. One of the first things that happens with a person that has an overabundance of energy and they go into some

project, if they do not see that that project is successful in bringing results, they stay a very short time with it. Because that's
the way those types of minds work, you understand. You see,
they're just that much open and they have to see all parts of
it. And instead of being a brother to the project, they're usually either the father or the mother; the tendency of possession
is very great, you understand. Yes. Does that help with your
question?

Very much.

Yes.

*How do we explain a person who, by all outward appearances,
for many, many years lived on the earth plane and was anti-
everything and very negative, who didn't believe in anything,
really, other than their own satisfaction, who didn't believe in
helping others, and yet was never ill a day of their life? Are we to
assume that all this is going to destroy the soul?*

Oh no! The soul cannot be destroyed. Thank you. That's a
very important question. I'm glad you brought it up. You see,
our thoughts and attitudes of mind, they form and they deform
our astral body, and that's the body that we have to function in
when we leave this physical body. And when you look into those
astral realms, if their soul has merited for their experience to be
in those astral realms, then that's where they'll have them. And
sometimes it's for many, many centuries. There is no escape of
divine law, for God, the Law itself, is never mocked. And so we
may see people here in this earth realm and we may see the
type that you are mentioning. And they seem to enjoy perfect
health, etc., but we do not know their inner being. And if you
open your eyes and view the lower astral realms, you will have
great understanding. There is no escape. None whatsoever.

Can someone like this on the earth plane be helped?

Definitely. They cannot only be helped while on the earth
realm, but they can be helped after they've passed to the astral
world. Absolutely and positively. There are many rescue doctors.

See, no thought ever goes in vain and most of our students spend some time in their meditation in directing their thoughts of peace and light to those souls on the other side, you see. Yes. That's known as rescue work in the Spiritualist movement.

I would like to have some guidance on what a parent can do to help a child in its spiritual development.

Thank you very much. And that's an excellent question. The lady would like to know what a parent can do in helping their child in their spiritual unfoldment. Remember, friends, though it's only semantics, remember that the soul unfolds like the flower, like the rose. It can't develop. There's nothing it can develop to, but it does unfold.

Now, how can a parent help their own children in their spiritual unfoldment? Well, number one: The parent must feel the soul of the child. They must first learn to get their own mind at peace, so they can feel what that little soul is trying to express. So many times, with parents, a child has a natural soul talent, but that talent is never permitted to unfold and to express itself because the parents have their own desires of what they want their child to be. I would say to the parents, spend less time in thought and concern of what they want their child to be in a material, physical, money world, and spend at least a balanced amount of that time in what the child's soul is seeking to unfold and to express.

Many times a child will do certain things and the parent can see that, as far as they're concerned, that is not going to be productive or beneficial in this material world, and so they immediately suppress it or at least attempt to do so. Consequently, what they have done, in truth, is to cripple the expression of that little soul. And if the child is brought into a type of concentration and meditation at a very early age—the age of three is not too early to start a little child into concentration/meditation: that's a little silent time. And if the parents will not suppress the so-called invisible playmates that the little child has, because the children, you understand, are usually very psychic and they have these different little playmates and children that they play with from the world of spirit. And if the parents will gain a little more understanding about interdimensional communications, that there is no death and there are no dead, and tries to gain an understanding that the soul is not brand new, here, this time in a little body—because the soul is not.

You see, a soul in a two-year-old child, the soul is not two years old, friends. Goodness sakes, only that vehicle, you see, only the vehicle is two years old. The soul is centuries old and has untold amounts of experiences, but it is limited in its expression through the two-year-old body that it is expressing to. If the parent will consider treating the child on spiritual levels like the adult that it really is, then they will get a much better response and it will be a greater benefit to the child's spiritual unfoldment. Thank you. Yes.

I was just nodding in agreement and against conventional Sunday schools for their handling of spiritual unfoldment for little children. They get bored so quickly and so early.

Yes, because they're usually programmed.

Because that is not food for their soul.

That is not food for their soul.

They're playing little coloring games, as a rule.

Yes.

This is rather a loaded question, but I would like to have your and your teacher's understanding—

All questions are loaded to the loader.

Thank you. What is the difference between the psychic realm and mediumship?

A vast difference. The question is asked, What is the difference between the psychic realm or a psychic and a medium? Now the psychic realm, you understand, is something that all of us, to some extent, are being affected by. Now, many people have impressions or this or that, which is psychic. They have an impression or they see a vision, for example, that there's going to be an earthquake. Well, they see that because it exists in a psychic realm. But it was created by the mass fears of the people, either in this plane or in another plane. Now that's psychic. Usually what comes to a psychic are disasters. Now the reason for that is because so-called thoughts of disaster have a great deal of energy behind them and they make a strong impression in this so-called invisible realm.

Now the psychic, in and of itself, has absolutely nothing whatsoever to do with spiritual unfoldment or with your soul expansion. A person can live in this world a lifetime and never experience any psychic experiences and be very spiritually evolved and go into a very high spiritual realm, if that's the type of person, good person, that they basically are. So we must first understand that psychic has nothing whatsoever to do with your soul expansion and your spirituality. Nothing whatsoever. In fact, one of the grossest materialists the world has ever known could be an expert psychic, you see, because that has nothing to do with your soul faculties and your spirituality.

Now in reference to what the Spiritualists call mediumship— a medium being one who, through his instrumentality, is able to establish contact with those who have passed to a spirit world— that is something that a psychic is not capable of doing, because they may see people in a psychic dimension, but they are not seeing the souls of the so-called departed, because they do not exist in that psychic realm. Now, a person may say to another individual, "Well, now, I see your mother here." And they may be able to describe her in detail and not be a medium at all, have nothing to do with mediumship. The point of the matter is that they see the individual in that person's aura, because that is coming either out of the subconscious of the individual they're talking to or it's coming from their conscious thought. And what they do, they see a flat image, you see. They see a subjective image. They do not see it dimensional. They see it like you see a television: it's very flat. Now that is psychic: that is not mediumistic.

And we have to recognize, to realize, that mediums are psychic, but psychics are not mediums. And that mediums may be giving from the psychic. They may be giving from their mediumship and their contact into the spiritual realms or they may be giving from the astral realms. They may be giving from the mental realms. They may be giving from the thought world and all these different dimensions. There is no guarantee, my friends, that every message is coming from the realms of light. There is no guarantee that every message is coming from the psychic or from the mental world. You see, that is entirely dependent upon the true motive of the individual. That's what it is really dependent on.

If your motive to establish contact with other dimensions is to serve God, not for your ego's glorification and your senses' gratification, then you will do it because it's right to do it. You will not be concerned whether the message was accepted or rejected. You will not be concerned whether the prophecy came to pass or it didn't come to pass, because you're giving it in the service to the Divine. And so it has nothing to do with how good it makes your head feel or how bad it makes your head feel. You give it because it's right to give it and you care less what people do with it. Now that's the basic difference, in my understanding, between genuine mediumship and psychics. Thank you. Yes.

You mentioned that consideration is necessary to have understanding.

Man cannot understand what he does not consider.

Can he consider what he does not understand?

So there you find that they are totally related and cannot be separated. You cannot separate total consideration from understanding, and you cannot separate understanding from total consideration.

Could you relate those to awareness?

Man cannot consider, nor understand, what he is not aware of. It's impossible. If we're not aware of the book that we're holding in our hand, we cannot consider it and we cannot understand it. And so, without consideration and understanding, there's no awareness.

In last week's class it was mentioned that we are more than one form within this form. May I ask how many forms we are?

We are nine. Yes. Does that help with your question?

Definitely. Thank you.

You're welcome.

Would you please explain the divine merit system?

I'll be happy to share my understanding with you, according to what I myself have merited. The lady has asked in reference to the divine merit system. Perhaps it would be best to share our understanding in this way: there is no thought that man can entertain in his mind that does not leave his universe and return unto him. If we have a thought of envy, if we have a thought of greed, if we have a thought of anything or anyone, that always returns unto us. And that is the divine merit system. Man, in his soul's incarnations and his evolution, sooner or later, man will learn that it pays to be good, for it is his own survival. Now how many centuries this will take different souls is dependent, of course, upon the individual soul.

You see, my friends, be good to yourself, then you can be good to the world. Now most people are not good to themselves. And the reason that they're not good to themselves is because they don't consider their true self. They might consider one level or a few levels of consciousness, but they're not considering the eternity which they truly are. They're not considering what's truly in their best interest. Because if they were, if they were truly considering all these other levels inside of themselves, then the world, which is peopled by people, would not have all the problems that it has. So often man is not good to himself, basically, and therefore he can't be good to the world, you see. It's not possible, because he doesn't consider his full being. If he doesn't consider his full being, he doesn't understand his full being. And the reason that he doesn't consider and doesn't understand his full being is because he has not yet made the effort to gain the awareness, you see.

Now, I mean, everyone within this room here this evening knows the word *subconscious*. But how many people have spent how many hours and how many years to try to find out how it works? Well, you see, my friends, it is a part of us, but we haven't spent the time and the energy and the effort to find out about it. Oh, we've read about what the psychiatrists have said and we've read about what the psychologists have said. But what have we, as individuals, done about it? Here's a part of us that runs our whole life and we haven't given it very much consideration. Wouldn't you, perhaps, consider that that's not being too good to oneself?

I agree.

You see? Now why is it we haven't given more study and investigation to what the psychologists call the subconscious?

Would that be because of fear that we have not investigated it?

It's an interesting question. Could it be of fear? Does man not investigate what he fears? Well, it would take a little courage, wouldn't it? Yes, it would take a little courage. So it could be, for many, a type of fear, of course. But more, it's a lack of understanding of how much that inner mind controls our life, you see. When the world becomes aware that every experience that we encounter—when you truly become aware that every experience that you have, you and you alone have set into motion, regardless of appearance. If you're unhappy and people are bothering you and you don't like the way they're talking or acting, you and you alone, my friends, have merited that experience. Like a great magnet in the universe, you have pulled the disturbance to you.

You cannot cure it by looking out there at people. You can do nothing for yourself, believe me, by trying to go out there and change someone else. You can do everything for yourself by going inside and asking in honesty and in truth, "What inside of me is pulling these experiences into my conscious awareness?" Because, my friends, it's always something inside of ourselves. That's where to start. If you're not happy with the way things are going, if you're short of money, which is the usual cry of the world today, if you're going through poor health, don't look outside. There's no answer there: it's only illusion and delusion. Stop and go inside of yourself. If you don't have friends, ask yourself, "What is it inside of me that is not a true friend, because I have none?" Don't you see? Again and again, the words are brought forth, to think, my friends: it's inside of you.

But don't think in despondency and say, "Oh, what's the use? Life is so miserable." Well, you're not going to get out of it that way. You know, it's a great change to the emotions to switch from blaming people for their experiences and blaming people when things don't go right and blaming circumstances. It's such a switch for the mind and the emotions to turn around and say, "Look what I'm doing to myself." Do you see that, students? Take the time to go inside. It's not your husband's fault. It's not your wife's fault. It's not the fault of religion. It's not the fault of the government. It's not the fault of anyone or anything outside yourself. Don't blame your parents, because your soul merited those parents, do you understand? Don't blame that you're born in the 1970s, because your soul merited being born in the 1970s, see. Don't blame the country that you're born in, because you set that law into motion and you merited birth in that country. And don't blame the students you're involved with, or uninvolved with, because you also merited them.

I tell you honestly, it's the only way I found to be free: Whatever happens to you, say, "Well, Lord, I set that into motion. I didn't do it consciously, but help me to find the way out, because I don't want to stay there too long." Can't you see? Why waste your life-giving energy constantly blaming something outside of yourself? You'll never be free that way, either here or hereafter. Remember, we take our mind with us, and if we're on the wheel of delusion, of blaming things outside of us for our detriments or our benefits, then that's right where we stay until we finally grow out of it. Yes.

You said there are nine forms.

There are nine minds and, therefore, there are nine forms. Yes, because mind is form.

Mind is form.

Yes. The only thing that's formless and free is the Divine Spirit. That is formless.

Thank you.

You're more than welcome. Now, you know, friends, that we have spoken so much on thought and the mind, and it's important that we should do so, because so little attention is given to it, it seems, in religions and philosophies today. There is a great need to understand, not to understand somebody else's book or writings or this or that, but to understand the way we feel. Think about how you feel when you wake up in the morning. Think about how you feel in the course of a day. Now, you know, sometimes a person will meet a certain person and they'll say, "Got to stay away from that person. Every time I see them, I feel just terrible." Well, let's stop and ask ourselves, "What is it that that person is expressing that causes my intolerance to rise and control my soul?" What is it inside of ourselves, you see? That's where the change can be made.

I admit, you know, we're all working to expand our tolerance and I find it a bit difficult sometimes, in that area, with different experiences, you know, in working with the public. But I have to pause to think and say, "Well, I have a choice. I can let them control my soul and rob me of my peace or I can just cut them out of my thoughts this instant. I have the choice to do that."

Now which is the wisest thing to do? Now someone else had a question.

With all this negative thinking, suppose we've become ill. What does the Teacher think about going to doctors? We must take drugs at times; how does this tie in with helping ourselves? Is it permissible to go to others for health?

Thank you. Remember, a wise student does not go beyond his understanding at any given moment. And if it is the student's understanding that he needs a doctor and he needs to take a certain medication to help him, then that is, of course, what the student should do in that area. Also, the student might recognize, of course, and realize that the doctor is simply working on the effect. They're not working on the cause and they'll readily admit it, if they're a good doctor. They are working on the effect. And so the student must make the effort to go inside of themselves—while the doctor, of course, is working on the effect—to work on the cause, because only by finding the cause and removing it are we going to be freed from that particular condition.

Could you please speak on the principle of healing in regard to the Law of Solicitation?

Yes. The principle of healing in reference to the Law of Solicitation: If a person solicits—"Knock and the door shall open; seek and ye shall find"—if a person solicits help with a health condition and the individual that they are soliciting the help from is in a position to offer—if they are a spiritual healer—their services as a healer or a counselor, or just to sit in silent meditation and direct this perfection from their own aura, if that is solicited, then it can be beneficial. But unsolicited help is ever to no avail. It is ever to no avail.

Now let's look at it another way. Let's look at it in energy fields. Say, for example, a person is very, very ill and the people that are around this ill person have absolutely no faith and no thought of what is known as spiritual healing, and someone asks for spiritual healing to be done for that person. You must understand and realize that there is a negative field that this energy must penetrate before getting to the patient or to the recipient. Now a lot of people, I know, don't understand what a negative field looks like. A negative field is like a solid cement wall and it is not the easiest thing in the world to penetrate, either with spiritual healing or with communication or psychic or anything else. It can be penetrated, but in the penetrating of the negative field, it dissipates so much of the energy, do you understand? It dissipates so much of the energy. This is why unsolicited help is totally to no avail, you see. Those who are seeking, those are the ones who are ready, and they will knock. And if they have patience, the door will open for them, you see. Does that help with your question?

Thank you very much.

You're welcome.

To continue on with what you were just discussing, for example, the person who is in need is in the center of this negative field and realizes his need. He considers the possibility of spiritual help and solicits spiritual help. Does this act on his part penetrate that negative field?

It depends on how strong and how much energy is emanated from the patient. Yes, in other words, how strong their faith is and their positive feelings in their seeking. You know, you must realize that when a person is doing absent healing, number one: the person that is seeking the healing—the healer must see the person, through the processes of concentration and visualization, in perfection in their own magnetic field. Then, they release that. Then, that image actually goes and, like water reaches its own level by its own weight, that image will find its own mold. Do you understand? However, if there is a strong negative field when this image goes to reach the person that's back here, it gets dissipated in this negative field. You see, even the Nazarene said, "Because of your lack of faith, ye shall not be healed." Read the Bible. It tells you all about healing in there. Because of the lack of faith of those particular people at that particular time, he could not do any healing. He was no fool, you understand.

And it's the same thing when they go to mediums and they want this proof and they want that proof and they want them to work in this material world and find ways of getting money for them and all that foolishness. It doesn't work. You see, it just doesn't work. That's why we have fortune tellers in the world to take care of the money for people, not spiritual mediums. There's a big difference. And so it's the same thing with healing. If the unbelievers want you to go out in the street and they want you to demonstrate your so-called gifts and this and that, well, the demonstration goes all the way down there, because that's not the purpose of it. Don't you see what I mean? You're going to dissipate your energy through these negative fields. Yes, even this fellow, he was on television, I think, he had such great difficulty in bending these forks or spoons with his powers. Well, why did he have such difficulty? It's most understandable. So much of the energy was dissipated on the negative vibrations and negative fields that he had to work with. It's very understandable.

See, it doesn't mean that a person must believe in communication or that a person must believe in spiritual healing. It means the motive must be pure, you see. They don't have to believe, but their motive coming from their soul, to be helped, that's where it is, you see. And they're open-minded enough to accept wherever the help comes from, it comes from God; it doesn't matter what person it is. And then there's a big difference. Thank you very much.

We are taught that every living thing or everything has soul. Are we not like rocks?

Everything is soul and has a form, yes.

All right.

Now soul is only the covering of the Divine Intelligence, known as Spirit. The divine, formless Spirit enters form—individualizes in the covering known as soul. Yes, go ahead.

With rocks, for example, at what point does soul take flight? Whereas in humans or in the animals—

Rocks disintegrate at varying ages and so do other forms.

Well, I mean, if you take a big rock, and it slowly—

I see what you want. And somebody splits it in half, does the soul leave?

Yes.

Yes. Well, I would like to ask you a question. If the doctor amputates your arm, does your soul leave your body?

No.

You have your answer.

It's an inanimate object, but it still has a soul, let's say—

What do you mean, "It's an inanimate object"?

Well, it's not . . .

Moving?

You know what I mean. It's just there.

Well, I don't accept that, because, you see, the rock, in and of itself, is in a constant state of motion.

Right. Right. Weathering or something.

Within itself.

Yes. How does one rock merit being in the astral world after it passes and another merit being in a higher spiritual world? I mean, how are they chosen to go to these different worlds?

They're not chosen. Well now, I see we're getting into a very, very deep discussion here. Number one: What is it that sends us into an astral world? Well, of course, it's the astral vehicle, the astral body. Did someone say that the rock went to the world of spirit? I wasn't aware of that particular teaching, and there seems to be some implication there. Of course, now, we could say, on the other hand, "Well, who wants to go to the world of spirit? I'm a geologist and they don't have any minerals or rocks there, so I'll stay in the lower realms." Well, now, we have to do a little thinking, you know. It's like the animal lovers. They're not about to go to heaven, if there aren't a lot of dogs there. And I don't blame them, I wouldn't go to that heaven either.

But now, remember, friends, you have to go beyond the limitations of form. All right, we say that there's a rock and that has a soul. Of course, it's a soul, because the effect is a form. All right. Now, we understand, hopefully, that the individualization and the awareness is not the same as it is in the higher-developed forms of creation, all right? Now, for example, the question is, then, Does a rock know it's down here on Earth or does a rock now know it's in the astral world? Well, it doesn't have, in the form, that much awareness. Do you understand?

Now, the dog is aware, well, that it's here. And then it leaves its little body and it is aware that it's still aware. It's still a dog, it still sees trees, and it sees people, etc. But the dog, you understand, though it has its understanding and it has its awareness—the span of understanding and awareness broadens as the forms evolve.

And so it is a great responsibility that the seeming most developed forms on earth, known as the human race, have to help all the other forms in their evolution, you see. We have that responsibility. We have the responsibility with the dogs and the cats to treat them kindly and to help them to educate themselves, you know. Because, you know, animals, they have strong egos, also. If anyone's ever had a dog or a cat, they ought to know that. And so they have a need for the expansion of their little consciousness and the education of their ego and to learn some type of self-control, that they can't have what they want, when they want, any time they want it. And so we have that responsibility. But who is man responsible to? He usually gets what he wants, when he wants, or he gets all upset and gets all excited and then he learns the hard way. See, society has a way of teaching him.

I wonder if you could expand a little more on the Law of Merit. Am I correct in assuming that before we incarnate to the Earth planet that we pass through the Allsoul?

Before we incarnate into the Earth planet, we reviewed all experiences yet to be experienced, yes.

If we had reached that level of consciousness, wouldn't we have been pretty highly evolved before we incarnated to this planet?

Well, if you want to put it that way, then that's known as the Law of Descent and Ascent, which, of course, is the law that governs form. That is the duality, you understand? You rise to the peak, to go to the depth, to rise to the peak. That is the Law of Creation. And the Law of Creation, you understand, is the Law of Form. And soul is the covering, which is the form, of the divine, formless Spirit. So in that sense, yes. Yes. We came from the Light to go to the darkness, to rise to the Light, to return to the darkness, to rise again. That is true, yes.

I'm still not entirely clear as to why some people merit certain experiences and bodies, based on what you've just said, when they incarnate to any planet.

Because, you see, there is a 10 percent free will. People choose different experiences; therefore, they set different laws into motion. Now, say you give a person a $5 bill—give it to two people. Each one, a $5 bill. And you send them to the grocery store. Do they come back with identically the same products?

Not—

It would be quite rare, would you not agree? And so it is with the soul's expression, you understand. Different souls react to different things in different ways and set different laws into motion. Consequently, on their evolutionary incarnation, when they enter here in this earth realm or in any other realms, you find that they have varied experiences. See, God's manifestation—form—is variety. And every soul is different. Does that help with your question?

It just seems—

Or do you want to know why some particular individual is experiencing a certain experience?

Well, generally speaking, yes. Because, it seems to me, that we would have been through, in some previous incarnation, some of the experiences.

Perhaps this will help you. When a soul has gone through the dungeons and the pits of darkness and rises to the thrones of Light, compassion—a soul faculty—dictates that it return and help the others to rise. You see, it knows what it's like, because it has been there. Do you understand, perhaps, now?

Yes. Thank you.

And so it is with even the teachers that come from the realms of Spirit, and they lower their vibrations here ofttimes to this mundane world to help the souls in their mundane bodies, because they've been here and they know what it's like.

Now, for example, if you have a teacher or, say, a guide attracted to you to help you with impulsiveness, that simply means, if that's a guide from the realms of Light, they were one of the most impulsive persons there ever was. That's how come they can help you, you see. They did all those things. Do you understand? And so they're attracted to you. Your need is to grow through that level. And so you attract them into your universe, do you understand? And they're pretty well versed because they've been through all those pits. And so it is with the soul's experiences.

We've been speaking this evening regarding varying varieties of form and forms, and that the soul expresses in many ways, even in the rock. And it would seem, in observing throughout the many universes, that each thing is a state of consciousness, that

each atom, electron, and molecule, each thought in all time is a
state of consciousness.

Absolutely! Because the Divine Intelligence is the Divine
Intelligence. There is no place that it doesn't exist. There is no
place, *no place,* students, that you don't find God. Because God
is everything and everywhere. Yes?

We are guided to understand eighty-one levels of awareness.
Could you relate, perhaps, how the eighty-one become the infinite
variety observed?

How they become the infinite variety of what?

The infinite variety observed.

Well, now, remember, friends, we're going to take first
things first. And first become aware of the levels of our own
subconscious. Because we cannot jump, you understand, from
one step up another twenty. So we're going to go step-by-step,
and understand not only the levels of our conscious mind, but
the levels of our subconscious mind. Because if we don't go
step-by-step and understand those levels, then we're going to
find that we do not have a solid foundation upon which to build
our understanding. Now I know that you are all aware that
these classes were never designed to build for you a foundation
of understanding, but they are designed to show you a way, and
many ways, to help you to help yourself to build those foundation blocks. Because we do not—and it is not our purpose
to—pour more information, more facts, into your computer.
It is our purpose to show you that it is in your best interest
to gain freedom, to remove the many, many things that have
already been entered into the mind. Because of the multitude
of thoughts that are entertained by the mind, the conscious
mind is not able to establish direct, observable contact with
its own soul. And this is why we're going to go very slowly
through the eighty-one levels of consciousness and the eighty-
one levels of awareness.

First, we want the students to find out for themselves what tape they're playing that makes them feel a certain way. What tape in their own subconscious are they playing that causes them and prompts them to do certain things? That is the first level to become fully versed in and aware of. When you wake up in the morning, students, and you have a feeling and you are able, through your own conscious effort, to find out what tape bank that is, you're beginning to become aware of your own self. We can never be free by awareness without. We can only be free by awareness within. And so first we must become aware of our thoughts and our feelings, and then we will be able to control what tapes we're playing from the depths of our mind. And when that happens, my friends, you will have self-control. And when you have self-control, you're on the path to truth and freedom. Thank you.

I would like to know your understanding as to the value of hypnosis in altering the tapes of the consciousness once some understanding has been gained, as to, say, certain tapes are giving you problems, certain things that are outmoded and need to be removed. Let's say you've had them for quite a long time and are having some difficulty removing them.

Yes, you want to know, in reference to our understanding, concerning hypnosis in your efforts to change your tapes of your own mind: is that your basic question?

Yes.

Number one: If you place yourself under the influence and control of another mind, then, what you've done, you've leased your soul for a time, do you understand? Because, you see, you have denied your own divinity, your own capabilities of controlling your own mind. Now I admit, it may appear to be a shortcut, but in the long run it isn't a shortcut at all. Hypnosis serves certain purposes nowadays in dentistry and things for the medical profession. But when you permit yourself, you understand, to come under the influence and the control of another human mind, what you have done, you have given up your divine right. Now, say that, perhaps, the question arises, then, in your mind, "Well, if that's the case, then what about a self-imposed type of hypnosis?" Right?

Right.

Well, at least it's better than the first question. I'm sure you will agree when you look into it thoroughly and investigate. Well, what does man mean by a self-hypnotic trance? What does he really mean? Does he mean that he has given control of his body and his thoughts to his subconscious? See, these are the questions we must ask ourselves: What do we mean by these things? Or does he mean that he, his consciousness, has stepped out here objectively and is aware? His conscious mind is thinking this way and his subconscious mind is thinking this way, and he's over here and he's working on the two minds to bring them into harmony. Now, if that's what he means by self-hypnosis—but that's not my understanding of self-hypnosis— then it can only be beneficial to him. That is given in *The Living Light* under the Law of Disassociation. And when you practice that, you see, you'll be here and you'll be able to see those other two beings and you will be able to bring them into balance.

The first thing is, friends, become aware. Aware of what? Aware of one's own true self. See, there are all kinds of teachings in the world. They can teach you a multitude of things, but they will be of no value and of no benefit if you do not apply the law and get in yourself and find out what's really going on. You can study a thousand books and a million philosophies, but they will benefit you not if you do not demonstrate the Law of Application. If they help you to get inside yourself and find God—because that's where God is, ever in. And when you find that, then the teaching has served its purpose. Otherwise, it is of no value to anyone.

Thank you, friends. We're past due. Let's have refreshments.

SEPTEMBER 20, 1973

CONSCIOUSNESS CLASS 25

Good evening, students. This evening we'll continue on with our classes. As we have in the past—and I'm sure that in time all of us will know our "Total Consideration" affirmation. Because this evening, as we did before, we will say it with the lights out and it will be most difficult to read anything. Now in your concentration and your meditation times, friends, if you will not try so hard, you will find that you will experience this peace within. Try not to use the mind in directing this peace, but let it flow up from the depths of your own soul, that you may experience this spiritual feeling. Now, if we're all ready for our meditation—

[The class holds a short period of mediation, after which a student reads Discourse 17 aloud.]

We'll speak forth the affirmation of "Total Consideration:"

I am the manifestation of Divine Intelligence. Formless
and free. Whole and complete. Peace, Poise, and Power
are my birthright.

The Law of Harmony is my thought and guarantees
Unity in all my acts and activities, expressing perfect
Rhythm and limitless flow throughout my entire being.

Without beginning or ending, eternity is my true awareness
and sees the tides of creation, as a captain sees his ship.

As the Light of Truth is sustained by the faculty of Reason,
I pause to think and claim my Divine right.

Right Thought.   Right Action.   Total Consideration.
Amen.   Amen.   Amen.

Before we get into our questions and answers this evening, I would like to share with you for just a few moments the barometer of understanding: how it is possible and quite easy, in truth, to gauge the depth of the extent of one's understanding in any particular area or in life itself. There have been many words spoken throughout his teachings on criticism and tolerance and understanding and the various soul faculties. Whenever we find ourselves in the level of criticism, what, in truth, we are doing is experiencing within us our own weaknesses, our own lacks and limitations. And so if you will become consciously aware of the times that you are experiencing this criticism, or at the times that you think you are being criticized, this is the barometer that tells you clearly and effortlessly exactly to what extent you have expanded your own spiritual understanding. And therefore, we have not been left in blindness or darkness: there are ways for us to know exactly where we are spiritually. We don't have to ask anyone. And I wanted to share that with you this evening before we got into our question-and-answer period.

Now you are free to ask any questions that you have concerning the teachings and spiritual matters, if you would just be so kind as to raise your hands. Now I know that some of the students that are new to this course—that this is their first class—have been a bit hesitant, some of them, in asking questions simply because they, perhaps, feel a little bit timid. But remember, if the question is important enough to you to entertain your thought, then it is important enough to be spoken forth.

In the affirmation, the first line ends with, "Peace, Poise, and Power are my birthright." I presume that peace, poise, and power are faculties.

Yes.

What are the corresponding functions?

Yes. The student has asked in reference to the affirmation of the words, "Peace, Poise, and Power are my birthright." And he stated that he presumes that they are faculties and what are their corresponding functions. Those have not yet been given, but they will be given at the appropriate time. Thank you very much.

Last week you spoke on the importance, when one is in confinement and on the great responsibility there is to the embryo, which, like a computer, is jotting everything down. The question now is, If there is a great negative feeling about the forthcoming child during the time of confinement, what effect will these negative feelings have on that child?

Thank you very much. In reference to a child in birth and the influences that were stated, negative or positive, that affect the child: Now some forms are created into this world with certain, what we seem to consider, defects. And some of them have a difficulty in retaining, difficulty in memory. Some of them have physical defects. Now, during this nine-month period, when this child is in the embryonic stage, the effects of these negative thoughts, or positive thoughts, register in the embryo. What we must consider, friends, is this: that the brain, the physical brain, is only the physical vehicle for the mental body, so that it may express in a physical dimension.

The mental body, the soul body, and the astral body: all of those bodies are contained within the seed. It's just like the mustard seed. In the mustard seed itself, very, very minute is the entire mustard tree. It exists in the seed. And so it is that the moment that those negative and positive poles come together, you see, those forms that are invisible to our physical sight have entered. And they are recording, like we are recording this very moment, mentally, various experiences that we are encountering. And so it is with that little child, that little embryo: it records all of those feelings and all the attitudes, especially of the mother. It may be negative or it may be positive. Now, the mother may—and it has happened many times—have an insatiable desire for her child to be a pianist or a this or that, etc. This can and does have an effect upon the life of that child in this earth realm. Does that help with your question?

Yes, thank you.

You're more than welcome. Does someone else have a question now?

It stated in tonight's discourse, "The soul can and does all things create. It is the power that flows through the soul [Discourse 17]." Could you explain the statement, "It is the power that flows through the soul"?

Yes. Thank you very much for your question concerning the statement in the discourse that was read this evening, "The soul can and does all things create. It is the power that flows through the soul." Now, my friends, we have repeatedly stated that God is not a creator. God, the Divine Intelligence, is a sustaining power that sustains all forms. For example, man thinks in his mind and he creates a certain object, but it is the power that moves through his mind, you understand, that actually sustains those forms that his mind conceives. So it is with the soul. In other words, the soul is the vehicle through which the Divine Intelligence expresses itself and sustains the vehicle. It is also the power which sustains whatever forms that are created by the intelligence that is within the soul itself.

We have created the bodies that we now are expressing through. Now, we say, "Well, if that's the case, does that mean that each soul, prior to entering this earth realm, has created they'll be 5 feet 6 or 7 or 11 or 12? They'll have brown hair and blue eyes, etc.?" In truth, that is correct. It does not mean that the soul has gone into a time of meditation and said, "I will express myself through a certain body that weighs a certain number of pounds with a certain family." But it has set laws into motion in its expressions through incarnations. It has set laws into motion that have guided the soul, just like a ship upon the sea, to a certain lineage, where this particular form would be created by those particular parents. And so it is, here and now and throughout all eternity, that we are, in truth, the captains of our ship, that we are, in truth, the masters of our destiny. But we have to accept that master ship within us. We have to claim our own birthright to realize, to recognize, and to accept that we are making this world, our world; and our world is a part of the whole.

You see, my friends, there is a level of consciousness in which all things are inseparably united. And so what affects one, in truth, is affecting, to some extent and to some degree, the whole. This is why, with the so-called catastrophes that we seem to have in this world, like earthquakes, tornadoes, and cyclones, etc., the Earth planet itself reacts to the disharmony, the discordant thoughts of the people that inhabit the planet. Now if we want better weather conditions, then we must learn to release from our beings—not that we pray for sunshine— but to release from our beings more harmonious, more joyous, more spiritual type of thinking. Because when those types of thoughts are emanated, they are of a high, fine rate of vibration that is extremely harmonious. And consequently, everything responds to it because it is a part of the whole. And so it is that the Divine Intelligence that flows through the soul sustains the form that the soul creates. Does that help with your question?

Yes, thank you.

Thank you very much. Someone else has a question.

We have been given the faculties of duty, gratitude, and tolerance, and the corresponding functions of self, pity, and friendship. Duty and self, gratitude and pity, and tolerance—I don't perceive friendship and tolerance. Would you please help me?

Yes, the lady is referring to the soul faculty of duty, gratitude, and tolerance and especially, how does it correspond, the particular triune faculty of tolerance, to the function of friend-ship. Is that your question?

Yes, it is.

Number one: Let us try to explain our understanding of the word *friendship.* Our understanding of the word *friendship* is true friendship, being use and not abuse, respects the rights of difference and will weather any storm. We understand this to be a function. Now, my friends, don't look upon the functions as bad and the faculties as good, because that's ridiculous. We're not teaching you that your functions are all bad. I mean, after all, the function of moving my mouth to speak isn't necessarily bad: it depends upon the listening ear and what they think and what I think at the time of doing it. And so it is that we do not look upon the functions as bad and the faculties as good. But we try and we strive to bring about some degree of balance between the two.

The lady does not see the reference between tolerance and friendship. Have you ever experienced friendship that you did not express some degree of tolerance?

No, of course.

It is not possible. And so it is in friendship, my good friends, if you do not have the energy, which is your consciousness, balanced between the function known as friendship and the soul faculty known as tolerance, then the friendship, my dear friends, will no longer be a friendship. It will either be a posses-sion or you'll make enemies out of each other. Because, you see, tolerance, which is the soul faculty corresponding to the sense function of friendship, is indispensable for the harmonious con-tinuity of the function. And so it is with all of your functions. If you want to experience a balance in your functions, then simply direct an equal amount of energy to the corresponding soul fac-ulty. Does that help with your question?

It certainly does.

Many Spiritualists talk about vibration and you hear a lot about vibes and it is really rather confusing. How do we use the word vibration? *What is* vibration, *as used in the Spiritualist churches? Would you explain that?*

Well, I cannot speak for any church outside of the one that we're trying to express through at the given moment, because everyone has—and even within our own church—everyone has a different understanding of what is meant by *vibration.* We have, on many occasions, tried to express a simple understanding of *vibration,* of how vibration is created, because, of course, it is a created thing. Now, again and again, it has been stated that our thoughts create our attitude of mind. If you go step-by-step, our thoughts create our thought patterns, our thought patterns create our attitude of mind, and our attitude of mind is our rate of vibration.

Now I'm sure you will agree, all students, that you experience different attitudes of mind. You experience them here at the class. You experience them when you leave. And we're constantly experiencing different attitudes. Some people like to have the attitude that it was such a beautiful day and they felt good with this day. Others have a different attitude. Well, it's a rate of vibration. Now what actually happens when you're entertaining an attitude of mind—and there is no time when we're not entertaining some attitude of mind. Because, you see, if we're out of vibration, we're no longer in the form, we're no longer expressing. This vibration we're speaking about is an emanation, an electromagnetic emanation, from our own aura.

Now following with that teaching of vibration is the simple teaching that like attracts like and becomes the Law of Attachment. Well, it only stands and follows that a vibration—these electromagnetic impulses that leave our aura—they attract their own kind. And so the teaching is very clear that whatever is happening to us is caused by us. But, my friends, we must get through the barrier of the illusion of self. You see, we have become oriented in what is known as self. And being so oriented in self, we cannot reach the level of universal consciousness where we can see and know beyond a shadow of any doubt that we are an inseparable part of the whole. Now being an inseparable part of the whole, we do not waste our time and energies to try to make everything else in form like ourselves, because if we do, we're defeating our own birthright of our own soul's expression.

I'm rather confused by the plural, "bodies". I believe you have stated there are nine bodies.

Nine bodies within one.

And nine minds.

That is correct. You see, anything that has body, has intelligence. Therefore, we understand it has mind. Otherwise, it couldn't be a body, you see.

Are these bodies sustaining—or is this what the soul creates in a form to express on different levels of awareness?

Yes, in other words, you're asking the question, now, for example, did the soul create the mental body? Is that the question you are asking? Because, you see, my friends, if it created that body, then it created all the other bodies it is expressing through. So, you see, that's the principle. You know, in these classes we want to get to the principle and not get bogged down with all these effects and things. Now, yes, the particular soul, your soul, created your mental body and it is in the process of refining it, just like everybody else's. You see, it merited the body that it incarnated into. Now, it merited that through laws it established along the pathway and the laws that it established along the pathway created that particular type of a mental body. Do you understand? See, there's a difference between that and saying that someone sat down and they created and said, "That's the kind of body I want to go into," you see.

I'm not speaking of bodies per se—or are we?

Yes, we are.

Like a sheath over—

Well, you see, the physical body is an effect of the astral body. It's an effect of it. And the astral body is an effect of the mental body. And then you have all these other bodies. And you have your vitality, your energy field. Well, that's your vital body. And those are all created, yes.

So it's like kind of a transparent, translucent layer of bodies?

Yes, one's inside the other, so to speak. You see, for example, it doesn't mean that my vital body is half an inch underneath my skin. It permeates all my skin, you understand: it permeates my whole being. And so it's the same thing with my mental body. See, my mental body permeates every part of my physical body. And whatever degree of a spiritual body that we have, that starts to permeate all this other, this piece of clay. Do you understand? Yes. And, you know, many times a person has their foot amputated or their leg. Well, they still feel that foot or leg because they're feeling it with another body, because, you see, that body has a foot and leg. Yes, it certainly does.

Now this body is very gross and it's a very heavy body. If you've ever experienced spiritual flight or even astral flight, when you leave this piece of clay, this physical body, and you return to it, it's like going into a very heavy laden body: tons and tons it seems to weigh. It really does, because it is the gross body, the physical body. Now, the spiritual body is very luminous: it emanates light from all parts of itself, you see. One body is inside the other body and they're permeating the whole. Does that help you with that question?

Does it relate, then, to certain degrees of vibration or different expressions, different levels?

Oh yes, absolutely and positively. They most certainly do. Definitely. And this is why some parts of the anatomy have been given, you know. But when you think of the anatomy, friends, just don't think of that physical body that we're used to: that's only one of nine of them. You see, we must consider all of them. Yes. Thank you very much.

Just the other day, a little boy that I know died. I don't know, but I believe that he probably died the moment of the accident, but he was kept alive by machines. And I was just wondering, at what time did his soul leave him or . . .

Well, in reference to a question of that nature, we must realize that the moment the Isle of Hist separates in this old physical body, it doesn't matter, the moment that separates, the soul leaves on its flight. It actually leaves the body. Now whether or not they've kept that isle together by artificial means, etc., you see, then the soul's going to remain there until that moment.

Now, I know that some people may entertain the thought that the body is being kept alive artificially. The heart's being pumped, etc. My good friends, it doesn't work that way. That soul stays inside of that house of clay until that moment—and when that moment arrives, that soul leaves. Believe me, it's left. It's really left. Now some other teachings may refer to it as when the golden bough is snapped, when the silver cord is broken. It doesn't matter what they call it, but when that happens, there is no return into that physical body. It is contrary to natural, divine law and there is no return.

Now, because we do not understand that some people could appear to be what our eyes seem to say is dead, and that some doctors could give an examination and say, "Well, that person is absolutely dead," and they've been gone maybe seven or eight days, but, you see, the Isle of Hist has never separated. Consequently, the soul can return; whether we think they're dead or not dead is immaterial. The point is that that separation never fully took place. But once it takes place, my friends, it doesn't make any difference who it is: you don't get back into that particular physical body. No. You see, the disintegration process has already been established at that moment, you see. It just starts in immediately. Of course, we understand there's a constant chemical change going on, around the clock, every minute, inside all of us. But once that separation takes place, there's no return.

When there are no longer any electrical impulses from the brain . . .

Yes.

The heart is kept alive by artificial means for seven or eight days.

Yes.

But for seven or eight days there has been no activity.

The soul has not left. It has not severed—

It is still in the body?

There's still a connection. It may or may not be inside of the body, you understand. It may be out there in some other dimension, but that silver thread is still connected, and until that is snapped, there is no real so-called transition. Does that help with your question?

Yes. I'd like to know how it is snapped. Also, does freezing the body at the time of death cause the individual soul to linger with the form, rather than to go on and let go of the Isle of Hist?

When the consciousness is completely removed from the nine bodies in which it is expressing at this time, when the consciousness is fully removed from the nine bodies, there is no return. The Isle of Hist separates when that consciousness is fully withdrawn. Now, the consciousness cannot express through what it cannot identify with. And once it has fully left, it can no longer identify. And therefore, the transition is, and there is no return. Do you understand?

Yes.

Now let me make that a little bit clearer, because I feel that some people do not yet understand. When the consciousness fully withdraws its identity—and when I say fully, it must withdraw through the nine vehicles, you understand. Say, for example, it's in the physical body. When the soul body, the vital body, and all of the other bodies fully withdraw the consciousness from its connection to the physical body, there is no return to the physical body. Thank you very much.

Parts of his body were donated for a transplant. Now, does the soul or his spirit continue on with those parts of his body?

It doesn't matter, because the only parts that they could donate would be the physical ones. They couldn't donate his mental ones. They couldn't donate his soul body. They couldn't donate his psychic body. They couldn't donate his vital body. All they could do was donate the clay, yes. Now, for example—and I'm glad you brought that point up—many people have asked me in reference to donating parts of their physical anatomy. If a person is mentally and emotionally attached to this house of clay and they donate it to science or whatever they care to, to the degree and extent of the attachment to that physical body will they experience what happens to that physical body. You know, it's just like, my friends, if you're greatly attached to, say, a pair of shoes, and you have the shoes, but you just love those shoes, and if they're misplaced, you just go into an emotional trauma. Well, that's the way many people are with their physical body, you see. And so when the day comes that their soul and those other bodies leave their physical body, the attachment is so great, many people hover over the graveyard. Many people, you know, stay bound in the earth realm and they witness the different parts of their anatomy being donated to science, etc. So that doesn't mean that we don't care for the body that we're in, but we certainly entertain the possibility and the thought that we're more than the shell. Because if we don't, we've got a little problem when we leave it. I can assure you of that, because I've witnessed many, many souls over the graveyards and they hover for, sometimes, untold centuries, yes. I hope that will help you folks with your questions.

If one casts off their physical body, do they then have eight bodies?

No, no, they don't. Thank you very much for bringing it up. You see, my friends, death is nothing more than birth, and birth is nothing more than death. And whatever you lose, be it a physical body or anything else, you gain something else. Now that does not mean to imply that when you lose your physical body—when it returns to the elements from which it was taken in the first place—you really don't lose anything. You're just returning it to its source, you know.

It only goes to prove there's nothing we own in life. See, we've borrowed everything. And if we can remember that, you know, because we don't own anything. If man owns something, he can choose to do what he wants with it. Well, we own nothing. Everything returns to its source. And so the physical body is brought up from the elements of this Earth planet. And Mother Earth has the divine right to claim what is hers and it belongs to her, and so she takes it back again. But I do not mean to imply when that body returns to Mother Earth that you automatically look and you find you have that other body. That body is there, but your consciousness may not yet be fully identified with it. Do you understand?

Now, this is of great importance, friends, when you're seeking spiritual awakening, and by that, I mean an awakening of your mind, so that you can get it out of the way and let it be at peace and experience that spirituality. We cannot experience what we do not identify with. So what is the logical thing to identify with if we want experiences that would be beneficial to us? Isn't it simple? We identify ourselves with peace, for peace is the power known as God. And so when we identify with that, we become the thing we identify with. If we are not aware of these different bodies that our consciousness is expressing through at this time, it simply means that we have not consciously identified with them.

You know, it's just like in the church service in this church or in spiritual communication and interdimensional communications: if the people do not give the thought of the possibility of communion, then they cannot possibly experience it. Now that doesn't mean that you sit and say, "Well, I feel everybody's here and that's fine and dandy." But you see, friends, you *can* feel that; you can feel anything. You can feel the ocean roaring there in Hawaii. I just saw it that instant, before I could get my mouth open, because that's how powerful thought is, do you understand? So choose wisely what you identify with, because whatever you identify with, whatever you entertain in thought, which is identification, then, of course, my friends, that's what you're going to experience, that's what you're going to become. So you identify spiritually; then you become spiritual, you see. Now, that doesn't mean to imply that you sit back and say, "All right, I'm identifying spiritually," and go out and do everything that is not in balance with what is known as spiritual awakening. Of course not. It doesn't work like that. You start identifying spiritually. You will find yourself changing inside yourself, whether you like it or not, you see. It pays to be good: it's known as survival. It's known as survival.

Would the nine bodies or nine minds—does that represent nine areas of growth within each mind?

If you consider by your question that that's totality, then your answer is yes.

And is this how you reach the eighty-one levels?

Well, you see, you would have to go more deeply into your thoughts that prompted your question before I could answer your question in the affirmative. In other words, we're taking this out of context, you see. I'm only getting a part of what your full meaning really is. If you mean by your question, the totality of expression, then the answer is in the affirmative: yes.

I read an article this morning that said that forty million years ago, a horse was the size of today's cat. And it seems like today we have more tall people than we had twenty years ago. I was wondering what would prompt this evolutionary process?

Well, thank you very much for your question. And you're speaking in regard to the evolution of the forms and not particularly of the soul incarnation expressing through them.

Whenever energy is directed to any part of the anatomy, it simply helps to increase the expansion in that particular area. Now that doesn't mean that it happens overnight. It doesn't mean that it happens in one or two centuries, you understand? But it does mean that that's what takes place. Say that you took all of the people, or say you took a hundred people and you sent them to Tibet, where they'd look at the sun, the bright sun shining on the snow-capped mountains, year after year, century after century after century after century. Well, what you would find in the centuries yet to be is that they would have very slanted, squinted eyes. Well, of course they would. Because nature is the great adapter and so nature adapts. Do you understand? And so it is with all forms. Thank you very much.

If one wishes to send absent healing to an animal hospital or to a human hospital, what is the most effective way of doing this? And also, how do our spirit doctors use this directed thought in treating the ill person or animal?

Thank you very much. And that has been covered in one of our other discussions, perhaps in a little different way. If a person is desirous of helping an animal or a plant or a human into what is a fuller expression of its divine right, which is known as perfect harmony or health, they may bring about, through the process of visualization, an image: the perfection of the form that they are trying to aid. Do you understand? They must first create that. They must create that image in their own aura, in their own consciousness and then—and this is where most people have great difficulty—they must release it to the Divine Intelligence. Now if they do not release it, then what is simply happening is they're working on mental levels. And there could be some benefit in the mental level, but the mental level, you see, is only the mind body and that's only one of several bodies. You see, if a body is affected—now hear this—if the physical body is affected, don't just work on the physical body. Work on the mental body and the vital body and all those other bodies.

You can't just work on one body, my friends, when you're trying to help an individual. You must work on all bodies. So you bring this about inside of your own consciousness; then you release it to the Divine Intelligence.

Now then, you want to know, how do the spirit doctors use this energy to help another individual? Well, it's really quite simple. This image is created in your consciousness, in your mind; then you release it. They take that balanced, harmonious energy, which is what it really is—you've got it into balance, you see, you've got that feeling—hopefully you have; that's the way it works—then that is impinged upon the form that is suffering. Now, when a person is truly in need, the chances of help are at their greatest, because the barrier of resistance has been broken down. Now this is when a person can receive the greatest help: when they have the greatest need. And so the teaching is very clear and simple: unsolicited help is ever to no avail. That's why unsolicited help is to no avail, friends, because the barrier, known as the ego, is up like a wall. But when they're on the bottom, way down here, that barrier is down and you can do the greatest work. Does that help you with your question?

In helping our loved ones in the spirit world, is this done the same way: picture them in . . .

In the perfection.

In perfection . . .

And then release it.

And then releasing it, that's the best way to help them also?

It works.

How does our teaching feel about hunting for sport and killing animals?

That is a level of consciousness. The teachings respect the divine right of the individual. And if an individual has not yet grown to the level of consciousness where they no longer have the desire, you understand, to hunt, then, of course, that is the divine right of the soul's individual expression and its education through that level of consciousness, you see. Yes. Now, of course, in reference to hunting or fishing and things of that nature, as we evolve within our own consciousness, the need for what is known as the sport starts to disappear. What happens is that other things are entertaining our mind on different levels of consciousness. But we must remember that each soul has its divine right to express itself. And so they have those different things that they call sport, you see.

I can feel with you in that respect and I'm so grateful that we don't have those so-called bullfights here in this country. Because if you ever saw those souls, those animals after they left this physical world and the torture that they go through—it is almost inhumane, for sure. Because, you see, friends, animals, like humans, have feelings, you see. And so if we remember that—now, of course, we can go a little bit further and we can say, "Well now, of course the vegetable has feeling." And that is true, because all of life has feeling. And so when man finds it necessary to kill something, then let him do it with the same feeling that he would like to experience if some giant were killing him. Because, you see, we don't escape anything. We're going to experience all of those things.

I've heard this mentioned by some people that a person may have a killer instinct in them. Say, for example, a person might want to be the world's greatest prizefighter. I would think he, then, has some instinct of that nature in order to achieve that goal.

No, I wouldn't call that the killer instinct, because it just may be the poor soul's need for attention, you see. And, of course, it would be a vast difference between the killer instinct and a soul's need for attention. Now if the person in his experiences found that he was able to get more attention by being a boxer or a wrestler, that would not necessarily, in and of itself, imply that he was expressing the killer instinct. Now, remember, friends, what we call the killer instinct is nothing more than a total imbalance in the instinct of self-preservation. It's just gone out of balance, you see. And so it is just an imbalance of the natural instinct of the form for self-preservation, you see. Yes, it's just an imbalance.

Then, you would identify it more with taking the life of something, more than the sport of it?

Well, yes, now I am sure that many people find sport in going deer hunting and killing the deer. Just as I am sure that many people find sport in making money, but, you see, that's up to the individual. It's entirely up to the individual. Now, that doesn't mean that I approve or disapprove of hunting. I have my own choices in that matter, which is my divine right, do you understand? But it is not within the purpose of the teachings to decide whether or not it is right to kill an animal or to make it a sport. It is within the realm of the teachings to share with you the understanding of the causes that you are setting into motion that direct the soul into those experiences. Because once we remove the cause, friends, the experience is gone and the effect no longer exists. So our interest is in showing you a way that you may find what is the cause of your need for any particular experience. Yes. And as the causes are removed from within you, and that means as your soul gravitates to a higher level of consciousness, you no longer have those needs.

Now, remember, friends, we never lose anything: everything is indelibly recorded in our memory par excellence. And so the hunter and the fisher, the judge and the jury, they all exist in all of us. All we have to do is to let our soul express on that level of consciousness and then we can find out personally for ourselves. Because, you see, what exists in one exists in all. Now, whatever one person is capable of doing, all people are capable of doing. Otherwise, you must disregard totally that God is a universal Divine Intelligence expressing through all, and then you must make God a man on a throne that's partial: gives this one something and takes it away from that one. No. What exists for one, exists for everyone: the good, the so-called bad, and the indifferent. Yes.

Do you have to be on a certain level to be able to heal someone or to be able to perceive an aura of someone who is physically ill?

Well, you must be on a level of receptivity to the emanations of the electromagnetic vibrations coming from form to perceive the aura, yes; and I'm sure you will understand, that this, in and of itself, as we discussed before in reference to the psychic, does not imply or guarantee any type of spiritual awakening, because that is a psychic field. Now, perhaps it's better put in this way: No good thought ever goes in vain, because no true good thought ever does. And so if it is a thought that has healed a soul, then that's a healing. Sometimes, you know, my friends, it's only a word of kindness at the right moment in the right place with the right person that heals them. But perhaps we don't get to see it because they pass us by in the traffic of Life herself. And so it is that each one serves the Divine in their way. You know, so many people think, "Well, that person is not very spiritual. They've never attended church and they don't attend classes. They don't do this and they don't do that." But do we know how many other things they may or they may not be doing? So God's work is done around the clock. Whether we see it or not is really immaterial.

Would you please expand on instinct in both animals and man?

Yes, I believe that we discussed that at our last meeting in reference to the instinct, both in animals and in the animal known as man. Because, after all, I'm sure we're all humble enough to admit, you know, that we are an animal. Let's face the truth about the matter: we tagged a name to ourselves called human, but we're still an animal, you see. And we're an animal on two feet. Perhaps that will help us in our understanding of the animal kingdom. Maybe, you know, we'll look at them a little differently when we feel that they are, in truth, our brothers and sisters, because that's what they really are. And after all, some of the so-called animal instincts in what they call the human form is pretty strong many times, you see.

Now you want to know a little more, perhaps, about instinct in the animal and instinct in the human. Well, it is obviously a natural instinct for any form to survive; that is, the instinct, self-preservation, is their first instinct. That is for the continuity of the species. Now whether that is the human, or the two-legged animal, or it's the four-legged one or whatever it is, that is an instinct and it serves a very, very good purpose. Now from this basic instinct, which has been designed to serve the purpose for the continuity of the species on the particular planets in which they're expressing—from an imbalance of this instinct, we've got all kinds of problems. But that basic instinct that is in the four-legged animal is the same basic instinct that's in the human being: it's known as self-preservation.

Now many of our acts, many of our thoughts are governed and controlled by the first instinct expressing through the animal: self-preservation. If that were not such a strong, potent instinct in our animal nature, which we are, you see, then we would not be so hungry for money and materiality and the so-called security. That's that instinct, you see. That's that basic animal instinct: that we must be sure we've got enough money, so that we can be sure we've got food when we want it, do you understand? So that's the same instinct: it's the self-preservation.

You talk to anyone in your work and your activities. What is the basic thing—say that you give them nine choices on nine subjects to discuss. Just try it as a little lesson to yourself. Say, "I would like to know the nine things that really interest you." I guarantee you, my friends, that number one would be either the top one or close to it, because the mind has accepted that that represents its security, its self-preservation. And that is the basic instinct governing our lives. And that's why we have so much discussion of money and materiality in the world, because of that self-preservation instinct, you see.

But now we have the potentiality of becoming aware that we are all things, that there is no death, that there are no dead. So what is this fear mechanism caused by this basic instinct that we're going to go hungry? See? Think, my friends. My goodness, the four-legged animals have better sense than that. They really do. Take a look at nature. Now the squirrels put a little bit away for the winter, when there's not going to be any nuts available. They put a few away. But, you see, the dog doesn't go and store up a whole bunch of garbage in his little doghouse. He has better sense. He knows that God has provided all things and he has a basic instinct, an instinct of survival: self-preservation. But he's got, really, at least he demonstrates more sense. Thank you very much for bringing that up.

Would instinct be related to ego?

Well, all forms have ego and all forms have instinct.

Materiality is what I'm talking about.

Well, it's self-preservation, you see. That is a basic instinct: to preserve the self. I mean, you must realize, friends, that that instinct of self-preservation, that's a soul principle. That's a soul principle, so that the soul may have its vehicle to express, no matter what form it's expressing through. But that is a principle. The only thing that we see—that it's done so much havoc in the world—is because it is not brought into balance with our soul faculty of reason. What does the average person entertain in thought? "I'm not getting any younger. In fact, I'm getting older. I don't want to be old without any money and have to have someone take care of me." And all of that foolishness entertains their minds. And so they base all of this, you see—the things that they don't want—on having all of the money in the bank, just in case, for a rainy day.

Well, now, this is usually what happens to the American public and I'm an American like all the rest of us. This is usually what happens. I used to fly for the airlines, for over nine years. And you would have been amazed. Most of the people going on tours around the world were ladies in their fifties and early sixties. The husbands had long been gone. They had worked themselves to death making money for their old age. They were on the other side. Now, I'm not saying that the women didn't work, too. I'm just stating a fact. I'm simply saying that, obviously, the wives didn't worry about it quite as much as their husbands did, because the husbands were over on the other side and the women were still down here, enjoying life. So, don't you see, what is this foolishness, stemming from this basic instinct of survival and self-preservation, that causes us so many problems?

That leads into a question of faith. And—

It has a great deal to do with faith. Faith and awareness.

Yes, now when we're aware of the fact that life is eternal and we're not afraid of that little sum in the checkbook—I had this experience today because I wanted to write a check for something, and I looked and I said, "I'd better wait until payday." Was that applying the faculty of reason or was that a lack of faith on my part?

Well, now, that's a very interesting question. What prompted you to think that you'd better wait until payday? Is that a tape that you have played for years or is that something that just came out of the blue? What prompted that thought?

I'd have to think what prompted the thought.

Give thought to what prompted the thought and you will have your answer, be rest assured. And you will know in your inner being and in your mind whether it was a lack of faith or whether it was common sense. There is a big difference.

I would like to know more about the nine bodies.

What would you like to know about them, please?

I would like you to list them for me.

Oh, I see, you would like me to list them for you. Several of them were listed, indirectly. They weren't called "being listed." And I would like to ask you a question, if I may, at this time in reference to your question. Do you feel that a listing of the different bodies that we are discussing at this time will benefit you in expanding your consciousness, in helping yourself this moment in your day-to-day activities? Or would a further discussion of how our mind works and our spirit works be of greater benefit? Now, the reason I'm asking you this question, ma'am, is very simple: I'm trying in every way that I possibly can to get the mind not to go by the letter of the law, not to become locked and bogged down into details. For, you see, when we come under the control of the letter of the law, we lose the spirit of the law. And it is the spirit of the law that we're trying to share with you. I will be happy to repeat what has already been given in reference to those nine bodies and I will say it once again: the physical body, the mental body, the vital body, the astral body, the soul body, the spiritual body, and now I stop. And I'm sure that will give you something to consider.

I am sure you have discussed this before, but I do not understand entirely the "Divine Abundance" affirmation that is on the back of the bookmark.

Thank you very much. I'll be more than happy to share that with you. And you are the first student that has asked that in class, to my knowledge: an explanation on the affirmation of "Divine Abundance." And what does that affirmation say? Would you be happy to share it with the class?

As I read it, it goes, "Thank You God I'm Moving In Your Divine Flow."

All right. Now, stop with each word. Stop with each word, because there's a principle involved. What does it say in parentheses under the word *thank?*

Gratitude.

Gratitude. Read on.

You (Principle).

Gratitude for the principle, yes.

God (Divine Intelligence).

Of the Divine Intelligence, yes.

I'm (Individualizing).

"I'm" is individualizing. Yes, the Divine Intelligence is individualizing.

Meaning through me?

Of course.

Moving (Rhythm).

Through rhythm, rhythmically.

In (Unity).

United.

Your (Realization).

The united realization, yes.

Divine (Total).

Total.

Flow (Consideration).

Considering all things.

[This is the text of the affirmation, as it appeared on the bookmark:

DIVINE ABUNDANCE

Thank
(Gratitude)

You
(Principle)

God
(Divine Intelligence)

I'm
(Individualizing)

Moving
(Rhythm)

In
(Unity)

Your
(Realization)

Divine
(Total)

Flow
(Consideration)*]*

When the students not only perceive that simple affirmation, when they start demonstrating it through the laws that
are involved in it, they will have no need. Now the "Divine
Abundance" affirmation is not an affirmation to abundantly
bring you all of the gold in Fort Knox. It might be good health
you're seeking. It might be peace of mind you're seeking. It
might be release from a certain situation that you are seeking.
But when you truly perceive the law involved in that "Divine
Abundance" affirmation, your soul will be freed every time you
demonstrate through that level of consciousness. Does that help
with your question?

Thank you.

You're more than welcome. And I can be happy to share with
the class that I say my affirmation at least a thousand times a
day. Perhaps it would help you, if you find that to be a chore to
say that "Divine Flow" a thousand times a day, to become aware
of how many times in the course of a day a thought is distasteful to you. Every time you have a distasteful thought, say your
"Divine Flow" affirmation and you'll be amazed. It'll be at least
a thousand times a day. At least. Yes.

Could you help me to understand better—cruelty to animals?
I don't know if acceptance *would be the right word.*

Perhaps understanding would help more than—you see, my friends, it is difficult for the mind to accept what it does not understand. It would be difficult, would you not agree, to accept cruelty as you presently understand cruelty?

Right now.

Now, wouldn't that be difficult for you to accept? So therefore, we do not work on acceptance. We work on understanding. So we broaden our understanding to a point where the mind is able to accept this so-called experience known as cruelty. Now what is most beneficial to ourselves—and that that is beneficial to ourselves spiritually is beneficial to the whole spiritually, because we are an inseparable part of the whole. So we must ask ourselves the question, "I see cruelty to animals. That has an effect upon me that is not beneficial to my peace of mind." Would you not agree?

Yes.

Fine. So what is the wisest thing to do, or at least some wise path to follow? And it's really quite simple. Number one: Gain a broader understanding of the Law of Divine Merit. Do not deny the four-legged creatures their right to their divine merit system. We wouldn't want ours denied from us. If the animal comes into this world and is to experience what our minds call cruelty—now that doesn't mean that we sit by and we let it take place. That's why we have animal leagues and the Spiritualist movement is extremely active, especially in London. In fact, it was the Spiritualist movement of Great Britain that brought about the antivivisection laws in Great Britain many years ago and have been active and still are to this day.

It doesn't mean that when we are in a position to prevent cruelty, that we do not prevent it, because our own conscience tells us that it's wrong. But when we experience what we call cruelty and we are not in a position, you understand, to do something about it at that moment—like, for example, say that some owner of an animal is cruel to that particular animal. Well, you don't go over and take the club away from him. Reason does not dictate that. You may call the Humane Society, etc., but you do not interfere to that point, because you might get someone that's in a state of furor and you might get the club, instead of the animal. Isn't that intelligent? So we work on an expansion and a broadening of our understanding of the divine right for the animal to have that experience. Do you understand?

Yes.

Now, that does not mean in the broadening of our understanding of that, the soul of that animal, having that right to that experience, that it has merited it—because that's the truth of the matter—that doesn't mean that we don't try to do something about it. Because we have obviously merited trying to do something about it.

Does the Law of Attraction come in here in any way?

It most certainly does. If a person is greatly disturbed about cruelty to animals, and that thought entertains their mind, they may be rest assured, they will call the experience necessary to them for greater understanding.

In that realm I can understand, but can it be applied to animal versus human? In other words, getting back to the bull in the bullring. That bull didn't come there through the Law of Attraction. He had no choice. He was put there.

Oh no. No, no, no, no, no. That soul that expressed through that bull set laws into motion to enter that particular bull, who would, in turn, be in that particular arena, who, in turn, would suffer those experiences. Oh yes. You see, the law that works for the human soul also works for all souls in all dimensions, yes. Oh yes. It's one law, infinitely expressed. Definitely and positively.

And, you see, in time we will grow to a greater understanding. Animals know more than we give them credit for. They have a degree of understanding. Oh yes, they certainly do. And that can be gradually expanded. You see, one of the great benefits in properly domesticating an animal is the evolution of its soul. Man has that responsibility. Definitely. Now, you know, you don't bring a dog to church Sunday morning. When we get our own building, you might, because we'll have our animal healing center. But usually we don't bring a dog to church to hear a lecture or something. But he receives his spirituality and understanding in the way that you treat him and talk to him. You see, many people don't bother to talk to animals, because their ego says, "Well, they wouldn't understand. How do they understand? You know, they never studied English." Well, my friends, it's way beyond that. It's way beyond that. You see, the animal responds to how you're feeling. You know, there's one thing about animals: you can't fool them. You can talk to humans, you know, and you can feel differently than the way you're talking, but you can't do that with animals, see. You can tell an animal you love him and you think he's beautiful and all the time you're emanating a vibration of animosity or hatred to him, and that animal knows which is which. Oh yes. Yes, they're extremely psychic.

I have heard that it's frustrating to the animal to talk to it. I do talk to mine, but I'm wondering if I am doing the right thing, because I have heard from veterinary science that the animal is trying to respond and, of course, cannot.

It is not a bit frustrating to the animal. The animal responds in the way that it is designed to respond. It might whine. It might grunt. It might bark. It might lift its paw or blink its eye. No, the animal is not frustrated. The animal is expressing back to the limit of its expression. Do you think that two dogs talking to each other are frustrated? They communicate beautifully.

Just take a look at them. No, that's just an understanding, perhaps, of that particular doctor.

Can we assume that these bullfighters will perhaps be incarnated as bulls?

No. No. If we could, that would be transmigration, which is not the teaching of the Living Light philosophy. However, you may be rest assured, from the years of experience I have had in looking into those dimensions, that they will get to live with the bulls they slaughter. Yes, that you may be rest assured. The laws are very impartial, yes. They will get to experience the feelings, the emotions, the frustrations, and all of the feelings that the victim went through. Whether the victim was two-legged or four-legged, they will have that blessed opportunity, yes.

I have a great concern about waste.

About what?

Waste. I don't like to see vegetables or fruit that's growing on my property go to waste. I don't like to see anything that exists go to waste. I'm a great recycler. I'm having difficulty putting that together with the Law of Merit, because, as I understand what you're saying, if I see somebody waste something and it upsets me or I get upset about it, then I have merited that experience. And I don't know where else to go with that.

That's true. Well, perhaps you might consider a broadening of understanding, because the moment you broaden the understanding, your mind will be able to accept that nothing, in truth, is ever wasted. See, nothing is ever wasted. You say you look at the garden and the vegetables are going to waste. They're not going to waste at all. They're going back to Mother Earth to come up with the chemicals once again. Mother Earth is constantly in a process of recycling, you see. So nothing, in truth, is ever wasted. Now, if our mind decides that that object was made to fulfill that particular purpose, and it's not fulfilling that purpose and therefore it's wasted—now that's a lower level of consciousness, do you understand?—then we've got problems and we keep seeing waste. But that's limitation.

It's not the fruit or the vegetable going back to the land I see as waste. I think it comes from—

You see the lack of use of it?

Yes, it's more the way people handle it.

But don't you see, it *is* being used. Mother Nature, she doesn't waste anything. She's taking it right back again, to use it over again. But you see, that's what I'm talking about. You're seeing waste through the limitation of the mind, of the conditioned, programmed, taped mind, you see. In other words, that's why I tried to explain to you that you're seeing limitation, because you said, "This is designed as a book: it's meant to be read. If it isn't read, then it's wasted." But it's not wasted. You must at least try to consider to see these things in a broader perspective. And if you will do that, you will not be attracted to witnessing what your mind calls waste, because you will have broadened your horizon and you will no longer have those experiences. Because the adversity created by the mind attracts the experience, you see. And when the adversity disappears, you no longer channel energy to that particular level of consciousness and therefore you will no longer experience it. Yes, does that help with your question?

Very much. Thank you.

You're welcome.

I'd like to ask you, what is the Wise One's definition of marriage, and does it and can it serve a spiritual purpose, rather than bondage?

Well, we must look over the centuries of civilization and ask ourselves in honesty, "How did marriage start? How did it start in civilization? What was its purpose?" Now I know that some people, perhaps, feel that it was ordained in heaven. Well, I honestly haven't found that heaven yet. Not that I'm for or against marriage: I just haven't found that heaven where it was ordained. I do, however, believe that it was brought into being out of necessity for the protection—you hear me?—of the children that were being born and to form some type of what we call civilization.

Now, marriage can serve a good purpose. It can also serve the opposite. It depends entirely upon what the two individuals interested in marriage are willing to accept and to understand. Now, if two people enter marriage and their motive for entering marriage is to become more secure, then in that very instant they have denied their own divinity, that their security is in their own soul. So if that's their motive, they're headed on a bad track. Now, if their motive is that they may experience life in a greater fullness and that marriage is necessary for that experience, then they're also placing themselves in bondage, because they have placed themselves into limitation.

Remember, friends, whenever you entertain in your mind that your joy or your sadness, that your beauty or its opposite comes from anything outside of yourself, your own soul—the moment you entertain that in thought—you are adding another link in the chain of bondage. And you are giving your power, the divine power of your own choice and your own birthright, to something outside of yourself. But that is the divine right of an individual to choose, if they want to put themselves into bondage.

Now, I am not saying that two people cannot get married without placing themselves into bondage. I am saying there's a possibility of probably one couple out of one hundred thousand that can stay free from bondage in marriage, because they give power to each other. And then the day comes that they recognize within themselves that they have given away their birthright, and then they start to take it back and problems come and then society calls it divorce.

Well, friends, let's look at cheery things. We're past our time and let us go have some refreshments. Thank you very much.

SEPTEMBER 27, 1973

CONSCIOUSNESS CLASS 26 ✧

Good evening, students.

Now, friends, as usual, we will go into our concentration and meditation. And, as has often been spoken before, when you go into your concentration of peace, try to let yourself go. Don't try so hard to mentally concentrate upon the word *peace*. Concentration is a very natural thing: it is not something that we force. If you force your mind to hold to the thought of peace, then you're going to guarantee all the other thoughts to enter your mind. When you concentrate, do it peacefully. That is what you are trying to experience. And in that experience of that peace that passeth all understanding, you begin to find your true self.

Now remember, as with all affirmations, if they're used like a rote, then they will be of no benefit to you. Each word must be thought upon as the mouth speaks it. Then the affirmation will have power in your universe to help you with right thought, with right action, which is your individual, divine right to life's expression.

Before going on with the question-and-answer period of this class, I would like to share with you our understanding of questioning. Many people ask questions and they are not aware from what level of consciousness they're asking their question. Now there are two levels from which a question is prompted in the human mind. One is from a level of the soul, which is a soul faculty, and that is the soul faculty of information. The other level through which a question is prompted in the human mind is from the level of the mind, of the function of confirmation. Now whenever we ask a question, we either are prompted, which is our true motive, by the level of confirmation or by the level of information. If our question is prompted from the level of confirmation, then we already are entertaining in mind, though we may not be consciously aware of it, an opinion concerning the question that we are asking. And what we are truly seeking in the question is not information concerning the question, but a confirmation or a support of the thought, the opinion that we have already accepted in our mind. Consequently, when we hear the answer, there are one or two things that take place. If it has been prompted by the level of confirmation and it does not fit into the opinion we already have, in either our conscious or subconscious mind, then we are unhappy, disturbed, and dissatisfied. If it is prompted from our soul level of information, then we take what is received in the answer and we put it into that vast computer. We do not feel satisfied or dissatisfied. Information is information. It's an addition to our knowledge and to our awareness.

So, friends, when you ask questions—now don't be timid about asking your questions—but give your questions some thought. Ask yourself in all honesty, "What is prompting this question that I have?" For we're all here to broaden our horizons or to be informed. Now, we are informed by laws that we set into motion within ourselves. That does not mean that you have to agree or disagree with whatever answers that you receive, but it does mean that you are seeking from a spiritual level to broaden your horizons and to find the truth which is within your own being. You see, friends, no one can give us truth. The only thing they can do is share with us their level of consciousness or the understanding that they themselves are receiving. Truth to the individual is, of course, an individual thing. Therefore, each moment of your conscious awareness is a moment of truth for you.

Now there's a vast difference between facts and truth. And so when we ask questions from the level of confirmation, what we are doing is adding facts upon facts. So let us ponder with our thoughts and let us ask ourselves in silence, "What prompts this question?" just before we ask it.

Now you are free to ask whatever questions you have.

Before the soul enters into form in accordance with the Law of Merit, is the soul fully aware of the form that it's going to partake in?

Thank you very much. Yes, we have discussed in one of our previous classes that the soul reviews all the experiences prior to its incarnation. And the soul is aware of the body that it is to inhabit in any particular incarnation. Yes, it is.

Why is it, then, that the soul is not aware of it upon the soul's entry into the form?

That is not a teaching of these classes: that the soul is not aware. The soul is aware, but it is blocked in its expression by the mind. The soul is aware. The soul is aware of all things past, present, and future, for its incarnation. However, the mind blocks the information from coming from the soul level into the conscious level of what is known as the conscious mind. Yes, thank you.

Now I don't want you students to be timid about asking your questions, because there's no one here to judge you from which level it is being prompted. That's a very individual thing. So don't feel a bit timid about your questioning. Yes?

Would you clarify the word judgment, *please, as particularly used in Discourse 36?*

Yes, now in what particular line are you referring to that word? Would you care to read that line to the class, because the class is not, I'm sure, consciously familiar with that particular line you're referring to.

The word is used several times throughout the discourse. "I was at that time what you may refer to in your day as a judge or magistrate. It was my responsibility to pass the judgment upon those who came before me. . . . Many were sent into the

nothingness: their life ended because they had transgressed, in
my understanding, the law. . . . Each judgment that we pass is
another prison that we place ourselves in and they are so easy to
get in, so difficult to get out."

In reference to the use of the word *judgment* in the last line
that was read: Think, my students. The moment that you judge,
you must have a basis or a foundation for your judgment. Now
this basis or foundation that you establish is a form or limitation. Consequently, all judgment is limitation and is governed
by the Law of Creation, which is the Law of Duality. There is
no such thing as neutral or impartial judgment. All judgment
is based upon the understanding of the person that is doing
the judging. This understanding may at any time expand or
broaden itself and, in so doing, the judgment of one day is not
the judgment of another. Therefore, it is our teaching and our
understanding that the Divine Intelligence does not judge, that
man and man alone judges all his thoughts, acts, and deeds,
the judgment, of course, being based upon the foundation of his
own understanding. Remember that our God is ever equal to
our understanding. Now that does not mean that an individual
transgresses a natural law and does not reap the effect of that
so-called transgression. But the judgment, you understand, is
done by the individual and his degree of receptivity to those
natural laws.

What if you don't make an actual judgment or statement?
What if your mind has a thought, but you correct yourself? Are
you just as responsible for saying or making a judgment?

Perhaps it would help in explaining judgment in this way. My
friends, thought is the judge and act is the jury. So the moment
you entertain the thought, you have the judgment. The jury en-
forces it. And consequently, when you entertain the thought,
you have made the judgment. And this is why it says in the
Bible that it is the thought of lust that is the sin. Well, by *sin*,
they mean "the error." For example, the actual act is an act in

another dimension, known as the physical dimension, but the judgment takes place at the moment of the thought. Because, you see, thought is a world. There is a mind and there's a world of mind. And whatever thought you entertain, that is an action and that is an activity in a mental world. So we begin with that world and we begin working on our thoughts. Now I have been asked before, How many forms does the soul experience? Now I would be more than happy to answer your question in this way: How many thoughts can your mind entertain?

You see, my friends, each thought is a form and each form is an act and an activity. So the first thing to guard and to guide in our spiritual awareness is our thoughts. That's what we begin with. Then what happens is, we begin to change our mental world, our mental world being an effect of our spiritual world and our physical world being an effect of our mental world. So the thing we're so familiar with now, of course, is our mental world and that's where we should begin. Begin with the thing or the dimension with which we're most familiar.

Now you tell a person, well, "Guard your thoughts." Well, you can't guard something, of course, that you're not aware of. So the first step is awareness and so we work with awareness. "What am I thinking about? From what level is my thought prompted?" Because all those thoughts, you see, they are forms and they exist in a mental world. You see, we're all united. What is it that unites us? Why, my friends, it's not only our spirit that unites us, it's also our mind that unites us. And so all of our experiences in this physical dimension are simply effects of attitudes of mind or thoughts that you're entertaining.

Now we experience so much disturbance, discord, and disharmony because our thoughts are so discordant. Our thoughts are battling each other. You see, a thought is an actual form. If you'll only get that into your realization: that whatever thought you have, that creates a form in your aura in the atmosphere, and it goes to work for you. You are the master of it—until it becomes your master. And that's what happens with thoughts, which, in truth, are forms. Someone else have a question?

Well, we have thoughts which are good, bad, and indifferent. Is there a way of being able to step away from all this negativity? Would this forgive all that we were not aware of?

Thank you very much. It is our teaching, in our private class work—it's just very simple: to forgive is to free. You see, that that we hold destroys us, and that that we free unfolds us. So the first thing to do is to forgive. And forgiveness must begin within oneself, because you can't forgive another until you can forgive yourself. When you start forgiving yourself, you start to free yourself from the bondage of that particular level.

Now one of the many difficult things—there do seem to be a lot of difficult things in growth—is to release a thought to the Divine. Now a person will get hold of a thought, especially if it brings them a lot of attention, and they will not release it. Now they do not consciously want to keep that thought in their mind. They really do want to let that thought go, but that thought is serving a purpose for them. So the key is to become aware of what these thoughts—what purpose they are serving for us. When we become aware of what purpose they are serving for us as individuals, then we will be able to reeducate them or to raise our consciousness to another level of awareness. Yes, then we will be free.

Some months ago, you gave us an exercise to learn to visualize, to really think about our desires. I've tried this, but perhaps not long enough. I wonder if you could shed more light on it. Would you suggest continuing with that one or trying something else?

Well, may I first ask you to share with the class the particular exercise that you have been attempting to demonstrate?

To think about your desire. Well, find the desire—something you really, really want.

Yes.

And then try to visualize it.

Yes.

I find that my material desires are not as strong, since I've come to this understanding, I would like to think.

Yes.

It just hasn't really worked for me.

Well, have you considered the subject matter that you have chosen?

I've tried different things.

You've tried different subject matter and what seems to be your problem? You are unable to visualize?

There's nothing happening.

Nothing happens. Fine. Tell me something. Do you visualize Boris?

I've tried to.

Has it been possible?

No, it hasn't been.

Have you asked yourself why? Because, after all, that was a dog of yours and you know what he looks like, etc. Have you asked yourself why there's difficulty in your visualization process?

Well, I'm sure there must be some emotional block.

Are you able to visualize anything at all?

No, I'm not. Not consciously.

Not consciously.

No.

Are you able to visualize the house where you live?

Not really. I can see something way in the back, you know, but not in an ethereal, plastic kind of sense, not three-dimensional in front of me.

Well, if you're able to see something in the back of your head that in any way or shape or form resembles the home in which you reside and you are grateful for that as a crumb, you will guarantee the loaf of what you truly desire. You see, we're talking about a visualization process, friends. But we must remember this: Sometimes we desire something and we say, "Well, I can't visualize anything." The truth of the matter is, we are visualizing. It's back here in the head. It's very fuzzy. It's very small. It has a resemblance to it. It's simply from a lack of practice. And if you're grateful for that small crumb, that you can see it back in the back of your head, very fuzzy, the day will come when it'll appear right before your vision. Because that is the power of the mind, yes.

Thank you very much.

You're more than welcome. It's known as the Law of Supply. You see, what you are seeking is supply in your visualization. Well, the Law of Supply is guaranteed through the faculty of gratitude. Duty, gratitude, and tolerance is the faculty necessary to complete the exercise you're trying to do.

Thank you.

You're welcome. Yes.

What is it that makes prayer so effective?

That is entirely dependent from which level it comes. Many students would say that "prayer is not effective for me," or that "I've prayed for many things, etc., and I have no results whatsoever." Another student will say, "I simply said a little prayer and it came to pass." What makes it effective is the soul's aspiration, if it's from the soul's level. Do you understand? Not all prayer, you understand, is motivated by our soul. You know, some people pray for, maybe, a few million dollars, etc. They pray for all kinds of things. Not that there's anything wrong with a few million dollars, but, you see, it is not stimulated, it's not motivated by the soul level.

Is that a deep desire with a pure motive?

An aspiration from the level of the soul. If a person considers prayer in the sense that they are praying to be receptive to right action manifesting in their life, and then they accept the experiences they encounter, you may be rest assured, right action is taking place.

Well, that is considered as prayer, then, isn't it?

Well, it is in my little book, yes.

I understand that Spiritualism is a religion, a science, and a philosophy.

Yes.

I'm trying to correlate the three. I understand that the three are integrated. What I'd like is your understanding of God, which is religion; atoms with their protons, electrons, and neutrons, which is a science; and the relationship of those to our human soul.

Thank you very much. I believe we did discuss, in one of our courses, in reference to a question of what is God or a definition of God. And I believe we did state at that time, a few courses ago, perhaps, the moment that we define anything, we limit it. And to define or to give a limitation of one's understanding of God, the Divine Intelligence, would simply put it into limitation or into form. Now you cannot explain or define Truth or God. It *is*. It is. Now we can share our understanding of our perception of it, perhaps, but we cannot say that it's this and it's that and it's that and put it into a form, because the moment that we do that with Truth, with God, with Spiritualism, what we have is form and limitation. And we have dogma and we have creed.

Now, my understanding I can share with you to a degree, concerning Spiritualism, the religion of Spiritualism, its science and philosophy. To me, Spiritualism is the three things mentioned, but it is more than that. It is a way in which a person may find their own soul and express their understanding of their God. Whenever we define God and these things and we impose that upon the human soul—the world is filled with religions. The world is filled with philosophies. The world is filled with sciences. But what it is truly seeking is a way to find its own soul,

to learn to think. Our children go to school and they're filled
with all kinds of facts. What we are truly seeking is initiative
thinking, that we can think for ourselves.

What we have become in the world are parrots: parroting
what we have read, parroting what we have had confirmed as
our own opinions. And we are losing—and in many areas have
lost—initiative thinking. Therefore, we have placed our soul
into bondage, the bondage of the masses; that this is the way
to think because "that one agrees with me and that one and
that one and that one." We're not seeking, truly seeking, truth,
which would free our soul and find our own God and express
that God.

As long as I'm in the movement of Spiritualism, I shall constantly strive to prevent it from coming under the shackles and
bondage of dogma and creed. For the moment that happens,
you have lost Spiritualism, because you no longer respect the
right of a human soul to find God in their own way, in their own
thoughts, and in their own expression. Now, that is also one of
the many reasons that true Spiritualism is not a strong organization, because you cannot strongly organize truth. It's very,
very individual. I hope that has helped you with your question.
I am very free in my thought and I hope that all of my students
will remain so, also. Thank you.

*When you're speaking of prayer, it sounds like prayer becomes
an asking. I would like to know what your understanding is.*

No, I do not look at prayer as an asking, but I do look at prayer
as an aspiration, a soul aspiration, and an affirmation. You see,
man is a law unto himself. When man affirms or declares right
action in his life, he sets a law into motion. He doesn't tell the
Divine Intelligence what that right action is, do you understand?
But he accepts right action as taking place. Now, you know,
man constantly questions what he calls God, but this Divine
Intelligence, in its great humbleness, never questions man. Stop
and think about that for a few moments. We constantly question

this Divine Intelligence, but that Divine Intelligence never questions us. When you affirm divine right action in your life, you will come under the Law of Divine Right Action for your life. But when you experience that divine right action, beware of the pit known as judgment and trying to enforce that divine right action on another human soul, because there are many factors involved in spiritual work; and one of the great pits is to force upon another human soul one's religious convictions. Now the reason for this seeming need within the human mind—to force a belief upon another—is really quite simple, and it is also a guarantee that that soul is not secure in their own convictions: they need confirmation and they receive confirmation by converting everybody else in the universe. Do you understand? Does that help with your question?

Yes. I have another.

Yes, ask it, if you would, please.

From the learning that I've had about meditating, I've been instructed to have a goal in mind. I have trouble making a goal for myself and accepting what occurs. What's your understanding of how to keep those two in balance?

Well, you state that you have in your meditation some type of a goal that you have set up for yourself?

I've been told to have a goal. I've tried it and I get myself into a lot of conflicts, because frequently the goal that I might select does not, in the long run, turn out to be the goal that seems to be what happens or what fits for me.

Thank you very much. Well, the only thing I could say to you is I try to share and teach my students, the thing to seek is peace, for there is nothing that peace will not harmonize with. Do you understand? So if you wish to call that a goal, you may. But you will find that if you are truly seeking peace, it doesn't go through a whole process of change and won't fit into this attitude of mind or that attitude of mind, because there is nothing that the mind can encounter that peace will not harmonize. Do you understand? And I am sure if you will consider using peace for your direction, that you will find what you are seeking and you will not need to go through these constant changes with your goal.

Thank you. That gives me relief already.

You're welcome.

Is the thing known as intuition, which seemingly comes from above, a mind function or—

No!

A soul function? Things that we know, without knowing.

An inner knowing is a soul knowing, yes. Definitely, positively.

Is conscience affected by the tapes or value systems which we have adopted or is it strictly a soul faculty?

Yes. It is and it is not affected. For example, conscience, being a spiritual sensibility with a dual capacity, knows right from wrong, does not have to be told. However, in the expression of this conscience is where it is affected. If a tape is playing—you know, we are habituated or addicted to various tapes. One of the first things I try to teach the student is to become aware of their addictions, because, you see, we're all addicts, you understand? Addicted to our tape patterns, to our desires, and to our adversities, etc. So when we face that, we start going to work. We don't take a pill to get rid of it. We take constant, daily thought to get rid of it or to change it. So our conscience constantly strives to express itself: it knows right from wrong. However, if some of the tapes are very strong, that means that they've been fed a lot of energy and they're playing at the time our conscience is trying to speak, we cannot hear our conscience, you see. And in time we're totally deaf and we no longer sense it, especially when a certain tape is playing. Does that help with your question?

Yes.

Conscience itself continues to try to express itself, to dictate to the mind, you understand, to get through to the mind that

that's wrong for your soul, because that is a spiritual sensibility. But remember, friends, that when we start to work with our thoughts, with our patterns, which are our tapes, the greatest struggle comes with the tapes we are strongly addicted to. Now if we're addicted, for example, to the tape of criticism and we look around and we always have to criticize or we have to complain about something, and if someone brings it to our attention that we are constantly playing that tape, that a day never goes by that we're not complaining or, as some might say, "bitching" or criticizing something, and someone brings that to our attention, we get very upset emotionally. Remember, whenever a tape to which you are addicted is revealed to you by another human being, the reaction is always traumatic. It is always emotional. It is always defensive. Does that help with your question?

Yes, thank you.

You're more than welcome.

I wonder if you'd explain why The Lord's Prayer is said in our Sunday services and is it consistent in its present translation with this understanding?

Thank you very much. The lady has asked why The Lord's Prayer is said in all of our devotional services and is it consistent with the understanding or the teaching of the Serenity Association. The essence, the spirit of The Lord's Prayer, is most consistent with the teachings of the Living Light and the Serenity Spiritualist Church and Camp Association. Now, by accepting the essence and the spirit of The Lord's Prayer, as it was originally given—and please do not ask for it—we are expressing the understanding in the present light of the Serenity Association. Because each individual has their own understanding of The Lord's Prayer does not in any way affect the true motive or the purpose for which The Lord's Prayer is said at all of our devotional services, yes. But if you will consider The Lord's Prayer in the sense of The Law's Affirmation, you will, perhaps, get a broader understanding of it. Thank you.

In Discourse 36 it says, "Is my duty a true responsibility or is it a fabrication of the illusions of my mind?" Many times I've had to ask this question of myself. When does duty stop being duty and when do we know it's an illusion? I mean, are we given this to know?

Thank you very much. The lady is asking, When is our duty an illusion and when is it a fabrication of the mind and how do we know it? Are we given this? Like all things in eternity, class, we merit it.

Now, we receive many things because we seek many things. And so it is that one's true duty, their first duty and their real duty, is to the Divine that is expressing through them. The vehicle itself—the physical body, the mental body, and all the other bodies—is simply an automobile that you're driving. The real you, which is the power, which is the fuel—you know, the automobile doesn't go very far unless it has some gas in it. And so it is that we are, in truth, that power expressing through these vehicles.

Now, when a person makes a daily effort to find the causes of things, they begin to come out of the illusion created by the senses. The mind is filled with a multitude of thoughts and a multitude of forms and its very nature is constant creation. That is why so many students have such difficulty in stilling their mind, but the mind must be stilled if you want to view your own eternity. And so it is that when we ask ourselves the question more frequently than we do, Why this and why now? whatever experience enters your mind and enters your life, then you will start on the path to find the cause and will stop spending so much energy, so much time looking at the effect and all of the illusion.

You know, look at life. We have the illusions of twenty years ago and we have different illusions today. We have the illusions even of yesterday and they're changing, moment by moment by moment. You see, my friends, security, in truth, is not in this passing panorama of which your consciousness is flowing through. That is why that that we free unfolds us, because, you see, when we hold to anything, we're trying to hold our consciousness to form or to an object. See, consciousness—God is my consciousness—consciousness is a constant flow, see? Truth is like a river: it continuously flows. Stop trying to stand still, and let this Divine Intelligence flow through you as an unobstructed vehicle. Stop trying to entertain your minds with so many different forms and so many illusions and delusions, because, my friends, they only retard the day that you're going to reach your own freedom.

Now a person says, "Well, I feel it my duty to help this person over here." Now the question is asked, Is that a true duty or is that a fabrication of my mind? If it is a true duty, then one will know within oneself. One will not have any emotion or any thought of mind connected with what is known as duty, for duty is a soul faculty.

Now many times we accept in our lives what we call a duty and we accept that because of certain errors that we have made in the past. For example, it's like a mother that has a son. She leaves home and she doesn't see her son for ten years. After ten years, all of a sudden, she feels that it's her duty to raise the child. Yet she's been away from him for ten years. Well, now, the question arises, Is that a true duty or is that a fabricated duty, fabricated by the guilt complex of leaving the child for ten years? That's the question that one must ask oneself. "Am I doing this for another person because of what my family will think? Am I doing this for so-and-so because of what other people are going to say if I don't do it?" There's where your illusion and your delusion come in, and the mind calls it duty. But if you will be honest with yourself and you will be sincere, you will know what is your true duty. And you will not have to ask the question of any human soul, because you and your God are a majority, and it knows what's right for you and it knows your spiritual duties. Thank you. Does that help with your question?

Thank you.

You're welcome. Yes.

When one is meditating and he hears the "om" inside his head, should he key in on it as much as possible or just ignore it?

Well, I would like to ask you a question, if I may. Would you be willing to share with the class how you have been able to judge that particular experience as the "om"?

Well, just from the books I've read. It's just a humming sound and that's literally what it is: an "om", like a heavy, deep drum. And it's consistent. It's there every time I meditate and sometimes during the day. It's very pleasing to listen to, very relaxing. I was wondering what it was.

Does it do anything else for you?

Nothing other than just give me a complete relaxation when I tune into it. That's about it.

Yes. Well, in reference to that particular question, I always like to tread softly in certain areas because, number one, we must give great thought to the experiences that we encounter psychically and from these other dimensions. Now, if you are able to remain in control of the experience, that means, if you are able to have a meditation that is peaceful and spiritual to your understanding without it, then it could only serve a good purpose. If, however, that experience is absolutely necessary for a meditation or a communion with God, the Divine Intelligence, then it is time to question and to outgrow it. Does that help with your question? Because, you see, my friends, that that becomes a crutch pulls our soul into the realms of the cripples.

I know in this type of work that many people require various paraphernalia or crystal balls or Ouija boards or tarot cards or all this paraphernalia. There is no need for anything outside of your being to commune with God. It is inside your very being.

There is no need for any paraphernalia or anything outside your being to establish the contact. And so it is, friends, remain free souls. And remember, to rely upon the spirit that is within your soul is the only reliance that is safe or secure. Thank you.

Perhaps I didn't understand. About two weeks ago I believe you stated that we should not send unsolicited healing. Was this meant in general if a person is negative? Or is it also meant for those that are not negative?

It's meant for everyone. Unsolicited help is to no avail. The door has not been opened.

It stated in The Living Light *that in order to help someone, the person is to change his aura first to white and then, in a sense, broadcast it to that person.*

That has solicited it, yes.

To change his aura.

Because when the aura is white—a white aura is the effect of a pure heart and a sound mind. And that is why it states in *The Living Light* an aura of white, for white will purify. It is the color of purity and will purify any of the colors of the aura.

In the healing, do the different odors that one senses, do they emanate different colors? Or in the healing is sensing odors— and also color—is that separate?

It's all the same.

The color is coming from the odor?

No. Not at all. The odor comes from the color.

Pardon me?

The odor and the sound come from the color. Everything is color. Everything. When you speak, there are emanations of color coming out of you, like everyone else. You hear the sound, but the eyes have not been yet tuned to see the color. When they're tuned to see the color, as well as hear the sound, then they will know truth from falsehood. That's why, in certain realms of the world of spirit, you see, there's no such thing as a lie. It's impossible. Because the moment that the thought goes out, the color goes with it. And this is why we teach the colors. The things you're learning here, my friends, are not only helping you here, but they're to help you in the hereafter. They help you spiritually. Remember, in the world of spirit you don't have a physical voice box. Your communication is telepathic. And if you learn about color here and now, its vibration and its meanings, then you will learn the language and you will be able to discern, you see.

I happened to be in a doctor's office this week, and my appointment was at a certain time and had to be delayed because someone came in as an emergency. They were screaming at top voice and because of some of the practices that I have learned, I called upon the spirit doctors to help this person. Now is that still unsolicited help? I mean, that person was in desperate need to be quieted and I thought of the class work saying that unsolicited help is to no avail, but my spirit wanted to help.

May I ask you a question?

Certainly.

Was your motive for helping the individual, was it from the level of judgment?

No. Just to stop the screaming and to help. I knew what his condition was. I was told what it was.

Yes. Well, this is what I'm asking, because, you see, this is up to the individual. Now remember that we, in life, go through many experiences; that each experience is the effect of a law that we have set into motion. For example, say that I have an appointment with the doctor, you understand, and that I go to the doctor's office for a set appointment. However, an emergency comes in at the time that I am scheduled for my appointment. Now we must remember, no matter who it happens to or anything else, that is simply an effect of a law that we set into motion. There are no coincidences and there are no accidents in the universes. They are simply effects of laws set into motion. So if a person has an experience of that nature, they have a golden opportunity, which I believe we mentioned a little earlier, to ask themselves, their soul, the question, "Why this and why now?" That's the question. Then what would happen, the person would go within himself and a light starts to go on and he sees many things that are hidden from the mind. Does that help with your question?

Well, I'm—

You see, I'm asking the question in this way: Now, are we prompted or are we motivated to ask for a healing for the individual because they have interrupted—you understand what I mean?—a certain law that we have set into motion? Now, what is the motive for our seeking help for the individual? For example, it could be, like, a person might call me and say, "Mr. Goodwin, I'm not feeling too well and I have an appointment with you in an hour." I book my appointments so many months in advance, usually. Now I could very easily say, "This is ridiculous. Now here I'm going to be here. That person's canceling out because they're not feeling well." Now I could ask my doctors, you understand, to please get over there and heal that person, because she has an appointment with me. You understand what I mean?

Yes.

But now, I would not permit myself to do that for a very valid reason. Number one: I'm demonstrating the Law of Interference. Number two, and probably most important of all: I'm motivated by my own personal desires. Now this is what we must be on the lookout for. What is the motive for our seeking to share our understanding or to help humanity? We must be honest with ourselves and say, "What is my motive?"

I have many people call me and many people come to me asking me for classes, development classes for the psychic, development classes for mediumship. Well, I have never given development classes for the psychic or for mediumship. I don't even know what kind of classes those things would be, because I have never given them. It is not within my realm of understanding to give them. But for spiritual awareness, for one's own soul, yes! Because when we find our own soul, we will know what it is that we're supposed to be doing in this life. But if we're motivated, my friends, by the mind levels of desire, then we are in deep water.

Let us not deny the facts. Let us not deny that we are all motivated by desire, because, of course, we're all motivated by desire. We just have to become aware of what desire it is that's motivating us, so that our soul can be free. A person says, "Well, I'll go and have a cup of coffee." Well, they're motivated by the desire to have a cup of coffee. The thing is, desire is not a bad thing. It becomes detrimental to one's soul when they're no longer aware of it and they can no longer control it. When it is so subtle that we become its slave anytime it decides to prompt into our brain, then, my friends, it's a sad, sad, very sad day for our soul. When we cannot say no, then, my friends, look out. We have fallen into the pit of pits. Just a little bit of self-discipline and self-control—that's all it takes—will free our soul.

It is very important that we become aware of what is motivating us, what is really motivating us. Are we the captain of our ship and the master of our destiny or have we given that great power of mastership and destiny to certain programmed tapes of desire that our soul has become so addicted to that we can no longer recognize what's happening to us when it happens? That's what I ask you to do, friends: to stop and to think, and to think more deeply. So that you can know where you're going, because you will know where you are. Now, no one can know where they're going until they become aware of where they are. And that's the fact.

I can't help but feel in reading The Living Light *that if we feel that our motives are right, that we should share all that we have here with others. Not for any reassurance, but I have the feeling that this is what the Wise One did. He came and shared.*

Yes, he did.

Do we just have to feel compelled to do this or if more of us were not so afraid to talk about our beliefs to others—I have talked to many and some have not reacted the way I expected, but it doesn't bother me. I feel that maybe they're not ready for this. But if we just wait for the people to find this church on their own, without anyone talking about it, does that matter? Does that mean they don't merit it, and we shouldn't, maybe, strive to bring it to more people?

No. I think in reference to your question—I'm glad that you brought it up. You see, each soul is prompted to do what is right for them to do. Some people are prompted by a feeling to mention their understanding or the understanding of Serenity, its Spiritualism, to another individual. They must go by those inner promptings. When they go by those inner promptings, what happens is really very simple. If they are motivated by a spiritual level of consciousness, they will not be concerned or thoughtful to any extent of whether or not the person rejects or accepts it. And they will be free, because the motivation is from their spirit; and therefore they are not attached, you understand, mentally, by the functions, to the effect.

Now, when that is practiced throughout our whole life in all areas—do what you have to do, care less what the world does with it, because you care less yourself. Be not concerned with the fruits of action. Take all of the joy that you're going to take in the doing, because that's the only place true joy exists. True joy does not exist in the effect. And when we slip into the illusion that joy exists in the effect, we're on the path to what is known as greed, because the desire can never be fulfilled, you understand. See, one desire only guarantees a repetition of it and an expansion of it, constantly. It doesn't matter what one's desire is: that's the way the Law of Desire works. And so if you can do that from your soul level with your spirit and your feeling and have no effect and no concern whatsoever whether they ever show up, then you are free and doing the work that's right for you to do.

In the Bible it is written about leaving the flock of sheep for one lost sheep. I feel that if we tell many people and just one finds their way here and is helped, it is worth all the rebuffs.

How right you are, because the right ones always come! Many are called, remember, but few are chosen, for few choose God. That's why that statement: Many are called and few are chosen. Thank you.

You mentioned the Law of Interference, which I'm not familiar with. I'm wondering how that law would apply to compassion.

Oh yes. Now compassion—when compassion leaves the guiding hand of reason, it inevitably opens the door to credulity, which means easily imposed upon. Now remember that compassion, you understand, under the guiding hand of reason, knows the Law of Noninterference. It is sympathy that interferes and sympathy is a function, not a soul faculty. What does sympathy do? A person sympathizes—you know, the so-called sympathy cards and things of that nature. What are they really doing? What is a person doing when they sympathize with another human soul? Are they helping them to grow out of their level or are they helping them to stay in it? Usually, of course, what sympathy does is, it helps them to stay in the level they're in and puts you in that level too, you see. A half a soul with God is better than no soul at all, you know. If a soul is drowning and they are stronger than yourself, it is your duty to your own soul to let them drown. And that is the duty to one's own soul if they are stronger than yourself, yes. Does that help with your question?

Returning for a moment to color, may I ask if each planet emanates a predominant color?

Yes, each planet does emanate a predominant color. Would you like the color for Earth? Perhaps you all know: brown.

Thank you.

You're welcome. Now brown doesn't mean just confusion, you understand: it has some other meanings too, but that is the color for this planet. And I know that some of you would like a color for one of the other planets and I'll share one more color only. The color of Saturn is purple.

With regard to the colors, is the color manifested dependent upon the observer also?

Do you mean, "Is the color of a planet dependent upon the observer?"

Yes. It was stated that the color of Earth, for example, is brown.

Yes.

Is that brown to the viewer, man's view?

That is the emanation and without the viewer it doesn't exist. Remember, nothing exists without a viewer. If you don't have a viewer, my friends, it doesn't exist. It's impossible. It does not exist.

May I ask the second part of that question?

Yes.

Would it perhaps appear a different color to one in a different level of consciousness than it would to one on this level of consciousness?

Oh, absolutely. Because, you see, each level of consciousness views an emanation a little differently in its emanating, because, you see, they are receiving it a little differently. For example, you know, the dog, the animal, sees things differently than the human because there are different levels of consciousness and that's why he sees them a little differently. Now, of course, medical science will probably say, "Well, it doesn't have this or that physically." Well, the reason, for pity's sake, it doesn't have this or that physically is because it doesn't have this or that mentally. Because, you see, the physical is only an effect of the mental, which, in turn, is only an effect of the spiritual. Yes.

A few minutes ago you said that everything is color. I have a friend who is working in the area of physics and the spiritual, and he tells me that he has discovered that everything is music. I wonder what your understanding is and how those two interrelate.

It states in *The Living Light* that everything is color and that all color is sound. And, my friends, all sound is odor, and on through the senses.

In the receiving of healing, what seems kind of strange to me is the color purple in the receivingship of it. I don't know, I just was thinking it would be red or some other color.

Would you clarify your question, please?

In the receiving of healing, for myself, I would sense the color purple.

Yes, well, that's most understandable.

Is that a certain level of consciousness that is purple? I mean—

No.

Pardon me?

No. It simply means that you were receiving a healing of your understanding.

It could have been any color, only I thought that it was purple.

No. It doesn't mean that at all. It simply means that you are receiving a healing of your understanding. Purple is the color of understanding. And if you were receiving it during a healing, then it simply means that you were receiving a healing of your understanding at that particular time. Yes, does that help with your question?

Very much. Thank you.

You're more than welcome. We have time for just a few more questions.

I guess all forms incarnate with forty faculties and forty functions. I mean, the soul—

I don't believe that's been stated, but go ahead.

The soul carries with it forty faculties to be unfolded during this incarnation and the forms have forty functions to express. What I'm really trying to ask is, Is there anything in animals comparable to humans with respect to the faculties and functions?

Yes. What exists in one form exists in all forms in potential, under the Law of Creation or the Law of Form.

I just wanted to ask, Is there such a thing as the hereafter? How can you be here and after? Or is it just a word? We hear so much about the hereafter. Are we ever hereafter?

Well, in reference to that word, *here after*, it brings to my mind that when our hindsight becomes our foresight, we'll have insight. And I think that's what they mean by *hereafter*, you know. Most people, don't you see, they are not working with insight, but they're controlled by their hindsight. So when we move hindsight up to foresight, we'll gain insight, and then our hereafter will be now, instead of after here. All right?

According to The Living Light, *in order to heal a person, the healer must transform the color of his aura to white. Then if the aura of the sick person is brown, the healer would have to superimpose a white and sort of interblend the colors. Can you tell me on what level of awareness the healer would have to be in order to be able to have these qualities, to be able to produce these auras in himself and also to transmit them to someone else?*

Certainly. A sound mind and a pure heart is a white aura, and that's what the healer would need to be in to truly to be able to emanate that and for another soul to be receptive to it. A pure mind and a sound heart, or a sound mind and a pure heart: it's one and the same. Now that takes a little bit of awareness and a constant effort at it, because, you see, one must learn their motives for their thoughts, their acts, and their deeds. One cannot be pure of heart and sound of mind until they are aware of their motives and gradually evolve to a level where the motives are not controlled by their personal desires.

Now one of the simplest ways of seeing one's motives is to become aware of how much you are interested in the effect of your efforts. To the degree of your interest in the effect will reveal to you, as an individualized soul, how much your motive is guided and controlled by desire. That's why we do what's right because it's right to do right and we are not concerned whether the world believes us or doesn't believe us. We do the job and in the doing we have all of our pleasure and all of our joy and all of our happiness. But if we must have constant feedback of how great we are or how much we did or how much everyone appreciates us, then we must give more thought to what levels our motives are coming from, so that we can be free. You see, what happens to a person that gets addicted to having everybody telling them how great they are? My goodness' sakes, what happens to them when there's a change in their life and nobody tells them that anymore? Well, they suffer unbearably. Unbearably. So that's what we want to become aware of. Do we need, whenever we work for God, do we need someone to constantly tell us how much we're doing? If we need that, then we've got to work on our motives, so we can be free.

Thank you very much, friends. It's time for refreshments. Thank you.

OCTOBER 4, 1973

CONSCIOUSNESS CLASS 27 ✖

Now let us begin our meditation period this evening, friends, and we'll speak forth our "Total Consideration" affirmation, followed by our concentration of peace, followed by our meditation of awareness.

[After the meditation, the Teacher continues.]

Let us turn to Discourse 45.

[A student reads Discourse 45 aloud.]

I want to speak for a few moments on application. Now we have already had several weeks of discussion of the laws that govern our universe: how the mind works, the spirit, and the soul. Now, we also know that knowledge, without application, has no value. And so it is in the remainder of this particular course that greater effort must be made by us as individuals— if we want to get the value from this course and from these teachings—to apply what we have already learned.

Now we have learned various things. We've learned about the soul faculties. We've learned about the magnetic field of our subconscious. We've learned about the electrical impulses of our conscious mind and we've learned about the taped patterns of our mind. Now the time comes when we should consider, upon awakening in the morning and going to sleep at night, just exactly what levels of consciousness we're in. What tapes are we playing in our mind? What experiences are we encountering in the course of our day-to-day activities? The teachings are very simple and they are very clear: whatever happens to us is caused by us. Now many, many years we have spent in seeing the causes of things outside of our control.

Friends, it cannot be stressed too strongly that effort must be made daily on our part if we wish to receive the true value of these teachings. Effort must be made daily by us to apply the law. And that law is very simple; it is very clearly stated. You have your divine birthright: that birthright is total freedom and total awareness. But that is not possible for anyone unless he makes the effort to control. You see, freedom is control. Truth is control.

And so we're here to learn awareness, self-improvement, but we cannot receive it and we cannot experience it unless we learn to discipline our mind. The reason that we have so many disturbances in life, the reason that people upset us, the reason that we encounter so much unhappiness and so much grief and misery in this world is because we have not and are not practicing spiritual discipline. We are not disciplining our mind to decide, to choose, which level of consciousness our soul is going to express through. We have permitted ourselves to be the victim of whatever vibration is predominant in the atmosphere. We have continually and repeatedly given away our divine birthright to people, to circumstances, and to things.

Now, it is a known fact that the mind desires to control things that it sees. It is also a known fact that we cannot control outside what is not being controlled inside. Now the first job that faces anyone on the spiritual path is self-control: to control the thoughts of the mind, to control our reactions before we express ourselves. And discipline is the key, strict, daily discipline. If you have reached the point where you have disciplined yourself that you are awakening each morning, seven mornings a week, month after month and year after year, to sit down in your spiritual meditation and your concentration, then you are on the way. If you have not at least reached that point, then you have a long, long way to go. Because our soul, our spirit, must mean more to us than all of the attractions of creation.

So we awaken each morning and we get up and we brush our teeth. It must be more important than even brushing our teeth. It must be more important than going to our job. It must be more important than the emotions that we are entertaining at the moment. Your soul, your spirit, God, the Divine Intelligence—whatever you care to call it—has to be number one. Now when that Divine Intelligence, that spirit within you, is your first choice in all your choosing, when that is number one, then you will not have any need in your life, because, you see, that Divine Intelligence is everything. You don't need to tell it what you need because you don't need anything. You already have everything. It is simply a state of consciousness. It is a matter of becoming aware on a level of mind that you are indeed whole and complete, formless and free. Because that, my friends, is the truth.

Otherwise, without that effort to apply each day, without that application, we will continue to go through the storms and the creation of this earth life and we will not find that spark of divinity that frees our soul. So let us make a greater effort to sit each day in concentration and meditation. And let us make even a greater effort to expand that level of consciousness throughout our entire day. Now a person goes into their meditation, and they feel so good and they feel so peaceful. Well, you see, you can feel that way all of the time, if you make the effort to control yourself, to control your thoughts.

Several times it has been mentioned that very few people are aware of the thoughts that they entertain in ten short minutes. Now the reason that we are not aware of these thoughts is because we have not made the effort to control ourselves, you see.

Now I would like to discuss, also, before going into your questions and answers, the "Total Consideration" affirmation, line by line. And I would like to also know what it means to my students. I know what it means to me, but I would like you to give it some thought, if you haven't already given it some thought. What does that affirmation truly mean? And why is that affirmation so important to our awakening? So let us begin with the first line, "I am the manifestation of Divine Intelligence." Now what does that truly mean? What are we, in truth? The first line says, "I am the manifestation of Divine Intelligence." Now what does it mean to my students? Does anyone have an answer? What does that line mean to you?

In my understanding at the present time, it is essentially the same thing as the expression, "I am that I am." That I am a special instance, that which I appear to be is a special instance of that which I am which, in truth, is all things.

What does that line mean to you?

That God expresses through me.

Thank you very much. What is your feeling of what that line means?

I've got the feeling that each individual life on Earth, whether it be a paramecium or us, has a purpose.

Thank you very much.

The spirit that expresses through me is of God, is a direct part of the Divine Intelligence.

Thank you.

I think that this means that everything is God and I am God, too.

Thank you. Does anyone else have an expression of what that means to them?

I am part of God and expressing in infinite variety; as other people are also a variety of the same expression that I am.

Thank you.

To manifest would be to make manifest, and manifestation is reality.

Thank you very much.

I see the "I am" not as I, but as soul, as soul is the living demonstration of your will of Divine Intelligence.

Now remember, friends, you're supposed to be saying this affirmation daily as many times as you feel that it is necessary to free you from any thought or condition that is not beneficial to you. The line says that "I am the manifestation of Divine Intelligence." I am the realization of this intelligent energy. Now if you are the realization, the manifestation of the Divine Intelligence, then you cannot possibly entertain thoughts of want or need.

Second line: "I am the manifestation of Divine Intelligence. Formless and free. Whole and complete." So if we are the realization of God, of the Divine Spirit, we are formless and free; we are whole and complete, and peace, poise, and power are our birthright. Now how do we, as individualized souls with our limited expression of this Divine Intelligence—because indeed have we limited it—how do we truly become aware that we are the Divinity? Well, let us go forward in the affirmation and start to think. "I am the manifestation of Divine Intelligence. Formless and free. Whole and complete. Peace, Poise, and Power are my birthright. The Law of Harmony is my thought and guarantees Unity in all my acts and activities, expressing perfect Rhythm and limitless flow throughout my entire being."

My good friends, without the Law of Harmony in your thought, which brings unity and that limitless flow, then you, as individuals, are denying your own divinity. Now how do we get our minds into a state of consciousness where we are expressing this Law of Harmony, this unity, and this limitless, divine flow? Well, it's very simple: Every time you entertain a thought of controversy, you are denying your godhood. Every time you permit your mind to go into a battle of "This is the way it should be. That's the way it shouldn't be." Every time you permit your thinking to get into those levels of consciousness, you become the slave of the contradiction that you are manifesting and you have lost your freedom, your peace of mind, your poise, and your power, which is your inherent right.

The entire process, my friends, takes hold in the mind. This is why we discuss so much about the mind, because it is the mind that's causing us so many problems in this world. We will not stop and control our thoughts. We are not used to disciplining ourselves. We haven't established, yet, that pattern. Now, we know what the other type of thinking has done for us. So we're not satisfied with that kind of thinking or we wouldn't be in this classroom tonight. So that implies that we at least are ready to some extent, to some degree, to try another way of thinking, so that we can free ourselves from patterns that we're not pleased with. Otherwise, we would not be here. So let us make this effort.

Do we need to suffer more to make the effort to control our thoughts? If that is what is necessary for us, friends, you may be rest assured we will guarantee all of the suffering necessary until we become so weary of the suffering and of the torture that we put ourselves through, that we will make up our mind that we have had enough. And we'll come back inside of ourselves and we'll say, "I'm ready and I'm willing to make the changes necessary in my thinking to free my soul at last."

Now you're free to ask whatever questions you may have.

I find myself wanting very much to change, but it seems like when the time comes, when there is a situation where my mind has been pondering it, there seems to be a reluctance inside that wants to hold onto it. I feel, I guess, my own spirit is fighting against me. And is this one of the consciousnesses that I may have programmed the other way? How can I break that strength? Because there is a lot of strength there holding onto that and it's tough for us all, I'm sure. Is there anything we can just really jolt it with to break that tension?

Yes, there is. First, we will discuss why the—when people want to make a change in themselves, that they have reached the point where they desire the change because the patterns that they have entertained for a lifetime are no longer satisfactory to them, the first thing that they face is the security of the patterns of mind that they are familiar with. Now there is a false security to our emotions with the patterns that we have entertained for a lifetime. So when we reach the point in spiritual awakening where we honestly are striving to make this change, the first thing that we're going to face is the war of the emotions: the battle that goes on within. Because, you see, what you're striving to do is to leave a home that you are so familiar with, to venture on out into space in uncharted waters. Now, that's going to take not only faith in the divine that's expressing through you, but it's going to take will. One has to learn to direct their will. Everybody has will. For example, if it were not for will, you would not feel so secure with the patterns of which you're familiar. So the very same principle must be used. You must use that will to go into new horizons and you must use that will, strengthened by your faith, and then you will move out of the level that controls your soul.

I have several questions regarding awareness. I wonder if you would be good enough to explain the faculty of awareness, attention, and appreciation in Discourse 27.

Yes.

Can I give you the other questions now?

If you wish.

I have been trying to really determine what criteria to use in trying to figure out what a level of awareness is and I wonder if you might talk a little bit about that.

In reference to your first question, the lady is asking for, according to one of the discourses that has been given, perhaps an expansion of understanding on the soul faculty of awareness, attention, and appreciation. When man directs his thought, his attention, there is a degree of awareness that it is an inseparable part of attention. Now, the expression of appreciation, of course, would depend upon the individual. For example, sometimes a person has a thought and they feel they do not appreciate that thought or that awareness. The truth of the matter is that you cannot have awareness without attention, and you cannot have attention without appreciation. Now what really happens is that you are expressing appreciation: you are expressing your appreciation of your intolerance, of your dislike to the particular thing that your attention is drawn to. And so it is that a triune faculty of awareness, attention, and appreciation is inseparable.

Now, when man directs his thought, his attention, to any subject, to any field, person, place, or thing, when he directs his thought to it, he opens and exposes his soul, his awareness, and he guarantees the appreciation thereof. And so it is in these teachings that we have tried to share with you the importance of directing your thought, to choose wisely who or what you direct it to, because that is guaranteeing your awareness for the moment.

Now, let us bring it down to, perhaps, a more simple process or perhaps we can give an example. Say that a person thinks of a particular individual. The moment they think of that individual, their awareness is limited to what they know concerning that individual and to what that individual really is. Now, the person consciously is only aware of what they know about the person, but there is another level of consciousness that, through the Law of Attention, they have become in rapport with. Therefore, the degree of attention you place upon the person will depend on how much you are affected by them. Do you understand? That's known as coming into rapport.

Now, we come into rapport with a person, place, or thing through the Law of Attention, Awareness, and Appreciation. Now a person says, "Well, I got into rapport with that person because I was totally unaware." Well, that's not the truth of the matter at all. They got into rapport with that person through the triune faculty of attention, appreciation, and awareness. You look at a person: there's your attention. And then maybe you like the way the person looks: there's your appreciation. And the awareness is guaranteed. And so the teaching is, choose wisely your associates and with whom you spend your life-giving energy, for the contents of the book are never like the cover. And so it is with all forms in all universes. Direct your attention ever upward to the Divine and you shall view the paradise which is your true home. Direct it otherwise and you will view the opposite throughout life.

Now I know you want to know about levels of awareness. Well, how does a person best express something that another person is not yet experiencing? How does one express and have the mind accept, unless the mind is receptive to what is yet to be expressed? We have to go within ourselves. We have to become aware of ourselves. There is no use and there is no value to any study unless that study, that investigation, in some way, no matter how small and no matter how great, but in some way causes us to make a greater effort to find our soul. That's where the true awareness is. Now a person could say, "Well, this is level twenty-six and that is level forty-eight." But unless another human soul, through an inner awareness, finds that for himself, it will be of no benefit to the receiver. It will not illumine them. It will help the mind to intellectualize and to theorize, but it will be of no benefit to the students unless the students themselves, through their own efforts and their own constant application, find it out as their own truth. Someone else have a question?

It's probably not a question, but I do want to express my gratitude for the "Total Consideration" affirmation, even for the limited awareness that I have of it. I had a very painful week, and at midnight and at other hours of the day, I read it and it really lifted my heart. It really did. It works. It really, really works. I can't say anything else but that. I'm grateful. Thank you.

Thank you very much. You see how important it is, friends, to go inside of ourselves. And that's where peace, prosperity—everything that we think would fulfill our life, it's all waiting in the depths of our own soul. It's been waiting there for many, many lifetimes and it will be waiting for many yet to come. So we have merited somehow in our evolution this moment and this opportunity to start directing our attention to the spirit within us and letting ourselves be free. Now someone else had a question?

You mentioned the will and we also mentioned tonight a discussion of a portion of the "Total Consideration" affirmation. I wonder if I could ask if you could go one line further, "As the Light of Truth is sustained by the faculty of Reason, I pause to think."

"I pause to think." To do what? "To claim my Divine right." "As the Light of Truth is sustained by the faculty of Reason . . ." Without the expression of your soul faculty of reason, you cannot, in truth, pause and claim what is rightfully yours. It is not possible. Only through the soul faculty of reason, which sustains the light of truth in your universe, only then can you truly pause to think and claim your divine right. Now why is it that only when the soul faculty of reason is expressing that you're capable of pausing to claim your divine right? Well, it's very simple, my friends. When any other level of consciousness is expressing, you are not free to claim your divine right: you're only claiming what that level is limited to express. Because it is only through reason that truth and freedom are expressing through our universe.

And so the first thing that we do is to stop, to rise our consciousness to what is known as the soul faculty of reason. "Now what is reason?" the question is asked. Well, reason is total consideration. If totally all is not considered, then reason cannot and does not flow. So you see the importance of your affirmation. You see how, when you are in total consideration—total consideration considers every level of consciousness; that's all eighty-one of them. If you are having an experience, then you pause to think and you claim your divine right. You do that by considering everything involved, seen and unseen, and then and then alone will you be free and have your divine right in any given situation.

In the third line, "Peace, Poise, and Power are my birthright," this word "power" has bothered me.

Yes.

What kind of power?

Thank you so very, very much. The word *power*, as used in the affirmation, is power over whatever is selfish and wrong in ourselves, not in another. You see, my friends, power over the lower states of consciousness, known as the animal form, in which our spirit, our soul, is expressing itself—that is our birthright. It is power. Peace, poise, and power are our birthright. Power over the form in which our formless spirit expresses itself; that this form goes back to the elements from which it was created. You have the power over it. You see that?

That is self-control.

That most certainly is. Self-control is power. You see, concentration is the key to all power. But concentration, my friends, doesn't come to anyone without self-control. Any person that thinks they're concentrating and they are not exercising self-control is not concentrating in the first place. Because concentration is placing the mind pointedly and fixedly upon the object of your choice until only the essence remains. That is the power itself. The essence of the thing, that is the power of it, you see. That's the very core of it. That's the power that holds it together. That's the essence of a thing. And so when you are truly concentrated, you're in one; that is the God within you. You see, there are no distractions. You have power over all those things that keep pulling at your consciousness. That's what that means.

I was going to ask a question about reason. You gave such a wonderful discourse on it, but I still would like to have explained to me, How does one come into this reason? I mean, some of us just do not have this reasoning power. You sit in meditation and you take it to total consideration. And I ask myself, "What have I done? Now let me release this to the Divine and let me see how I can protect myself and not do this again." How does one contact reason?

That's a very fine question. And the lady has asked, How does one contact this soul faculty of reason within oneself? I'll be more than happy to share with you my understanding. When you first take count of all of your desires, known and unknown—and the question arises, "Well, how do I find my desires that are unknown?" By searching one's own soul, by searching one's own subconscious. When you take stock of all of your desires, and you list them all and then you make the choice to let them go—that they have no control or power over you—you will rise to what is known as the soul faculty of reason. Now many people, they like to use reason. And they ask themselves in any situation, or perhaps they've had an experience, "Well, what have I done?" And they cannot find within their mind what they have done. Well, it's very simple. It's because we don't yet know all of our desires, those hidden desires. We must first list all of these desires. We must also become aware of how important they are to us.

Now, for example, a person goes to work and say that the boss doesn't say, "Good morning" one morning. And so the person says, "Huh! What's the matter with *me*? No, something must be wrong with *him*. He didn't say good morning to me." Now, why does a person think like that? Why do they think that way? Why is it necessary for the employer to say "Good morning" each time they come to work? Because they have become addicted to the pattern of the employer saying "Good morning" to them. Therefore, that has become important to them and on the morning that the employer does not say "Good morning," they go through all kinds of emotional frustration. Now why do they become frustrated on that particular morning? Well, it's very simple. Curiosity is the cause of frustration. The mind is curious what happened that he didn't say "Good morning." That's why they get frustrated, you see. It's that old curiosity killed the cat. Well, information brought it back. So go to your soul faculty, where information is, and then you will have the answer. And you will not be concerned that he didn't say good morning on Tuesday, when he said good morning for the last twenty-five years, you see. Because you will know inside of yourself that it doesn't really matter to your soul. It doesn't matter.

It's just like a person who is used to seeing certain people on a certain day of the week, and then one week something comes up and they don't see those people. Well, they go through all kinds of emotional trips. Well, that shows the degree of attachment they have to that pattern.

You see, friends, the mind—the nature of the mind is to attach. Well, if that is the nature of mind—and that is demonstrable—then let's, for goodness' sakes, attach it to something that's formless and free and something that's intelligent, not something that's going to bind us and control us, you see. I mean, some people are addicted to food. They're addicted to certain types of food. Some people are addicted to automobiles. Some people are addicted to airplanes. Well, my God, we're addicted to all kinds of things. And you know, the moment we start working on this addiction and that addiction and another addiction and we start removing them from our universe, we'd better be on the alert, because another habit pattern is already manifesting itself, but we're not yet aware of it. You see, that's the nature of the mind. That's the nature of form. It must hold and attach to something. So it constantly is manufacturing some new pattern to get addicted to, unless we make the constant effort to let it be attached to the divine, infinite, formless, and free Spirit. And that has to be done constantly.

You see, the moment something happens, that's the moment that we know how addicted we were to it and that also shows to what extent and to what degree we sold our soul. See, my friends, the degree of suffering always reveals the extent of the attachment. Now, if you're attached to your job and you lose your job, then it's a most difficult experience. If you're attached to your husbands or your wives and they decide to go or they go off to the other side over there, and you suffer, well, you sold that much of your soul and that's why you're suffering.

It's a rather funny question, but is it true that we are getting rid of our attachments—husbands and wives and children and all this—because when we get to spirit we may not be in the same level as they are? And because of our love or our dislikes, we may not have known that somebody hated us and we may have become attached to someone we can't be with. Is this true?

Well, from what I have seen in this world and the next one, it is a rare husband and wife that land up in the same plane of consciousness. But, of course, you know, you don't have to wait till you get to spirit to find that out. You can find that out while you're still in the flesh. I mean, how many husbands and wives really, truly are in rapport spiritually? I mean, you know, you mustn't expect that you're both going to go to the same plane of consciousness when you're not even on the same plane of consciousness while you're still in the flesh. How can you expect to be on the same plane of consciousness when you're out of the flesh? You see, you go in there with a mental body, you see. And so, my friends, you know, if you feel that you've kind of weathered the storm in your marriage and it's been thirty or forty years, well, you can look forward to when you leave. Because if it's been that difficult while you're in the flesh, you undoubtedly won't be on the same plane when you're over there, because you haven't been on the same plane here, you see. What is there to hold you? There's no money in spirit. You know, there's no material substance, so that's not going to hold you to him. So if you want your husband to be with you or your wife to be with you on the other side, get him on your side here and now. That's the only thing I know, the only way I know, if you're ever going to have him with you. Yes, does someone else have a question?

Would you discuss a sense of lack as an attachment?

Absolutely and positively. If one is experiencing it, if we're experiencing lack, then we are attached to what lack has to offer us. So what we have to find out first is, to honestly say to ourselves, "Now let me see, I'm experiencing lack. Now in this experience, what am I gaining?" Because we're gaining something from the experience. Now if it helps us to feel humble, if that's what we've computed and we want to be humble, then that's what we're gaining. If it brings us attention and compassion from people, then that's what we're gaining. And if we have computed in our computer that it's making us more spiritual, then, of course, that's what we're gaining. But that depends, you see. We cannot experience lack unless lack is doing something for us.

See, lack does a lot for us. It depends on each individual, you know. Lack for some people will help them educate their desires, you know. Not because they want to educate their desires, but they'll be forced to, don't you see? I mean, after all, if a person is experiencing lack and they want a new car, well, that desire is going to get educated one way or another, because they don't have the money to get it. Lack certainly serves a purpose.

Now with some people, you know—I find that with most people—lack does bring them energy. It brings them attention, you know. I mean, after all, it's like a woman that's had a kidney removed: she can talk about her operation. Excuse me, a man also. And so if lack is a topic of discussion for us—don't you see?—then it helps bring us a little energy and attention. Of course, I think it's much, much better, myself—I finally, hope-fully, got to that level of consciousness—better to talk about prosperity. That brings you a lot more attention than the other. I found that out for a fact. Nobody likes a loser, you know, and everyone gravitates around success, you see. And so if it's atten-tion we need, well, let's use prosperity for an attention-getter. It's a much better one. Much, much better, yes.

Now sometimes, perhaps, we go into a little more detail. Sometimes, you know, it's like, perhaps, when a woman gets married and she raises her children, etc. And things start to change, don't you see, which they do as the children grow up and then they get married. And so the things that they used to have, they no longer experience. So something has got to be experienced, and the mind is a very intricate mechanism. And if they need lack to bring them the experiences that they desire, then lack is what it's going to be. Now, if they need prosperity to do it, then it's going to be prosperity, you see. It's very difficult to grow out of patterns that we've become familiar with. You know, we might say, "Well, now, I always prepared myself that my children were going to grow up, that I was going to face that day. You know, I've thought about it for years." But the truth of the matter is it's a very rare person that's ever prepared, a very rare person, you see. I mean, after all, it is the nature of women to mother. It is the nature of men to father. So let's face the reality of the forms, because that is a reality and it's a fact. So it is our nature to mother something; it is our nature to father something. And so it is when the family grows up, then we'd best find something else, you see. And I think that everyone, if they will give it some thought, will agree that we do not easily grow out of these patterns that we've been habituated to.

But you see, if lack is no longer serving its purpose in our universe, we can very quickly change to prosperity and fulfillment. I have given all of my students the way; we've even printed it on our bookmarks: "Thank you God I'm moving in your Divine flow." And when you really get that into your computer, you may be rest assured, my friends, it just works beautifully. Every Monday morning it's in, and every Monday morning it goes out, so that it can come back in again. And so that's the way it is. But I don't hold it with my tight fist. I let it go, because I know when I let it go that God is already bringing it back to me. If I let it go with a vibration "God, that's all there is left and I don't want to have to pay the bills," then, don't you see, I will guarantee the experience. I'm not that foolish anymore. I used to be, but no more. So when I sign the check, I say, "Thank you, God, I'm moving in your Divine flow." And I let those hundreds of dollars go out, because I know they're going to turn right around and get multiplied and come right back again and that's exactly what happens. But if I let my mind get into that level of consciousness that, "Let's see, well, how much money will we be able to make this week? And I've got this many bills," and I get into that level of consciousness, you be rest assured I'll experience all the lack that I desire, even though I'm not consciously aware of it.

That that we let go freely comes back freely, you see. And the material world: how sad, it has become our master and we have become its slave. We're the creators, not it, you see, but it has taken control of us. For what? It's in our thinking. If nothing else gets through your mind, friends, remember that lack and limitation is only in your thought. It doesn't exist in truth. It isn't something that God brought into being, or anyone else. The only place that exists is in your levels of mind. And when you get your levels of mind retaped, you will never again experience lack or limitation. It is not necessary. Now if you want to suffer, if that's what you need, then lack and limitation continue to control your soul. But that's up to you, you see. That's entirely up to you as individuals. Let it go freely and it will come back freely. But that takes a little bit of faith.

What do you think of the phrase sometimes used in a time of heartache or trouble or lack or limitation or what have you, "It just doesn't matter that much anymore"?

If it really doesn't, then you will be freed from it.

Well, I can free myself from almost anything by saying that.

That's right. Because when it no longer matters—

Is that a wise person's attitude? Does it really solve a problem? Or does it just take your attention away from it for the moment?

The only way a person can experience a problem is through attention. Our problems are only companions as long as we love them. You see, as long as love, energy, attention is directed to a thing, then we create the problem. When it no longer matters, your soul is freed.

No matter what the problem?

It doesn't matter. It doesn't matter. You can free yourself that way. Now there is a better way than that.

In other words, just completely be lazy and say that it just doesn't matter.

No, that's not the way. That's not being lazy. What you are doing when you say, "It doesn't matter anymore," what you are really doing is, you are removing your state of consciousness from a level known as concern. Concern is a function. If that is the way you have found to remove your level of consciousness from the function known as concern, then you are freed from it.

Now there is even a better way. There is a way of stating, "This has no power over me." Now you've said it in words that are different, you understand: you've said it doesn't really matter. Well, you're really doing the same thing. It has no power over you. See, the only power a thing has over us is the power that we give to it through our awareness, attention, and appreciation. Do you understand? We discussed awareness, attention, and appreciation earlier, and so this is the very soul faculty that you're dealing with. When you say it no longer matters, then your awareness, attention, and appreciation are no longer directed to that particular circumstance or condition. Is that not correct?

Yes.

And then you are freed from it. Certainly. See, the only thing that really matters in this life, and in any life, is our soul. Because this keeps changing. It changes all the time; it's changing moment to moment. The time here is very, very short. Very, very short. And if you don't think so, just go past forty and you'll see what I mean. It keeps going faster after you hit forty. At least, it seems that way, because that's the way the masses are programmed, you know. When you get to be forty, you're on the—it goes much quicker. So what does it matter? That's the thing. It only matters as much as you permit it to matter to you. A house, it comes and it goes. A car, it comes and it goes. Well, if everything material goes, and we don't have peace of mind when it goes, then we don't have control of our soul. Don't you see? And remember this: In creation, by the law of coming to you, it's guaranteed to go. Whatever has come to you in life, or anyone else, by the Law of Coming, it is guaranteed to leave you. So hold not to form, because if you hold to form, you will never be free, no matter what the form is. Any individual that holds to form is bound to slavery and that is the law that is demonstrable. I don't care whether you call it a child, a husband, or a wife: if you permit yourself to be bound to form, you will never be free. Ever. Because the thing that you're bound to controls you.

A topic was given for discussion tonight on application. It was just spoken that as you hold to things, you are bound by them; and that it is the nature of the mind to attach to things. And so when we tell the mind to release, release, release, give, give, give, then the mind has a tendency to react to that.

It does, because it isn't yet attached to the Divine. It most certainly does.

Then—

The automatic emotional reaction. I know, I'm a fund-raiser. Thank you.

The question that would follow would be, then, the release, release, release, obviously to the mind, is not a satisfactory path. It may, perhaps, be the most desirable path or the most "aspirable" path, if you prefer.

The mind will seek something to attach to, if you constantly tell it to release all of this creation. Its very nature demands that it attach. So in the process of releasing, it constantly seeks to attach. Finally, it will be directed to the Divinity.

So in the releasing, then, I assume that there is a counterpart to this little exercise, which will, if not satisfy the mind, at least keep the mind busy applying. Could you expand upon that?

Yes, I'll be happy to share with you our understanding on releasing to the Divine. You see, what happens when a person, a student, is constantly taught whatever the seeming difficulty or the desire that they have, to release it to the Divine, which means to free it from the bondage of the mind—and the nature of the mind is to attach to something—now the first thing that the mind goes through is a state of frustration. You see, it has all these multitude of desires. It's constantly creating new ones. That's the way our minds work. And so here it is, the mind is being told to release this to the Divine, release that to the Divine, release something else to the Divine. Now frustration is the first thing it goes through. It gets angry. It doesn't want to give. It doesn't want to serve, doesn't want to do this, doesn't want to do that. It sees that everybody else isn't doing as much as it is doing.

That's the process it goes through, because, you see, when you say, "Release it to the Divine," the mind becomes curious. What Divine? It hasn't spent the effort to find out what the Divine is. And so curiosity takes control of the mind. And it says, "Well, now, if I release this to the Divine, number one: I don't really know what the Divine is. I haven't satisfied myself in that level yet. Number two: I haven't had enough experiences in releasing it to the Divine to find out that it comes back to me." So it goes through all of that level of curiosity, and its curiosity keeps increasing and the frustrations keep growing.

Now when the frustrations reach a certain point, they do one of two things: they either take the soul completely away from the light that they're trying to find inside themselves or they break them down (the habit patterns they're attached to in their own brain.) They break them down and, through the soul faculty of humility, gratitude is born. And from gratitude comes tolerance and duty. And that is the first soul faculty. And when that starts to open the eyes, a person sees a little crumb that they're getting and the gratitude increases even more, because they say, "My God, it does work. It's only a crumb, but it works." And that's exactly what happens when a person finally has enough frustration and they have enough battle inside of their brain and their emotional patterns, and they really do finally free it. They become very humble souls and they are so grateful because the soul faculty of humility has opened up. Now the soul faculty of humility—if you will study your study book [*The Living Light*], you will find that the soul faculty of humility has something to do with healing. Anyone remember what that discourse is about?

Well, I remember the Law of Harmony flows through the faculty of faith, poise, and humility. Now the question about humility and—

What is the soul faculty of humility? They're all triune.

The soul faculty of humility?

Yes. It's a soul faculty and it's triune. What are the other two points of the triangle, of the faculty? You just read them.

Yes, faith and poise.

Faith, poise, and humility. And what flows through faith, poise, and humility?

Healing is involved.

What else does it say? The Law of . . .

I'm reading fast.

That's all right. Take your time. The line says, flows through the soul faculty—faith, poise, and humility. Well, what is it that flows through?

Could it be the Law of Harmony?

The Law of Harmony. Now what does the Law of Harmony have to do with? Now, we've discussed the Law of Harmony in this classroom before. Yes?

Peace.

Peace. What does it bring? I want the students that were here in the last course to tell me about the Law of Harmony, because it was given to you—not this course but the course before—and it was spelled out about health, wealth, and happiness.

Health, wealth, and happiness are governed by harmony, rhythm, and unity, in the order given.

And what does harmony deal with?

Harmony deals with health. It's also given in that particular course that the body is referred to as vibration.

All right. Now, you see, friends, this is all tied in. What does your affirmation say? "The Law of Harmony is my thought." Think. If the Law of Harmony is my thought, then, my friends, we have faith, poise, and humility. The Law of Harmony flows through the triune soul faculty—as it says in *The Living Light*—of faith, poise, and humility. The affirmation says, "The Law of Harmony is my thought." If the Law of Harmony is your thought, then you are expressing faith, poise, and humility. Now, go back to the affirmation. It says, "The Law of Harmony is my thought and guarantees Unity in all my acts and activities, expressing perfect Rhythm." And what is perfect rhythm?

Harmony?

Limitless flow. "Expressing perfect Rhythm and limitless flow throughout my entire being." My friends, if you are expressing through that soul faculty, then you cannot help but have health, wealth, and happiness. You can't help but have it. Think about it, friends.

Let's go have refreshments.

OCTOBER 18, 1973

CONSCIOUSNESS CLASS 28 ❦

Good evening, students. And before getting into your questions and answers this evening, I would like to discuss for a few moments—in *The Living Light* and throughout our classes, there have been many techniques given to the students to help them to help themselves. Of course, that is the true purpose of these classes, both the public and the private ones: that we may become aware of what we really are, who we truly are, and that we may, through our own personal efforts, not only become aware of that, but be able to free ourselves at any given moment.

Now a great deal has been spoken not only in this particular course, but in all of our classes, both public and private, on the mind. And I know that it does seem to some that perhaps there appears to be a great dwelling on the mind, on how the mind works, on how to control it. But my friends, it is not wise, nor beneficial, to move to higher levels of consciousness until the levels which we are so familiar with, in the sense that we are using them all of the time, until those levels of consciousness are understood. Because we cannot control, nor can we discipline, anything that we have not spent the time and the effort to understand.

How does a person truly begin to understand himself? It has been stated that when man takes the essence from an experience—which is the indispensable ingredient for the reeducation of the senses that have, in the first place, created the experience—then man will start upon the path to free his soul. Now, I know that to many, the word *soul* or *spirit* seems to be very nebulous and formless and something that we can't seem to grab or to grasp or to really understand the import of. But you see, the soul, my friends, your soul is the true you. Your attitude of mind at any moment is only the cloak that you have chosen to express through. But that is not you, not the true soul, your real being.

Inside of all of us is a level of consciousness which knows all of its experiences. It knows why it came to Earth. It knows where it came from. And from that knowing, it also knows where it is going. Now that may seem to be some distant thing that is not important to our daily activities and to our conscious mind. But my good friends, it is of great importance, for it is the true cause of all of our experiences. We came here into this physical form. We came with certain attributes. We came with certain lessons guaranteed in this incarnation. We are not going

to escape those lessons. We are not going to escape what we have
established as our destiny, because, my friends, we are our own
destiny. But you see, when we think that we are our destiny and
we do not perceive on deeper levels of consciousness, then we do
not, in truth, see our true destiny.

Now many have said over the years that if there is something they have to do, they have an eternity, of course, in which
to do it. But we must remember, students, that eternity is not
some far distant thing that you're moving to. It is something
that you *are*, this moment and this moment only. For eternity is
your conscious awareness at any given moment. So a hundred
years from now is not yet perceived by our conscious mind. But
the eternity of this moment is what we can do something about.
Now we can't do anything, of course, about yesterday. It has gone.
We cannot directly do something about tomorrow. It has not yet
arrived, in the illusion in which we believe. You see, we believe
in time and we believe in space. And because we believe in it,
we have created it. Time and space do not exist, in truth. It is a
created thing, created by the mind substance.

Again and again it has been said that all things, to a certain
level of consciousness, are possible. And indeed, all things *are*
possible to that level. If there is something that is of such great
import to us to accomplish, if there is something that our very
being wishes to fulfill inside of us, if we and we alone will make
the strenuous effort—it is strenuous because there are so many
levels to rise through—if we will make that great effort to rise
our conscious awareness to a plane of consciousness inside of
ourselves that is beyond the belief, the illusion of creation, the
illusion of time and space, and we will accept that that we are
seeking on that level of consciousness, it shall indeed come to
pass in the order that we and we alone have established in our
own path.

Now many have asked about their prior expression of life. I
can understand the reason for the inquiry. But let us view it in

the eternal now. Let us see that this eternity of this conscious moment is indeed the effect of many things that we have set into motion along the way. Now, it is not within the realm of divine justice to set laws into motion and to wave the hand and remove them. Because if that were within divine justice, then we would have chaos in the world. There would no longer be a law of what is called cause and effect. And the system and order of the universes would go into turmoil and you would not have a harmonious life expression.

Whatever there is, exists. Whatever we wish, exists. But we, my friends, must make that conscious, constant effort to get to it in consciousness. We say, we want to go, perhaps, to Florida. Well, Florida, in our mind, exists X amount of miles away. And so we believe that we must do certain things to get there. I am speaking of things that are higher and greater than the created illusions of our mind. There are other ways to get what we are seeking. There are greater ways to our fulfillment. But we cannot reach that, my friends, unless we're willing to let go. When we let go, we can gain another step. But we cannot gain another step of consciousness until we're willing, ready, and able to let the other step, whatever it may be, leave our universe. So let us give, perhaps, a little more thought to what we're doing—not to the world—let us think what we're doing, in truth, to ourselves now.

We're here to enjoy a world that is a true wonder. We see but such a small fraction of that great wonder. We get a fleeting glimpse of the divine and the true purpose of life. But it's only a fleeting glimpse because we are not giving more thought to why we came to this planet. You know we did not come by chance. We came to learn what the planet has offered to us. And it offers different things to different people, because those are the laws that were set into motion in the life before this one and the one before that. But my friends, your life and my life are not the form. It is not the vehicle through which we are moving. It is greater than all things, it is greater than all experience, and it is greater than all that the mind can possibly imagine.

You're free now to ask whatever questions that you have.

I have two questions. Number one is, I've heard it said that one can see the soul. I was wondering what enlightenment you could give and what that would be composed of or if different ones look a different way. And number two, I was wondering what it is that makes the body age, the physical body. Is it the mind semblance of self or what?

Thank you very much. In reference to your first question, you have heard it stated that man can view or see the soul. Whenever the soul is viewed or whenever it is seen, it is seen by the soul and not by the mind or the physical eyes or even the psychic eyes. We see mental things with a mental vehicle. And we feel physical things with a physical vehicle. And we perceive spiritual things with spiritual sight. So in reference to that question, it would be the soul of a person that is viewing the soul of another. If that is what they are truly viewing, it would be from that level of consciousness. What was your second question, please?

What is it that ages the physical body?

The physical body is a direct effect of the mind. And whenever the thoughts in the mind are in controversy, contradiction with each other, whenever there is discord, there is an aging process that takes place. There is, in the natural law of things, no absolute need for the form to age. However, this has been created through the discord in the mental body. Now a person may justly and rightly ask, "If that is true, then how come the dog or the cat ages? How come I look at creation and I witness its aging?" Well, it's very simple. You see, man has been given charge over all creation. And when man's thoughts are discordant, nature responds to the discord, and you have what is known as the aging process. Does that help with your question?

Thank you very much.

You're welcome.

If man does not age naturally, then does man not reproduce naturally?

That's a very fine question. And the question is, "If man does not age naturally, then does man not reproduce naturally?" No. The aging process, as he's explained, is the direct effect of discord or disharmony in the mental levels. The reproduction of the species is something that our present evolution is experiencing. That was not always the case in creation. There is an evolution and a devolution to creation. It evolves to a great refinement and then it goes back on the cycle to evolve again. That is the Law of Creation. That is the cycle of creation and that is the duality of it. You see, man, by his own experiences and his own thoughts, can see, without a shadow of any doubt, that he is high one moment, only to be low the next. So the cyclic pattern is the Law of Creation herself. Thank you very much.

My question regards destiny. Until one reaches the level of consciousness of knowing one's destiny, how does one deal with changes or decisions, as opposed to just flowing with the stream of life?

Yes, thank you very much. The lady has asked the question, Until one rises to a state of consciousness within oneself where one may perceive their destiny, how does one deal with the normal experiences and the things of life itself? There are varying levels of consciousness. And the first time a person encounters an experience, the normal, let us say, the average thing that takes place is that the mind reaches its decisions. Now the mind reaches her decisions based upon the experiences of the past, based upon the facts that it has in its own computer.

Now, that isn't necessarily, in and of itself, the best for the individual. That depends on what they have fed into the mind in the first place. It also depends on the tendency of the mental body from the moment of conception, because, you see, this mental body and this astral body do enter—and the soul—at that time.

That is not necessarily the best thing for the individual, because one is acting or reacting upon facts, upon experiences that are stored in the mind.

When one has an experience and they will make the effort to be objective, number one: They will consider what their mind is dictating, recognizing and realizing that the mind that we're consciously using is basing its decision upon its own experiences and its own facts and its own brain. If then they will be at peace within themselves and be receptive to the highest level of consciousness that they are able to be receptive to, then they will get another set of guidelines.

Now, then they must make a choice. They must choose between what their mind and the computer has dictated and what their higher level of consciousness is trying to dictate. Now this is known as the war of the emotions. This is the battle that goes on within the self. This is the battle between creation and truth. And it is not an easy battle for any form and for anyone in anyplace at any time. But the battle can be won. If a person really wants to win it, it can be won.

And you will find that the guidelines that are coming from your higher level of consciousness are usually very simple. The mind cannot see how it's going to work, but give it a chance. Make a choice in some little matters and you will be amazed if you demonstrate the soul faculty of patience.

With regard to an earlier question, if the mind of man can age the mind of a cat, dog, or a tree, can the mind of man age other men? And relative to that, one thing that I am concerned about, say, with reference to our current political scene, What is the mind of man, one man or a group of men, able to do together?

Thank you very much. And I'm very happy you've brought the question up. What affects one mind affects, to some degree, all minds, for there is one universal mind. And so it is that when the mind, the mass thinking of the planet is disturbed, then we have disturbances in our physical world. And this, my friends, is the true and great value of peace. If we as individualized souls become disturbed in ourselves, we disturb all things that we are not only in rapport with, but associated with to any extent. Now because we have not spent the time to study and to investigate the universality of mind is no reason to say, "Well, that's impossible." We are individualized souls inseparably a part of the Allsoul. We are individualized states of consciousness inseparably connected with the universal consciousness.

If you have five people thinking "peace, poise, and prosperity", and they are truly feeling it and they are united in their thought, then you will move, truly, a mountain. Because that is the power that is within the human being. But you see, friends, because we have permitted the experiences of lifetimes to affect our thinking, we have lost this power to move the mountain. We have lost it because we have contradictory thoughts in our mind. Nothing is more destructive to the human being than a vibratory wave of contradiction. Because the moment you entertain an attitude of mind known as contradiction, you are a house divided and, being a house divided, you do not have the power to do what you desire to do.

A person decides they want to do anything and the moment they reach the decision, they have the battle going on within. They're either conscious of it—usually they are—or they're not conscious of it. But you have this duality of the mind going to work. You have this contradiction. And the energy—you see, thought is the vehicle through which energy expresses itself— so this energy, being expressed through thoughts that battle each other, dissipates itself. And you see, friends, this is your true cause of poor health and disease. This is your true cause of lack and limitation. It is the contradiction in your mind. And then you lose the power of the Divinity. You lose it in the sense that you dissipate it by the war within yourself.

Now, each student in this Association is taught, the understanding is shared with them, that peace and peace alone is the power. Now that has to mean more to you than a thought. It has to mean enough to you to apply it. No matter what your eyes may view, no matter what your ears may hear, nor your senses feel, the power that moves all things in all places is known as peace. That is the thing that the students are instructed to concentrate upon, to direct their thought and their energy to. Whatever you may see in your life as an obstacle can be disintegrated by one power, and that is known as peace.

Could you give us your understanding, Serenity's understanding, on principle and how to apply it?

Yes, the lady has asked the question of the understanding of the Association on the word *principle* and how to apply it. It is ofttimes, and usually, through comparison that we're able to perceive, perhaps a bit deeper, in our questionings in life. And so we'd like to take a few moments to compare principle, that word and that meaning, *principle,* to what is known as *person* or *personality.*

Now when a person is truly striving to flow, to express what is known as principle, they are freed from the seeming obstructions of what is known as form or personality. There is no thought of judgment. There is no concern for effect. There is only the all-consuming love of the principle that they are trying to express. For example, one may say that they are working in the principle of spiritual understanding. If we are truly working in the principle of spiritual understanding, then spiritual understanding, the love of it, is the one and only thing that entertains our thought.

Now, when we say, "I'm working toward spiritual understanding. That is the principle I've placed myself under. But these other people that are supposed to be working for that are doing the opposite." In that type of thinking and in that moment, we've lost our principle. That's when we've gone into personality. Because, you see, principle is a faculty within our being that has no judgment. It has no thought of what everybody else in this world, or any world, is doing with it. Its all-consuming love is the principle itself.

I, perhaps, may share with you my understanding in the reference to the word *principle*. Principle is an electrical vibration and it is not affected by the emotions. The emotions are the magnetic field, and you do not have principle in the magnetic field. You only have principle in the electrical field. Therefore, when you're in principle, you don't have emotion and you don't have feelings and you don't have concern and you don't have worry and you don't have all of the emotional experiences. That's when you're in principle of anything. Now when your principle, you understand, becomes personality, then you have emotion and you've lost your true principle. Perhaps that would best help you.

Could you make it a little clearer for me regarding magnetic and electric and also water?

Yes, I'll be happy to share with you what understanding that we have. The student is asking, perhaps, for clarification on what is the magnetic field and what is the electrical field and water. I know that we all understand what a magnet is. A magnet is that that attracts things to us. Now, in the magnetic field we find all of the emotions, all of the feelings, all of the personality. Without the magnetic field, there is no personality. It does not exist. Because the only other field left to us is the electric and the neutral, or the odic. Now, without this magnetic field, we could not—it serves, also, a very good purpose—without this magnetic field, we could not experience what our minds call love or affection. We could not experience attracting things to us. And so we would be very electrical and very, very barren.

Now each individual is tipped on the scales between the electrical vibration and the magnetic one. We find some people in the electrical vibration. They have no emotions, they have no feelings, they have no concern about anyone else, and they're totally wrapped up in their own intellectual thinking. That's when the scales within us, we have tipped ourselves more into the electrical vibration.

Now it is true, like in worldly business, that a wise man uses a great deal of the electrical vibration. But you don't stop there, because if you do, you see, that's what you send out. That's clear-cut. If you stop there, everything goes out and there's no magnet to pull it back to you. And this is the purpose of the separation of your daily concentration, meditation, and manifestation. You see, your concentration is your electrical field. Now, you have no emotion when you're concentrating. You have no emotion whatsoever. You're concentrating on peace. Now when you concentrate upon peace, you're sending that out of your aura. You see, it's going right out and touching what is known as peace.

Now when you start to feel that peace, you see, which is an emotion, then you are in your magnetic field. And so you pull that great peace back to you. It's the same thing with man and his desire. Now, you see, what happens, say you have a desire. Well, when you have that desire, you project it, you see. It becomes electrical and you project it out into the atmosphere. Well, like attracts like and becomes the Law of Attachment. Well, the reason that like attracts like, you see—that's known as the celestial marriage. The thought goes out electrically, it attracts another thought that's coming out electrically, and when they come together, they become magnetic. And then that is the attraction. So you see, everything, everywhere is electric and is magnetic. That that goes out electrically comes back magnetically.

Now, when you take the essence from these experiences, when you take the odic force from them—that's what it is—when you take that which is known as the neutrality, you take the very essence out of it, then, my friends, you're in neutrality. You have become objective to creation. You're up here where truth is and you're watching the duality which is creation. Now until we learn to separate this truth, this odic force, from the electromagnetic fields of creation, we're not going to be free. It is not possible because we're going to be constantly fluctuating between the electric and the magnetic field over and over and over and over again.

But you see, you take the very essence from the electromagnetic. Now how does one get the essence from an experience? How does one get the odic force out of the electrical-magnetic? By bringing it into balance. Now that's what takes place within our being. When we bring it into balance, the positive and negative, we rise it to what is known as the soul faculty of reason. And this is why the teaching is, "Keep faith with reason: she will transfigure thee." And that's what takes place with all experiences every day, every moment, everywhere. That is the law which is the trinity of truth. That is known as manifestation.

So we try to make our effort to stay at the apex of that triangle, because from up there, we have a clear view. But it's not, of course, particularly easy for any of us to stay on the point of anything. Why isn't it easy? Well, it's simple: the point is sharp. And our magnetic field doesn't want to stay up there. Of course it doesn't, because it hurts and it takes great effort. And you see, friends, everyone has to make effort. We all do. We're not alone in our struggle in life. "Why, why," someone asked me just this very day, "why do we have to struggle so much? What is the sense of the soul coming into this life, and the spirit, with all of this struggle, with all these trials, and with all of these tribulations?" Well, my understanding is very simple. The purpose of the soul's incarnation into physical form is to raise, or to purify, those forms, that in time, in eternity, they may know of their true source, of the true Divinity.

See, everything is being refined. The diamond doesn't reveal the beauty and the luster until it's chipped and it suffers through all of that struggle. Everything, everything, my friends, that's form suffers and struggles, because that is what we say it is when it's going through the refining process. Now, you see, you go out and cut the tree down and you have no thought that it is suffering. Well, of course, it suffered, because there's a life expression in it. And there are feelings in the tree. If you kill the dog, the dog goes through a suffering experience. But you see, my friends, that suffering is the form and it belongs to the form. And it's simply a transmutation, a refining process. So why get caught up in the suffering when you can be objective and be free?

When you can look at the form and say, "Yes, it's being refined. Thank you, God, I'm not controlled by it. Therefore, I can witness it going through its transformation. I can witness it going through its changes." Learn to be objective and indeed you will be free. Does that help with your question? Yes. Someone else have a question now?

It was stated, I believe, that if a desire is projected, it is sent out electrically. And it is when we become magnetic that this is brought back to us.

That is correct.

What happens if the desire is thwarted by another individual or by circumstances?

Yes. That's a very good question. What we're stating is that a desire leaves our aura, goes out into the universe, and it is electric. And it meets another desire that is expressing, which is electric, and when the two desires meet, then, of course, you see, the magnets pull it back to the both of us and the experience, of course, is encountered.

Now the lady has asked the question, Well, what happens to the desire if it goes out into the universe and it's stopped? Well, you see, what really happens to that desire is this: The desire goes out—you hear me?—and it meets its kind, because one thought attracts its own kind out of the universe through that very principle. Now what we call being thwarted or meeting an obstruction is a change during the process—now bear with me, please—is a change within our own being. For example, the desire goes out and it's going out electrically. The moment— that instant—that it is leaving, a person has an instantaneous thought change. Maybe it will be fulfilled, maybe it won't. There's all kinds of things that take place. What happens is, you ground the desire. You see, you ground it, and you ground it through your magnetic level of consciousness. Do you understand?

Let me put it another way. The desire, the thought, leaves your mind. As it's leaving your mind, you have a feeling maybe it's not going to work, or anything that is negative or magnetic. Do you understand? When you have that, this thing, the great illusion, says, "It didn't get fulfilled." Well, of course, it didn't get fulfilled, because you grounded it. You grounded it in that instant. Is that clear to the class?

With a negative thought.

You grounded it with a negative feeling or thought, which is the magnetic field. And the instant you did that, you changed the law and this is the effect.

When a desire has been grounded, then . . . if I could understand—

It returns home, unfulfilled.

That's probably good, though, because maybe you want to reprogram yourself.

That's so true. What we desire on Tuesday, we ofttimes change on Thursday.

That would be good then, wouldn't it?

It could be. Thank God for the divine wisdom of those universal laws! You see, they all have a built-in safety guard. All of God's natural laws have this built-in safety guard. Yes.

Well, friends, it's time. Let us go have refreshments. Thank you all very much.

OCTOBER 25, 1973

CONSCIOUSNESS CLASS 29 ✖

Beginning this evening, class, we'll have a slight change in the format of our Thursday night classes. And I do hope that all of you have brought your pencils and notepads, because you will need them this evening and from now on. We're going to help you to clarify your understanding of the discourse that was just read [Discourse 24], known as the creative principle. So if all of you have your notebooks and pencils—if not, I'm sure that someone will share some paper with you.

[The Teacher draws a diagram on a blackboard.]

In the center of your notepad, if you will, kindly draw a triangle with the apex down and one with the apex upward, shaped like a diamond. In the center of that, would you kindly draw a straight line, and that is known as *faith*. The bottom triangle is *love,* the top one, *belief.* At the apex, the point of the downward triangle of love, kindly put the word *duty*. Right here. Directly across from that, *tolerance*. At the bottom of the apex of the love triangle, *gratitude*. At the apex of the belief triangle, the word *attainment*.

Now, faith in our duty equals motive. Beginning at the point of faith and duty, kindly draw a circle up through belief and attainment, returning through gratitude and back to its point of origin, and that is known as *acceptance*. The acceptance of our faith to our duty equals our motive, whatever that may be.

Now, we're here returned to this point of motive. We're now going to cross this line or this bridge of faith to this point of tolerance. And we cross the bridge of faith once. Here you make another circle, returning through gratitude to tolerance. That is known as *adaptability*. Adaptability.

This left sphere is your *magnetic sphere* and is *feeling*. The sphere on the right is your *electric sphere* and is the sphere of *thought*. If I'm going too fast, just raise your hands.

THE CREATIVE PRINCIPLE

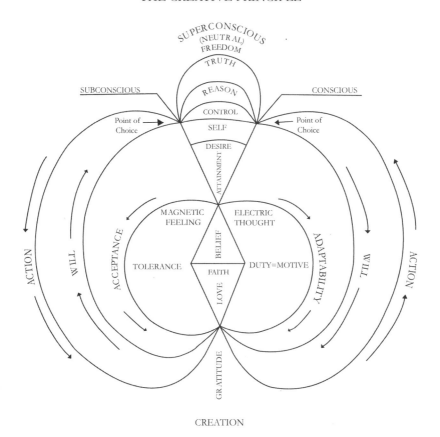

CREATION

Now we're at the point of tolerance and we have just gone through our adaptability. Now remember, adaptability also means harmonizing. To harmonize is to come into rapport with. So we're at the point of tolerance in our magnetic sphere or our emotional being, and we now must cross the bridge to our motive. Second crossing. At this point with our motive, we descend through love and gratitude and encompass our magnetic and our electric spheres, returning to the point of tolerance. That circle is our *will*. And it goes clockwise.

We're at the point of tolerance, where we have returned with our will, and we now cross the bridge of faith again to motive, which is the third crossing. At this point, we rise with our action through belief, attainment, acceptance, and we encompass both our electric and our magnetic spheres and return once again to the magnetic field of feeling and tolerance. That is *action*. And it moves counterclockwise. Does everyone have that?

Now in this sphere between will and action is *creation*. Halfway between our acceptance, adaptability, and will, kindly draw a curved line. That is known as *desire*. Above that is *self*. Above self, kindly make another half circle connecting to each junction, to each point. And that is *control*.

I've made it a bit high because I'm running out of blackboard space, so you bear with me a moment. Control. Above that, another half circle, and that is *reason*. Above that one, another half circle. That is *truth*. Now, above that is *freedom*. At this point, where will, action, control, reason, truth, freedom, and self come together, is the subconscious. It's in the magnetic field. Over on the right, the electrical field at this junction, is our conscious mind. Now from the sphere of will upward, which includes control, reason, truth, and freedom, is neutral. Now remember, that that is neutral is the perfect balance between the electric and magnetic vibrations. That's what the odic, or neutral, really is. Does everyone have that?

I'm not clear. If it's above, what is included?

Control—it's above will. Will upward is neutrality. That includes control, reason, truth, and freedom. That is called the *superconscious*. Superconscious. Control, reason, truth, and freedom is the superconscious.

Is that up there, way up by freedom?

The superconscious includes control, reason, truth, and freedom. That is the superconscious.

Is that associated with the subconscious?

There is a junction—we'll get to that, yes. Now, we have found on our last journey through the mind that we ended up in the magnetic field at the point known as tolerance in the soul faculty of duty, gratitude, and tolerance. Now we must, once again, cross the bridge of faith. That will be our fourth crossing. To cross the bridge of faith, to descend now with our will—the circle here—through love and gratitude into creation, and go, and we reach this point in the subconscious, this junction of the magnetic field, where we view self, desire, and attainment. At this point we make a choice, subconsciously. The choice, usually, is to go down through self into desire to attainment. But we do not receive attainment without the power of the superconscious. Because the superconscious is that power where the electric and the magnetic fields are brought into perfect balance, which is the neutrality. So this is known as the portal of the mind. This is where we stand guardian.

Now if we stand guardian, we're now in the frame of consciousness known as will. If we stand guardian at this point, and we look and we choose to go across through the superconscious with self-control or to even go higher with reason control or reasonable control or we go across through the superconscious with truth or freedom, we will come over here to the conscious mind at another junction.

Now say that we have chosen to use control with what we are desiring. We will cross through the superconscious to the conscious mind. Once again, a choice is made. We either choose to descend into self and desire at that point or we complete the circle of will, coming up through creation and returning to the soul faculty of tolerance.

Now, we have one more journey to make and we're at the point of tolerance in the subconscious mind. We must cross the bridge of faith, which is our fifth trip across, and now go upward into action. As we go up into action, we view our attainment, our desire, our self and we're at the point, once again, of the portal of the mind in action at the subconscious. At this point, if we choose to go around the circuit, we will come here to the conscious mind and again have to make a choice. If we choose to go through the superconscious, where the power is that truly brings us whatever we desire, either through self-control, reason, truth, or freedom, we return to this point in the subconscious and we descend back here to where our motive originated. That is the creative principle.

This is the fifth planet in the solar system in its size and in its purpose. And we are here to learn one of the many laws of nature and creation: the principle of creating. Because we are, in truth, the creators.

Now, at these two points in the conscious and the subconscious mind, at those portals, this is where we look across and we cannot see the fulfillment of our attainment. Because, as we look across in control, reason, truth, and freedom, we do not see: the attainment lies here. And so this is where we trip ourselves up with frustrations. At this point, through our curiosity, which is the cause of frustration, we look down and see attainment and we become frustrated. And we do not receive fulfillment, because we do not complete the circuit with our will and with our action into creation, where the fulfillment truly lies.

Now anytime you set anything into motion, you start with motive. And your motive is your accepted duty to your faith. If you have faith in your ability to drive an automobile, then this is what you go through. No matter how small or how great your faith is, if it is accomplished, you must go through this process in the planes of consciousness and the spheres of your own mind. Now you must use not only your conscious mind, but your subconscious mind and the superconscious. Because the superconscious is what actually moves it into creation. This is where the power to move it truly exists.

Now you're free to ask any of your questions.

From what side of the bridge of faith did we start with number one?

Well, you started right here, if you'll remember. You started with faith and duty and acceptance. You started at the point of motive. That's when you set your desire into motion, when it started, you see. You set it in motion from what you accepted, your duty to that acceptance, which is known as your faith.

The desire is set into motion. The area labeled desire, *I'm having some difficulty correlating that . . .*

I see. You're having some difficulty following that. Well, now, let's visualize, you see, these triangles. Love, the Divine love, descends into creation through the consciousness of belief. Now when this love descends—we say descending from above—down into creation, it comes down through this triangle, this sphere here, which is known as belief. When the love is balanced with the belief, that is, perfectly balanced, you have what is known as faith. That's the bridge of faith. Now faith is a triune soul faculty that is inseparable from poise and humility. The first two soul faculties are indispensable to the creative principle, for they are an inseparable part of the creative principle. There are actually three soul faculties that are here on the blackboard.

When that descends and comes into balance—in other words, when your love of a thing is 20 percent, your belief of that must equal and must be 20 percent. Then you have the perfect balance, so that you have what is known as this bridge of faith on which to move.

Now, when that takes place—love and belief balanced—you set into motion what is known as the Law of Desire. And so, here desire is. When desire is set into motion, you have awareness, awareness of form, of self. Now remember, friends, the creative principle not only involves your soul's entry into a world of form—your divine spark, the Divine Spirit entering soul, which then, in turn, enters other forms—but it also is the same principle and the same law involved with any thought or desire that you have. The same law applies to the incarnation of the soul that applies to your driving an automobile or becoming a millionaire. It is the same law; it's the same principle. It is the principle of creation.

I would appreciate, perhaps, a further clarification. It was said that the desire is set into motion from the point of motive.

That is correct. You see, from the point—well, where is the point of motive? The point of motive is at the bridge of faith, where love and belief have come into perfect balance. Now if you don't have love and belief in balance, then, don't you see, you don't have your motive, which rises you to your attainment and your desire. You see, here's your junction: acceptance, attainment, and adaptability. Any desire that you have, you must pass through the soul faculty of acceptance, adaptability, to attainment. Because if you have a desire, you understand, that is a motive in motion. So you already have part of that soul faculty opened, because you've opened acceptance. But the moment you accept anything, you must go through the process of adaptability. Now I said in the beginning that adaptability also means harmonizing. So if you accept something, you set the law into motion to adapt yourself, your own electromagnetic being, to become in rapport with the thing that you have accepted.

On gratitude, are we on the circle of adaptability?

Gratitude is right here. It is the apex of this point of the soul faculty of duty, tolerance, and gratitude—right here at the apex. This is the soul faculty of love.

Are we grateful because we adapt? Or do we adapt because we're grateful?

All right, we'll go through that once more. The student wants to know, Are we grateful because we have adapted or do we adapt because we're grateful? So let's go through this point of adaptability. Now we've found that we're here. In order to get into adaptability, number one: We start off with motive, and that faith and duty, which is our acceptance. All right, you have a motive; you have an acceptance. Now that acceptance goes through your magnetic field and your emotions and your subconscious and through tolerance and feeling, and when it gets through there, with its acceptance, it reenters into its motive with gratitude. You see, it's gotten through the subconscious area and through this magnetic field. It has accepted. In other words, it has accepted your thought. Does that help you?

Yes.

All right. So therefore, in the acceptance, in the passing through that dimension of that emotional realm, through tolerance, through that magnetic and that feeling realm, you reenter your motive that you started with. And you enter it through the soul faculty of gratitude and duty.

Now, you want to know about adaptability. All right. Now we're here in this soul faculty of tolerance. We come up through and view our attainment, and in the process in our thought and in our conscious, electrical mind we pass through these different areas and we return with gratitude back to our subconscious, where is our feeling. Does that help? You see, my friends, you have gratitude after the event. You don't have gratitude before it. You have it after. You know, you're grateful that it's over. You're grateful that the experience is a thing of the past, not that it's a thing you're yet going to go through. That's the way the mind works. And that's why you enter through gratitude, after you have passed through all of this.

Well, if tolerance is in the magnetic field, is tolerance a feeling?

Yes, definitely. It's in the magnetic field and tolerance has to do with our emotions and with our feelings: that we have tolerance for the levels that are difficult to grow through within ourselves. This, here, this soul faculty is expressing through your magnetic and your subconscious, yes. That is a soul faculty, yes.

Is there an element of time?

That depends on the individual. Most people, as we discussed earlier, either subconsciously or consciously, stand guardian at the portal of their thought and remain there with frustration. Now some people only get part way in adaptability. That is why the teaching is, Be ever ready and willing to change. Because, you see, if you're not ever ready and willing to change, then you cannot adapt or harmonize or become in rapport with the thing that you desire. Therefore, you will not attain it. You will constantly view it—right here, the attainment—but you will not have a fulfillment here in creation. No.

How does thought enter into this?

How does thought enter into that? Because, you see, out of our magnetic field of feeling springs thought. And the thought is here, in our conscious mind. Now remember, as was stated before, that the conscious mind is electric; the subconscious mind is magnetic and feeling. Now a thought goes out from the mind; it goes out electrically. It attracts its kind and it returns magnetically, as the diagram shows you, from the universe. Now you cannot attract anything into your life without the magnetic, feeling dimension. It is not possible. It doesn't work that way. Yes. Does that help with your question? Any other questions on the creative principle?

I should like to know how one could keep balance between belief and love.

How one can keep balance through belief and love? Only through faith, because faith is what balances love and belief.

Would you say that again, please?

Only through faith. Faith is what balances love and belief. And without faith, your motive does not bring your fulfillment. See, faith doesn't necessarily mean something religious. Faith is the Law of Creation. It is the five creative principles. It is the steps of creation. You see, you had to cross the bridge of faith five times to receive your fulfillment. Now this law is operating for us all of the time. It doesn't matter, my friends, whether or not you've been consciously aware of it. Most of us have not. We have lived quite a lifetime without that awareness. But the law itself is still operative and continues to operate in all forms here on this planet. This is the planet of faith. And this is the Law of Creation.

Now, ask yourself the question, in the process that your thought in your mind and in your feeling goes through in any day and in any moment, ask yourself the question, Where have you stopped on the diagram? I know that you will know where you stopped. You either stopped in adaptability, which, if you will recall, has stemmed from tolerance, from your soul faculty, because of an unwillingness to make necessary changes to attain what you desire to attain. Now, because of our lack of awareness of how these laws work, we cannot see the relationship between certain changes in our being and what we desire to attain. The only reason that we cannot see the relationship between what we desire to attain and the changes that are necessary to be made within us is simply because we haven't spent the time to become aware of ourselves. We haven't spent that time.

Does this diagram take into account the fact that the motive is the channel, that our motive starts all this going?

That's right. Our motive starts that. Our accepted faith to our duty is our motive. That's what sets the law into motion. You see, we had a discussion in this church here, I think last month, on acceptance, the divine will. Well, acceptance is the divine will, because without acceptance, you do not have this whole creation. The mind cannot experience or go through this process in anything that it does not accept. It's not possible.

Is freedom neutral or is that a different—

No. These are all neutral. Control, reason, truth, and freedom are neutral; that's your superconscious. That is indispensable, and without the use of the superconscious, you do not bring your desire into fulfillment or into creation. It's impossible.

Well, then, do we rise to self-control, reason, and truth? Or do we come down to self, which is desire—self-desire, the desire of things?

Now remember, desire is not a bad thing, like negative isn't necessarily a bad thing. Desire is a part of the creative principle of all creation. If we descend at either the subconscious or the conscious portal, down into self-desire, viewing attainment here, we only have frustration, because we do not have the fulfillment in creation of the attainment. Now we can have it mentally, but we do not have it in this physical dimension. It's not possible, because it is the superconscious that brings it into this dimension.

What if we go down the little path in self-desire: how do we get out of that? Do we have to go all the way around again?

The way that we got into it is the way that we come back out. If we got into it through the junction of the subconscious, which is through our feelings and our emotions, then that is the way we have to come out of it. Because we're now trapped in the magnetic field. If we got into it through our conscious thought, then that's the way we have to come out of it, because, you see, that's the way that we went into it.

I was wondering if desire is wish.

No. No, if you have a wish, then you have not completed this complete circuit. No. People wish for many things and, you see—let us put it this way: a wish does not express sufficient energy to bring something into manifestation. That's why wishing is a waste of time.

It may just be my trouble reading diagrams, but I don't understand how you get into creation.

Because what you have done—you don't understand how you get here?

If you're on those tracks, it looks like that's in a space to me. And I don't see how those . . .

Well, it's impossible in this dimensional world for me to give the four dimensions of which it truly should be. However, you don't understand how your will came down into creation? My friends, this here is creation, between your will and your action. Your will in action is creation. But you see, your will in action is an effect of your love, belief, and desire. You see, without love, belief—brought into perfect balance by the bridge of faith—desire, you do not have will in action and therefore you do not have creation. Does that help with your question?

I'll think on it. Thank you.

Very well.

Is there a label for the space between will and acceptance?

You're asking about this area between will, acceptance, and adaptability?

Well, I was thinking just on the magnetic side, the space between—

You want to know what is the meaning for where? This space here?

No, between will and acceptance.

Between will and acceptance?

Yes, that whole space that goes clear into—

This entire sphere here?

Yes.

Now that's your magnetic sphere of your subconscious. See, now a person says, for example, that maybe they want this or that and they say, "Well, now, I accept that possibility and I accept that I have it." But they do not accept it—they accept it into the conscious, electrical field, but they do not accept it into the emotional subconscious and the feeling dimension in the magnetic field, which is the part that helps pull it to you, you see, from your superconscious.

Isn't belief a function? I see love and belief and desire. And I believe that I was told that belief is a function and faith is a faculty.

Faith is a soul faculty. Yes.

Well, love and belief are the center of the—I'm a little con-fused, excuse me.

Perhaps you can understand it better this way. Love is a spiritual expression of the Divine Intelligence. When it enters, on its process of entering form, when it enters, it enters the universal mind, which is belief or image or enters form. You see, we are formless and free spiritually. Our spirit has no form and therefore it has total freedom. However, when it descends into form (so that it may have an awareness of itself), it descends into what is known as belief or into the mental realm, the universal mind consciousness, where images are created.

I have two questions. Is there a reason for the action going one direction, and the will going the other direction? And the other question is, Could we use this in reprogramming our sub-conscious?

Yes. And in answer to your latter question, you most certainly could. And in answer to your first question, will goes in a clockwise direction and action in a counterclockwise. That that goes out, returns. Again and again, the teaching is the same in all philosophies of truth: Whatever goes out from the mind, whatever goes out from your universe returns unto your universe. And that is why it is taught that man is a law unto himself. Whatever happens to us is caused by us.

Now because we, perhaps, may not yet have a full awareness or an understanding of the laws that we are setting into motion does not in any way exempt us from their effects. Because the law itself is not—the universal laws are not manmade. They cannot be transgressed without reaping their effects. So you see here, in your creative principle, that man is a law unto himself. And each experience that we encounter in life is an effect of a law that started down here at the accepted duty faith, known as motive. This is why we try to share with the students to become more aware of the thoughts and the feelings that they are entertaining. Because if you do not have the awareness of these laws from your realm of motive that you're setting into motion, then you're going to constantly have frustrations.

Can you explain to me why we have the symbol of the triangle? I understand that the world is supposed to be round, and we more or less believe this. But why do we in our diagrams have triangles?

The question is asked, Why do we have in these particular teachings all triangles? Well, we don't have all triangles, but we have a great deal of them. The triangle, equilateral triangle, has three points. All things that are made manifest are triune. That is the trinity of truth. We've said, repeatedly, that creation is dual. It's the number two: it is duality. But that that moves creation, the power that moves the form, is that third point. That is the apex of the triangle. That is the trinity of truth, and this is the reason, in these teachings, that we use the triangle. All soul faculties are triune. All sense functions are triune. And that is the purpose of using the triangle in these teachings.

In the last class, you mentioned something about setting a law into motion the previous day. Can you show me how it would work if, for instance, two days ago we were talking about an individual and somehow we both knew this particular man. And coming back from Sausalito on the freeway, I saw this individual that we were talking about, just riding along beside me. Now how would that work?

How would that work? It's really quite simple. The first thing: You have to become aware of your motive. Now the motive of anything, that is the most important, because that's going to reveal to you your experiences. Whatever your true, pure motive is, that will tell you what you're yet to experience, as you start to travel through these spheres of consciousness and planes of action.

Now if you started here with your motive—and you have a particular case that you were discussing. Now you came up through here from your point of motive into your acceptance. Of course, you have acceptance or you wouldn't be discussing the individual. Is that not correct?

Yes.

All right. Now depending, of course, upon how much feeling, how much energy you are releasing here, would reveal the experience yet to come. Now you say you discussed the person and a few hours later you met the individual?

The next day.

All right, the next day you met the individual. Well, if you want to ask yourself, number one: What was your motive? Number two: How much magnetism did you release from your aura, from your universe? And number three: When you got into your electrical field, did you go through an equal degree of adaptability? If you did, then what would happen is you would have that experience, if it were absolutely equal. Absolutely. You would have the spontaneous experience of meeting the person. In other words, you would be speaking of the person and he would appear. Yes. But then, of course, your feelings, your emotions, your thought in your discussions would be perfectly, equally balanced, and the power of the superconscious would bring it into being. Yes. Now that comes about, of course, by a perfect balance here, which is known as the bridge of faith.

Well, this would be twenty-four hours. In other words, in your sleeping and in your dreaming, this still is in effect.

Oh yes! Yes.

In your dreams and your whatever, astral flights, is still . . .

It's taking place: that is correct. It is taking place. Yes. Now, most people are not consciously aware while they're dreaming. You can be consciously aware, but that's up to you to make that type of an effort. You can become consciously aware that you're lying in bed, that you're sleeping, and you're dreaming. You can be aware of what your dreams are and how you are feeling concerning those dreams. But as I say, that takes a little effort and that takes some practice. Are there any more questions on the creative principle?

Say you're thinking of someone and you do throw out a lot of feeling or love or whatever, that you want to see somebody. Does this necessarily mean that you're going to attract someone the next day?

Or you can attract them much sooner. You're setting the law into motion. Yes. Now, you're setting the law into motion. Now don't misunderstand, friends. If you misuse—misuse, of course, is simply an ignorance of God's divine, natural laws—if you try to misuse—which is an imbalance—the powers that are within your being, you, and you only, will be the victim. And you, and you only, will suffer the consequences. Now I bring this point up because, you see here, at the point of motive, one may say, "Fine, I want a particular person to appear," and they start with that type of a motive. Now here they are at their motive and they're going through their magnetic feelings of acceptance. What happens when you do those things? In the depths of your own subconscious, you're going to face experiences that you have had. And I can assure you that no one, and I mean no one, appreciates giving their divine right of free expression to the control of another individual. So don't misuse the laws of the divine creative principle. You will only destroy yourselves in the process. I caution—

How could you do that?

Because many people try to use what is known as thought power or influence of the mind. The bookstores are loaded today with books on how to control other people. I caution you against even the temptation of it, because I can tell you what it does to people. I've seen people go through this before. It is extremely detrimental and, in time, will destroy you. Are there any other questions?

What you just said has to do with hypnotism?
Absolutely and positively. It has to do with that.
Could you speak at this time a bit on time?
On time? What man calls time?
Yes.
It won't be many, many years before this world will realize and accept, from that realization, that our concept of what
we call time is wholly and completely an illusion. Because we
have so fully identified with what man calls time, it is no longer
possible for the masses, with rare exceptions, to experience the
eternity which they truly are. Our minds, of course, through
acceptance, have created this great illusion and delusion. And
so we wake up in the morning and we think that the day is such
and such a time, that there are so many hours in it. We look at
the sky; during the daylight hours we see light. At night, we see
what we call darkness. Now we believe and, of course, through
our belief have created, that there is a day and that there is a
night. But the truth of the matter is that the day and the night
do not exist outside of the creation of our own mind.

Now I know that this is difficult for many to accept, because
you're going to have to work at it within yourself, to raise your
consciousness to a level of truth, of eternity, where you will know
beyond any doubt that you have always been, that you will ever
be. It is not some theory to entertain the mind. It is the truth that
sets you free. However, in expanding the consciousness here—
expanding our mind—a slow growth is the only healthy growth.
Because as you expand your consciousness into the universal
consciousness, you become aware not only of people's thoughts,
but you become very aware of their feelings. And unless you
demonstrate, daily and constantly, spiritual self-discipline, and
I mean discipline, you will not be able to maintain your sanity
in this dimension. And so do not seek things, but seek the truth
that sets you free. And don't ask for more than you are able to
endure at any given moment.

This illusion of time is only one of many illusions. The only reason that we do not walk through the wall here, in creation, is because of our belief. We are so identified with our belief, it is not possible for us to pass through the wall. And fortunately for this Earth planet, very, very few people have reached the state of consciousness where they can accomplish so many of these so-called spiritual wonders. It is indeed a blessing for the continuity of the form on the Earth planet that more people in their present state of consciousness do not have the ability, through lack of understanding these universal laws, to control these things known as form.

For a matter of clarification, I've often felt that, for example, this chair doesn't exist. It's just that the mind's created it and you just know that you're going to sit on something solid. Is this correct?

All creation is through belief. That is correct. It's only solid to the belief. Now, for example, a person says, "Well, then, I don't believe that it's real." Well, how ridiculous! You are a part of what is known as the mass mind, and the mass mind has that belief in creation, and you're going to have to rise above the mass mind, which takes self-control. You're going to have to rise above the mass mind, of which you are a part, if you want to pass through it.

I would appreciate knowing—talking about light. You talk about the light of truth, the great, white, eternal light. Is the darkness, which we call night in our part of the world, an illusion? Is it light? Or is light enlightenment? Why do we have night? I know it's in creation, but why do we have it?

Anything that's in creation has to have the poles of opposites: it's the Law of Duality, which governs creation. It's the entering of the divine love into the mental realm known as belief. So in order to bring about creation in the first place, you had to have these two poles meet. And consequently, anytime that you're in creation, then you're going to see these constant opposites, you see. You're going to see the positive and you're going to see the negative: you're going to see the so-called good and you're going to see the so-called bad. You're going to see what you call the light and you're going to see what you call the night.

Now your question, basically, was, Why do we call truth light, etc? What does *light* really mean? Does anyone in this class know what *light* means?

Would it be clarification? Everything in the light is clarified, clear.

How are things clarified?

Through belief?

Thank you. Anyone else?

I think light means "energy." And as we exert energy, we clarify our thinking.

How do we exert energy?

By applying ourselves to the question at hand.

Would that mean control?

Yes.

That's what light is. Without control, you don't have truth. And without truth, you don't have freedom. And so one of the first things we do is discipline inside of ourselves. And that, my friends, is known as control. Now there are two types of control we can use. We can use the control of the self, which is known as self-control, or we can use the control from the superconscious, which is known as reasonable control. Now, reasonable control is not denying anything, but it is controlling it, so that it will come at the right time in the right way for us. In other words, we remain in control.

Of the two types of control that we can use, reasonable control or control under the soul faculty of reason, of course, is the wisest. And this is why the teaching is, to keep faith—the bridge of faith—keep faith with reason: she will transfigure thee. And that's exactly what takes place. When you keep faith with reason, you have a transfiguration taking place, a transformation within yourself. What you're really doing is bringing perfect balance between your electric and your magnetic spheres of action, which permits the superconscious, the perfect balance, to bring into being whatever it is that you desire.

You have said in the past, emphasizing about the ability to think, to think about anything that we're going to say. If we were to think about what we're going to say, then, actually, we would control the action and wealth and more or less everything on that board, wouldn't we?

That is absolutely true. When you start to think, when you no longer are satisfied—remember that irritation wakes the soul and satisfaction lets it sleep—when you are no longer satisfied with the way things are going in your life, then you'll start to think. And when you start to think, the first level you start to think on is the electric one, the conscious one. Now remember, that's one step. But you've got to go beyond your conscious thoughts and you've got to find out what your emotions, the magnetic field is doing to you.

Now when you start to think and when you bridge the gap between your conscious and your subconscious, between your electric thoughts and your magnetic feelings, and you bring them into rapport, you start to control your life. Now when you control your life, you're controlling ignorance and error. And when you control ignorance and error, then you're going to be free. And that's how it works.

Friends, I see that we've gone past our time. Thank you and good night.

NOVEMBER 1, 1973

CONSCIOUSNESS CLASS 30

We will have a short review of the creative principle. Now I'm going to draw this triangle of love first. That is the first principle of this creative principle: this divine love. This is the power that descends down into creation, through what is known as *belief.* Whatever we believe, we love. And whatever we love, we believe. And in so doing, we desire it. The top of this triangle is *attainment.* And you remember the steps of creation are love, belief, desire. So whatever we love, we believe; whatever we believe, we love. And that sets the law into motion, which is known as desire.

[Please see page 177 for the diagram of the Creative Principle.]

Now over here on this lower triangle of love we have, at this point here, *duty* (which you have already been given), *gratitude,* and *tolerance.* Now, when we express the first soul faculty of being, known as duty, gratitude, and tolerance, then this divine love is able to flow freely or unobstructed.

On this top triangle, which encompasses our belief, we have *attainment, acceptance,* and *adaptability.* Now you remember that *control, reason,* and *truth* is the superconscious or the neutral power. So let us begin. Because I've found that most students, number one: they don't remember where to begin, and number two: they don't recall the five steps across the bridge of faith. Now what does duty to our faith equal?

Motive.

Our motive—or faith to our duty is our motive and our starting point. All right. Now we start here, here in the realm, from the point of tolerance, from our magnetic, our acceptance, and with our feeling. And from our feeling—this is the point we start at—from the depths of our subconscious, through our own acceptance, we cross the bridge of faith. Does everyone have that? That's one crossing. We cross from our accepted feeling, from the depths of our subconscious, across the bridge of faith, into our conscious mind, where our motive begins to express. Has everyone got that? You start in the magnetic field. You cross the bridge of faith to your motive. All right? That is one crossing. When you step into your motive consciously, that's where you accept the thought and you return to your motive. Does everyone follow that? Now if you don't, please raise your hands.

I just didn't see that. I was writing this out.

You started here with your feeling. You crossed the bridge of faith into the thought realm and your electrical field, where your motive is. All right. Then, you entered through the circle of acceptance, through your magnetic field, and you returned to your motive. All right?

Yes.

Now you must cross the bridge of faith back to your sub-conscious—that's your second crossing—where you must make the necessary changes. And that is known as the sphere or the plane of adaptability, where you must come in harmony with your desire.

So you go here, now on the circle through your electrical field of thought, on your changes, and you return here, to the subconscious. Everyone have that?

Could you trace that one more time, please?

Yes. You see here, this was your second crossing. You see, now, if you will notice, you go either clockwise or counterclockwise with every move. There's a perfect balancing that takes place. All right, now you're going to make the change. You must make the change necessary: the adaptability. You must come in harmony with that that you desire. And in order to do that, you must swing in a clockwise motion through your thought realm, your conscious mind, and return to your magnetic field. Does everyone have that? Now if you don't, raise your hands. All right.

Now we're going to cross the bridge of faith a third time to our motive. We must cross it this time in order to set the will into motion. And here, we start from a motive. Will moves in a clockwise motion and we go through these realms, across here, and on back into our subconscious.

I'll do it once more. We cross the bridge of faith the third time to get to our motive, to descend down through love and gratitude into creation, setting our will into motion, crossing the superconscious. Remember, you must cross into the super-conscious before you can put anything into creation. Otherwise, your desire, your motives, whatever you're seeking stays here in the mental realms, in the daydream, the wishful-thinking realm. It does not get out into creation. You must use reasonable control or self-control or truth and freedom to put the power of the Divine into your will. You must cross this, here. Otherwise, it remains here in your daydreaming. This is your daydream-ing realm. You think about it, but all you do is experience it mentally or emotionally: you never experience it in the creative realm of physical dimension, you see. And that's your wishful thinking. Because you have not put your will out, through some degree of control, to tap the superconscious and return, here, to your magnetic field.

Now you must cross the bridge of faith in order to take that will into action of creation, which is your fourth crossing. And here you are, you're in the subconscious. You cross back to your motive, here, in the conscious mind. And here you rise up, through the subconscious; you're going now in a counterclock-wise motion. You go all the way through creation and you get here, to the conscious mind. Well, you have not yet tapped the power of the superconscious. You must cross this. If you descend, here, into self and into desire, you will view your attainment, but it will ever be like grasping for the rainbow. You will never get it.

Many times we descend right here. You must cross, across here, back around through your action, and descend down into your magnetic field, cross the bridge of faith back to your motive, and you have your attainment or your fulfillment.

Tonight we're going to discuss success. Before we discuss this word, however, please write in your notebooks the word *success*. List the five things that success means to you. Now, success means many things to many people. You're not going to have to show your list to anyone, so be honest with yourself. It is very important to *you* to be honest with yourself, because you're the one that is seeking that success.

If you say, "Well, I just want to be successful," well, you want to be successful in *some*thing. Say that a person wants to have success, that they want to be successful financially or materially. Well, you've got to go beyond that. What does success in a material world mean to you? What does it mean? Does success of having money mean to fulfill your desires whenever the desire strikes a blow to the mind? Well, if that's what it means, then that's the law that you're setting into motion. But you will never have fulfillment. Because, you see, friends, the material serves a very good purpose in a material world. But there are some things that are beyond purchase. So write down what it is that you want to be successful in. You want success. And write the five things down that you want success in.

And as I say once again, be very honest with yourself—you don't have to show it to anyone—because that is important in understanding where you are at this moment and why you're there and how to move onward. And that we will discuss after you have written that down. As soon as everyone is finished—if anyone isn't finished, just raise your hand, please.

I find that I can't write the five things down.

I can't either.

Are you able to write the word *success?* Everyone? Then we'll move from that dimension onward.

Now, it is the nature of the form to seek success. It is the nature of the form to desire. Desire is the third step in the creative principle. Desire—what does desire mean? What does success mean? What does the word *success* mean?

Attainment.

The attainment of one's desires. That's what success means. To attain one's desires. So we find that it is the nature of the creative principle, in its third step, from love, belief, to desire.

So all form desires. In other words, all form seeks to attain, attainment of its desire, which is its success, and a fulfillment of its purpose in this earth realm. Therefore, some time ago we discussed—in fact, before we even had this church—never to suppress desire: to fulfill desire or to educate it.

All right, now we're going to start with this principle, known as success, and the third step of creation, known as desire. "Why, why," we must ask ourselves, "do we want to be successful in any particular area? What does success bring us?" I'm not interested in whether it is your desire to be successful financially, your desire to be what you think is successful spiritually or mentally. What is it? What does it mean to the mind? What does it mean to us? Does anyone know? What does it bring?

I think it brings freedom.

You think that success brings freedom. Yes?

I think it would mean peace to the individual seeking it.

Thank you. Yes?

Fulfillment.

Fulfillment. All right. So we find that everyone is seeking to be successful. But it means more than what's been mentioned. What does success bring us? Because without it, we no longer will seek it.

To the mind, it means security.

Security. Thank you.

Happiness.

Happiness. Success, friends, brings recognition. Without recognition, you will never seek to be successful. That is a proven law. Success brings recognition. Now what is recognition? What does recognition mean? Yes.

Love. Admiration.

Thank you. Anyone else?

Realization.

Realization. Yes?

It means energy directed toward us.

Energy. Therefore, recognition is attention. Write it down in your notebooks. Everything in form is seeking attention, which is also known as the divine energy or God's love. This is why we go out into creation. Remember that this success that we're seeking is never, in and of itself, permanent. It cannot be permanent. So we chase from one star to another repeatedly through creation. For what we are truly trying to find, what we are truly seeking, is energy.

Now we're going to go a little bit deeper in this discussion, because it applies to all of us, moment by moment, in all of our acts and our activities and in our thoughts. If you have computed in your thoughts—and this is why the prophets have taught, Man, know thyself. And when you know yourself, you will know the truth. And when you know the truth, you'll set yourself free. A person is seeking success, we have all agreed. Is there anyone that disagrees that we are seeking success? Because we're all seeking recognition, which is attention, which is energy, which is the divine love, which is the law and the first principle of the creative principle.

Everything goes back home. It is the nature of creation to return unto itself. So everything returns unto itself, and the self, the beginning, is what is known as love. So we're all in a constant process of going back home. We're on many different trips to get there, but we're all going back. We're returning to the source from whence we have come. That source is called by many names; in this particular teaching, it is known as love.

Now, if success, what you're seeking, means to you a new car each year, a home of your own, and all of the things that your mind has accepted that goes with it and you have those things, then you have your attainment, if this is what you have accepted as your success. Now, when you do not have any of those things—and that's why I asked you to write *success*, and the things that it meant to you—if you at any time do not have one of those things, say, for example, a year goes by and you don't have a new car, you immediately set the law into motion of lack. You immediately go into the emotional realm and like attracts like and becomes the Law of Attachment. If success or being successful or happy means to you that you have steak seven days a week and you go a few days without it, consciously, but definitely subconsciously, you're going through this process. You have accepted that you are no longer successful.

Now, why do we need encouragement in our seeking, no matter what we're seeking? The statement is in life that "nothing succeeds like success." Well, of course, nothing succeeds like success. The attainment of one desire guarantees the continuity of the desire if—and remember, it's a big *if*—sufficient recognition is received by the attainment of the desire. Therefore—I'll be with you in a few moments, class—therefore, everyone needs to be encouraged. My friends, you plant a little tree in the ground and you encourage it by caring for it. And so this is what we're all seeking.

Now, what happens in this success drive that is within us, which is a very natural thing, from the third step of the creative principle, known as desire, what happens is simply this: when we get to the point that we have all of these things that our mind has computed that represent success, we find something lacking. There are only so many houses you can live in. There are only so many cars you can drive. There are only so many suits you can wear. That's fine and it serves its purpose. But you will always find something lacking. That something is known as peace. This here, known as peace, is the only thing that brings balance in our life. This peace—the divine peace, the perfect peace that's known as passing all understanding, that is beyond the human mind to understand—is the intelligent divine power that harmonizes all these multitudes of desires that are within the human mind that are all seeking supremacy.

We're going to go back to our little success trip, because that's so important to everyone, to everything that's in form.

We decide that we want to be successful in a certain area. All right, fine. We accept that; that is what we want. Now we accept that in the magnetic field of our subconscious, which is known as our feeling. We have a feeling that perhaps we want to be successful in business, perhaps we want to be a good carpenter. It doesn't matter: it all represents success.

And so we set this law into motion, we move across the bridge of faith to our motive and our thought. All right, we start out and we go on to this acceptance and we get about to this point here, about halfway through, and that thought and that desire, that feeling, meets another one that's ahead of it. That's a desire from maybe a year ago and maybe a week ago and maybe just yesterday. So we can't quite get through. It takes a lot of thought; it takes a lot of energy. Because you don't have just one desire battling to get around: you've got about fifty thousand of them battling to get around, all seeking their own fulfillment, because that is the nature of desire. That is its very nature.

Now what does this cause within the human mind? It causes frustration.

Confusion.

It causes confusion. It certainly is not conducive to peace. It isn't even conducive to success. And so this is what happens, my friends, until we learn how our mind really works.

Now there are many teachings on how to get what you really want. There are all kinds of teachings on the market today. Now the question is, fifty people read the same book and let's even agree that they put in an equal amount of energy, but only two of them succeed. Now why is it that the other forty-eight fail? Now that's the big question. Why, out of fifty, have forty-eight of them failed, but two of them were successful? And they all applied the same teaching. And they all gave it sufficient energy: an equal amount of energy, an equal amount of attention, an equal amount of effort.

Well, we've got to go deeper than what the teaching states. It doesn't mean that the teaching was incorrect. It doesn't mean that, because if the teaching were incorrect and false, then it couldn't have worked for two out of fifty. It couldn't have worked. So we find that the teaching is right because it works. But it's not working for all of them. So we have to go into the mind and have to find out what took place.

Now, it all deals with what is known as acceptance. And what is acceptance? What is acceptance? What does acceptance deal with? It deals with our belief and our love. And acceptance is the divine will. The reason that acceptance is the divine will is because that is the Law of Creation. How can love express itself if it's not accepted? And that is the divine will: acceptance. Because the Divine is what is called love.

All right, two of the people accepted it sufficiently, right here, the moment that they read it. They so fully accepted it, they utilized sufficient energy to propel themselves through these planes of consciousness and they became successful. Perhaps, let's say that they accepted it: 50 percent of their mind accepted it, 50 percent. And the other forty-eight people, they only accepted 20 percent. But it took 50 percent worth of energy to bring it into fulfillment and into creation. So you see, my friends, it's a matter of how much of anything you really accept. Now, you can teach the same teaching to everyone, but it is not going to work unless the person that is receiving it accepts it sufficiently, sufficient for it to work for them. You may only have to accept 10 percent of that and have that work for you fine. Someone else may have to accept 90 percent in order for it to work for them.

Now I'll be happy to entertain some of your questions.

Am I to understand that, as recognition is attention, that also attention means energy?

Yes, attention is energy directed. Whatever you put your attention on, your energy is going in that direction. Yes.

Secondly, in dealing with the Law of Merit, am I to understand that that is acceptance? In order for the Law of Merit to work?

Yes, that has been accepted, absolutely. The Law of Merit—remember, friends, a soul is not brand new here and now. So we all come in with certain merit systems that are very individual to our own soul. Consequently, some of us have the ability, the tendency, to accept 50 percent and some other soul can only accept 2 percent. Yes.

Then my question is, realizing that nothing is improbable to attainment; at least I've found it so—

There are no impossibilities: that is correct.

Then my question is, working on that thesis, then why—and, of course, there are a number of laws in effect—why is it that on the attainment one has to wait? Say that you have exercised many phases of this law for this attainment and then they say, "Well, be patient. It's not in divine order."

Why isn't it in divine order?

That's why I'm asking.

Is man a law unto himself?

True.

Is man, in truth, his own divinity?

Most definitely.

There's a part of man known as the Divine that expresses through him. And that is where divine order and divine action take place. Now if a person, for example, is seeking, let us say they are seeking success in a certain business venture and the person is told they must be patient. All right. Well, if the laws that they have set into motion along their own life's expression are such that it is going to take time for them to work through them, and time to the mind is represented as patience, then, of course, patience would be necessary. Yes.

In other words—let me understand a little more clearly, not to take up everybody's time—if one would, shall we say, clean up . . .

All these desires that are ahead of the present desire?

No, no. I'm not thinking of that at all. Say that they clean up a past effect that has not been too strong in their favor. If they clean that up first, shall we say, so it seems like, "Let's test it out to see if the person is really ready."

No. Past effects are nothing more than desires that are standing in the way of your own attainments.

Say that once more.

Past effects are only desires standing in the way of your own attainments. What are effects? Effects are the result of causes. And what is desire? What is desire? Desire is the effect of love and belief. It's an effect.

I don't mean to waste this time, but it is something I'm trying to understand. Personally, I've never seen anything financially, when it comes to money, that was hard to attain. It's always been rather easy.

Well, that depends. For some people, the material success comes very easily. For some people, it's most difficult.

So then, again, with that attainment, it seems like one must wait before this junction works. That's what I don't understand.

Well, the waiting, class, is dependent upon the time that it takes us to work through all the desires that are screaming for priority, of all of our past desires that are bogged down in our own subconscious. Now, these things sometimes can be forecast. It can be forecast that it's going to take, for example, perhaps it takes this person two years to clear out what is in front of their present desire, you see. But you must remember, if desire is not fulfilled, then it must be educated. Now if it is not educated, here it lies as an obstruction to your new desires. Today's desires are rarely what yesterday's desires were, you see. Does that help with your question?

Yes. Thank you.

Yes. And so first off, it will benefit and behoove man to become aware of what he's got locked here in his own subconscious.

And all of these desires—what happens, my friends, this is the conflict of your own mind. A house divided cannot stand. This is why the teaching is to "keep your eye single." This is why the great importance of peace. Now, what will peace do? Peace will bring a harmonizing of the desires that are fighting for priority in your own magnetic field. It will harmonize and balance your so-called magnetic field, so that when you set a law into motion of your desire, instead of coming up halfway into the depths of your own subconscious and fighting with all your conflict and your emotion—this is what your emotion is: your emotion is nothing more than a conflict of your prior desires that you forgot all about. That's where your emotion is, you see. And this is the field of feelings. So you see, there's that conflict that goes on.

Now when you make the effort to truly tune yourself into what we call peace—peace is the great balancer. Peace is the power, because it brings all things into balance. When a man is at peace, when he's truly at peace, he makes very wise decisions. Whether those decisions are spiritual or material, the principle of the law is the same. But if you are not at peace, then what happens, your decisions are being made according to the priority of desires in the depths of your own subconscious. And usually, when decisions are made from this level, they're not wise decisions. They may appear temporarily to be, but they are not.

You see, when you permeate this with peace, then all of those years of desires that were not fulfilled—and our minds are filled with a multitude of them—all of them literally lie down and sleep in perfect peace as that permeates the atmosphere. And that desire can go out into the laws of creation and into your fulfillment.

Then to reprogram those desires, would be by peace?

Yes, now you have been given many affirmations, several affirmations, to help you to bring peace into the depths of your own inner being. Now one of the very simple ones, if you accept it, is, "Thank you, God"—that's the divine Power—"I am at peace."

But you see, it does you no good to say it by rote. It's just like saying the "Divine Abundance" affirmation: "Thank you, God. I'm moving in your divine flow." Well, what is God's divine flow? God's divine flow is perfect peace. That's what brings all of the good that you're seeking into your experience. But you have to feel it.

Why do you have to feel the affirmation? It's like your "Total Consideration" affirmation. If you don't feel your affirmation, you're simply repeating it in your electric vibration, in that plane of consciousness. That's all you're doing. You haven't got it into your feeling, so it can't do anything down here, because you're not feeling it. Peace doesn't even enter here until you feel it. This is your magnetic field. Now your magnetic field is very important, friends, because your magnetic field is what pulls things out of the atmosphere to you, you see. Take a look, just take a look at your life and experiences. Take a look at yourself. Our hindsight, you know, usually has a lot of light in it. When our hindsight becomes our foresight, we're granted insight. Of course we are.

Now when you feel badly at any time, stop and think. When you feel badly, you pull experience upon experience on top of you. That's the law of your own subconscious. So this is why it's so difficult when you go down. Because when you go down, friends, you go into the depths of your magnetic field. There is no balance between your electric and your magnetic: you're totally down into the emotions. This is where your emotions are. And you're in the depths—all of us, we're in the depths of our own desires. The forgotten ones. The present ones. The ones that were twenty years ago. And here, we go through all the war, known as the war of the emotions, the battle and the conflict for supremacy of the entities, the children that we have created. These are our children.

And this is the great importance of not only *thinking* peace, but *feeling* peace. Because it's the only way that you're going to be free. And once you start doing that, then when you set a law into motion, you're not concerned whether it's going to take two days or two years. Because it doesn't matter. You see what I mean? It doesn't really matter. It's going to happen. You know it's going to happen, because you're in perfect peace. And it does happen.

But you see, when you're in peace and your mind says, "I accept that," you not only accept it in your conscious mind fully, wholly, and completely, but you feel it. You feel it with such an intensity. And when you do that, don't you see, you are the magnet that pulls it out of the universe into your life.

Concerning the attainment, or I should say, the prophecy of attainment, if this prophecy were given at a certain amount of time—like you said two years—does a person emanate a color at that time? And if so, say in this period of two years of the attainment of the prophecy, is there another color that would be fully emanated?

Certainly. Because, you see, whenever you come into rapport— number one: When you have a desire, you emanate the color or the vibration of your own desire. Now, many people have asked, "Why are most people's auras brown?" Well, it's most understandable, because brown represents confusion. And when you've got so many desires here and they're so contradictory with each other and they're in conflict and they're battling for priority in your own experience in your life, then you can understand why many auras are brown, you see. Now, that doesn't mean that everybody walks around with a brown aura all the time. The aura is brown when this here is expressing itself, known as the subconscious, you see. Because we haven't cleaned it up. Don't you see what I mean? Friends, go back to the principle of creation. It is our nature to desire. That is the law of the Divine.

Look, the plant desires nutrients from the soil. If it didn't desire those nutrients, it wouldn't make the effort to pull them up through its roots and through its leaves, etc., and survive. It is desire that we desire to eat food, that we desire to drink water. Desire is not, in and of itself, something that you try to push out of your universe. Desire is something, my friends, that you work at educating. And you can't educate what you don't understand. So if you don't understand desire, you not only can't educate it, but you can't even fulfill it, except by what seems to be chance. Then we say, "Well, I was lucky. I had a good day and I was lucky." It wasn't luck at all. We weren't consciously aware, but we did something in here. Somehow, we got through.

But isn't it better to find out what's down here and balance it? Or even better than spending all of the time seeking what's down here, to go right to the source, and that source, my friends, is peace. And anytime that you are truly at peace, consciously and subconsciously, if you are truly at peace and you set a law into motion, you may be rest assured you need to give it no more thought, because it is already on its way to you. You only need to entertain it in thought once. Because, what happens? It makes its full circuit: it goes through the will and the superconscious and the action and into creation—and there you have it.

Now I can answer a few more questions and then our time is up.

Can you define what it feels like to be at peace or in peace?

Well, let me say this: I have moments of it. I'm not a person that says I have it all the time, because I honestly don't have. But I'm so grateful when I do have it. You see, that's the blessing of creation, you understand? To define it, I can only say this: to me, it is a feeling of perfect well-being. There is no disturbance, there is no emotion, there is no concern for anything in you or outside of you. And that's the best I can describe that feeling. It certainly is a feeling of "Everything is well." You don't even have to think about anything, because you feel so good and you feel so well. And no matter what happens, when you are in peace, if you are really in peace, the things that would cause anger or anything else—any other emotion—when you're out of peace have absolutely no effect upon you whatsoever. In other words, there is nothing that can affect you.

Thank you.

Those are moments of peace and, God knows, they're well worth however much the struggle may be to attain them. But I can only say for myself they are moments of peace, which is also a sensing of perfect freedom.

In my meditation, when I say the affirmation and then I say the word "peace," I can feel the vibration after I say the word "peace." But how does a person actually convey it to someone in particular?

Well, to convey peace . . .

Or do you just say "peace" to anyone or to the world? Or does it just flow out to everyone?

No. You see, God's greatest work is done in silence. And many times peace is sent to individuals. It is not important, nor is it even necessary, that they are aware. What is important is that it works.

Now of all the classes, tonight there was one thing that the minds might say we forgot. Now what was that? We're working on awareness. Anybody remember what we forgot from our usual routine tonight?

[Many students speak.] *The affirmation.*

That's right. How many remembered? That is what deals with awareness. Well, friends, I don't like to erase *success,* but it reappeared, so it's all right. We will be off for Thanksgiving. That means we have two more classes. Let's go have refreshments. Thank you all very, very much.

NOVEMBER 8, 1973

CONSCIOUSNESS CLASS 31 ✖

Good evening, everyone. This evening, before going into our questions and answers, we'd like to discuss for a few moments the word and the meaning of *belief.* Now for the last two classes, you have been studying what is known as the diagram of the creative principle. You know that this divine intelligent power, called love, expresses through what is known as belief and that expression is through the bridge, what we call the bridge of faith. Now, it is the very nature of the mind to believe. For without belief, our soul would not be in this world of creation.

We find in our activities and in our daily acts and businesses that we are prone to believe certain things and we have tendencies not to believe other things. Man, in his present state of evolution, values what he calls his skepticism. In fact, man even takes pride in being what is known as a good skeptic. Now we must ask ourselves, "What does skepticism truly mean? What is the meaning of that word?" When we analyze and investigate the true meaning of the word *skepticism,* we find that it is a value of what we know as suspicion. The more value man places in his suspicions, the greater a skeptic he becomes. So we find that it is man's belief in suspicion that truly makes him a skeptic.

Now we all believe in different things. We have what is known as the mass mind of beliefs in which our soul is encased in this mental form. Again and again, it's been stated that man cannot experience what the mind has not first accepted. Now acceptance is our belief. And so it shows us, clearly and demonstrably, that our experience is directly the effect of our belief in anything.

Why has man become so suspicious and so skeptical in this world? It's really quite simple: man, believing in people, in personality, being discouraged and dissatisfied, becomes suspicious.

So we find the first step into the pit, on the downward path, is what is known as personality.

We have been, and are, to some extent, expressing our faith in form, in people. We have lost the true freedom of our belief in our own home, which is the source from which all of us have wandered. There is a way out of that great jungle of disturbance and distress, but the way out of it, my friends, is to truly become aware of what you really believe.

Now if you ask a person if they believe in God, they may say that they do. But remember, they have their own understanding of what God truly is. And that understanding sustains us, usually, when things are going well or in accordance with our desires.

In the past two classes, we discussed that desire, as we all know, is a part of the creative principle. So the truth of the matter is that nothing lives without desire, because without desire there is no completion of the form. So we find that our soul enters this world under the divine laws, and the Infinite Intelligence, known as God or Love, enters into a realm of mind stuff, known as belief.

When we were very young in age on this planet, we were taught many, many things. We've been taught that it's raining outside. Now, we believe that, because we believe the person that was teaching us that. And consequently, according to our belief, we experience. Now if a person does not believe that it is raining outside, then they do not have the experience, because it is impossible. A person may say, "Well, the facts speak for themselves. It is a reality that it is raining." Our realities, my good friends, are only the effects of our beliefs. And this is why we have taught, and continue to teach, that man is a law unto himself.

Now a person may say that it's raining or the sun is shining and that is a fact of life. The only fact that it is, is our acceptance of it. That is the only fact. Remember that facts are mental acceptances: they are not truths and never will be. Because truth is something that is beyond the mind to perceive. We conceive with our mind and those conceptions are ever in accord with our accepted beliefs. And so let us ponder and consider what it is that we are truly believing at any time, at any given moment.

We believe in things. We believe in people. And according to our belief, do we experience our sadness or do we experience our joy. Whenever, my friends, you believe in form, you must prepare yourself for its duality, because that is the law, that is the nature of form itself. And so in that understanding, let us give more consideration and more effort to where we are directing our beliefs, because wherever we are directing those beliefs, we are directing our lives and will continue to experience this discord in our lives.

Now, for many people, I know, it seems difficult to believe in something that the mind cannot conceive. It is difficult to believe in a formless, divine Infinite Intelligence. But we can make those gradual steps by not being concerned with the effect of our directed energy.

The only thing that truly brings us this unhappiness is our concern, which, of course, is a self level. When man goes to work, he's concerned about how much he's going to receive. Well, why is man concerned about how much he's going to receive? Because he is concerned about how much he is giving. That, my friends, is the pit and the trip downward.

Now when we spend some energy, we make some effort and we do that from a level of consciousness where concern does not exist: we are doing it because there is something within us that knows that we should. We are not concerned with how many minutes we have spent doing it, or hours or years; therefore, we cannot be concerned with what the effect is going to be.

It is a very, let us say, *average* thing to be concerned with our efforts, because we have found in our life that by being concerned with our efforts, we receive more recognition. And we discussed last week the need of recognition, which, of course, brings success and this divine energy back to us. But we can, if we want to, recognize our true divinity. We can do that. And remember, friends, that that we recognize, recognizes us.

When we feel alone, it is because we have shut the world out from our life. That's what loneliness is. We have closed the circuits of our own spirit to express in this world of creation. And when that happens to a soul, there is a great inner turmoil, followed by a cloud of depression. It's commonly referred to as loneliness. We do that, of course, to ourselves.

Many times it has been taught that service is the lifeline to your own divinity. Only through serving, which is the purpose of the soul's incarnation into this world of form, only through serving are we truly fulfilled. Now I know that many people feel that they serve in many ways and there is no question: I am sure that they do. But if you are feeling out of harmony, if you are feeling and experiencing discord in your lives, be rest assured that you are closing down. You are not expressing your own spirit, your own soul.

Living in a world of variety, it is not the easiest thing, it is not the easiest step to make, to find one's own home, because we are distracted by so many things. But as the years go by and as we get a little older, we begin to think a little more often and we ask ourselves the question, "What am I doing here and where am I going?"

There is more to life, my friends, than eating and sleeping and enjoying the form. That does not mean that we should not have some balance in our life. But remember, what is balance to one is imbalance to another, because we have our own set of values.

And so this evening, in discussing belief, remember that we believe and our beliefs are revealed by the experiences that we encounter at any given moment. So the first step, of course, in freedom is the step of self-awareness. So more time and more effort must be spent by ourselves in finding our own soul than we have spent so far, unless we already believe that we are free and we experience our lives accordingly.

Now you're free to ask any questions that you have.

My first question deals with personality. In the early stages of my awareness in this area of thinking, the questions that arose at that time were about how man thought, say, fifty thousand years ago. I realized, while I was searching, that I found the answer that man has not changed his thinking from then to today. So then we have this sort of religious fable about Adam and Eve. My question is, How did man actually begin personality?

Your basic question is, How did personality begin? That's the question that you asked?

Yes.

Yes. What is its origin? Whenever or wherever there is form, you have personality. Because *personality* means "personal." You have individualization. There are no two forms identical. And so from the laws of nature, the Law of Creation, you have form and from form, you have what is known as personality. Yes. Does that help with your question?

I'm probably concerned more so with—I thank you—how form actually began?

How form began?

Yes. I mean, other than this self-creation.

Well, form began according to the laws of the creative principle. You see, if you will read a certain discourse in *The Living Light*, it deals with form and it deals with belief. And so, you see, form comes from belief, according to the laws known as faith. That's the beginning of form.

You see, the Divine Infinite Intelligence, formless and free— it says, "I am Spirit, formless and free"—it's on your church programs—"Whatever I think, that will I be." Because, you see, that's our belief, and belief is one of the laws of the creative principle. From love, belief. The moment you believe something, you understand, you put it into form and through that Law of Form, you have desire. So whatever you believe, you desire. And I believe we discussed, last class, that the continuity of desire is dependent upon the degree of recognition that we receive from the fulfillment of the desire. You see, man does not continue with a desire if he does not receive sufficient recognition. Now the recognition, you understand, is an experience that takes place within oneself. But if a person no longer receives—say that they have a desire and they continue on with their desire for a number of years. And then they have an experience and they've always received, say, 75 percent recognition for the fulfillment of the desire. Well, say, now that the years have passed and they're only receiving 10 percent recognition. Well, very soon, my friends, there will no longer be a continuity of that particular desire. It will start to diminish, you understand. Because recognition, you see, is attention and this divine energy follows the Law of Attention. So if there is not a continued energy influx, then the desire dies on the vine and that deals with the Law of the Creative Principle and the Law of Form.

In Discourse 34, there is the exercise of visualizing the fountain, which I've also heard recommended in the Sunday services. And all it says is, visualize a fountain before you think of a word. That leaves me kind of cold. I don't know exactly what to think—

Yes, thank you very much. How many weeks have you spent in the daily visualization process?

How many?

Weeks have you spent in the daily visualization process of the exercise?

I have been trying it about two weeks.

You've tried it for two weeks daily?

Yes.

Yes. Now do you feel that that is sufficient time to experience what the discourse is discussing?

No, I just—I'm not really sure that I'm understanding what to do.

I see.

For example, "the word": I don't understand what that means.

You don't understand "the word"—

Think of a word.

Think of a word. Yes.

Any word?

Any word. A word of your choice. Yes.

I'm using the word light.

Yes? Read the rest of the exercise.

I hear you say, keep trying.

Read the rest of the exercise.

It says, "Do the exercise you have been given and you will witness the changing of the colors of the fountain before you as you emanate the vibration from within."

That is correct. Now, do you believe that?

I believe that it's possible eventually. Yes.

Then for you, it will work. Nothing works for us unless we apply the Law of the Creative Principle. And love, belief, desire, will in action is the Law of the Creative Principle. Otherwise, my friends, you see, it cannot work. Nothing can work for us that we do not believe, because belief is acceptance and we cannot experience what we do not accept or we do not believe. It is impossible. Does that help with your question?

Yes. Thank you.

Another student has been waiting, please.

Last week—if I can get through this on the diagram and on tolerance. We cross the bridge of faith to duty and motive. In my thinking, I'm foggy. It might be that we'd have tolerance first and then cross to motive. But I thought we'd have to have a motive to be tolerant. I know that the teachings are correct. Would you explain why we come from the magnetic side of tolerance to the electric?

Because feeling precedes thought. And unless we have tolerance, we cannot have acceptance or motive. It's not possible.

Is motive acceptance?

Yes.

Thank you.

You're welcome.

May I ask one more question?

Certainly.

*We just talked of recognition. And, last week, I remember that
we spoke about encouragement. And everyone and everything
needs encouragement. Well, when we recognize some of our own
failings, how do we rise to encourage ourselves or others? I mean,
how do we give it out in truth so it is lasting and has light?*

Yes, thank you very much. We all, I'm sure, are aware that
the teachings state very clearly not to place your attention upon
your weaknesses or your frailties. Now, we all accept, of course,
that anything in form is not perfect, because it could not be perfect and be the Law of Duality. Therefore, the teaching is clearly
stated: to place your attention, which is your love, your energy,
upon what you want to become, not to put your energy (your
attention) upon what you want to overcome. Because, you see, if
you keep your attention, the divine Infinite Intelligence directing that, to what you want to overcome, the mountain keeps
getting bigger. Because you keep feeding it. You keep recognizing it. You keep giving it attention. You keep giving it energy.

So you see, once the mind has said, "Well, I'm going to work
on this area because this is a little frailty of mine,"—all right.
Now you start from that point, you see, which starts from a
point of tolerance from your magnetic field, and you move over
to your electrical field, to your conscious awareness. And with
that duty to your motive, you understand, that duty, you start
directing your thought to what you want to become.

I have never heard of a successful man that kept his attention on failure. The law is very clear. Every time you permit

your mind to accept, to entertain in thought, failure, you will continue to experience it, because you will continue to guarantee it. You see, the thing is that it is not going to be successful for us to think "success" without feeling it. You see, we must think it and we must feel it. And the feeling must be equal to the thought. Now you can think "success" around the clock. You can totally brainwash yourself with the word *success*. You're not going to be a bit successful, until you start to feel it.

Now how does a man *feel* success? Well, he first finds out what is in his subconscious that represents success. So he starts to work from that level. Maybe a new pair of shoes means some degree of success. Well, when he gets a new pair of shoes, he has a feeling of success. You see, your feeling—your magnetic field must be brought into equal portion and balance with your electric field. And when they're in this perfect balance, my friends, that is when the Divine Power that moves all things in the universes, that's when you're receptive to it.

Every Sunday morning we ask our congregation to be still in thought, to be at perfect peace, so they may be receptive to that Divine Intelligence, which is peace. Thank you.

You mentioned "the Divine Power that moves all things in the universe." It has also been stated, I believe, that which moves a thing is the will. Now I would like to ask a two-part question. Is the divine will the Divine Power that moves all things in the universe?

The question is asked, Is the divine will the Power that moves all things in the universe? According to the Law of Acceptance, yes, it is. Nothing can be moved that is not in rapport with it. We can't experience God unless we're in rapport with what we understand to be God. Yes.

It was also given that acceptance is the divine will.

That is correct. Acceptance is the divine will. Yes.

The question arises, is that acceptance, to me, in my present understanding, implies a duality: that which must be accepted and that which is accepting.

That is correct on the mental level.

And my understanding of the divine will is that it is totally impartial and not individualized.

The divine will is totally impartial and is not individualized, except through form or individualizing expression. And acceptance is in accord with the creative principle. Love, *belief.* Belief is acceptance. And that is the second step of the creative principle.

Is belief in duality, then?

Belief. Man believes in many things. So belief, in that sense, could be called dual. Yes. For example, you may believe in the understanding you're receiving or you may choose an alternate path and believe something else, which is known as rejection, you understand. That is a mental belief. We're talking about belief that's on a higher level than the conscious, mental acceptance. Yes.

That is not in duality? There is a belief and acceptance that is not in duality?

Belief is the second step of the creative principle. The second step is the dual step or the Law of Creation. One is God, two is duality, and three is manifestation. And so the second step of the creative principle is belief. And when the divine, neutral Power, known as Love, moves to belief, you have the beginning of creation or duality. Does that help with your question?

That answers a multitude. Thank you.

You're very welcome.

As individuals, how can we find and recognize our own personal purpose in life?

That's a fine question. As individuals, how can we find and recognize our purpose in life? My friends, the moment you recognize anything, you will find it. So the first step is recognition, for finding follows recognition, as the day follows the night. So the first thing is recognition. That is why they say, you know, man looks all over the world to find God. And the last place he looks is inside himself, because he does not pause to think that he may recognize within his own being his own divinity.

Now, we teach a certain system of daily concentration and meditation. We teach a concentration upon the word *peace*. The reason that we teach this particular word, *peace,* which is the power of God, which *is* God, is because when you truly accept—which, of course, is belief—peace, you will bring yourself into harmony within your own being. And when that takes place, you will recognize your own divinity. And when you recognize your own divinity, through those simple steps, then, my friends, you have found yourself. And having found yourself, you will know the purpose of your life. Thank you.

If I may ask about this personality business—because sometime you're in that an awful lot. We notice that a person can go to a cradle and the child has a reaction. The child has not grown to think, at least not outwardly, "This is someone I do not like," or "There is something about this person that I don't know what it is, but I feel a wall." We grow up with this feeling and we meet people constantly. Some we like and others that we, well, not dislike, but we just don't feel very warm toward. How does this start in a little baby? I mean, it's just a few weeks old and it sometimes screams when somebody comes near it.

Thank you. And that's a very good question. And let us begin with the understanding that all things respond to God's love. All things: a plant, a dog, a tree, a cat, a mouse, an elephant, a human being. All things respond to what we call the divine love.

Now when a person has an experience with a three-year-old child and they go to pick them up or to cuddle them and the child screams, there is a reason for that. The child's vibration at that particular time, its feelings—you see, most of us have been conditioned that a three-year-old child doesn't have a developed mind yet. So unfortunately, we're conditioned and we believe that. We've accepted that and therefore we believe that a three-year-old child does not think, or at least it doesn't think like a fifteen-year-old child. That's not true, my friends. It is simply that the physical form, the brain, is not yet sufficiently developed for the mind to express itself.

Now, there are some children in this world who doctors call geniuses. Well, how does this take place? What is this? It's simply, my friends, that this physical brain is in a greater rapport, unusual for a child that is five or six, than the average child that is born. Now, it's just like a dog. Most people have accepted, and they believe, that a dog, a four-legged creature, has very limited ability to think or choose, if it has any. Consequently, if we have a dog, the dog, in truth, is going to be a mirror of what we, as individualized souls, are expressing. And that's exactly what the dog is going to be. The truth of the matter is that a dog—and many animals—they think. They have feelings, they have emotions, they have frustrations, they feel rejection, they retaliate. They do all of the things that a human mind does, only to a lesser degree. And that is the truth of the whole matter.

Now, getting back to a three-week-old child, that child is thinking, but unable, because of its physical development, to express itself. If it could, it would say at three weeks old, "I don't want to be picked up. I don't feel like being picked up right now." And so it expresses the best way it can and it screams.

You see, friends, it's a lack of communication. We don't talk, as adults, to a three-week-old child. We don't talk, as adults, to a four-legged creature. What is it within us that doesn't permit that to take place? I can tell you what it is. It's what is known as our ego. It is our acceptance and our belief that they are more ignorant than we are. So if someone or something is more ignorant than you are, you are supposed to treat it accordingly. And so that's what we have done. And that's what we continue to do, you see. And then, we have a breakdown in communication.

Because we believe that a three-week- or a three-month-old baby doesn't understand what we're talking about, doesn't have the feelings that we have, and we treat it like some toy to pick up when we want to pick it up, etc. And that mind has its own individuality. It has its own feelings of its own rights. Perhaps it's saying, "I'm cold and I don't want to be touched," or this or that or something else. But you see, it's not yet capable, physically, of communicating those feelings and those desires.

And after all, my friends, there are people even in their twenties and thirties and all age brackets that don't like to be touched, that don't like to be cuddled. So it's not exclusive, you know, to a three-week-old baby. Many people don't like to be touched, including myself, which is my personal choice and my personal desire. But considering that I respect the rights of other people and try not to run around cuddling and touching them, then I have a right to demand the same respect for myself. I do hope that has helped with an understanding of a three-week-old child. Yes.

I understand that the way to free a soul is through selfless service, but what happens, what does a soul experience when it reneges on a spiritual commitment?

Usually, when a person is striving to serve the Divine and they make a decision—of course, what you mean by *reneging* is deciding not to do something after you have accepted the value of doing it, is that not correct? So what it deals with, of course, is the second step of the creative principle, known as belief-acceptance. When people have accepted and believe and have demonstrated to themselves that what they understand as selfless service has benefited them and is benefiting them, and then they make a decision not to continue with their efforts— this is what you're speaking of, aren't you?—they have varied experiences. Now those experiences, of course, are dependent upon their original acceptance and motive. Yes.

Now, it could cause certain guilt feelings. It could cause a discord emotionally, mentally within the individual. But they are indeed varied. You see, it will do something, because a person feels better when they're doing something.

I know that many religions have taught that there is no greater sin than idleness. And how just and how true that is. Because, you see, what happens is we just get grounded. What do we get grounded in? I mean, if we're just sitting, you see, like a toad, and we're just basking, I mean, how long can we do that? How long can we remain grounded in our own small, little, minute universe without suffering the consequence of blowing out the circuits? Well, that varies with each individual, you know. A person goes on an extended vacation—what that means is extended to the point of their own tolerance. That means, "How long can I tolerate myself will depend, of course, on how long my vacation will be," you see.

See, friends, it's not so easy to live with oneself. Just shut yourself up in solitary confinement for seventy-two hours. Do yourself that favor. And then you'll understand what it's like to really be grounded in yourself and to really see where you are. Because, you see, then, you know, we'll think about this and think about that, but only for so many hours. And then we start to experience the greatest depression of all. Solitary confinement is a great suffering to the senses. Phenomenal suffering. Because, you see, all of the things that have kept us from viewing the true self are now all taken away. And now we stand naked and bare and we have to face our real, true self. And it's not so pleasant, you see. So service, indeed, is not only God's divine lifeline back home to where we started, but it is a path which helps us to keep some degree of balance and sanity in our life.

What does *sanity* mean? What does it really mean? Does anyone know what *sanity* really means?

I think I know. And that would be reason.

The student feels that *sanity* means "reason." If that's the case, there's very few sane people, few sane ones of us left in the world. In fact, they haven't found one yet, including myself. Because if sanity—and thank you very much for your understanding—if *sanity* meant "reason," let's be honest and let's say, "Well, now how many minutes in a day am I reasonable? How many minutes am I really using reason? Is it reason for me to be all frustrated and concerned about a so-called gas rationing?"

You know something, friends? Let us think. If we accept, through belief, that there's going to be a gas rationing in our country—by the way, there is, but that's not the point—if we believe that that's going to have an effect on our lives, you may be rest assured we have just guaranteed it. I assure you, friends, I do a lot of driving; it will have no effect on my life at all. You may be rest assured. Because I do not accept or believe that it will. But if we accept or believe these things—this is what I'm talking about—how many of us are using reason? See? How many of us in the world are using reason? We believe those things and then we experience them, you see. In other words, they have a greater effect over us because we gave them a greater acceptance, we gave them a greater belief. If we're going to believe in anything, let's believe in peace. Let's believe in freedom. And then act accordingly. Then, my friends, we will have sanity.

Now Andrew Jackson Davis, the father of our philosophy, stated in 1863 that the Earth planet and its inhabitants were known in the universe as the "lunatic fringe." And he stated that over 110 years ago. Now I know that what Mr. Davis, a very fine spiritual man, stated in 1863 was not well accepted by people. In fact, even in the spiritualist movement today there are very few people that care to accept that the Earth planet and all of its inhabitants are known in the universe as the lunatic fringe.

Well, you know, friends, there are moments when we say, "Well, that's not a very pleasant thing to think about." But you look around and you see this rat race of creation, and I'm sure there are moments when we will all agree. So what is it that keeps us in some degree of reason? Is it not peace?

Man values freedom only when he's in bondage. But it's oft-times difficult to be aware when we're in bondage. I'll tell you when we're aware that we're in bondage. It's when we're coming out of it. And it's a wonderful feeling. Because we start to sense a degree of freedom. It's a beautiful feeling to start to rise up out of jail, out of the bondage that we put ourselves in. It is a very rare person that is aware when they're descending into bondage.

Now the purpose—and one of the main purposes—of your awareness classes is to help you, your perception, so that you will know when you're on the descent. Not only that you will know it, but that you will have the method necessary to keep you from descending any further. You see, we slip easily, but we work like the dickens to come back up. And that's the way that it is in this world of creation.

I thank you all very much. I see our time is up. Let us go have refreshments.

NOVEMBER 15, 1973

CONSCIOUSNESS CLASS 32 ✖

Good evening, students. I would like to discuss a few things concerning our soul and our spirit, before we go into our meditation this evening.

It does seem, in review of the courses that have been given in this church, to some, it does not seem that there is much change in their lives, if any. However, if we could look a little deeper into the lives of people and we could see, on the different dimensions which they are expressing, all of us, we would see that there has been accepted the possibility of a new way of thinking.

And by accepting that possibility, there are, in certain levels of consciousness, gradual, but very slow, changes that are taking place. No one outgrows any type of mental pattern that they have expressed for a lifetime overnight. It is a slow, gradual, and a very stable process, if it is going to be a lasting process.

Now in review of these twelve weeks, we have seen and we have discussed a great deal about the importance of our thoughts, what they do to us, how they attract different things to us. We've also discussed how our feelings—that things originate with our feelings. You know, a person says, "I feel good." They don't say, "I think good and now I feel good." They feel good and then they think accordingly. Now we must work both ways. We must work with our feelings and we must work with our thinking, because that is, as we all know, what our life really is.

In this world of this dense matter, we can't immediately see the result of a thought. But when we leave this physical body, the moment you have a thought, my friends, you immediately see the effect or the form of that thought. When you have a feeling, you see the effect or form of that feeling. This is what these classes are, in truth, all about: to become aware, for your own salvation, for your own protection, for your own preservation.

Now we know that our soul is indestructible, in the sense that it is not composed of matter that can be destroyed. However, it can be covered by a conglomeration of mental substance. This is why we strive in our ways to think, and think clearly, because if we don't think clearly, we're not going to experience a beautiful life; we're not going to experience a life that is worth living at all. So we try to make our efforts, if we are wise, daily, giving more thought to which levels of consciousness we are expressing at any given moment.

Let us look back at the beginnings of just this particular class. Let us look around this little log cabin, this room here, and let us see how many are called and how few, in truth, are chosen. Remember, friends, the choosing is ever up to us. Some of us have had sufficient experience in life, in our evolution, that warrants a greater effort to continue to free ourselves from what we call a world of creation.

Again and again, we look out each day in the world and we see an interest, a desire. It never lasts. And we discussed one time—a student asked the question of—the difference between *desire* and *aspire*. Well, there's a great difference between those two levels, friends. Not only is desire part of the creative principle and a function, but aspiration is an expression of the soul faculty. When we aspire for something, we have, with that aspiration, the awareness that it is coming to us and that it is coming at the right time and it is coming in the right way. Now that is the freedom of the soul faculties. We know that beyond a shadow of any doubt. And that knowledge, that awareness, sustains us through what is known as the time-consciousness level that demands patience. And patience, friends, demands faith. Without patience, there's no faith. And without faith, there is no patience. So you see, it behooves us to aspire to the goals that we have established and not to desire them, but to move from the functions of desire to the faculties of aspiration.

You cannot, you *cannot* deny the creative principle of existence. The more you try to deny it, the more problems you are going to be in. That energy must be expressed. If it is not expressed, you're going to suffer the consequences. So let us aspire to free ourselves. Let us aspire to the wonder of life itself. And let us try not to give this great power to people, places, and things.

Our minds are so conditioned to put the blame elsewhere: it's either the world or it's people. Now this is a trap of personality that we all fall into. The reason that we fall into it is because it takes a strong spirit to face one's own frailties. None of us like to admit that we have frailties or weaknesses: that is not something that anyone cares to think about. But there is no perfection in form. No matter who we are and no matter where we are, we all have certain tendencies, known as weaknesses or frailties. Now if we stop worrying about them and we start doing something about them, then we're going to free ourselves and we're really going to enjoy this life. Because, you see, friends, if you cannot enjoy *this* life, there is no chance of enjoying the next one. See, we're not going to leave here—we're not going to leave and find a wonderful spirit world with all the joy and happiness that our heart desires, if we don't take that with us.

So let us give a little thought each morning, each day: "This may be the last day that I'm down here. What am I going to take with me?" Because what you take with you mentally, emotionally, that is the realm of consciousness that you will be trapped in, just like myself. So let us give more thought to that when we open our eyes in the morning. And if we will do that, then we will be prepared for what is known as the inevitable. So very few people think about what they call the process of dying until they get up into their sixties, seventies, eighties, and nineties. Then, they give it some thought. Ofttimes, my friends, it's almost too late then, because the patterns are so well established. It is so very, very, very difficult. We do not know the time, the day, nor the hour when we're going to leave here. And it behooves us, sincerely, to give that more thought. Not in an emotional fear, because that will not be of any benefit to you—in fact, it will be quite detrimental—but to give it some thought of reason.

Try to sit back for a few moments in the morning and look at your thought realm. Now, by that I mean the types of thoughts that you habitually entertain in the course of a day. If you have someone that you are adverse to, if you have someone that is difficult for you to tolerate, to communicate with, that, my friends, is what you're going to find in the next life. Now, you may leave that particular person here on the earth realm when you go, but you are taking your mental universe with you. So there'll be a substitute—and usually a few thousand of them—waiting to greet you at the door. And when you go over, that's what you will find. This is why we teach that our adversities become our attachments. We direct energy to the things which we are adverse to and to the people we are adverse to; and by directing that energy, or God's love, we pull them, like a great magnet, out of the universe. This is why, when you have a problem, if you keep entertaining that problem in thought, if you put emotion into that problem, if you put your feelings into that problem, you will guarantee that problem to multiply and to increase in your universe, because that is a natural law of creation. So doesn't wisdom dictate for us to think more clearly? Let us feel what we really want to be and then let us go about doing it.

But patience, my friends, is not only a soul faculty. It is the patient man that sees all creation pass and yet stands alone in his universe, knowing that something else will come and, also, something else will go. Whatever you have to this moment and to this day, you and I and all of us, we have earned that over a period of untold thousands of years. We are at this point in time because this point in time is the effect of what we have done all of those centuries before. We came into this world into certain families and certain circumstances, with certain desires and certain weaknesses. Our soul entered that type of a body, that type of a mind, because that was what we had earned to that point. Now by looking at today, we can see how far we have come. And when we see how far we have come, if we will express the soul faculty of gratitude—not disgust or discouragement, because that's as far as we got in all those centuries—but if we will express the soul faculty of gratitude that we are at least at this point in time, then we will go further to our eternal destiny.

Remember, friends, each soul is destined, according to the laws that it has established, to reach its own goal in its own way. No one entered this earth realm by chance. You entered on the path known as destiny and that is the effect that we have today.

[The class meditates. Following the meditation, a student reads Discourse 61 aloud.]

We will now open the floor for discussion of your questions, if you will be so kind as to raise your hands. Yes.

In the diagram of the creative principle, we have two triangles, which are the triangles of duty, tolerance, and gratitude; and faith, poise, and humility. Each one of those points expresses a soul faculty. How do we relate the functions to that creative principle and the functions, which are attached to each one of those points?

Thank you very much. In reference to your question on the creative principle, first, if we did not have the soul faculties, there would not be any sense functions. Now, the teaching is a balance between the soul faculties and the sense functions. Now some of the functions and their corresponding faculties have been given in *The Living Light*. Those that have not yet been given will be given as time progresses. Was there a particular soul faculty that you were interested in?

No, all six of them.

You're interested in duty, gratitude, and tolerance; faith, poise, and humility?

Yes, and their functions.

Yes. If you will study *The Living Light*, you will find your answer. Because your answer is very obvious with regard to one of the triune faculties. A little bit more thorough study to find the other one. Yes. And if you haven't found it by the beginning of our next course, I will be happy to discuss that with you privately.

Yes, sir.

Thank you. Does someone else have a question?

I know this is our last class for this year, but I wanted to ask about something that has been with me for a long time. What is the importance of finishing that which we start here on the earth plane? And if we do not finish classes or sewing or whatever that we start to do, do we really have to finish it on a spirit side of life?

Thank you very much. And with my experience of the past thirty-some years, friends, there is no endeavor that man begins that he does not finish at some time in some life. Now, we have entered this world with a lot of unfinished work and consequently, some of us—each one differs, of course, according to what we've set into motion. Now the Law of Cause and Effect is an immutable law. You see, you don't establish a cause without its effect. Therefore, one of the basic teachings of the Living Light is the Law of Continuity. So man should consider choosing more wisely what he accepts and when he accepts it as *his* personal responsibility.

Now I have witnessed many people on the other side still writing to finish some book that they had started. I've seen them in various projects in the different dimensions. And to some of them, it was most difficult and to others, they couldn't understand why they had to do that. The only reason that they had to do it is because man is a law unto himself. And so they had established that beginning and—you see, my friends, what you establish, you are a part of: you become that thing. That's why we choose more carefully what we get ourselves involved in, because we are becoming a part of it.

Now we might say, "Well, that doesn't bother me. I can do this. I can do that and etc." But you see, it's like the boomerang: it always comes back. Now what we are trying to do is to become aware; so when we have an experience, we will be able to follow that experience backward in so-called time, so we can find the cause. Because when we find the cause of the experience, whether it's a beneficial experience or it's a detrimental experience, when we find the cause, we've got the cure. Then, the next time, when we start to have that type of thinking, we'll say, "Just a moment! I well remember what experience that brings into my life." And so we will stop to think. No, there are no beginnings, my friends, that don't have their own endings.

It says here, in *The Living Light*, that man is responsible unto himself and to all his creations. What does that mean? That means that man is responsible: he has the ability to respond to all his thoughts, acts, and activities, which are his creations, which are his children. Now those creations, or children, are all with us, and when our eyes open, we get to see them. There are quite a few of them, you know; it depends on the individual. I hope that's helped with your question. Now that doesn't mean, friends, that we should start going backward in time and saying, "Oh, let's see, I've got five hundred projects that I haven't finished." And then go through the delusion of the time-consciousness realm. *This* is your moment. *This* is your beginning. What has gone yesterday, it hovers in our universe to be faced another day.

There's an old saying that "history repeats itself." Why, my friends, look at our own personal history: it repeats itself. Every so often we say, "Oh, that happened to me ten years ago, and I did identically the same thing and here I am all over again." Certainly, history does repeat itself. Why does history repeat itself? Because of the impartial law: you create something, you're responsible for that creation, whatever it may be. You are directly responsible, because it's your child: you gave it birth. And until you fulfill what you gave birth to, until it grows up and becomes an adult, stands on its own ability of response, you have to lead it by the hand or it waits, for the day comes that you can see it and then take care of it. Let us not be discouraged or down in the mouth. Let us just be aware. *This* is the moment we start from.

Remember, it is taught that hell is paved with good intentions and broken promises. You see, my friends, when a person breaks a promise or a commitment, they're not doing that to someone else. That's the illusion. When we break a commitment, my friends, we are breaking the back, not only of our own character, but we're breaking the back of our ability to stand on our two feet and build a solid foundation. That is what we are doing. To be honest with you, my friends, it's very bad business. Someone else have a question?

Would you be good enough to discuss in more detail the illusion of time-consciousness? Where does one draw the line between being practical and being caught up in it?

Thank you very much. In reference to the illusion of time consciousness, where does one draw the line of being practical? Well, my friends, you see, what is practical to one is very impractical to another, because, of course, this is dependent entirely upon the motive, you understand, of their thinking practicality. Now, for example, a person can feel under emotional pressure and at that moment they say to themselves, "Now, I have to be practical here. I have to cut out this, this, this, this, this, this, and that." All right. Now on another level of consciousness, you understand, perhaps two minutes later or two days later, one sits back—perhaps now they're expressing through the faculty of reason—and they say, "Now I have to be practical. I only have so much time that I can work with." All right? That's the number one mistake: "I only have so much time that I can get so much done." The reason that that type of thinking and attitude of mind is the number one mistake is because in that statement and in that thinking, you have given power to limitation.

Now a person may say, "Well, now, there's twenty-four hours in the day." Do you understand? "And I've got this to do and it's going to take so long and etc." When man says that a job is going to take so many minutes or a certain amount of time, man establishes that law. God doesn't. Man establishes the law that it's going to take twenty minutes to do this particular job. Now, the truth of the matter is there is the possibility that it can be done in two minutes. So we'll go a little further and we'll say we're living in a world of mechanics: this is how it operates, this is the way it's timed, and etc. But we don't stop to think that perhaps we may receive some type of assistance and it will take us, now, two minutes instead of twenty. So this is known as the time-consciousness illusion. Man creates that.

Now, if we go into peace and clarification, and we sit back and we strive for organization—an organized mind is a healthy mind, and it is the most practical mind that can exist. So organization is the first thing that we seek. Now what does organization really mean to the mind? When the mind is organized, it sees clearly the levels of consciousness. When a thought strikes a blow to the mind, the mind is aware, aware from what level of consciousness the thought has originated. Being aware, knowing the pattern of the levels of consciousness, then a person becomes organized. They don't have to be told what to do. They know what to do and they are no longer controlled by the illusion of the time-consciousness level. I hope that's helped with your question.

On the paths of incarnation, it is my understanding that we come from the Allsoul before we get another incarnation.

That is correct.

My question is, On the past incarnation, as with the present incarnations, and the so-called forms or children, what happens to them when we have returned to the Allsoul from the past incarnation? And another part to that question is, How many children do we inherit upon the function of birth?

Are there any more questions?

I hope that you will answer those.

Thank you very much. In reference to the soul's return to the Source from whence it came, the reabsorption into the Allsoul, and when it is impulsed again into incarnation, into expression, the so-called children or responsibilities that we have created, they do go with us from incarnation to incarnation until they are fulfilled. Do you understand? We're talking about what man has responded to. And this is why man comes in—the soul comes into different types of bodies, different circumstances, etc. That is what governs that condition. That's what governs whether you're going to be born in this family, in this country or that country, this area or that area. Now, that's what governs it. Our responsibilities, our creations govern that, you know, not some God sitting up there. And it's the evolutionary process. But that's governed in that way.

Now, how many do we have? That depends upon the individual, that depends entirely upon the person and what they have set into motion. You see, it's just like a man; he gets married. He has a choice. He might have two children. He might have ten. So it's the same thing. You know, that depends, of course, upon your own desires and what you have set into motion as the laws that you have established.

You see, we come into this world and we always have this, what we call, 10 percent choice or 10 percent free will, while this other 90 percent is what has been established. Now each moment, we keep establishing these causes. And so we're moving from cause to effect, moment by moment, constantly, in creation. Now we cannot be in this world of creation without these laws, because that *is* the Law of Creation. You see, the thing is to establish a thought from what we call a pure motive. In other words, become aware of the level of consciousness when you have a thought. Now, if you will become aware of the level of consciousness when you have a thought—I'm saying one thought, not a million that are spinning around in our heads, but just start with one—you will know exactly where that's going to lead you. Because, you see, my friends, if you start working on that—say that man has a thought. OK, the thought is, "I want a new car." Now, if man will be truly at peace when he has that thought, he says, "All right, I want a new car." OK, then he goes into a peaceful vibration. He will see the level of consciousness that prompted the thought. He will also know the payment for its attainment, because he will see the pattern of that level of consciousness. Then, he might decide he doesn't want that new car right now, you know.

Thank you. I would like some clarification. It's my impression of the Allsoul, of it being in complete purity. Would that be correct?

The spirit is formless and free and therefore pure and is the peace. The soul is the covering of the spirit and it has its individualization or form, which guarantees imperfection in order that it may have form. You see, you don't have perfection in form. You see, you can't have perfection in form, because you wouldn't have the pairs of opposites. You wouldn't have the duality, which is the Law of Creation. You must have this so-called balance and counterbalance: that *is* the law. Yes.

Thank you.

You're more than welcome. There are good souls, but I never saw a pure one. Spirit is something different.

I don't know whether I had a perception, but the "Total Consideration" affirmation is very dear to me and I am studying it. [See Consciousness Class 25.] It says, "The Law of Harmony is my thought." I found in Discourse 41 that harmony, the Law of Harmony is faith, poise, and humility . . . is my thought . . .

That's right.

And guarantees Unity.

"In all my acts and activities."

Well, I understand, to a degree. I'll try to practice it. This is right, is it not?

That is correct. The Law of Harmony is my thought: faith, poise, and humility.

Is my thought.

Now when you have a thought and you have that soul faculty operating—faith, poise, and humility—now what does faith do? Faith is the power of the universe that brings it to you. What does poise do? If man is at poise, impatience cannot exist. In other words, the emotional realms no longer exist when you are poised. And what does humility do? What does humility do? It opens wide the door of the divine will, not man's will, but the divine will, which is acceptance. And so when the Law of Harmony becomes your thought, when faith, poise, and humility guide your ship—but remember, friends, you don't get to faith, poise, and humility—you know what that is, don't you: that's the faculty of belief—until you've had duty, gratitude, and tolerance, which is that faculty of love.

And so if you, as the student has mentioned the Law of Harmony, you study, you apply the pieces, they all fit together. They're brought together this way because man is on a multitude of levels of consciousness. And no matter what level of consciousness you're on, you can pick up the book [*The Living Light*] if you have just a moment of sincerity and you open it; and if you do that faithfully, under the Law of Continuity, you will open it to the discourse that's meant for you. Of course it works, because, you see, you are greater than a book. You are the power that moves the book, that opens the page. It's your spirit, that's your god, your godhood within yourself. It cannot help but open to the page that's meant to help you at that instant and that moment if you demonstrate an ounce of faith and a pound of continuity. Yes, does someone else have a question, please?

From the comment that you made earlier, I wondered if organization is a soul faculty.

Organization is a soul faculty.

May I ask if you could discuss this in relation to the other two faculties?

In reference to love and belief?

Well, I was thinking, whatever it goes with in the triune . . .

Organization is the first law. It is the law of the universe. Organization is not only the law of the macrocosm, it is the law of the microcosm. And so the first thing that man sets into motion is the effort to organize his thinking, so he can become aware of what is controlling him.

Now you cannot, my friends, control your life until you organize it. You can't control something that you haven't organized. You see, it's a total waste of energy. It's ridiculous to try to control anything that you haven't organized. But once you organize it, my friends—in that process of organization, that's your responsibility—then, my friends, you are in a position to control it. Not to control people, places, or things. People, places, and things are controlled by our own control. You control yourself: everything around you will be controlled. If you are the peace that passeth all understanding, all things that touch you, they will bow to that peace. Don't you see? It knows its kind. That's the power that we're talking about. Peace is God and that is the power. But, you see, you don't have peace and say, "Now that person is to do such and such." You've lost your peace that instant. What you want to do, what we want to do, is to work here on peace. And when we do that, we have organization and we have control. And when you have organization and control, my friends, you have success. And when you have success, you have recognition and your purpose in life is being fulfilled.

I don't know how exactly to put these all together, but you're talking about organization and also the duality of form, the creative process. One of the things that bothers me is that when people organize themselves, they tend to freeze in that organization. So it is very hard for them to change. I'm applying this now, because if I organize my thinking, do I then freeze myself in a way that will make it difficult for me to change?

Not unless you desire to do that. You see, if you organize yourself, you understand—your own mind—then you become aware of the levels of consciousness. Then, we become aware that whatever one soul does, all souls are capable of doing. And by becoming aware of that, we are granted understanding. Then, when we see another person expressing on level twenty, we know that level twenty exists within us, so we're able to have tolerance within ourselves, granting each individual their right to express on their level of consciousness. You do not freeze unless you desire to do that. For example, if you're on level thirty and you feel comfortable—you feel comfortable within yourself—then you will seek all souls that are on level thirty, you understand? And you will only be in rapport or happy with them when they're on level thirty. Now that could cause a type of freezing: you understand that, don't you? But that is something that you, as an individual, would choose to do.

Now, in reference to organizations out there in the world, yes, there is a very strong possibility, because of the type of organization, that you could be frozen into that particular level of consciousness. That is very, very true. You will not find that, I'm sure, if you have investigated to this point, in the Serenity philosophy, because it not only recognizes the eighty-one levels of consciousness, but it respects the rights of each individual to express on any of those levels. Does that help with your question?

Yes, thank you.

You're more than welcome.

Could we use the same organization and continuity in the hours we sleep at night, so that we won't have these feelings of tiredness? And, well, at some point, it's a type of programming. Well, at a certain time I'm tired, you know. Through organization of, let's say, set hours, could keeping the continuity of those hours, maintained every day, bring a balance in that kind of thing?

Absolutely. We could certainly bring a balance into any part of our lives, whether it's one's sleeping or whatever it is. But usually what happens when the student attempts to cut down on their sleeping hours, usually from twelve hours to ten and then, hopefully, sometimes to eight or seven, what usually happens is, they try to do it overnight. Now let's remember, friends, that we didn't start the twelve-hour sleeping habit pattern in a year or two. You see, when we were little babies, we slept and we slept and we slept and we slept. And so we have a whole

lifetime of programming. So we don't try to just automatically
say, "Now I'm sleeping twelve hours a day. Now that's just too
much. So I'm going to cut that down to eight," because you're
going to guarantee a reaction from that level of consciousness.
I have found the wisest thing to do, very consistently, but very
faithfully, "Today is Thursday. I cut out five minutes today.
Tomorrow is Friday. I'll stick to my five minutes. And I'll demonstrate that for a week or two. Then, I'll try seven minutes."
But be consistent: the Law of Continuity.

You see, that Law of Continuity puts you in control, because
that's part of organization. Don't try to do it overnight. The emotional body and the emotional levels react fiercely and, with some
people, they even react with their health. Usually, what happens,
people become very irritated. Well, you take the drink away from
the drinker, you take the cigarette away from the smoker, you
take the sleep away from the sleeper, you take the food away
from the eater, how do they react? Irritable. So you can see what
level governs those things, can't you? You see, according to the
reaction, that determines the level that controls it, which is
known as the emotions. Yes.

*About organization, upon coming into an office in the morn-
ing and finding your desk piled high—I got this while you were
talking: Organization is concentration, meditation, and manifestation. It would be in that circle. And thinking your business
into being before it takes place. If you could go into your office
and become quiet, would you just gravitate to the work that is to
be done first? I mean, would the spirit people, your band of spirit
guides, would you not attract someone who would help you with
organization?*

Well, I would say this to any student, including myself:
When I face an experience—whether it's on a job, whether it's
something that is disorganized or whether it's emotion, no matter what it is—the number one question to entertain in thought
is, "Why this and why now?" The experience is an effect. Now,

say that we go onto a job and our desk is piled heaping with disorganized papers and etc. Now the mind usually says, "That person is very disorganized. I just don't know how I merited that individual." But we have to go beyond that. We have to see that this is an effect. "That person is only instrumental in presenting disorganization to me. That is giving me a golden opportunity to organize myself."

Now if a disorganized experience repeats itself in our universe, what it means is, in some area in our universe, we are disorganized. Now, you see, where the mind gets deluded. It says, "Well, I'm not disorganized. I have all my papers neat and etc." That's the delusion, because we're trying to relate it specifically, instead of by principle. If the experience of disorganization keeps hitting us, that reveals to us on a level of consciousness we are disorganized. If it is a great disorganization, that is how disorganized we are on that level of consciousness.

Now, how do we find out what level of consciousness that is? It's very simple. When you have the experience of these disorganized papers, ask yourself, "How does it affect me? Does it make me angry? Does it affect my emotions? Do I get upset?" Now, if that is how we react, that reveals the level of consciousness that *we* are disorganized on. Isn't that beautiful? So you see, every day we are being taught. Whether we like it or not, we are being taught. The effect reveals the level of consciousness where we need growth. And you have that whether you go to the supermarket or you're on the telephone or you're driving your car. No matter where you go, the effect, my friends, reveals the level of consciousness where organization or growth is needed within. Does that help with your question?

Very much. Thank you.

You're welcome. Does someone else have a question? Yes.

One could say that we create our own challenges.

Oh, absolutely! We guarantee them. You see, even the challenge of being born by a certain mother and a certain father, we

created that. We absolutely guaranteed it. And here we landed
on what we call the earth realm. And some parents, you know,
they were quite a challenge. I think some will agree with me anyway. Yes, we create our own challenges. We create our own fail-
ures. We create our own successes. We create all of those things.

For growth?

Yes. Well, it's for more than growth. You see, what happens
when we meet a challenge and we are successful, what we have
done, we have refined the ingredients that compose the challenge. That's what we've done. That's the purpose, really, of a
soul's incarnation: refine those things.

You know, man looks around and he says, "Well, I see life
here." And, you know, he has to see things physically. If he'd
only open his eyes, he'd see all those other dimensions. They're
just as important. In fact, they're more important, because the
material-physical world is the effect of those other worlds. See,
those other worlds that we're moving in right here and now,
those are the ones to work with, because the physical one is the
effect of them, you see.

Now a person says, "Well, I have a physical pain. It's physical!" Well, it's not physical at all. The physical body is experiencing an effect of a mental creation. Now that's what it really is.
And the mental body is experiencing an effect of the other bodies, and on up. So my gosh, let's go to the horse's mouth. Let's
work at the top, where it's really effective. Why bother with all
this other stuff? Why not go to the source? You go right to the
source. Go right to the cause. Then, you're going to have real
results. You're going to have some substantial results. Go to the
cause of things. Go right to the source and work from that point
outward, yes. See, in other words, don't try to work on your
friends and all your business associates, because your friends
and business associates, friends, they are an effect of you, you
see? So we work on ourselves and then all those things, they
start changing according to the changes that we make. Yes.

I've been puzzled. Can I have an effect over what people call biological rhythms? For example, many women experience a lot of uptightness or nervousness before the onset of their menstruation. Is that something that an individual can affect, or mitigate the effects of, through her mind?

Absolutely.

How?

You want to know how you can affect the cyclic rhythms of another individual?

No, of one's own self.

Well, my goodness, you're not only affecting your own self, but you can affect other individuals; that depends if they're in rapport with you. Now think, friends. In fact, I believe we read that discourse just tonight. Stop and think. When you have a thought of a person, place, or thing, you, as a receiving reactor, are affected by the thoughts, feelings, acts, and activities of the individual that you are entertaining in thought at that time. Now, if that is what happens when you think about them, can you imagine what happens when you have a feeling for them?

Now, I want to talk to the married ladies in our class here tonight and I want to ask them if they haven't found that to be true. You certainly have feelings of some kind for your husbands and I think, if you're honest with yourselves, that you have some effect according to their moods. Wouldn't you agree?

Yes, that's true.

To some extent. You see, we are affected by these things, but we're doing it to ourselves. Now what can affect the cycles and the rhythms is your emotions. Your emotions can change it. Definitely, absolutely, and positively. The emotions interfere with nature's divine flow and that's how you can change those cycles. You can only change them through your feelings and through your emotions, but you can change them. Anyone can. I hope that's helped with your question.

In talking of the Law of Continuity, in keeping with it rather, for those who have been married and have instigated a divorce, is this a broken law that we will have to face? Or when we bring about a breaking of a relationship with another person and it isn't finished—and sometimes it's very bitter, over money or other things—is this something that is a broken promise?

Thank you. That depends, in reference to relationships with other people—husbands, wives, etc.—that depends *entirely* upon the level from which the motive was given birth. Now, for example, many people get married and, you know, that's a man-made law that man has created. And they say all types of things from certain levels of consciousness. Well, of course, they have the effects when they make the changes.

Now you must realize that when people are in an emotional level and they have a certain desire at stake, that those levels of consciousness, they're not very reliable, you see. They're emotional levels. They're certainly not reliable. I mean, I'd like to see any emotion that's reliable. I haven't found one emotion yet that's reliable. I do not consider divine love an emotion, by the way, but I have yet to find one, single emotion that's reliable. Has anybody found an emotion yet that's reliable? I haven't.

Now, if you're talking about a spiritual faculty of kindness or a spiritual faculty of divine love or something like that, it's something different. But when you're talking about human relationships and conjugal love, then you're talking about levels, my friends, that are most unreliable. And let's all face that truth. I think we should by now: there are so many divorces in the world! Let's face that honestly. Now a person might say, "Well, now, I'm in love with my husband. My husband's in love with me. We've been married fifty years." Well, I think that's wonderful. I think that's wonderful, but ever be on the alert, my friends. If you have given him or her that much power, you will guarantee to suffer. For the power you have given to form, you have denied God. And that is why man's only suffering is his denial of God.

It's just like a person that has a job. All right. And they say, "Well, I'm not making very much money. The reason I'm not making very much money is because in the business I'm in, things are pretty bad and the way the government situation, etc., is." All right. They place themselves under the control, the power, and the influence of that level of consciousness and everybody in all the universes that thinks that way. They have denied the true source of their supply, which is God. And in denying the true source, they're going to suffer.

So whatever it is that we desire, whatever it is that we are seeking, let us remember where it really comes from. Now if we remember where it comes from, you see, no matter where we go, we can always tune in, because "God and I are a majority." God and you are a majority. So you see, you'll never be without your source of supply, if you truly recognize your true source of supply and you don't tell that infinite eternal Intelligence through whom or what it's to express to fulfill your desire. Now if you really do that, friends, you will never be in need and you will never have want. But you must always remember that. There is one source. Remember, it says in the Christian Bible, There shall be no worship of any God besides me, for I am a jealous God—this God of Jehovah. Well, what did the prophets mean? It meant exactly what they said. When you deny that one true Source, when you do that, you immediately cut yourself off from it and you have your idols here and they all have clay feet. There's never been an idol in the universe that didn't have clay feet and everybody knows that feet represent understanding. Well, that's why idols have clay feet: their understanding, you understand, is not perfect.

Maybe I'm listening to you too literally, but I sometimes have a hard time understanding why people would get married if they were reaching for a spiritual direction. I'm having a really hard time seeing that.

I think that's most understandable, why people would get married, though they're seeking a spiritual direction, in this sense—perhaps I can share this with you. People get married for a multitude of reasons. And now, perhaps, some get married for what they call a material security, emotional security. Now that does not mean that they're not seeking God or seeking a spiritual understanding, but it does mean that they are not on that level of consciousness. That doesn't mean good or bad.

Now, for example, how many people can find fulfillment for their emotional desires with a formless Divine Intelligence? How many? So we have in society what is known as marriage. And so that simply means two people who come together, who believe that they have some type of rapport—but you see, the sadness, of course—and this is the reason we have so many divorces in this world—is that the rapport is on an emotional level. It's not on a reasonable, spiritual, awakened level. You see, they're very compatible on certain levels of consciousness, but they don't stop to think. Now they, perhaps, say, "Now, let's see, we are compatible on four levels of consciousness." Well, look at the odds against them. There are eighty-one levels of consciousness and they're only compatible on four. Now most married people are compatible, I would say, on an average of four to six levels of consciousness. And through fighting and bickering over the years, they become compatible on more levels of consciousness, you see. But that isn't usually the way that it starts out.

And so, you know, the thing is about marriage—and I'm really not against it, but then, I'm not for it either—is that people have some rapport on certain levels of consciousness. And, you know, they say they want to share in marriage. Well, sharing only lasts so long before it becomes possession and when it becomes possession, you've had it. You either decide, "All right, this prison cell isn't too, too, too big, but it's not really too small. So I'll stay in it because, after all, I have this and this and that and that and that." Now I'm not saying that two people can't love each other: well, of course they do. Love's what makes the world go round and increases the population explosion. Obviously. But the thing is, what is it really based on?

What is it really based on? Could we not use the creative principle and again return to motive?

Absolutely, absolutely. Well, the question is, friends, What is the attraction in the first place? Now I think that we have to recognize that, number one. Because the attraction, of course, is the level of consciousness, you see. Maybe a fellow marries a girl because he likes the way she blinks her eyes or something. Or maybe he likes the way she walks or maybe he likes her weight or a multitude of things. Now I'm not saying there are not a few people—I'm sure that there are somewhere—that get married because they feel that, united together and sharing each other's lives, that they would stand a better chance of finding God or their true Source.

I am not one—perhaps it's because I am a bachelor—that thinks in any way that it's necessary to get married to have the fulfillment of life. I really don't think so. If that's the case, friends, then we should all have been born here married. I mean, otherwise, what kind of a world, what kind of a Divine Intelligence is operating? That just seems a little bit ridiculous to me. But you see, there are many happy marriages, friends. But remember, a marriage stays happy when the people involved make great effort to stay in their own vibration and they respect the right of the other individual to express their emotions in their ways. And, you see, sometimes that's known as separate rooms. But anyway, I'm sure it works out for everyone. Now, friends, you have a question here, please. Yes.

Does the Law of Merit enter here anywhere as far as whether you're married or not?

Oh, absolutely and positively! Goodness' sakes, I know many people—I know one lady, she's been married fourteen times. She's a client of mine. A very elderly woman. Some souls, they can't survive without being married. They're totally lost. You see, they're not able—many men are not able to function, let alone women, unless they're married or there is someone in the house. They can't cook their breakfast. They can't make their coffee, let alone darn their socks or wash their clothes or change the bedding. So you see, they're programmed that way, you know. And that's the way it is: they can't survive. They're totally miserable unless there's someone in the house to fight with when they want to fight and to make love with when they want to do the other. Otherwise, my friends, they would lose their sanity. Many people are that way. They can't live alone. It's impossible for them. No, no. They must have someone to, it's preferable to say, share with, but it usually means possess. Does that help with your question? Yes.

The discussion seems a bit flavored to this point. Could you or would you discuss the principle of marriage?

Well, I'll be happy to share my understanding of man's created principle of marriage, yes. I do not believe in a divine principle of marriage.

Could you repeat that?

I do not believe in a divine principle of marriage. But man's created principle of marriage, I'll be happy to share with you my understanding.

Well, that answers my question. Thank you.

You're more than welcome. My friends, is a soul whole and complete or is it only half a soul and has to have, here in a world of creation, its fulfillment? Now if the truth of the matter is that a soul is only half and that it must seek in another physical body its better half, then history has proven for thousands and thousands of years that it is a rare man—and that is even questionable—that's found his other half, because the divorce rate has proven it. So let us stop and think. Would a Divine Love, an Infinite Intelligence, establish such a world where a soul comes into form and it has to spend a lifetime looking for its other half in someone else? Maybe it goes through all kinds of emotional disaster and it still doesn't find it. Well, I don't know of anybody that's so bad they'd merit that type of a system. Now, I really, honestly don't, friends. Now I know we've spent a great deal of time on marriage. It must be the time of the year or the wedding bells hanging in the rafters. But whatever it is, I believe honestly in divine justice. Two people married can be very happy, if that's what they choose to be. But I do not accept, nor do I believe, that an individual must spend their lifetime to find their fulfillment of their own soul by going everyplace else to find someone else. That denies the divine right and individualization and completeness of the soul itself. Thank you.

If a man is self-sustaining and feels complete within himself and marries a woman who is also self-sustaining and complete within herself, wouldn't you say that's as close as you can get to divine love?

Well, now, that's a very fine presentation. But now, if a man and a lady are self-sustaining, whole, and complete within themselves, I'm sure you realize there would be no children. If they're whole and complete and self-sustaining in all their levels of consciousness, there would be no desire.

But there would have to be balance.

What's the balance?

The functions and the faculties.

Certainly. So therefore, they would not be whole and complete and self-sustaining in all of their levels, would they?

Well, they—

They couldn't be.

But they—

Could they?

They would be self-sustaining. Self-sustaining is a person that stands on his own two feet.

Well, they would certainly be expressing some degree of need to have procreation.

Well, everybody—

If man doesn't compute the need, he doesn't have the desire. You see, my friends—now, students, seriously, you cannot desire something that you do not accept a need of. And if you don't accept a need of something, you can't desire it. You have to first accept the need. You see, first there is the feeling, then there is the thought. And then, there is the act, in all creation and everything. So you have to first accept the need. And if you accepted a need, my friends, you wouldn't be whole, complete, and self-sustaining, now would you?

Are you saying no one is self-sustaining?

I'm saying this: that there are eighty-one levels of consciousness; that man has a choice on which levels he cares to express on. All right? Now, he can express and—it takes a little effort—make the choice not to express on certain levels of consciousness, where she or he accepts what's known as need. Now, if you don't accept the need, you don't have the desire. Do you understand? You cannot desire to eat food unless you accept the thought that you are hungry. Don't you see how simple it is? Don't you understand?

No, I don't.

What is it that you don't understand?

I don't understand why people cannot be self-sustaining by balancing the functions and the faculties. Isn't this what it's all about: balance?

The teaching is to balance the functions and the faculties inside of oneself.

Right.

All right?

Right.

Now, the balancing of the functions and the faculties does not, by balancing, mean that the individual must accept need. It doesn't mean that.

No, we shouldn't have to accept need.

But if you don't accept need, then you don't have the desire. I think if you will think about it—we have time just for, perhaps, two more questions, friends. We're running overtime. I'm sure if you will just give it some thought—the teaching does not deny man's right to express himself in any of the levels of consciousness. Perhaps where there's some misunderstanding is that a person may think that they should express on all eighty-one levels of consciousness in order to have balance. That is not necessarily so. Let's take, for example, level six. Say a person spent twenty years expressing on level six. Well, they've expressed enough energy on level six that they don't need to express on level six anymore. Do you understand?

I understand.

But they have all these other levels of consciousness that there's been hardly any expression on at all. You know, it's a known fact that when we turn into our forties that we start thinking of spiritual things, you see. Well, why do we wait until we're forty? Well, there's a biological change that starts taking place. I don't care what they call it, those are the facts of life. Yes. Perhaps that will help.

I don't know which discourse it is, but in one of the discourses in The Living Light, *it says that the spirit is helping to remove obstructions from your universe and do not worry about the effects. My mind began to wonder if the guides help us remove obstructions from our universe, what did we do to bring this about? For a week I have been having a terrible time with my thinking. I really have. I've been entertaining a thought so strongly. I don't know where it comes from, but it has awakened me at night. And this record has been going on and on, and tonight, all of a sudden, it's not here and I'm back up in that higher level of consciousness.*

I see.

Was this a spiritual influence, was the other a thought form, and what happened? Because I feel great tonight and I really have had an awful week.

Well, students, let us ever remember this: No matter where we are or what we are doing, we have the ability within ourselves to choose the level of consciousness that we choose or desire to express on. Now, it is true that a person may be in a lower level of consciousness and they may walk into a spiritual student group or study group or even into a church or they may go even on a mountaintop. They are very open and receptive to whatever is the strongest vibration in the atmosphere. Now, this is why, wherever the need is, the supply is forthcoming.

When a person gets emotional, their stability, their ability to remain stable and in their own vibration, starts to quiver and it starts to fall down. That's their foundation, their own aura, their own universe. And this is actual electromagnetic energies that are doing this. The person is wide open to the strongest feeling in the universe. Then, they become a part of that vibration. Then, they start suffering in those levels of consciousness. Now the question is—of course, we're the ones that did it. Now the thing is to say to ourselves, "Now, what thoughts or attitudes, what feelings did I have before descending down to this level of consciousness?" Because if you will review what kind of thinking, what attitude of mind, if you review your feelings, then you will know—each individual—they will know their pattern. So they will know that they must no longer permit themselves to think, to feel, in that particular way, because that guarantees the descent down there. Now, when you do that, then you nip it in the bud. You start thinking a certain way, you start feeling a certain way, you say, "That is it!" Because you know where your soul is going to descend to. You know that from experience, you see.

Now, remember, we might say, "All right, I feel this way when someone does this or doesn't do that. I feel this way, perhaps, when my husband is in a bad mood or someone else is going through a struggle, etc." All right, we now know how we feel, so we can say, "Now I can't change that person's thinking. I can't change that person's act. But I can change my receptivity to it."

That we can do, friends. You'll never change another human mind, but you can change your own. And in changing your own, only those souls receptive to your level of consciousness can come into your aura. Now that, my friends, is an absolute demonstration, which we can prove to ourselves repeatedly.

Let us have some refreshments. Thank you all very much. Please, those who want to carry on, kindly register tonight *[for the next semester of spiritual awareness classes]*, if at all possible. And remember, that that goes out into the universe returns unto us as an immutable law of creation. Thank you.

NOVEMBER 29, 1973

CONSCIOUSNESS CLASS 33 &

Good evening, students. We will begin our class, the first one of this year. Although next Thursday, as most all of you know, is the final registration for this course. There will be a few coming that weren't able to make it tonight.

Now, we're going to carry on with the basic format of the awareness classes. And to those who are new this evening, that is a period of reading from our study book, *The Living Light*, followed by the declaration of our affirmation, which is known as "Total Consideration"—which you all should have received—followed by our concentration and our meditation. After the concentration and meditation time, you will be permitted to ask whatever questions that you have of a spiritual nature. Now does everyone have their study book? Because that is necessary for the course. And I would like to mention, again, next Thursday is the absolute deadline for entering this course. So there will be a few students coming in next Thursday.

And, also, I would like to mention the policy here of the classes: and that is promptness. Now promptness is consideration. It is consideration for the rights of another human soul.

And promptness also is an expression of the students' ability to organize themselves. Now without organization in our lives, we have chaos. And when we have chaos and confusion, we have nothing but problems. So I know that you will all make the effort to demonstrate the level of consciousness that you are truly on by being prompt at all of your classes.

Now I would like to give a short introduction of what these awareness classes are all about. I know that many of you—and it's most pleasing to witness—as students, are demonstrating the Law of Continuity. One of man's most difficult habits is to stick with anything long enough to be victorious. It seems just before the victory, in any endeavor, we have a tendency to quit and to seek something else. In these classes you will come to know that man himself is the law; that he establishes the law within his own being; that we live in a world of form, of which desire is the propulsion. We do not teach an annihilation of desire in these classes, because to annihilate desire would be to annihilate the form itself; without desire, our soul cannot remain in any form.

And so it is that we look around in our lives, and we see that we express desire and we experience what is commonly referred to as suffering. Now you will gain the understanding, as time passes, that suffering is nothing more than the experiencing of an event in our lives that we have not consciously desired. However, because all things that man experiences are the direct effect of laws that he and he alone has established, we see that, in truth, suffering is an effect of an imbalance or a lack of control of our own desire world. For example, if man desires to eat a certain food and he enjoys the food and he eats more than the laws of nature dictate are in his best interest, then he will have the experience, of course, which is known as suffering. And so it is, my friends, that we attempt to show you a way to rise above this flux and flow, this duality of creation, that you may be objective and be free from the entrapment of what is known as the illusion and delusion of creation.

Our teachings are to be with a thing, person, or place, and never be a part thereof: to be in this world and not to be a part of this world. Now many students have asked, "Well, just exactly what does that mean?" That means, my friends, no matter what experience that you encounter, no matter what you do or don't do, that you, your spirit, may view the experience from a level of consciousness where peace reigns supreme. Now that level of consciousness is within all human souls and it is possible for all souls to attain. The attainment, however, is reached by the effort to balance our own being. Each person knows what is balance for them. It is not something that someone else has to tell us.

How do we know what is balance for us in our lives? My friends, that is the benefit of the effect of imbalanced desire, which is known as suffering. When we suffer, depending on the extent that we do suffer, we start to awaken within ourselves and we start to reexamine our life and we start to look at our life patterns and see where they have led us to this point in so-called time. And so it is that we are freed from these entrapments, when we make the effort.

Now in this course you will find that through acceptance, appreciation, you will gain a greater freedom and a greater understanding. But you, and you alone, must make the effort. You will gain from these courses and from this class whatever it is that you put into them, for man does not receive anything that he does not put something into. So you put your time in, you put your effort in, you put your interest in, and you make the spiritual effort to apply some of the teachings that are shared with you.

We do not have any particular pattern where you must go rigidly by this or by that. But by an effort to experience a fuller life, a more complete life, by that thought, that interest, and that application, you will indeed experience it.

Now if there are any questions concerning what we have stated what these classes are about, you may feel free to ask them at this time. And if not, then we will go on with the reading of one of our discourses.

The greatest difficulty, for all of us, is to apply the knowledge and the understanding that we gain. And the reason that it is difficult to apply something new in our lives is because we are habitually addicted by the patterns that we have established for ourselves. And it is not easy for me or for you or for anyone in this world to make those changes. But because it is not easy, does not mean that it is not possible. Because, indeed, it is possible. Are there any questions at this time?

All right. If there are no questions, let us turn our Living Light study book [*The Living Light*] to Discourse 40.

[A student reads Discourse 40 aloud.]

Before going into our meditation time, does everyone have the "Total Consideration" affirmation? You will need to learn it because we usually turn off the lights for our meditation at the time that we say it. However, this evening we will leave the lights on.

Now, I know that many of you do meditations daily; some of you do them spasmodically. And, of course, like anything, our growth is dependent upon our own continuity and our own efforts. But in our meditations here, we do spend the first few moments and few minutes in concentration on peace. Peace is the power itself. Peace is what they call God, the Divine Infinite Intelligence. It also brings balance into the inner mind. So when we go into our meditation this evening and you sit relaxed in your chairs and you concentrate upon peace, do a little bit of slow, but deep, breathing, and let that peace of the Divine Intelligence permeate your entire being. After you have concentrated for a few minutes upon peace, then let the mind become that great stillness, that perfect blank. Following that meditation time, you may have your manifestations or your experiences from whatever levels of consciousness that you have managed to attain. So let us sit back and say our "Total Consideration" affirmation and, after that, if our chairman will kindly turn off the lights, then we will go into our meditation.

[After saying the affirmation, the class meditates for a few minutes.]

Now in our question-and-answer period, you may feel free, as I stated earlier, to ask any questions that you have of a spiritual nature. And if you will be so kind as to raise your hands, I will be more than happy to share with you my understanding of your expression and level of consciousness. So if you'll just raise your hands, please. Yes.

Would you please give your understanding of God?

Yes, thank you very much. And the lady has asked, Would we share our understanding of what is called God. Once before in one of our classes that question came up and, my good friends, we must realize if we understand God to be Truth itself and this Peace that passeth all understanding, that when we, in our humble way, try to make an effort to define it, then we're going to limit it to our own understanding and our own limitations. Truth is beyond definition, as freedom is beyond limitation. And so we can only state that man's God, his understanding of God, of course, is ever equal to his own personal understanding.

I wonder if you would explain the purpose of comets, like the comet Kohoutek. Is it on its evolutionary path to become something else? Is it inhabited by forms that are within our present concept? And could you tell us . . .

Thank you very much. In reference to your question on this particular comet that has been viewed of recent time, number one: Is it inhabited with forms of our conception that we would understand? In that respect, it is not, not on our present level of consciousness. It is a very natural phenomenon, as the comet, like people and all forms, is on its evolutionary path and in its growth process. Because what is one form this moment is guaranteed to be different the next. So it is nothing more than a natural phenomenon. I know throughout the ages, there have been many superstitions attached to comets. They have been, supposedly, the cause of wars and all types of catastrophes. Of course, we understand in this understanding that if a sufficient number of people believe a thing, then that becomes the thing for them, because it is created by, of course, our own creative principle of our own depths of our own mind. But other than a natural phenomenon, nothing else is attached to it. Thank you. Yes.

In Discourse 19, there was mention of the mantras that have been given to you—

That is correct.

I was asked to find them in order—

They are not published. They are given to some private students during their private classes. You, I'm sure, are aware that I do give private classes to members of the Association.

But they are not available—

They are not available for public use. That is correct. Thank you very much. Yes.

Perhaps you can clarify to some of the other students that in our soul's unfolding, we experience some manifestations. Especially to some of the newer students, this seems to be sort of an excitement, something that is very encouraging, something that you always are anticipating. Therefore, in our eagerness, we are anxious to, sort of, get a definition of this—a clarification. And I understand that there is a seventy-two-hour rule that should be, more or less, observed. Otherwise, the energy dissipates of this particular manifestation or experience that one has received. And I thought that maybe you could enlighten us on that. And I want to apologize to my guides and helpers and some of the other students for bending their ear a little bit too much last night.

Thank you very much. The student has brought up a very important point, in reference to seeing different things in different dimensions. We have an understanding here that there are eighty-one levels of consciousness and that we communicate with various different levels—some of them, of course, of a spiritual nature. A great deal of it is of an astral nature, a mental nature, and etc. Because, after all, let us face the truth. Now, I want to say one thing to all of my students that has not been brought up before and it's a very important thing. Whatever it is that we see, hear, or sense that excites the senses, is not— and I repeat—*is not* of a spiritual nature. If you will get that understanding into your consciousness, then, my friends, you will seek the light of eternity that frees your soul. Now I am not saying that psychic science does not serve its purpose. After all, this is an integral part of the science of Spiritualism and this Association. But that that excites the senses is not, *is not* of a spiritual nature. That that brings you peace that passeth all understanding, that awakens within your being a better way to think, a better way to live, is of a spiritual nature.

Now, we live in a world of form and form has, as its expression, what is known as the senses. We have these senses, these feelings. The reason that our students are taught to go by their feelings, what we call clear-sensing, is because the eyes deceive, and so do the ears. But when we first unfold our clairsensing, our true inner feeling—some people call it intuition— when that is the first thing that is unfolded, then, when your eyes view a vision and when your ears hear a voice, you will be able to test that vision, because you will be able to test it by your own soul feeling or knowing. Then, you will know beyond a shadow of any doubt whether or not, as Saint Paul put it in the Bible, to test the spirit that it is good, of God. Then you will know. No one will have to tell you. And this is one of the main reasons that we stress in this Association, Spiritualism, its philosophy and its religion, brought into balance with its science of communication.

My good friends, it is critically important that you get into your consciousness the laws that govern communication and not communication itself. For if you do not get into your understanding *and* your application, daily, of the laws that govern the science, then you will be controlled by the science and it will not be of any great benefit to your soul and its eternal journey. First we must study the laws that govern our mind, our body, and our soul. Having studied those laws, having applied them, then we will be the living demonstration of how to control our own lives.

Now, there have been many, and are many, philosophies and religions in the world that teach one to bypass, so to speak, the so-called psychic realms and what is known as the astral traps. The reason—and I spent four hours today counseling with a lady who is ready to take her eternal flight to the beyond, who had requested some instruction on her passing. And it's very important and I would like to share that with my students this evening. When we leave this physical body, we are going to experience what is known in this understanding as the reflections or projections of our own subconscious. We are going to pass through those dimensions and, hopefully, not be trapped in them. What is important, in passing through those dimensions, is to keep the eye single upon the eternal Light, known as God. If you have any strong, potent desires here and now, you will view them as temptations when you leave your physical body. If you are distracted and you stop with the lesser light, then you will be trapped on that level of consciousness. How long you will remain there, of course, depends upon your ability with self-discipline and control.

Now, I admit that there is great fascination viewing into the other dimensions. But I also admit that for multitudes of people there is great fascination viewing the television set or going to the movies. Now what is in our best interest? Is it in our best interest to be free while yet in form? Or is it in our best interest to entertain our senses? Surely, there has to be some degree of balance. Now, the student brought up a very valid point: that when one has experiences with these other dimensions, that they keep it to themselves for a minimum of seventy-two hours.

That has proven, over the years, to be most beneficial, because within seventy-two hours the enthusiasm of expressing what is commonly referred to as the ego has an opportunity, a chance, to get a little education.

We have repeatedly stated with our unfolding mediums and healers and students in this Association, to give, in the work that you have to do for God, what you have to give, to care less what the individual does with it. Now, I know, as a medium for over thirty-some years, that it is most difficult in the unfolding processes not to express these different experiences. Now what really happens when we express that we saw a light or we saw someone who had crossed the veil? Are we using that expression to strengthen our faith, that we really did have that experience? Let us honestly ask ourselves that question. Of what need is it within our being to share those personal, and, ofttimes, very sacred experiences, if they are truly of a spiritual nature, with our friends, our associates, and everyone else? What is the need within our own being? We must be very honest in asking ourselves that question.

Seek first, my good friends, the kingdom of God, and that is the throne of peace where all things in your life will be brought into balance. If you will truly seek that first, whatever is necessary for your soul unfoldment and for your own good and evolution will be added unto you. Do not seek the science of communication in and of itself. If you do, you will indeed guarantee for yourself a great deal of experiences that few in this world are ready for. Now, please do not misunderstand. Communication serves a very fine purpose, if it is wisely used. But it is not, my friends, the thing for any wise soul to seek.

I hope that helps with your question. Does someone else have a question?

Does the soul grow? Does a spirit grow? Or is it the consciousness that grows? Is there a need for soul growth or is a soul

complete already and then the mind grows? Does thinking grow?
I think you know what I'm trying to express. Is it spirit or soul
that grows?

Thank you very much. In our understanding, the spirit is
formless and free and, therefore, there is nothing it could grow
to. And our understanding, also, is that the soul is the covering of the spirit. And in other words, the Spirit, known as God,
the Divine, the Intelligence, is individualized by the covering of
soul. It is the soul that *expands* and its purpose in its evolution
is to expand and to raise the rates of vibration of the forms in
which it is encased. We are a physical body, a mental body, we
are a soul body, and several other bodies, including a vital body.
And so our soul expands, that is, it learns many lessons. But
our spirit is that formless and free Divine Intelligence that is
expressing through the soul.

Hope that's helped you with your question. And I think
that some of our new students this evening might, by this time,
have the courage to ask a few questions, if you have some. Just
kindly raise your hand. Now remember, I know, especially the
lady over there has some questions in her mind. Not that I'm
a mind reader, but I know that she does. And I want to express
at this time: Ofttimes a question entertains our mind and we
feel, "Well, I don't want to ask it because I might seem a little
bit dumb or stupid or something." And so we don't ask it, you
see. We get a feeling of timidity and whatever other feelings that
accompany it. Remember this, my good students, if a question
is important enough to entertain your thought, then it is important enough for you to speak it forth. And with that, would you
like to ask a question?

I don't think I have one.

You don't? You have just been sitting there thinking?

Yes, I've been thinking.

All right. We will let it go.

The universal laws, are they quoted in The Living Light? *Maybe you could clarify this. Are there, also, eighty-one laws, as the eighty-one laws or levels of awareness?*

The laws governing form are unlimited, because form itself is unlimited. You see, its variety is beyond what is called limitation. There is no limit to the creation or the creative principle.

Now there are universal laws that govern the universes of which we are a minor universe and a part thereof. And man *is* a law unto himself because man is a part of the universe itself. Do you understand? So, for example, a universal law is that all forms are composed of an electromagnetic energy field. That is a universal law. All form—it doesn't matter what the form is—is composed of that. It is a universal law that like attracts like and becomes the Law of Attachment. It is a universal law that all things evolve. It is a universal law that that which comes from a thing returns to the thing from whence it came. That, also, is a universal law. Did that help with your questions?

I was thinking, more or less, of the laws that we read about in The Living Light, *such as the Law of Love, the Law of Life* . . .

The Law of Harmony. The Law of Unity. Yes, those are laws that govern those levels of consciousness. Yes.

And remember, consciousness is not something that you can put into limitation, because consciousness is the Divine or God itself, you see. Yes. Now many people, you see, they misunderstand what we refer to as God. We understand God to be a divine, neutral Power that sustains all things and controls none, in the sense that it interferes with the expression of the individualized form, you understand. See, God is not something that passes out the good and hands out the bad to the others, or judges us. That is not the God that we understand in Serenity.

You were mentioning, with regard to laws, that there are several universal laws. Are there laws on different levels, that have their sources on different levels?

That is correct.

Could you speak a bit more on this at this time?

The difference between a universal law and a created law is one is limited, the other is limitless. Now universal laws are without limitation. They apply at all times and in all ways. Then, you have laws that are known as the created laws.

Now, for example, a man thinks a certain way. He establishes a law for himself. Because when he thinks a different way, he, of course, pays the price or he has the effect thereof. Now that is a created law that is created by that particular form or that individual. And that is a limited law. In other words, that law was given birth, do you understand? And therefore, it shall know its own death. It shall return unto its own source, you see, and destroy itself. But a universal law is a law that has always been in the universe. And, having always been, it will always be. Such as a few of the universal laws that were mentioned.

Now, when it is stated that man is a law unto himself, man, his soul, has entered a form that has certain tendencies to establish certain laws for itself. That's what man has merited. Now man, also—by man I mean all humanity—is in the process of changing these laws that he alone has created for himself. Now that changing is a renewing of the mind. That is what makes man free, is this renewing of his mind. It is a breaking down of established patterns which have become laws for him or for the individuals. Do you have another question? Go ahead, please.

Yes. I was so fascinated with what you were saying regarding the renewing of the mind. We were given, in our last course, a discussion on the creative principle, and the principle through which we create all of our experiences and so on. Well, now we're also speaking of becoming aware of our awareness, our growth, of becoming aware that we are all one and so on.

That is correct.

So in one sense, we seem to have this—we're spreading out all these creations all over, and yet at the same time we're all evolving toward becoming one. Could you speak a bit on that?

Yes, I would be more than happy to share with you our understanding. First of all, we're speaking of different levels of consciousness. The part of us that is whole, complete, perfect, and free is a part of the one Whole, known as the Spirit, of which we are all an inseparable part. Some people call that God. All right, now that Divine Intelligence, expressing through form, is variety. Variety is the manifestation of the Divine. And so if we're looking on the levels of consciousness of what we call creation, then we see, of course, a great variety; and we see discord, disease, instead of seeing harmony. Now the reason that we see that is because we are not looking beyond the covering, the illusion of creation herself. Creation, as you know, we've discussed, its very principle is the Law of Duality. And when this split or duality takes place, then this energy is released to create this variety.

Now, the mind, its very nature—because it is of the creative principle—its nature is a constant process of creation. If you remove from the mind this constant panorama of events for any extended period of time, the mind will lose its own balance. And then, it will no longer be able to express itself. Because its very nature is a constant, continuous panorama.

So we must go beyond this mind to find the true perspective, to be able to see that we are using what we call mind as we drive an automobile. But that is not where it's at. We are not the mind. It is a vehicle. We are no more a mind than we are a body. The body is a grosser vehicle of which its true cause is the mind.

Now, the mind is a vehicle for the soul's expression in its evolutionary process and according to the laws that this individualized soul itself has set into motion. For example, we know that some souls enter this world with very intelligent minds and some not so intelligent. Some bodies are very, very strong physically; some very weak. And so it is, my friends, that we have repeatedly tried to instruct the student to go beyond the mind and there you will find the truth. And when you find that, of course, you are freed.

Because the mind continues to move from one event, from one creation to another, another, another, another, and it is an eternal process. But we must take, through discipline, mental, spiritual discipline, control long enough to go beyond the panorama of what is known as mind stuff. I hope that helps with your question. Yes, you have another question. Then, I must get to the other students.

Yes. It seems as we go through creation, our mind goes through creation, we have an apparent expanding of creation, like creation just keeps expanding and expanding and expanding. There's more and more and more and more of this variety.

Why does that happen?

Well, that's kind of what I was getting at. When our path of evolution seems to be returned to the One, and yet our expression seems to be we're spreading out.

Nothing multiplies in anyplace in anything like love. And so it is that it is love or energy expressing through the vehicle known as mind that continues to expand outward. That's the mind, but not the spirit. So we must take hold of the reins and pull our soul inward to find our own spirit and find the truth itself.

I have a question regarding tonight's discourse. It says, "Think before the word is spoken for each word vibrates on the scale of expression." I have two questions, actually. First of all, regarding the scale of expression, and, secondly, Does it matter what level we are in or is it the word itself that vibrates?

The statement is in *The Living Light*, Think before you speak the word for it vibrates on a level of expression. Is that right? That's not literal, but it's close.

"For each word vibrates on the scale of expression."

"For each word vibrates on the scale of expression." A scale of expression is a level of awareness. Now, when you are communicating with anyone, before you open the mouth to speak the word, you think about that word. And when you think about it, it will help you to become aware of the level of consciousness of the person that you are speaking to.

Now, you know that many people can say many words, but someone can pass you in your daily activities and only say a few words, but they make a change in your thinking and a change in your life. Is that not correct?

That's true.

That means that the person who spoke the words was on a level of consciousness that was the same that you were on at the time the words were being spoken. Therefore, there is, and was, what is known as a true rapport. And this is why, if we would only stop, you understand, and think before we speak— because many times we speak and instead of bringing peace, we irritate the person terribly. Now why is it that we irritate them? Well, it's quite simple. Perhaps—and probably so—the level of consciousness that the individual was on—they were enjoying the level of consciousness, you understand. And you spoke some words which jolted them from that level of consciousness and they did not appreciate being awakened from their level of satisfaction. Is that understandable?

Yes, sir.

And so we have in this world so many problems, it seems, with what we call communication. Because we don't stop to think about the word that we're going to speak, and in thinking about that word, become aware of the level of consciousness, you understand, not only of ourselves—because, you see, my friends, you can't be aware of the level of consciousness of another human soul unless you are aware of the level of consciousness of your own soul at any given moment. That's what the exercise is about.

Thank you.

You're more than welcome. And there's someone else who's waiting.

Would you give your understanding on how emotion, alcohol, and marijuana affect our growth and our mind and our body?

Yes, thank you very much. I'm sure that would be an interesting discussion to everyone present. And your interest lies in how certain—you want to know about alcohol, marijuana, and what else?

Emotion.

You want to know about the addiction to it or the use of it?

The use.

There is a difference.

Well, both.

If we are discussing the addiction, which means that we cannot express a fairly normal and balanced life without its use, then we're speaking of addiction. You understand? Because we must get our footing solid before we go on with this discussion. And you want to know how it affects your spiritual growth?

Yes.

Yes. If we—no matter who we are—are controlled by any chemical, you understand, to the point that we lose our emotional balance and our reason when we are deprived of the chemical, then it most certainly and positively is affecting what we call our spiritual growth.

Of course, now this is a very individual thing. Now a person may choose to state, or to think, "Well, everybody has an addiction." Well, now if we want to look at it in that level, that is true. We can say that we are addicted to waking up in the morning and brushing our teeth. All right? And we can say that we are addicted, from necessity, to holding down some type of a job, so we have some money to fulfill our pleasures and our desires. So we can expand what we call addiction into many areas.

However, the wise students look at themselves and they honestly ask themselves, "How much control am I losing?" or "How much control have I already lost?" If you can be without the fulfillment of the desire and not be emotionally disturbed, still be able to function with reason and with logic, then it is not yet that detrimental to that particular individual. But I honestly and seriously question, in addictions and habits, anyone that can lay it aside and not have some emotional reaction. Because it is the emotions that have the need for it. It is not the soul. It is not your faculty of reason. It is not your intelligence. It isn't even your body, in the beginning, that has the need for the fulfillment of the desire. Does that help with your question?

Yes. May I ask you another?

Yes, you may.

What's the best way to change those habit patterns when you have them, so the emotions won't be affected?

That is entirely dependent, of course, upon the particular individual. Now, first off, the habit is serving, whatever the habit may be, you understand—because we're talking about addiction—and habit—to anything—the habit is serving a purpose emotionally. The first and wisest thing to do is to find out what emotional vacuum it is fulfilling. Having decided, of course, and having become aware of what emotional vacuum it is fulfilling for the particular individual, then a man is on his way to his own cure. Because he knows his own cause.

Now, say, for example, that the emotional problem or the vacuum is a lack of attention or a lack of love or a lack of affection or there are a multitude of lacks that the mind computes. Well, then a person simply sits down with himself and decides how he can get the fulfillment of his need without some particular habit that he wishes to outgrow. Is that helpful to you?

Thank you.

You're more than welcome. Now someone else has been waiting. Yes.

I don't know if it's a matter of semantics or what, but I was curious when you were talking about mind, and you said that the mind will drive a car. And I just want to understand, because my thought had always been that there is a brain and a mind, and your mind controls your brain, which is more of a computer. So if you could help me out with that . . .

That is very, very true.

Thank you.

The brain is simply a vehicle through which the mind is expressing, but the mind itself is simply a vehicle through which the soul is expressing.

OK, it's one step further.

And the soul is simply a vehicle through which the divine, free Intelligence, known as Spirit or God, is expressing. See, all things that are form—and mind is form, and soul is form— all things that are form are vehicles for the expression of the Divine Intelligence, known as God. Does that help with that? Clarify it? Thank you very much.

We're told to speak our affirmation with feeling. And this feeling registers in the universe to magnetize it and to go on to better purposes. What about every word that we speak? We do not speak every word with feeling. And we've been told that every word is registered. Well, we don't speak every word with feeling and we certainly say a lot of things, a lot of jabbering all day long that has no feeling or sense behind it. Do we have to work our way through all of this when we get to the spirit side of life? Or is it just the things that we have said, either negatively or positively, with feeling?

Thank you very much. And in clarification of your statement, all words spoken are accompanied by feeling. We are not consciously aware of the feeling. For example, a person says, "Well, I just talked on the telephone. I had no feelings whatsoever. It was simply a business transaction." Well, we had a feeling. But, you see, we have computed in our minds, unless we have a certain emotional sensation in our being, that there is no feeling. That is not true. There is feeling with every word that is spoken.

Now, the feeling, of course, with these words that we speak— and we've become so habituated, it seems, to talking so much in the world that we are not aware. It's just like washing your hands, you know. How many people go in and wash their hands and they are consciously aware of the sensation of the water running on their hands? Well, we're no longer aware because we've done it so much. But that does not mean that there isn't a feeling and a sensation of the skin as the water goes over the hands, because there is. But, you see, we've got to the point, from habit, that we are no longer consciously aware of that. And so it is as we speak words. We have spoken so many in the world that we are no longer consciously aware of how we feel as we are speaking. But we are still feeling, because there is no word that's ever spoken that is not accompanied by a feeling.

Now, a person, you see—and it's easily demonstrated. You carry on a conversation with an individual and after you've carried on the conversation, you ofttimes become aware you don't feel so good. Or you become aware that you feel much better. Well, that's only a living demonstration, my friends, that you're finally becoming aware that you are feeling all the time, but you just weren't aware of it, you see.

I have two questions. One is, I wonder if you would be so kind as to name the nine bodies. Secondly, does the soul have the same color before incarnation into this form? And also, does it maintain the same color while it's in the form? And does it do that as well out of this form?

Thank you. It's the same color; it's different shades. Same color, different shade. Yes, because, you understand, it expands and gains many experiences.

Now in reference to the mentioning of the bodies, we've mentioned before that you have a physical body, you have a mental body, you have a vital body, you have a spiritual body, you have an astral body, you have a universal body. Several of the bodies have been mentioned.

Now our classes are usually geared, of course, for one hour each Thursday evening. If there are any more questions, I'll be happy to share with you. If there are not, then we can go and have refreshments. Yes.

In regard to the student's question on addiction, I believe you were saying about trying to fulfill the need in a different way, maybe, so that you don't have addiction: is that correct?

To fill the vacuum. You see, there has to be a vacuum in the emotional body in the first place. There has to be an acceptance that—the emotional body has to first accept that it is lacking something. Do you understand? And that creates what we call a vacuum. Now, once the vacuum is filled, the addiction no longer serves that purpose, because it's filled with something else. Do you understand? Yes. And so what was your question in that reference?

Well, what I would like to know, if part of you realizes that you don't have any need . . .

Yes?

And you can observe this other part of you expressing a need . . .

Yes?

Is there a way to handle that situation?

Well, there most certainly is. Absolutely and positively. First off, you have an objective acceptance and realization that there is a part of your being, one of the levels of consciousness— and in this particular case we're discussing, it's known as the emotional level—that has what it computes is a need. There's a vacuum. All right, now, you, being seated on a throne of responsibility and reason to your own spirit and your own soul, looking objectively at how that level of consciousness feels, you can, using your reason, choose something that would be of benefit for your own growth to fill the vacuum. Do you understand?

You see, my friends, it simply is that, of course, we've got ourselves into certain patterns. Now in the first place, as we're expressing from youth onward, we have found that by doing this or doing that, etc., according to what we have accepted, we feel this vacuum or this need for expression. Do you understand? Now some people may say, "Well, I just need affection." Well, that's what they have accepted.

But think what the mind does. So the mind says, "All right, well, I need affection. And I get my affection in this way. Period." Do you understand? Well, now that is the law that that individual's soul has set into motion. Now that is not a universal law. Because, you see, if the emotional body says, "I need affection"—which we all know is recognition and attention, is that not correct? What else would one call it? So I'm sure we'll all agree that it's recognition or attention or energy that we really need. God's manifestation is divine variety. My goodness, you can get that by looking at a tree or something else. But, you see, it is a matter of a reprogramming of our own computer. Do you understand? Does that help you?

Yes, it does.

You see? Now, when a person goes through a process of reprogramming their computer, it's not the easiest thing in the world. Because now, for example, a person says, "Well, I was married and I had all this affection and this love." Well, that's how they got it at that time. That's what they accepted. A lot of people are married and say they don't get any at all. Because I counsel people and I know. All right. Now another person, you see, they could go out and look at the ocean and the seashore, they could see a bird flying in the sky, and they could get the same feeling, if that was what they wanted to accept. Do you

understand? But you have to make the effort to put that programming into your computer.

Then, do we actually create that attention?

Well, do we create the attention? We create the opportunity
for the attention or energy to express itself. Yes, we do do that.
People do it in many strange ways, but they do do that. They
create the opportunity, yes. Yes.

*Do you think there would be opportunity in the future classes,
like next week and so on, to discuss the forecast you had given
last Sunday?*

Of what benefit would it be to the students, do you feel? Of
what benefit would it be?

Clarification on things that were mentioned in the forecast.

You mean clarification for your own acceptance and understanding, is that what you mean?

Yes.

I think that would be better handled on a private basis, for we
have many things to discuss concerning the laws governing us.

Thank you very much.

Thank you very much. Are there any other questions? If
not, friends, let us go have refreshments. Thank you all very,
very much.

JANUARY 3, 1974

CONSCIOUSNESS CLASS 34 ✬

It is the policy of the Serenity Association not to impose its
teachings and its philosophy upon anyone, but it is our policy to
share with you our understanding of the purpose of life, as we
have found it to this point.

Now we will continue with our regular format, which is: we
will open up our classes with a reading of one of the discourses
from *The Living Light,* our study book. Everyone will need a

study book for this course and any future courses. Following the reading of the discourses, we will have our period of meditation. Now after the lights are turned out for our meditation we will, in unison, speak forth the "Total Consideration" affirmation. Following that, we will concentrate upon peace, for we understand that peace is the power of the Divine, of God, that brings a perfect balance into our life. Following this concentration period upon peace, for a few moments, we will have our meditation.

Now meditation, to us, means a complete stillness of the mind. The mind is blank and there are no thoughts within it. Following that meditation period, you will have what is known as manifestation. That means you may have different experiences, either with your feelings, which, of course, are the most accurate, or with your sight or with your hearing.

After the meditation period, we will have an open discussion, which means you are free to raise your hands and ask any questions of a spiritual nature. Now many students, I know, are a bit hesitant in asking their questions, because they can't seem to decide whether or not it is of a spiritual nature. Well, my good friends, anything that is important enough to entertain our thought is certainly important enough to our lives to speak it forth, if we want to know. Therefore, all questions, directly or indirectly, are of a spiritual nature.

Now I know they're presented in many ways. It is not the purpose of this class or this course to show you how to become a millionaire. That is your prerogative by applying the natural laws that are shared here with you. And so in these courses we will attempt to share with you our understanding of bringing a balance into your life. For when we bring balance, friends, then we truly find peace. And when we find peace, we know inside of ourselves what is, in truth, the purpose of our life. Some of us, already, have been giving thought to why we're down here. Certainly it means more than building a house or buying an automobile or all of those different things and, indeed, it does.

[A student reads Discourse 31 aloud. Following this, the class meditates.]

Now you may feel free to ask any questions that you may have. So if you will just raise your hands, please, I will be happy to share with you our understanding concerning your question.

On the affirmation that we are saying ["Total Consideration" See the appendix for the text of the affirmation.], *is any part of it dealing in the—well, I realize it deals with levels of consciousness. As an example, the last line would be in the superconscious. Would any other part of that deal with the magnetic or electrical flow?*

Yes, in reference to your question on the affirmation, Is the superconscious expressing in that affirmation? That is your basic question, isn't it? Now remember, friends, it is the perfect balance between the electric and the magnetic fields, of which all forms are a part; it is the perfect balance that is the superconscious. That *is* the neutrality. That is where peace reigns supreme. So in reference to your question, the entire affirmation is a balancing of the magnetic and electric fields, which would be an expression of the superconscious, yes.

We just read in Discourse 31 about the Law of Disassociation. Could you tell us how, in our daily lives, we can best begin knowing how to put this into practice?

In reference to your question, How can we best put into practice the disassociation, which, of course, we understand is an attitude of mind? Now, a person is able to reach some degree of disassociation when they bring their faculty of reason to the fore for expression.

Now we teach, Keep faith with reason, for reason will transfigure you. We all understand—most of us, I'm sure, do—that every expression, every action that we express is a reaction to an action that is taking place within us. Now when we're about our day-to-day acts and activities, a multitude of times in the course of a day, we are reacting to someone else's emotion, to someone else's desire, to someone else's attitude of mind. And because we continue to react to others, to circumstances and conditions around and about us, we are robbed, by our own acts, by our own choice, we are robbed of this peace that passeth all understanding. However, we do have within ourselves the ability to make a choice at any given moment and not be affected by or react to the emotional expressions and to the desires of people around and about us. However, that choice is only possible through some degree of discipline and self-control. Control of our own being.

Now when we make a greater effort at disciplining our own minds, a greater effort at the control of expressing our own emotions and desires, when we do that, we can and we shall experience this great peace. It is not an easy thing to work at disassociation, for the natural or, let us say, the common process of the human form is to react to stimuli. Now whether the stimulus is seemingly from without or within, we are constantly in this process of reacting. Therefore, it behooves the students to make a greater effort in daily meditation and concentration upon peace. Because when they are in their daily activities, if they have established a daily concentration-meditation time, organized it in an organized way, then when they are tempted to react, they can stop themselves and still that mind by coming into rapport to the moment of their daily meditation. I hope that helps you with your question.

The Law of Harmony—are functions and faculties involved in the Law of Harmony? Harmony, rhythm, and unity being the faculties, and health, wealth, and happiness being the functions thereof. That's the way I understand it.

That is correct.

However, there were some fellow students that disagreed with this interpretation and I'm a little confused on it.

Yes. I'm sure you respected their right to disagree.

Oh, certainly.

Yes. And that is one thing we must remember, friends—and when I say "friends," let us, for the benefit of our new students in this class, perhaps first share our understanding of what friendship really is. We understand that true friendship, being use and not abuse, respects the rights of difference and, therefore, will weather any storm.

Now if everyone agreed with us, there would be no growth, there would be no evolution, for there would be no challenge inside of ourselves to make the necessary changes. Therefore, we look around the world and see the great wisdom of God's manifestation, known as variety. It is my understanding, from what you have stated, that this "Law of Harmony is my thought" is the balancing between those functions mentioned and those soul faculties. Is that your understanding?

Yes, sir.

That is also my understanding. However, I respect the rights of the students to disagree with that understanding. Because we all know—most of us present—that there are eighty-one levels of consciousness and it is rare to find another individual on your level of consciousness at the moment that you are expressing anything. Does that help with your question?

Yes, sir. Thank you very much.

Thank you very much.

I wonder if you would discuss courage, your understanding of courage. And would you discuss it in relation to patience and faith? And would you also give us the corresponding function to courage?

I'll share with you as much as I am able to. I understand that courage is the ability to express a level of consciousness of which we have become firmly convinced is right for us. In reference to courage and the corresponding faculties—and you've asked a question concerning faith and patience—it takes some degree, of course, of courage to sustain what we call faith. Because when we are trying to express faith in anything, it is a matter of a growth process. A person may say, "Well, I have faith that life is eternal." And consequently, they're going through an expression with that particular faith which requires patience. Now, they may also, in that expression of their faith and their patience, come to a time, a point in time, when it is necessary to express what is known as courage. Now we want to remember something about courage, friends. Truth needs no defense. You cannot defend what is truly truth. You can defend, if you choose, your understanding of truth, but truth, in and of itself, needs no defense. Now if you are expressing truth, when you express it, you have a certain belief concerning it. That is what you defend; that is when courage expresses itself. So let us bear in mind that truth to one, to anyone, is individually perceived; in and of itself, it is truth and the light. I hope that's helped with your question. I know that all of your question was not answered, but we may come to it at another time.

Because I'm striving hard to achieve the Law of Harmony, I wonder how the Law of Harmony fits into the creative principle.

The less we strive to express harmony, the more harmony we will express. Now, first of all, when we decide that we must strive to express harmony, what we have accepted in mind, in thought, you understand, is that it takes a struggle and that it takes a great effort. It is not a matter of gaining harmony. It is a matter of letting go: just releasing what is standing in the way of the divine natural flow, which brings balance into our life. Now, where most of us seem to fail, on what we call the Law of Harmony, is that we decide what is harmony for us. You understand, it seems that at times we become more intelligent than the Infinite Divine Intelligence. Then, we decide that we're going to tell that great Intelligence what harmony is for us.

Now some people have computed into their minds that harmony is having a house with a two-car garage and a couple of television sets and all of the frills that go with it. Well, that is not the harmony of the peace that passeth understanding. I am not saying that with that harmony that those things will not come to us. I am saying that, in the seeking of harmony, it is not a matter of a struggle or a strife: it is a matter of acceptance. A man can experience the divine harmony whether or not he's in the cold or out of the cold. Do you understand? Does that help with your question?

Thank you, sir. Yes, it does.

You see, my friends, if we truly believe in what we call God or a Divine Infinite Intelligence or whatever you care to call it, if you truly believe in it, then you are going to experience it. And when you are not experiencing it, it simply means that we have slipped in our belief. I hope that's helped with your question.

Yes, sir. Thank you very much.

Now some of our new students, I'm sure, have some questions. Please don't be timid. It's your class and that's what it's all about. Remember, friends, man is a law unto himself. And if you choose to hear the questions of a few students, then that is your right. But you also have a right to ask your own questions.

I would like a little more clarification, if you please, with all due respect, on the incarnations of the soul. Am I to understand, as stated tonight, that upon the returning of a soul back into form, as we know form on this level of consciousness, that it has completed the eighty-one levels of consciousness? And if so, did the many savior gods in the many denominations of faiths, did any of them, or did all, return?

I would like to first clarify that it is not the purpose of these awareness classes to make a decision or a statement in reference to whether or not the so-called savior gods in which the world has believed, and continues to believe, have made a journey through eighty-one levels of consciousness. It has been stated in Discourse 31 that to the understanding, our understanding, at this time, that those who had reached illumination had gone into totality or total awareness and had returned on rare occasions to this particular planet. I do hope that that will help you with your question.

I've often wondered about the spoken word and affirming the good, as we do in most of these truth religions. I know we say our affirmation and we tune in with this, and this goes out as harmony. I try to make it as harmonious as I can, but are we not forcing our will when we affirm that this thing that is good or that I want—like I want my life harmonious and God is at the helm and my life is just the way it should be—are we not forcing, using force, rather than power and harmony, when we do this in affirmations?

We are not, if we are doing it correctly. We are simply accepting what is a divine truth, what is truth.

You see, my friends, many people pray for many things. What is prayer? Say that prayer is an aspiration of the individualized soul to the Oversoul, if it is truly prayer. A person goes into what they call prayer and they ask God, or some divine intelligence or some power that they believe is greater than themselves, to bring this to them or to bring that to them, to make an adjustment with this person, to change that person, and all types of things are asked in what is known as the name of prayer. All right. Now when we ask this Divine Intelligence for anything, what we are doing is declaring unto ourselves that we don't have it. That's what we're really doing. When we say, "God, would you grant me, please, good health?" we are making a statement that we are lacking good health. Now in making that statement, we are guaranteeing, of course, its continuity. You see, my friends, man is a law unto himself. So when you ask God for something, you are declaring, at least unto yourself, that you don't have it.

When you speak forth an affirmation, when you speak forth that you are moving in the Divine flow of perfect peace or prosperity, you are setting a law into motion. What you are doing is setting the law of the self into harmony with nature's divine natural law. My good friends, nature is not without abundance. However, nature is very thrifty. There's an old statement that nature wastes not. Look at the tree. She drops the leaves from the tree and leaves the tree barren in a season in time. The leaves go to the ground and they replenish it with nutrients. And the roots absorb it and it blossoms forth with its blossoms and its leaves, ever multiplying and ever increasing. Nature teaches the divine wisdom.

Now, we are a part of nature. We are, our form, an inseparable part of this Earth planet. What we think has an effect, to some extent, upon all forms of the planet, because we are form and an inseparable part of all forms, including the trees and the blades of grass. The type of thoughts that we entertain in mind, whether they are harmonious or discordant, has some effect upon the rest of the planet and all of its inhabitants. This is repeatedly being demonstrated in the laboratories and the effect that man has over plants and their growth.

The plants that are loved, they grow quicker and more healthily. Now why is it that this happens? It happens because we are an inseparable part of the whole. Man is not forcing his will, unless he thinks he is, and then, of course, he is stating his affirmation from a level of self-will. If you believe that you are speaking forth an affirmation from your own will and you put yourself in front of the allness of the Divine, then, of course, that is what you are doing. But that is not the purpose of the affirmations that have been given to the class and to the students of this Association. If there is any affirmation that any student has in question, that they do not understand, I'll be happy to share my understanding with you. Yes.

The Healing Prayer, in which we ask the unseen—

Thank you so very much. The Healing Prayer is something that has been handed to us by our national association. It is not an affirmation or a teaching of the Serenity Association. Of course, the question quickly rises, then why does the Serenity

Association use it? We use it because it has proven itself beneficial to those in levels of consciousness who are yet in the beseeching or the asking of the Divine. Does that help with your question? *[The Healing Prayer referred to in this discussion is not the Divine Healing Prayer, which was given through the mediumship of Mr. Goodwin. The Divine Healing Prayer can be found in the appendix.]*

Yes. However, if you assume, then, that at least some of the members of the Serenity Association are not operating in that level, what effect does it have for them to utilize this prayer on their own levels of consciousness?

That is dependent upon their belief. That is dependent upon the belief of the individual. Now, for example, is it better for man to experience some good in life and to be helped, whether he believes in a particular prayer or a rabbit's foot? If it works for him, is it better not to use it than not to have it at all? Which is the best? You see, we understand that all religions are serving a good purpose, if the people involved with the religion are putting some good into it. Remember, we cannot take from anything in life more than we, in truth, have put into it. Does that help with your question?

Yes.

Yes, now remember, this little Association serves a multitude of levels of consciousness. Its purpose is to serve humanity, not to dictate what they must think, nor to dictate how they must live. Thank you so very much.

With regard to healing and harmony that was discussed in a previous class, that harmony has to do with—I'm searching for a word. If healing may be thought of as maintenance of the body, is there a difference between maintenance and sustenance?

Yes, there is a vast difference.

And there is some discussion in The Living Light *on through what faculty the healing flows and so on. Could we have some discussion on that?*

Absolutely and positively. The discussion in reference to *The Living Light* is that the function which is the opposite of the soul faculty of humility is procreation. All right. Now, also in that particular discourse in discussion is a balancing between the soul faculty of humility and the sense function of procreation. We understand that this divine energy that's in all form, when it goes on its downward path, there is an increase in forms or a procreation principle. When the same energy is brought upward, then there is a balance and there is an illumination of the mind, a renewal of the mind. Now, the question has been asked in reference to that soul faculty and sense function and also a question that is concerning the healing, whether or not it is maintenance or sustenance—is that your basic question?

Yes, if it is maintenance or sustenance. If it is one, then could we have a discussion on the other one?

Yes. It is sustenance. It is sustenance. It is the divine light. It is the divine energy. And it's called by many names, one of them being prana. Now the body and the mind utilize a certain amount of this energy in order to sustain a perfect balance. When this energy is depleted and wasted on a downward path, there is a lack of the energy for the balancing of the soul faculties and there is, in turn, a discord or disturbance within the human form. Therefore, it is the teaching of Serenity for a balance in all things.

Now, each time we speak forth a word, each time we have a thought or a feeling, we are utilizing some of this energy. Now, man renews himself of this energy by being receptive to what is termed, in this class and in our understanding, as this perfect peace. When we are balanced with these faculties and these functions, when we reach that point of balance at any moment, we become receptive to this great power, this great energy that permeates the atmosphere.

And so it is, my friends, that in healing, what the recipient is, in truth, receiving is this divine energy, which the healer, by bringing balance into his life at that moment, is receptive to and is merely the channel to direct it to the one who is seeking what we call spiritual healing. Now, if a person goes to a spiritual healer repeatedly, and does not make certain necessary changes to bring about a balance in their own life, the healer is serving a great dispurpose in continuing to permit the recipient to come for healing. Because what is taking place is, the dissipation of the energy continues by the recipient and the healer is not establishing corrective measures. Do you understand? Now, this is why healing, for most people, is temporary. It is not permanent because the change necessary is not being made by the patient. Therefore, they continue to return to their doctors. They continue to go back for spiritual healing and do not make the necessary changes in their attitude of mind to bring about some degree of balance. Thank you very much.

Would you share your understanding of love, the life expression? In our daily lives we can't really go out and say, "I love you" or "I love everybody" or "Everybody should love one another." But that seems to be in one of the discourses, the magnetic power of the universe. Since our souls have been on different planets in our universe and the soul knows all and has been everywhere and seen everything, why can't we express a little bit more love?

Man expresses love in a multitude of ways. It is not necessary to tell an individual that you love them in order to express the love that you may feel for them. That is not, in any way, necessary. It may help the individual to have the recognition by the recipient that they know that they love them, but that is not necessary for your soul. You see, you can love many things without saying that "I love you." Now, why is it that man has to say to anything or to anyone that he loves them, you understand? What is it inside of us that needs that recognition? If we love a person or anything, it is not necessary for us to tell them so. However, if we are on a level of consciousness that needs an obvious reaction or a feedback of that love, which is energy, then we must either see or hear the person say, "That's very kind of you." Do you understand? Because what needs it is this thing here, you see. It's a three-letter word known as our ego.

However, you see, we can look out at the sunset and we can have a feeling of love for the sunset. But it is a very rare person that looks out at the sunset and says, "Oh, you know, I really love you." Because this is not the way society is presently programmed. Do you understand?

Yes.

All right. Now, we understand that love is nothing more nor less than an expression of the divine energy. Now you can love anything that you want, anytime that you want. That is entirely dependent upon the individual. However, man, usually, has restricted, at least in his thinking, that love is a conjugal relationship with the opposite sex. Otherwise, love doesn't exist. Well, of course, I'm sure we will all agree that that is certainly a very narrow, limited expression of God. If we understand that God is love and then we decide that the only way we're going to permit ourselves to express God—think, now, the Divine itself is in one particular area in a certain relationship—then, surely, friends, we are in a very sad, sad state of consciousness. Some people, they go out and eat and, well, they just love that food. It's very tasty to them. Or they build a house or they buy a new car: they're expressing energy.

It says here, "Love all life and know the Light." That does not say abuse what you want, get what you want, and know the light. That isn't what it says. It does say to "Love all life and know the Light." What does that really mean? What does that mean? It means, in our understanding, to recognize that you, on a level of consciousness, are inseparably a part of all things everywhere; that you have always been inseparably a part of that whole and, therefore, you will always be. So what you are doing, my friends, you are loving the God, the cause of all things. You're loving that divine energy, which is the true you, without all of the coverings of so-called variety. Does that help with your question?

What is happening to the soul, if anything, when a person partakes of intoxicating beverages and it changes his whole personality?

Thank you very, very much. The lady has asked, What happens to the soul, if anything, when a person takes intoxicating beverages and it changes their whole personality? Well, number one: My friends, it is not the purpose, of course, of our classes to decide whether or not the consuming of intoxicating beverages is, or is not, in the best interest of the individual. We take no stand on those matters, recognizing the divine right of all souls. However, if a person is addicted to the taking of intoxicating beverages and that addiction is proving detrimental to the individual in some degree to the peace or balance in their life, to some extent, then, of course, it would be detrimental to that particular individual. However, we must go beyond that point and we must go to the cause of why the individual has merited that particular tendency to become habitually intoxicated. Now that, of course, is a very individual, evolutionary process of that particular soul, which is, also, their divine right. Therefore, there is, no matter what the form expresses, an effect, of course, upon the soul that is within it. For the soul, my friends, is the covering of the divine, formless Spirit. And, in turn, we have many bodies. We have, of course, our astral body and our mental body, our vital body and, of course, our physical body. Now any habit, whether it's drinking or smoking or anything else, that is an addiction, unless there is some degree of balance with it, is going to have an effect upon our body, which, in turn, has an effect upon our mind, which, in turn, has an effect upon our astral covering and on down the line until it reaches our soul. I do hope that has helped with your question.

Coming back to speaking, "I love you." We are of the belief, I believe, in Serenity that speaking is life-giving energy. So you

might as well give energy to the highest thing. I don't mean be-
tween men and women, just say, like, "I love the sunset" or "I
love you as my friend" or something like that. But—

Yes?

My question is, Is it higher still to refrain from saying it?

That is entirely dependent upon the individual. First, we
must ask ourselves, "What is it in myself that needs to express
my feeling of love in words?" Remember, friends, it is always the
motive that reveals the truth that is within us. Now, if we need,
you understand, if we need to say the words verbally, that does
not, in and of itself, give it more energy. Because, you see, a person may say, "Well, in order for me to really feel this God's love,
this power, I must speak it out in words." Now, as long as we
believe that is necessary, then, of course, we're going to need to
do it. We do teach that the spoken word is life-giving energy, but
we must also remember, "From what level of consciousness am
I speaking the word?" Now, a person could say, "You know, I'm
really your friend." But we have to be honest with ourselves.
We have to first know what friendship is; we have to accept it
as a truth to ourselves; and then we have to feel it. So speaking
the words "I love you," is not, in and of itself, a higher level of
consciousness and it is not, in and of itself, a lower level of consciousness. That is entirely dependent upon the individual, of
course, and their motive. Does that help with your question?

Yes. Could I just add a little more now?

Certainly.

Isn't it, in a sense, the highest form of spoken prayer, if we are
to speak at all, to say that since love is the objective of—

If it comes from that level of consciousness, yes.

Thank you.

Yes, if it comes from that level of consciousness, yes, it is.
Because we are but the vehicles of the Divine.

I should like some information regarding apologies. Is it
possible for one to apologize to someone who is no longer with

us? I don't mean that they've passed to spirit, but perhaps they
don't live in the locale. Is it possible for that individual to receive
the vibration of the apology?

When man apologizes, he's apologizing to himself. That's
who he apologizes to. Man thinks that he apologizes to another
human soul, but he does not. Man apologizes to himself. This is
what really takes place. Now, it is the need within the individual
to express what he believes is an apology to the individual that
he believes he has offended. That is the need of the individuals
themselves. Do you understand?

Yes.

Now if somebody does something and then, you see—they
call that their conscience. And their conscience dictates that
they have made a transgression or perhaps it dictates they have
made an error, but the apology, in truth, is to oneself. It is to the
level within us, you understand, that made the transgression in
the first place. Now if man does not recognize that, he can spend
his lifetime apologizing to everyone and keep right on doing
what he's been doing: transgressing all over the place. Because,
you see, it hasn't really gotten here. See, that's where it is.

Then, that is part of forgiveness, where you must forgive
yourself first.

Now that is correct. Yes, indeed, it is. Because, you see, if
you don't forgive yourself, you're not in any position to forgive
another. You cannot, my friends, grant unto another human soul
what you have not first granted to yourself. That's impossible.
Absolutely impossible. You can't give to another what you have
not given to yourself. Now I'm not talking about this illusion
known as creation and that you decide, "Well, I want to give
that person a book," and you haven't given yourself one. I'm
going beyond that level of consciousness to the true cause. No
one is in a position to give to another human soul anything they
haven't given to themselves first. How can you give something
that you don't have? It's not possible. Yes.

I'm still confused about what I have, in the past, termed reincarnation, which I understand in this teaching would be incarnation.

Evolutionary incarnation. Yes.

Evolutionary incarnation: I'm understanding more all the time.

Yes.

Somehow it doesn't go together for me. I'm not clear whether the teaching says that once you come into physical form, unless you get to this place of disassociation that you never come back into physical form on this Earth again. I don't understand that. Could you clarify it, please?

We teach evolutionary incarnation: that the soul is evolving through the forms and the planets. The basic difference between the teachings of Serenity and its evolutionary incarnation and the popular theory of reincarnation is this: Serenity's teachings are that the soul evolves through the planets of the solar system. The present theory of reincarnation teaches that the soul leaves the physical earth form and through what is called karma or the Law of Cause and Effect, it returns to this particular Earth planet to outgrow the transgressions that it has made and that it finally escapes, supposedly escapes, the cycle of return when it reaches a state of bliss, so that it is no longer trapped in this circle of return.

Evolutionary incarnation teaches that the soul evolves—constantly, continuously—through the many forms on the many planets. It teaches that this present form is an effect and not a cause; that the soul evolves, like you go to school from the sixth grade to the seventh to the eighth and onward; that the soul is evolving or expanding its consciousness in the various forms. I hope that helps with your question.

Would you please share with us your understanding of bliss and joy?

Well, you know, that is like trying to express what God is. You have to put it into the limitation of expression. Now, some people, I am sure, have a certain understanding of what bliss means to them and what joy means to them. And therefore, what joy means to one does not necessarily, in and of itself, mean to another individual. So I do not feel at this time that it would be, necessarily, in the best interest of the students to express my particular understanding of joy or bliss. I'm sure that you have had moments when you have either felt joyful or blissful. I hope that's helped you. Yes, you have another question?

I wasn't sure of the difference between the two and if they're faculties or not.

I see. You didn't want a description of joy or bliss. You wanted to know if they are soul faculties.

And the difference between the two.

Well, joy and bliss are both soul faculties. Bliss is—we could, perhaps, share it this way—is even a higher level of consciousness than joy. Bliss, let us say, is more of a refinement. It is a finer expression, bliss is, of what we call joy.

When you say the soul goes through the solar system, are we aware of all the aspects of the solar system? Are there rings or other places that we are not conscious of?

There is a part within us—Are we aware of the different parts of the universe? There is a part within all souls, here, now, this moment, that is aware. And that awareness comes to us in glimpses, very short moments, and is known as a total awareness or an illumination or they've called it cosmic consciousness. But it is within the realm of all souls, everywhere, to glimpse what they really are, yes.

Now I've heard there are souls here on this planet who are able to tune in and know things and have special healing powers.

Yes, they have. That is very true. Now that means that their particular soul has merited that particular expression in this level here, known as earth. Yes. You see, we go to school and we learn many different things, would you not agree?

Yes.

And remember, it's just like people that have a healing potential. Everyone has the potential, you see. But it's like playing the piano: not everyone is going to be a virtuoso. Is that not correct?

Yes.

So everyone, my friends, has these potentials. Remember, what one human being can do is within the realm of possibility for all human beings.

And are we progressing all the time? I mean, when somebody comes back if they have been very good in one area, then they come here, they're going to be very good in—

We're constantly refining and processing: it is the Law of Evolution. The form is constantly evolving. You see, all we need to do, friends, is to study nature. Nature reveals the evolutionary process. Now we look out at nature and we see it constantly evolving, would you all not agree? All right. Now, we know that the soul, you see—that that is individualized—to individualize it is to form it. So we know that the soul is the covering or form over the spirit, the formless and the free. So you see, we look at Nature and Nature herself teaches us that all forms are evolving. And so it is that we are evolving because we, too, are form.

I'm puzzled how if joy or bliss—you said bliss may be a higher—

More refined state of consciousness, yes.

I'm puzzled how, how bliss—

Let me put it best this way: the senses respond to joy, you understand. The senses, the feelings, the form responds to joy, but not to bliss. Perhaps that will help you.

I'd like to finish my question.

You may.

You also teach that neutrality, divine neutrality, to my understanding, is like the epitome of where I would like to go.

That is correct.

I don't understand. Why would I bother to tune into bliss if I were going to neutrality? To put it very bluntly.

Thank you very much. You want to know why you should bother to go to neutrality.

No, to bliss, if I'm heading for neutrality. I don't understand.

But, my dear student, that is what neutrality is. I just stated, before your question, I believe, that the senses or feelings respond to joy. They do not respond to bliss. The reason they do not respond to bliss is because they are in perfect balance and that that is in perfect balance does not react or respond. Does that help with your question?

Yes. Thank you.

So if you are seeking balance and neutrality, then you are seeking bliss.

I don't know if I have my question formed, but something triggered me and I can't quite get my question together. But it is about harmony and friendship and accepting people. I have to do this personally. There are certain people you find who really take your energy.

Yes.

And they bring you down. It's very hard. I would prefer not to accept or be around them, because they do drain me.

Yes.

And then, I feel, perhaps, that is wrong. That's not where I should be, because that's putting a law into effect against me, because there are places where I want to be accepted and I won't be.

Yes. Would you like us to share our understanding with you in reference to being drained by what you call "friends"?

Please.

There is—and we have brought it up in our other classes. The first law of the form, of this form, of all form, is self-preservation. That's the first law of the form. Man's first responsibility is to his own spirit and to his own soul. That is man's *first* responsibility. Therefore, if it is necessary for you, or any soul, to be discrete in demonstrating and expressing the first law of the form of self-preservation, then, of course, wisdom dictates that you be discrete. Does that help with your question?

Yes, it does.

Yes. Now remember, my friends, we must ask ourselves the honest question, when we attract—remember that like attracts like and becomes the Law of Attachment. So we must ask ourselves honestly, when we have an experience—you see, experience is the mirror that reflects a level of consciousness that we are expressing. So we must look here and we must say, "My, I'm attracting an awful lot of freeloaders in my life." You see, freeloaders are people who take energy from you with no balance back. You see, there's no reciprocation. So we must say to ourselves—no matter who we are—"Just a moment. Just a moment. There's some level of consciousness that I am expressing somewhere, because I'm attracting this to me." Do you understand?

Yes, I do.

Because, you see, my friends, you want to grow out of it, you know. First of all, you have this self-preservation and that's it. "I spend so much time there, there, there, and there," you understand. But we must go beyond that, because that is only an effect. It's a reflection and it's telling us—the experience—that somewhere, somehow we are out of balance. Does that help?

Thank you. And, friends, we're way past our time. Thank you all very much and let's have some refreshments.

JANUARY 10, 1974

CONSCIOUSNESS CLASS 35 &

Good evening, students.

Now before getting into our question-and-answer period, which, as you all know, of course, is a part of our regular class, I should like to take a few moments this evening and discuss with you communication. And by communication, I'm not referring to the communication with these other dimensions, but communication with people here and now in this old earth realm. There seems to be, here in this earth world, a difficulty in people expressing their thoughts, their ideas, and their desires. There seems to be an obstruction for being understood by others. And this seeming obstruction that so many people appear to experience in their daily activities causes a great deal of problems for those who are trying to express themselves.

So we must ask ourselves the question, What is this obstruction that is within us that seems to be a barrier for our being understood by other people? Now if we are honest with ourselves and a little objective, we will find that we cannot be understood by anyone at any time, unless we are making a conscious, serious effort in understanding ourselves.

So I wanted to pass it on to you this evening, because so many people think that they're not understood or that, perhaps, people don't love them or they're hurt or they're alone. There are so many of these obstructions within the minds of people here and now. So let us look clearly and make the effort on working on ourselves, because people, my friends, that are attracted to us, around and about us, they're only the mirrors that are reflecting the level of consciousness that we are expressing.

And, of course, the sadness, my friends, when we are expressing through a level of consciousness known as desire, is that there is no light. Desire is absolutely blinding. And the more of it that we express, the more blind we become.

So if we will make the effort, each moment, with all of life's experiences, with all of the joys and all of the sadness, with all of the ups and all of the downs, and we will remember each moment—not just once a day—but remember *each* moment that we are experiencing a reflection of the level that we insist upon expressing, and if you will do that, you will no longer have any obstructions or any barriers to being loved, to being understood, or with communication.

Thank you all very much. Now you're free to ask whatever questions that you have, if you will just kindly raise your hand, please.

In the journey of the soul, in its evolutionary process, my question is—I just happened to see some ants down there, so it made me think of it. Can the animal stage . . .

Yes?

For example, someone might be incarnated as an ant or an elephant. Now is that just the one stage that that soul would express in, regardless of its size?

Well, the seeming proportions of the soul are not dependent on the proportions of the form, of the physical or mental form. Do you understand?

Right.

So therefore, you know, we understand that God, the Divine Spirit, expresses through all things, the little ant, you understand, or the elephant or etc. That does not indicate that the ant has a very dinky, little soul and the elephant has a gigantic one. No, it does not mean that at all.

The soul is evolving through forms and forms unlimited. It has already been evolving and is constantly in a process of evolution. But be not concerned, my friends, about coming back as an ant or something, because that is not our teaching. That is the teaching, however, of transmigration, which is not the teaching of evolutionary incarnation. I hope that helps with your question.

I'd like to ask you a question regarding the discourse for this evening. I'm very aware that this reflects my beginning state. It says, "Open your vision, you will perceive [Discourse 33]." Is there more to opening one's vision than the meditation practice in which I'm already engaged?

Yes.

The other question that I would like to ask is that it says very simply to change your own aura to white. And it sounds very simple, but I don't know how to do it.

Thank you very much. In reference to your question on the changing of one's aura to the purity of white, when you have a sincere heart and an open mind, then your aura is transformed into the purity known as white.

In reference to your first question and the process of perception or opening your vision, one of the seeming sadnesses in this world with so many people interested in the psychic is that they think, in unfolding and desiring to see into these other dimensions, that it is advisable to attend a class that specializes in it. This is a great sadness, because what we're trying to teach to the student is an unfoldment of the soul faculties. Now there are many techniques, of course, of awakening the psychic. But what you open up to, of course, is a psychic dimension, which includes the astral realms and the mental realms and all of those different dimensions, which is not advisable.

In awakening one's vision—and what they were referring to in the book [*The Living Light*] is our spiritual vision—in awakening one's vision, this comes about not simply by a daily meditation process. That is only a very minute part of awakening the spiritual vision. It comes about in a process known as selfless service.

It is through selfless service that the energy that is flowing through our being is directed and expressed through what is known as the soul faculties. The reason that we, seemingly, have so many problems and emotional pits in this life is because the energy that has been, and is being, directed in our lives is out of balance. Most of it is going down to the functions. So when you take some time each day and bring about some degree of directing this energy to the soul faculties—now, you see, some people might think, "Well, if I think of the soul faculties, then I direct energy there." Well, of course, that is true. But it's a very minute amount of energy. It is when you put it into application through service—and you know your soul faculties, you know enough of them to at least try to use one or two of them—when you do that, then you begin to open what is known as your spiritual perception or vision.

Can a person engage in selfless service in their own day-to-day work?

Absolutely and positively. Yes, you can engage in selfless service moment by moment. Now a person might say, "Well, I have a job. I'm being paid so much money and so therefore that isn't really selfless service." My friends, we're not talking about that at all, in any sense of the word. What we are talking about is a conscious awareness, a conscious awareness of where the energy truly comes from. A conscious awareness that we, the so-called self, the brain, the ego is only a vehicle of the Divine Spirit, known as God. Now, when we have a conscious realization of that moment by moment, we are in selfless service. Because what that will do, you understand, that type of thinking, that level of consciousness will inspire us to do things in this world without remuneration. Does that help with your question?

Yes, thank you.

You're more than welcome.

I didn't think I had a question, but I do. "Your spirit is responsible, your soul, for all its thoughts, acts, and activities [Discourse 33]." I'm a little confused by "Your spirit is responsible." I realize that we are responsible for everything we say, do, and act, but in this sentence I'm a little mixed up. Would you please help?

Yes. Which part are you confused by? Your spirit is responsible for all of its thoughts—

No. It says that "Your spirit is responsible, your soul."

That is correct. The soul is the covering of that spirit and that's where the responsibility lies.

That is part of my confusion. The spirit and the soul.

I see. Well, we've discussed before that the Divine Spirit, of course, is formless and free, that the soul is the individualization of that spirit that it may express in form. So it is our soul, you understand, that is responsible for all of its acts and activities.

Now, how does this responsibility really work? Well, all we have to do is stop and look at ourselves this moment. We are here. We are in a state of consciousness that we are either enjoying or not enjoying. Now, we have merited this according to the laws that we, as individuals, have set into motion. We are, each moment, facing our responsibility. Now, we are not yet aware to the point where we can say, "I'm having this experience this moment and the reason I'm having this experience is because of laws that I set into motion at another time in another day." So, you see, man is constantly moving through his own responsibilities.

Now, it is true that there comes a time in life where it seems our responsibilities become a great burden. Well, what that really is, is a greater awakening to what we're really setting into motion. Then, when that happens man starts to choose very wisely. He starts to give some thought before he speaks. And he gives some thought before he acts. Because, you see, my friends, we're all facing that moment by moment.

Now, they say that ignorance is bliss. And in that sense, of course, ignorance *is* bliss. It is blissful in the sense that we are not aware of these laws that we're setting into motion. But when we start to become aware, we become a little bit more thoughtful about what we're thinking and what we're doing with our lives. Does that help with your question?

Yes. Could I ask another?

Yes, certainly.

In the "Total Consideration" affirmation, it states, "As the light of Truth is sustained by the faculty of Reason, I pause to think and claim my Divine right. Right Thought. Right Action. Total Consideration." The first part, "As the light of Truth is sustained by the faculty of Reason," does that mean that the light of truth within us is sustained by the faculty of reason? Because the light of truth is the sphere of everything, isn't it?

Without the faculty of reason, the light of truth is not expressed. The light of truth is expressed through what is known as the faculty of reason and, therefore, it is the faculty of reason which sustains it or permits its expression, you see. Now don't misunderstand and say, "Well, then, if there were no human beings on the earth plane without soul faculties of reason, then there'd be no light of truth," because that is not true. What we are talking about is the faculty of reason—the principle of reason itself, is what sustains this light of truth.

Now, unless we pause to think, we do not express reason. This is the thing, my friends: If you gain nothing else from the classes, at least put it into your consciousness that unless you pause to think, you are not using the soul faculty of reason. Because you are not in control. And not being in control, you are reacting. You cannot use the soul faculty of reason unless you pause to think. Now when you pause to think, your chances of using your faculty, of course, are much greater. In fact, it's the only way it's going to be used. Otherwise, we are constantly reacting from the emotional realm, that magnetic field of impulse. And that's what gets us into so much grief in this world, is all those impulsive thoughts and acts. What happens when you pause to think? You still the mind. And when you still the mind, your spirit, the soul can express itself.

You can't express your spirit, friends, through the faculty of reason, unless you pause, you take control. Remember, these classes are about spiritual discipline. Because without the discipline, there's no awareness. There's no awareness.

You see, friends, they say that no one likes to change. Well, of course, nobody likes to change, because they've found security in the patterns that they're habituated to. Now, if no one likes to change, then how is it that some people are changing? And we're really changing all the time. How is it that we are changing, if we really don't like to? Well, they say that necessity is the mother of invention. And because we do suffer, we do change. Thank you. Does someone else have a question, please?

Would you give your understanding, please, of strength? And is there any inter-relationship between strength and courage?

Thank you very much. The lady has asked the question, Is there any interrelationship between the word *courage* and *strength?* Not in this understanding. Now our understanding of the word *strength* is a spiritual reliability. It is when, through full acceptance, we truly rely upon the divine spirit expressing through us. That is where our true strength is. That is strength. Now I'm sure that many of you think that strength is something bodily, etc. We're not talking about that type of strength in this understanding.

Now, of course, our spiritual reliance, when we rely upon that divine spirit within us, of course, that comes through our faith. So, therefore, we need faith and patience before we can fully express. And I hope that has helped you.

I would like to know how we can tell whether our acts are truly guided by spirit or if they are promptings by spirit or if they are from our own subconscious desires.

Thank you for that question, because it is a very important question to all students who are seeking the spiritual light, regardless of the paths they have chosen. How can one tell whether or not what one is receiving is from spirit guides and teachers or the suppressed desires from the depths of one's own subconscious? Is that basically your question?

Yes.

Yes. Well, one of the first indications of whether or not it is suppressed desires of the subconscious is that it will always be pleasing to the self. Now that's one of the first indications. Now, I know in this type of work that many times, you know, people and students have heard a voice, or what they felt was a voice— and many times it has been a voice. And the voice is always telling them to do something, which, of course, will either bring them greater recognition, if greater recognition is what they are needing at the time. It will bring them more money, if more money is what they think they need. It will bring them what they call love or bring them pleasure, if that's what they think that they need. This is the importance of first finding the self, the true self, one's own being, the depths of one's own subconscious, before opening the doors to these other dimensions. This is one of the main reasons that I do not teach psychic development or unfolding mediumship. For that simple reason. It is extremely dangerous.

Now, when we first know about ourselves, we know about our suppressed desires and we know about what our needs are. When we're honest with ourselves and we go through the depths of those realms within our own mind, then we will know if the voice is from the voice of discarnate spirit or from the depths of our subconscious.

Now there's another area that must be looked into. It doesn't necessarily mean that the voice is from the depths of our subconscious, because it could also be something else. It could be discarnate entities on the astral realm who have not yet outgrown the particular desire that we have suppressed. And not having outgrown it, they are trying to impress us to fulfill it. Do you understand? Because like attracts like and becomes the Law of Attachment.

Now, which is best? To go very slowly and steadily and gradually find out about what we really are, not just on our conscious level, but what all of our suppressions are, recognize them, and work with them or be deceived, because the deception, of course, is caused by our own mind? Does that help with your question?

Thank you very much.

I hope so, because that's very, very, very important. Very important.

You see, the Bible says to test the spirit that they are of God. And we say test the spirit that they represent the good. Well, how do you test the spirit? You cannot test a discarnate spirit, unless you have the equipment to test them with. Now that testing comes about by first testing oneself. And one cannot test oneself, unless one knows truly what oneself really is. That is how you test the spirit. Thank you.

That confuses me a great deal. Because I work with people and I find a lot of people operate on the basis of finding out what somebody else wants them to feel like and then try to behave in that manner. And what I try to help them to do is to operate on the basis of how they feel from the inside and then operate like that in the world.

Why do you think that people try to do what other people want them to do?

Because it brings them energy and attention. It also—

It brings them love.

Yes. Most especially—

That's the reason that people do that. Thank you. Go ahead.

Especially it brought them love. Usually in the way they did it, it brought them love in their families, when they were growing up as little children. Well, what I find is that most people I encounter have a lot of trouble making the step, because they feel like they're going crazy when they move from acting from out there in, instead of from in here out.

You can understand why, can't you?

Yes. I've been there myself. So when you offer this, to look within yourself, I look around and I see people who are trying. I, myself, have tried to live by this discipline and yet I feel without more support, say, than merely this class or even the church experience, then a lot of people have trouble making that step. And I'm concerned about it. I really don't know what my question is, so much as how do you expect people to do that on their own?

Well, actually, we don't expect them to do it on their own, wholly, in that sense. You know, it's like a person that wants to be a golfer. He goes to the golf course and he associates with golfers. And so it is with spirituality. As people seeking spiritual awareness and true awareness of themselves, if they have any common sense or reason or logic at all, what they will do is, they will attend, you understand, any organization that is offering what they are seeking. Then, they will make it a point to associate with students, with people who are also on the path. Because through associating with them, they are supported in their struggle upward. Do you understand? This is very, very, very important.

Now, this is one of the reasons that we offer so many activities by this Association: dinners and bake sales and all these different activities. Because, then, the students are able to associate, you understand, with spiritually minded people. Now that doesn't mean that they like them or dislike them. That isn't where wisdom is revealing itself. It is revealing itself that there's someone else trying and struggling to come up through those levels of consciousness. They are not alone in the world. Do you understand?

Yes.

Now, what happens to the students? A few—like the Good Book says, many are called and few are chosen—a few demonstrate the Law of Continuity. They begin to learn to choose their associates wisely. Remember this: If you want to be a musician, you play the musical instrument of your choice and you associate with people who are interested in your endeavor. Because if you associate with people who are not interested in your endeavors, then what they are doing is, they are taking from you. Do you understand? Because they are taking your time and your energy on levels of consciousness that you are trying to grow out of. It is known in this study as auric pollution. And so one of the first things the student recognizes is, "How much time and energy am I spending on my chosen path of awakening and spiritual awareness in a day? And how much time am I spending in auric pollution?" Do you understand?

Now, since the founding of this Association, I have watched many, many, many students come and go. They have all received the same teachings. And they have all been cautioned about where they spend their energies. It is for their own good. What is the sense, my friends, of spending your time, your money, and your energy to awaken your own spirit, your own soul, within yourself, and going and casting it out in the world before the swine? That's not very sensible.

Now that doesn't mean that you should only associate with people who are interested in Serenity's concept of Spiritualism. But it does mean to choose more wisely your associates and to associate with people who are, indeed, spiritually minded, who aren't saying that they're spiritually minded, but who are really trying. Now how do you know whether they're really trying or they're just becoming a sponge to gain your energy and time? Well, you'll know very soon because you'll know how you feel when you're finished. I hope that helps with your question.

I'd like to know how to go about recognizing my suppressed desires.

Yes, thank you very much. When a person makes the conscious effort to pause before they express themselves, you see, then they can go to their soul faculty of reason. Now when you keep faith, your effort, with this faculty of reason, it transfigures

you. It illumines you inside yourself. Then, when you have a
thought, and before you express it, you pause, you see, you make
that a moment-to-moment practice, then what will happen, you
will see what the stimuli for that thought really was. And when
you do that, you will become aware of what your suppressed
desires are. And in becoming aware, you will be able to balance
them out and to express them.

Now remember, friends, everything in all universes needs
energy, which we call love. The plants need it. The trees need
it. The stars need it. The moon needs it. The sun needs it. It
needs it and it needs to express it. Everything needs to express
this energy and it needs to receive it. That is man's number
one problem. Number one. Think about it, because that's where
the problem really is. We do a multitude of things in life to gain
attention. A multitude of things. All we have to do is pause to
think. We'll have all the attention, which, of course, is energy or
love, that we could ever utilize. And having received it, we can
also express it. Yes.

*My feeling is that certain people have, well, each of us has, at
the core, a problem or several problems. For example, if, when you
were little, you were very lonely or you felt that no one loved you or
you weren't wanted in the first place, then a lot of your suppressed
desires or your subconscious is trying to reach back to get enough
love for yourself, or trying to reach back to get enough things for
yourself. And what I notice in people is that it seems to be a cycle. I
may, today, be in contact with the fact that I feel like nobody loves
me. I'll struggle with that and I'll get through it and I'll do all
right for a while. And then I'll come back up with that same problem again. And even though I'm continually dealing with it in a
cyclical fashion, the question or the problem still seems to come
up. My idea is that it keeps coming up because I haven't solved
it yet or I haven't let go of it. That's still the way I get energy, but
each time it comes up, I'm getting stronger and I can handle it on
a more subtle level. I'd like to know what your understanding is.*

I'll be happy to share with you the cyclic reoccurrence, the constant reoccurrence of any level of consciousness. The reason that a situation—which, remember, all these things exist on levels of consciousness—continues to reoccur in anyone's life is because it has not yet been fully accepted on the levels of consciousness. You see, it takes an impulse to send it back up into the conscious mind. Do you understand? So that means that the situation or the problem, whatever you care to call it, has not yet been fully accepted. And not having been fully accepted, it has a constant stimulus to drive it back up, you understand, for recognition. That's what happens.

I just got confused when you said that love is man's number one problem. It came to me that you're saying it's something that you should learn to do without?

No! Absolutely not! You cannot survive without love. It's impossible. Because love is energy. It's the divine energy. You cannot survive without it. We are not teaching to try to annihilate it or be without it, because you won't be in form very long. What we're trying to share with you is that you may receive it in a multitude of areas; that man has limited the channels through which he will accept this divine expression known as love or energy. Does that help clarify that for you?

Could you give some examples of other channels?

In broadening one's horizon? Well, for example, man—by man, I mean mankind—he can accept love, the love expressed by an animal, by a dog or a cat or a bird. He can accept the love that's expressed by the sunset or the rising of the dawn. He can accept the love that's expressed by the rain or by music. That's what we mean, you see. God's manifestation is variety. And all things in God are good. If you look for the good in anything, you will find God there, because there is no place that the Divine Intelligence does not express itself.

So what we're trying to share with the student is a broadening of one's horizon. Because it is the limitations that man has set up for himself, through society, through his own thinking, that has limited the expression of this divine love and, therefore, is filling his life with a multitude of problems. Does that help with your question? Thank you very much.

I have noticed in my own development that I get to a certain point and everything is beautiful. I am getting along with people and personalities are not in the way. I feel I've reached a certain, maybe, little peak in my consciousness, and then, all of a sudden, down I go. What is it? How can we avoid this pitfall? Sometimes my spirit goes way down and even though I know that other people are a mirror, still I don't feel in my own heart that I have done it. I may have done something unconsciously, but consciously I would not do this thing. What makes me do this thing unconsciously that makes me feel this way? And what is testing me? What is—or who is—testing me to leave this height where I'm very happy and go down so low at times?

Yes. Thank you very, very much for expressing the understanding which is a demonstrable truth: that all of our experiences and emotions take place inside of ourselves and they're all caused by ourselves. And it is the delusion and the illusion of the brain, known as the ego, that tries to put it out onto somebody else or something else.

So first we have accepted—we've recognized and we've accepted the truth that man is a law unto himself. All of our experiences we are willing into action and, therefore, we are the captain of our own ship and the master of our own destiny.

And the lady has asked, What is it or how is it that you're able to go along for so long a time and you're feeling fine and everything is beautiful, and then, all of a sudden, you go down to the bottom and you get very depressed? Well, my friends, it's really quite simple: that means that our consciousness has descended into a level of self where darkness reigns supreme or what is known as ignorance.

Now, how do we descend down there into those realms of darkness, those realms of self and ignorance? We descend there, friends, through uncontrollable desire. And when this uncontrollable desire—no matter who we are—is expressing itself, there's no light. So what happens is, we find ourselves down in the basement of darkness. We don't know how we got there, because the thing that sent us there has no light and we can't see it. And when we're down there, then we start to cry out like a voice in the wilderness. And when we do that, it's our soul that's crying out like the voice in the wilderness. And the light dawns, and we see and we say, "Look! We're down there in the basement again." How do we stay up out of there? I can only say this: through self-control, through discipline.

When do our problems start? When we start remembering that we are so important in life. It's known as the self-level. Now the moment that happens, we've got real problems.

When you feel down in the depths of despair, stop. Pause in that moment, and ask yourself what you can do to help the Divine. You will receive a thought, but you must act upon it in that moment. And when you do that, you'll come out of the basement. Does that help with your question?

Very much. Thank you.

And you'll feel a great deal better. Now we have, perhaps, time for a few more questions. Time passes very quickly.

I would like your clarification of a particular statement in The Living Light. *And I'll read it so that it will be in context. "Now you know, my good students, that the color white is the combination of the three primary colors in perfect harmony. You know the primary colors red, yellow, and blue; divine wisdom in action is spirit [Discourse 33]." I would really appreciate clarification on that.*

Yes. Well, you see, you're not expressing divine wisdom in action, which is spirit, unless you have a pure heart and a sound mind. And when your heart is pure and your mind is sound—by the word *sound* I mean balanced: that the faculties and the functions are in balance—then, this divinity expresses itself unobstructed. Then, there is a perfect blending of vibrations: the three primaries, namely, red, yellow, and blue. And when that perfect balancing takes place, then you have what is known as pure spirit. There's no obstruction. There's no contamination. Yes.

If we put the colors on a triangle . . .

Yes?

Is no particular color at the apex of the triangle?

Yes, there most certainly is. Yes. The right point, which is electrical, of course, is red. Divine wisdom in action is spirituality. And that is your triangle. Divine wisdom is neutral. You see, it's beyond choice because it came before choice. And when those are blended in perfect balance, you have the white, which is pure or uncontaminated.

Thank you very much.

You're welcome.

You've talked a bit about acceptance tonight in answering several of the questions and in a previous semester you gave us the soul faculty of principle, detachment, and acceptance. I wonder if it would be appropriate to ask for an explanation of that.

What do you mean by an explanation?

How do these three or how does this triune faculty operate as a unit or as a faculty?

You mean the principle of acceptance and detachment? Yes, we'll discuss that later on in the course. Thank you, but we still have quite a few beginners in this course.

I am looking for a crutch.

Then, that guarantees you'll find one.

Good. I asked a question in a preceding class about a mantra. I find that frequently my life runs at such a pace that I, all of a sudden, stop and say, "My goodness, I haven't thought about what I'm really doing here and what I really want out of this! I haven't really tuned in to God." And sometimes I'm in the middle of an activity where I can't spend my time going back to meditate or to really spend my thought on peace, per se, the way I would like to. And I wonder if you have something to offer that I may—something else to offer. I know I have the affirmations and that sort of thing that I may say in times when I'm otherwise busy, but I also want to help myself to tune in during the demands of the kind of world I seem to live in. I really don't know how to push it back at this point.

Yes, absolutely. And I can give you a few, very short words that were given to a three-year-old boy over a year ago that helped him tremendously. And it's helped all of my students ever since—a good portion of them—that have applied it.

When, in your busy acts and activities—and you only have a moment to do what you want to do to remember the Divine Intelligence that is your true source and supply and your true wisdom and intelligence—if you can just make the effort—and it's such a little effort to make—to say to yourself from the level of consciousness where it works, "Thank you, God. I am at peace," you will be amazed. If you are sincere with that statement, if you put your soul and heart into the words when you say them to yourself, you will rise to a level of consciousness where you will have all the help that is necessary for you to accomplish the job that you have to do at any given moment. Now the more you practice it, like anything else, the more it's going to work for you. I hope that has helped you.

Very much.

We have time for, perhaps, one or two questions. Yes.

I would like to give an example. I'm at the point, now, where, when I do something, I realize that I have two feelings. When someone wins an honor, I'm aware that I'm really happy for the person, and at the same time, I'm jealous or envious.

Yes?

Or when someone's boy ran away, I asked because I was interested. At the same time, I thought, "Oh, well, poor family." I have two feelings.

That's most understandable.

Well, what do you do then?

Thank you very much. Well, at least, number one, you're honest enough with yourself to state the fact, because it happens to all of us. But, you see, there are very few egos that would permit themselves to say that they have those feelings.

Now usually what happens, we go along in this life, we suppress one of them because, you see, we're taught that's not the feeling to have. We're not supposed to be jealous, we're not supposed to be envious, we're not supposed to be greedy, and we're not supposed to be all of those things. But I'm happy to hear that you have faced that in your life: that you have that recognition of those feelings.

Well, number one, the feelings that you are discussing, of course, have proven themselves, in our lives, not to be beneficial. Is that not understandable? Because they don't reap a very good harvest, right? So, consequently, we recognize that this is what some philosophies call the lower self. Now we don't spend our time thinking about it, because that that we give thought to, we create. And so the more thought you give to it, the greater will be your tendency to express it. You understand?

But if you will simply accept that we are a part of the animal form and those different functions are in the animal form for their survival—the first law of form is self-preservation. It's like the dog and the bone situation. The dog may have all the bones it wants, but it is a very rare dog that's willing to share it with another dog that's hungry. Do you understand?

All right. So we recognize, first, that our soul and the spirit are expressing through an animal body, because that's what our body is. It is the animal part of us, you see, and it has those functions. And we recognize that that's not what we really are—the form—and we make the effort, you understand, to bring about a balance in our life.

Now, we say we shouldn't be greedy. Well, what is greed? It's simply an imbalance of one of the expressions of one of the functions, right? Because a person, a wise person, puts away a few acorns for the winter. Is that not correct? The squirrel teaches us that lesson, or should teach us that lesson. And so we do recognize that there are some things that we should take care of and just not throw everything away and be a spendthrift. Now if we go out of balance—and by out of balance, we all know our own balance. If, for example, in setting aside a little savings, something happens and the savings are wiped out and we lose our emotional stability in the process, then, my friends, we've gone into what is known as greed. Do you understand? We've gone out of balance. Because, you see, the true source of all of our supply is God. And when we take so much and put it aside there, and that's wiped out and we collapse, then we have denied our own divinity.

So when you have these feelings, which you well recognize, you shouldn't feel guilty about them. That's not going to help you. But you recognize them as a part of the form in which your soul is expressing. You also recognize that every other two-legged animal in the universe, known as the human race, has the same thing. They may, or may not, be expressing it to the degree, perhaps, that someone else is, but it lies within all of us. And then, we see that wisdom dictates to bring about some kind of balance in those things. Because whatever it is that someone else has, it is within your power for you to have also, if you truly believe that God is the source of all your supply. Do you understand?

Now, when you have a feeling of envy or jealousy because of what someone else has and you desire it—and this, as I say, is a part of the animal form of man—every time you express that feeling inside yourself, you are another step away from attaining it. And that is the divine law of Nature herself.

If you look at someone else and you desire what they have, what you, in truth, are doing is feeding energy that they may have an increase of what they already have. You understand? So instead of looking out there with those thoughts and feelings, you look inside, knowing that it's on its way to you. Do you see what I mean? Now they say the rich get richer and the successful become more successful. Well, they ought to. They have multitudes of jealous people helping them get there!

Thank you, friends. Let's have refreshments.

JANUARY 17, 1974

CONSCIOUSNESS CLASS 36 ✖

Good evening, students. We've had a call this evening. Some of our students are a little disorganized and won't be here until a little later. However, we will continue on with our class. If you will, kindly turn your study book [*The Living Light*] to Discourse 36.

[A student reads Discourse 36 aloud.]

We will go ahead with our meditation and our affirmation. I do hope that all of the students now know their "Total Consideration" affirmation, so you may give it the life-giving energy of the spoken word.

Now when you go into your meditation, I know that you're all finding your own way to that God, or Peace, within yourself. But let us unite in thought with this affirmation. And remember, total consideration, of course, includes all levels of our own consciousness. So we can't consider anything outside of us until we have first considered it inside.

[The class says the "Total Consideration" affirmation aloud. Then, the class meditates.]

Before going into the question-and-answer period of our class this evening, I'd like to spend a few moments on discussing energy and tiredness, as was mentioned briefly in the discourse that you just read. Whenever man makes an effort to change certain patterns of mind, he really doesn't change them. We all know that. We just rise our soul consciousness to a different level of awareness and no longer express certain patterns of mind. Whenever we make this effort, this conscious effort, to make these changes, there is ofttimes an experiencing of tiredness or a depletion of energy. Now, the reason for this, and the cause, is that the energy is going in two different levels of consciousness at the same time.

To some people on the path—now, this is happening to all of us, whether we're in a spiritual class or we're not. We are constantly in a state of change. But it is when we make a conscious effort to make these changes that we find necessary for our own good and for our own peace of mind, there is this temporary depletion of energy. For example, if we are expressing on level sixteen and we wish to express on level nineteen, what happens is level eighteen demands the energy that it's used to receiving. And therefore, with our conscious effort to express on a higher level of consciousness, there is a great utilization of energy that takes place.

Now, how can we balance this energy within us so that we will not experience this tiredness and this lack of energy and enthusiasm? Well, it's really quite simple in the sense that if you are doing your meditations properly each day and you are really making an effort to tune into that peace, which is a perfect balancing, you will find a rejuvenation and you will find all of the energy that is necessary for your use. But you must make that effort, more than just once a day, to be at peace in your thinking, in your emotions, and in your feelings. And I did want to share that with you this evening, because there was a mention on this energy and the lack thereof.

Now you're free to ask whatever questions that you have concerning the study and things of a spiritual nature. If you'll just be so kind as to raise your hand.

I've been trying to understand the creative principle. And I wonder if I might ask a rather basic question. Would you give your understanding of both duty and motive? I find that some of these words we've used all of our lives—but when we put them in a spiritual context, they take on a far different meaning.

Yes, thank you. If you'll just be patient, because we're going to go through the creative principle diagram again with the blackboard in the coming weeks. And I think that would be of more benefit, especially to the new students, to get the entire diagram and the process of the energy going through the mind at that particular time, if you will be so patient. Yes.

Is it possible for two people living together to be on the same level of consciousness in order to live in harmony?

The lady's asked the question if it's possible for two people living together to be on the same level of consciousness in order to have harmony. The thing is, with each individual—of course, we are individuals, individualized souls. There are times that we are expressing on the same level of consciousness as another individual.

Now when two people live together, there is a natural tendency for the two people to come into rapport with each other's level of consciousness. What usually happens, fortunately or unfortunately, is because of a lack of understanding, they become bored at certain times, because they are experiencing the same level of consciousness too frequently. Then, we have what we call separations, divorces, and all types of problems. Now two people living together, if they will recognize and accept that every human soul vibrates on different levels of consciousness at different times, that there are times when we are on the same level—and when we're on the same level of consciousness as another individual, then we have the understanding that that individual has on that particular level of consciousness. That doesn't mean that it is a clear understanding. But it does mean that if we are in rapport with another individual, that means we're on the same level of consciousness and we have the understanding that that particular level of consciousness grants. Do you understand?

Now, it is not advisable for two people living together to spend too much time on the same level of consciousness, because it is the nature of form that opposites attract, you understand. So I hope that's helped with your question.

Could you define reasonable control *and* self-control? *What are the differences?*

Well, yes, thank you. The gentleman has asked for a definition of *reasonable control* and *self-control*. Well, first off, if we want to express reasonable control, then we have awakened, to some extent, our soul faculty of reason. Now, when we have awakened our consciousness to our soul faculty of reason, then we are expressing consideration. And if we have fully opened that faculty, then we are expressing total consideration. So that is reasonable control, by using the soul faculty of reason.

Now regarding self-control, ofttimes a person understands self-control to be a suppression of all of their desires. So, therefore, if we are practicing what we call self-control and if self-control means to us to suppress our desires, to control our emotions according to certain standards or circumstances or conditions which we have merited, there is a vast, vast difference. However, the first thing to do is to get a student to some degree of self-control in order to move their soul consciousness up to a reasonable control. Does that help with your question?

Yes, thank you.

Yes. In other words, reasonable control is, by far, preferable to what is called self-control. But we have to start with first steps first.

You mentioned that there are eighty-one levels of consciousness. You talk about level eighteen and nineteen—

Yes.

And I don't find anything about that in The Living Light.

That is correct.

Would you share with us at least some of the levels of which you are speaking and how to recognize them or else how to get in contact with them?

Yes. The lady has asked a question in reference to level eighteen—level nineteen is the level that was mentioned, I believe, and level sixteen—and just how to get into contact with those levels and what does each level mean. First of all, students, a level of consciousness is what the soul is expressing on at any given moment. Now, in order to become aware of the levels of consciousness, we must make a conscious effort daily, more than once or twice, to gain some understanding of our feelings and our emotions.

Now some people think that they have outgrown this or that level of consciousness or patterns of expression. Remember, you may have risen your soul consciousness out of a certain level, but it is ever waiting for you to express on that level again. Now, it will not be, to my present understanding, of any benefit to you to give you the various meanings and the numbers of the levels of consciousness until such time as at least 50 percent of the class has made the conscious, daily effort to find the different feelings and their own levels first. When that effort is made by at least 50 percent of the class, and they are able to demonstrate that, I will be more than happy to share with the class the names and the numbers of the eighty-one levels of consciousness. But, you see, friends, it would be like me giving you an advanced problem or a solution to an advanced problem of algebra and we haven't yet demonstrated the basic fundamentals of mathematics. I hope that's helped with your question.

You just mentioned that opposites attract—

In form.

Could you explain that a little bit further, please, in conjunction with what you've taught us, which is like attracts like?

Yes, thank you very much. And I'm very happy that you've brought that point up. The teachings of these classes are that like attracts like and becomes the Law of Attachment. It is the nature of form or creation that opposites attract. Now let us analyze and discuss that very important question. If a person is thinking love, they will not attract its opposite. I'm sure we will all agree on that. Is that correct? However, whatever the mind entertains in thought, we all, I'm sure, will accept, it experiences it in life.

Now when a thought leaves the vehicle of mind, it goes out into the atmosphere as a dual expression. It attracts of its own kind and, therefore, like attracts like and becomes this attachment. However, it is the opposite pole that attracts the opposite in creation. Now I'm sure that that seems like algebra to most of us, so let's go through it again. A thought is an electromagnetic impulse. That's what it is. It leaves one's mind; it leaves one's aura. It attracts the same out of the atmosphere from other minds. However, it is the magnetic pole of that thought that attracts the electrical pole of the thought that is waiting to receive it. Does that help you? And it is vice versa: it is the magnetic which attracts the electrical. However, the characteristic, you understand, the basic principle of the thought itself is the same. That may seem contradictory to you, but if you will study a little more deeply on the electromagnetic fields and how they operate, I'm sure you will gain more understanding.

Yes. Someone else? Yes, please.

How can you tell if you're giving out the vibrations or if they're coming in? I mean, how do you differentiate them?

Yes. What is coming in is what has been sent out.

That's what I thought.

Yes, yes, that's what helps awaken us, you see. All we have to do is just be at peace and watch what's coming into our aura, into our universe, because we can be rest assured that we were transmitting that at some time on some level. You see, our purpose here is to help you to become aware of these levels of consciousness, to become aware of your subconscious, and become aware of these different levels. Because so many times in life, so many times a person says, "Now, I wasn't thinking those types of things and look at the experience I'm having!" Well, the thing is, my friends, that those types of things were being broadcast on one of your levels of consciousness at some time or you could not possibly be experiencing them. It is impossible, my friends, and totally contrary to the natural law to experience anything that you, as a sending, transmitting, electromagnetic vehicle, have not been sending out. So if we have experiences in our life that we do not appreciate, then pause and think and go inside and find out on what level, you understand, in your own being you are transmitting those vibrations. Does that help?

Yes.

You see, my friends, remember that we are an individualized soul and a vehicle known as mind. But remember, that is an inseparable part of the whole and whatever one mind experiences, all minds experience on that level of consciousness. So whenever that level of consciousness is triggered in your own mind, you will have that experience.

Now they talk a lot about suggestibility and etc. Well, of course, we are suggestible to all things that exist in mind because we are an inseparable part of the principle of mind itself. And therefore, we can experience anything that any mind experiences anyplace at any time. It lies within our potential. Does that help you with your question?

Yes.

Yes.

I'd like to know your understanding of what is duty.

What is duty? Yes, thank you very much. Our understanding of the word *duty,* and I think we mentioned it earlier, will be discussed with this class on the creative principle, when the diagram will be given in the coming class. If you wouldn't mind being patient for just a few weeks. Thank you very much. Yes. I believe a question was asked on duty and motive and an understanding of both. Remember, all things are recorded in memory par excellence, you see. So it's only a matter of pausing before we speak, and then we can let that taped record come up. Yes.

Does someone else have a question, please?

Mr. Goodwin, can you help me, and maybe some of the other students, in meditating, to still the mind, to keep it focused on peace or keep it centered on peace. We all have a tendency—at least I know that my mind occasionally wanders. How long are we supposed to keep our minds still? Or what is the limit? Is there any limit to time that we can keep our mind still?

Do you mean while you are concentrating on peace?

Yes.

Yes. It's recommended five minutes of concentration, five minutes of total silence or meditation. And, of course, many students say they have such a difficulty when they go to concentrate, because so many thoughts and feelings come into their experience. And this is a wonderful thing, in truth, friends, because it reveals to us that we have no control of our emotions, though we think we are controlling our emotions and feelings. Whenever you go to do your meditation, your concentration and meditation, and if you have your mind filled with all types of experiences and all kinds of pictures and thoughts and feelings, this is revealing to you—to each individual student—that you have absolutely, a bare minimum of control over your feelings, your emotions. Because that's, you see, the way the mind is. There's been no practice. There's been no discipline. There's been no reasonable control, you see.

And so when you sit silently and you see all of those pictures and feelings and things going through your head, just think what's happening in the course of a day and night. You see, you're not being still. You're not trying to be still to see what's happening. The mind is a constant panorama. It's one image right after another with absolutely no control, no guidance of any type whatsoever. And so it is that man has so many problems, because, you see, these impulses keep hitting the mind.

Now anyone that has tried to sit down and truly concentrate, I know they've had that experience of all those pictures and all those feelings and things hitting their mind. Well, that's telling them, my good friend, "You have almost totally lost control."

And if some experience comes to you—you see, what happens is, a person says, "Well, I had a terrible experience out there." Well, the thing is that an image hit the brain and you set a law into motion. And, you see, by not having any control of yourself—this is happening to us all of the time. And so we're having all of these different experiences. And so we feel good one minute and we just feel terrible the next. And all this is caused by all of these impulses and these pictures, you see, and the mind stuff. And there's no control.

I can only suggest to the students and to the class, a greater effort, a greater effort before you speak. A greater effort before you express: to stop in that second—it's only a split second—that you can rise your consciousness to the soul faculty of reason and gain a little bit of control, so that you won't be batted back and forth in the seas of time. And so when an experience comes to you, you will be able to stand still for an instant, you see. And if it is undesirable, to have the faith and to have the strength and the energy to know that it shall pass. You see, my friends, no matter whatever happens in life, by the Law of

Coming to us, it is guaranteed to leave. So there is nothing in life that is so disastrous that it should cause us such great misery.

We're constantly, and always have been, expressing this great eternity, this spirit that's within us. It comes to us and it goes from us, and it's a constant panorama. So the best thing that we can do, my friends, is learn to be still, perfectly still. And when we're perfectly still, we're moving in the divine flow. And that's the only time we are really moving in the divine flow. Because when we're perfectly still, all the created mind stuff disappears and you're with your spirit. You're with your God. I hope that's helped with your questions.

[No hands are raised, so the teacher continues.]

If there are no other questions, we can have a short class this evening. I'm always grateful, of course.

I have found a great difference between simply becoming aware of something or perceiving something and understanding something or putting it into application. And I wonder if you could speak on this.

Thank you very much. Of course, we all know that awareness doesn't guarantee understanding. You see, man can be aware of the rocket ship that flies to the moon and not understand the principle by which it works. You see, there are so many levels on which to become aware. Now, if we're not aware on the full levels of consciousness, which, in this teaching, is eighty-one, then we're not going to have full understanding. But let's be honest with ourselves. I don't see any saints walking around the Earth in this day and age and I honestly question how saintly some were in the days and ages past.

But that's beside the point. You wanted a discussion of awareness and understanding. Now we do teach that without an opening of the soul faculty of duty, gratitude, and tolerance, there is no opening of the understanding. Because we cannot understand ourselves unless we have duty to our own spirit, which is the true self, we have gratitude for its expression, and we have tolerance for these levels of consciousness that are so difficult for most of us to grow through.

So we start with duty, gratitude, and tolerance for ourselves, you see. See, the great delusion of the mind is to try to work on somebody else. It's a total waste of effort, I can assure you. A wise man tries working on himself first. Then, he shares his understanding when it is solicited. And by doing that, he continues to work on himself, not on someone else. Remember, friends, you never change a thing in life. You change your own perspective. You change your outlook toward it. That's how it really works.

If you want, or you feel that you need, someone in your life expressing on a different level of consciousness than what they are expressing on, you do not go to work on that individual: you go to work on yourself. And when you go to work on yourself, you go through the soul faculty of duty, gratitude, and tolerance in here. Then, you rise your soul consciousness to a level where you see the good in the person that you wanted to change. Now by seeing that good and becoming that good in yourself, you will attract that goodness from another human soul or an animal or whatever it is that you are trying to be in rapport with on a certain level of consciousness.

Now the old brain says, "Well, this, of course, is an illusion. I'm just deluding myself. I'm feeling good, but he hasn't changed at all." Well, you haven't quite arrived if you still think that way. Because when you've really arrived, the person that you are in relationship with—at least as far as you are concerned and with your experience—will rise to that level of consciousness that you and you alone are expressing.

So, you see, my friends, as long as the mind insists—the brain—on seeing the frailties—now what it's really doing when we see the frailties and things outside, what we are really doing is seeing the frailties inside of ourselves. But this deludes us and we think it is out there.

So in reference to awareness and understanding, I can only say, make a greater effort on the first soul faculty of being, which is duty, gratitude, and tolerance. Now, when you make these changes, if that is your desire, when you make these changes to have a better life, a more enjoyable life, a more peaceful life, it's going to take faith and patience and continuity. Because that level of consciousness in a world of creation is not the easiest thing to attain, let alone to sustain. I hope that's helped with your question.

Very much. Thank you.

You're welcome. Yes.

It's my understanding that we had a preview of this incarnation before we physically entered this form. Could you describe what the review is when we go to another dimension? How complete is it? Or how does it take place?

Thank you very much. Whenever the soul enters form, and prior to its entering the form of the planet on which it is to express, it does go through a review of where it's been and a preview of where it is going. That is, all of the experiences and expressions that it had in its prior expression or incarnation are reviewed and, also, the various lessons that are to be learned in the incoming form.

Now, when we leave this earth realm, most of us will leave with what we call an astral body. Now the astral body, of course, is very similar to our physical body. The imperfections of the physical body are also in the astral body and, of course, the mental body. And we will express in an astral-mental realm if we have not garnered up spiritual substance, which creates, of course, our spiritual body.

Now, we leave this earth realm and we go through the experiences of this entire expression here on this earth plane. We will not only go through those experiences, you understand, but we will *live through* the transgressions or the errors that we have made. Now, this is not something that some intelligence or some power outside of us does to us. This is what our own conscience does to us. Now some people say, "Well, so-and-so doesn't even *have* a conscience." Well, of course, we understand the person making that expression is in the level of what is known as judgment, you understand. And it may seem to some people that there are others who don't have a conscience. And usually when a person says another person doesn't have a conscience, what they're really saying is, "The other individual is blocking my desires of what I want." Now that's what, *usually*, a person means when they say somebody else doesn't have a conscience. That's what they usually mean by that statement.

So when we leave this physical body, we are in our astral body. We live in those levels of consciousness, which we gradually grow through. Now, there is a reviewing, as I said earlier, of the life experience and there is also a preview of the future experience.

You see, it's a wonderful system. The divine law is a beautiful thing. By having a review and a preview, there is an inner urge within all souls to do better. There is this drive within us to try to work things out. You understand? And so when we touch that level of consciousness, we will know why we're here. We will know the great, divine justice of meriting the life experience we have and we will also know exactly what we did to get here. And when we know that, we will know where we're going. Now we usually don't like it, but that's not the point, friends. That's what we earned. And that's the way it really works. I hope that's helped you.

You said that most people will leave in an astral body.

That is correct.

What about the remainder?

There are some people who have merited, through their own efforts in this lifetime, or the ones prior, to enter a realm of spirit or spirit lands with a spiritual body. Of course, we cannot function on a plane of consciousness without the substance of that plane of consciousness for our vehicle of expression. And so it is that we do teach the soul faculties and the wisdom of making some effort to unfold them. Because when the energy is expressed through those soul faculties, that, in turn, is garnering up spiritual substance, you see, which is building our spiritual body here and now. Yes.

Thank you.

You're welcome. Yes.

In your theory of evolutionary incarnation, when a soul is born on this planet, does that mean that he has been, in his previous incarnation, on another planet? Or could he have subsequent incarnations on this planet?

Thank you very much for your question. Our teaching is evolutionary incarnation, which means that the soul is evolving from planet to planet. And remember, friends, a teaching is only a theory until we come to a level of consciousness where it is our truth. But that's up to us. Yes.

I would like you to expand more on meditation.

What would you like to know about meditation?

Just how to go about it and more on how it works. Is your mind supposed to be blank? Clear of all thoughts? And is this the vehicle to get to the different levels to know what we're all about?

It is for me, yes. And it has been for many other students. You see, the first thing on the path to understanding anything is to become aware of it. Would you not agree? And so, first, we want to become aware of what is controlling us. Now we can say, "Well, I control myself." But can we say that honestly or truthfully, unless we are aware of the levels of consciousness that are affecting our life or our soul? No, we cannot honestly say that. Because a person cannot say, "Well, I make all my decisions and I control all of my thoughts. And anything that I want to do, I do it myself. I don't have any influences. I don't listen to anyone." Well, that's a very ridiculous statement, because we are being influenced on levels of consciousness that we're not even aware of. Now the reason that we're being influenced on those levels, you understand, is according to natural law. However, if we don't want to be influenced on those invisible levels of consciousness, then we've got to become aware of those levels and we have to do something about it. Would you not agree?

And so that is one of the important parts in concentration and in meditation: to become aware and to be able to still the mind. To be able to reach your own soul and to awaken within your own being so that you, as an individualized soul, know where your thoughts come from. Where are your feelings, your drives, your impulses, and all of these things, where are they coming from? Are they coming from within your own being? Or are you receptive to the influence of someone else's desires in your life? You see, that's where most people are.

You see, now they'll be walking down the street and all of a sudden they'll decide, "Well, I think I'll go in that store." You know, it just comes out of the blue, they say, just all of a sudden. And they go in, and the next thing you know, they've bought something. Then, they get home and say, "Now I wonder why I bought that?" Well, you see, we're not aware. We're not aware.

Now years and years ago there was—in fact, it was outlawed by the U.S. government—there was what was known as subliminal perception. And it was something that they started in the movie houses way back in the early fifties. It didn't last very long, I assure you. They found, by flashing on the screen very rapidly, "Buy popcorn," that they were able to sell popcorn to over 90 percent of all of the people in the movie house. Well, it was outlawed by Congress and very wisely so. So, you see, if man is so susceptible, which, in truth, he is, you must realize, students, that you're not expressing your own real inner being until you become aware of what's influencing your lives.

You see, you could be driving along the highway and someone that you know might decide that they would like to see you. And then, the next thing you find out, you're driving on and you get home, and just out of the blue you decide to call this particular person. Well, now, if that works with one person, then it works with all people, because that demonstrates the principle of the law itself. And so we stress the importance of gaining, that is, reaching this point within ourselves that's known as peace. And that's why it's so important for your concentration to control yourself, to be able to put your thought on one thing and one thing only, and to keep your consciousness there, you see.

It's happening, my friends, all the time. Look at the people that have let themselves get into the mass vibration of the so-called energy crisis and all of this disaster and everything, you see. Why is it easier for people to accept and experience the disasters and the horrors in life and seemingly so difficult for them to express and experience the good in life? Why is that? We must ask ourselves the question, "Why is that true?" You have a ten-car accident down on the freeway and you'll have hundreds of people down there just to witness it. If somebody's murdering someone down the street, you'll have a whole mob of people to witness it. Now why is that? However, if there's someone out on the street corner trying to tell you about God's love and the good life that we really have a divine right to enjoy, you might see one or two people. Now why is that? We must ask ourselves the question. Disaster and those things excite the senses, the emotions, those feelings. And consequently, like a great magnet, we flock to them.

Stop and think, of all the words spoken in the course of a day, how many words are really spoken from the heart that says, "What a good person that is. How kind of them to do this or that!" No. It's usually, "Why didn't they do something better?" Well, think, now, why is this? Why is that? Because we are not controlling ourselves. We are letting our minds, our feelings, our beings be controlled by the masses of people. That's what caused the last depression: mass hysteria. And that's what will cause any other recession or depression. What do you think causes the earthquakes and the calamities in nature? It's man's disturbed thinking and nature reacts. Because that's what happens. Yes.

I have a question that has to do with matrimony and man-woman relationships. If you identify yourself with the spirit, then you, well, at least I tend not to be a gender. I don't know if it's something lacking within myself for not wanting a home life, but it seems like a pursuit of matrimony would be, like, backsliding on a spiritual path. Because eventually you come to a oneness with God, who is everybody. So why would you single out someone for a crutch through life and, perhaps, meet on the other side and continue? I think you probably, generally, sense what I'm trying to say.

The question is indeed a very deep one. In fact, a full class could be devoted to it. However, let us get to the point of the question, I believe, that the lady asked: Is it a so-called backsliding from a spiritual awakening or a spiritual nature to be married? Well, my good friends, we must realize this: It is no more of a backsliding from God or the Spirit to be married than it is to go and eat a dinner, to put food in our stomach. Because, you see, if we look on that level of consciousness, then when we have to say, "Well, now, matrimony or marriage has an appeal to the senses." Then, we're going to have to say, "Well, food has an appeal to the senses, because when I'm hungry I have those hunger pains in my stomach. And when I fill my stomach, then I feel better and, therefore, there is a fulfillment there."

The question is a very deep question. And we must realize that it is not the purpose, of course, of these classes or the teachings to recommend or not to recommend marriage. We do say this: There are married people who are very spiritual and it does not seem to be a detriment to their soul awakening. There are, however, also people who are not married who are very spiritual, aware, and awake, and being single does not appear to be a detriment to them.

Now, whether a person is married or single, in and of itself, has nothing to do with their finding their God. If a person is able to find God through a so-called marriage and family, then that is the way that that individual should find their God. If a person, however, is able to find their God by not being married or remaining single and not having a family, then that is the way that particular soul should find their God. Because, you see, my friends, it isn't a matter of just dealing with this moment in this earth plane. It is a matter of a whole process of experiences and education of the soul through a multitude of soul incarnations.

Now, when God is first, then all is well, whether it is a marriage or a person is single. I say this and I firmly believe it: A married man or a family can put God above all form. And many people do. That doesn't mean that they all do.

And so the question cannot be answered in the sense that it's advisable to marry or it's not advisable to marry. I do hope that's helped with your question.

With regard to what you were saying in answer to the preceding question, I wonder if you would comment on what you think the effect of newspapers is on people in terms of the mass hysteria and the excitement of the senses and that sort of thing.

Thank you very much. It has proven itself and continues to prove to be, on the whole, most detrimental in the sense that it continues to feed the emotional realm of the masses. It continues to feed the senses and disturb the mind. In that sense, it has proven to be most detrimental. Does that help with your question?

It gives me something to think about.

We're not recommending that they discontinue printing newspapers, but we are saying they have proven to be most detrimental. Because when you talk to people who, daily, read the newspaper, you understand, and they stop at every story of disaster and horror, see what state of consciousness that they are usually in. Then, I'm sure you will agree that it's most detrimental for most people.

My question goes back to meditation.

Yes.

I have tried to meditate in the past, but haven't been lately. And I've found that I would find some answers. But to be perfectly still—you said to find your God. Then, would you experience it through an emotional feeling rather than your mind?

No. It isn't an experience through what we usually refer to as an emotional feeling. Things that are of a spiritual nature, such as a meditation, do not excite the emotions or the senses. If they do, they're not from the higher levels of light, you understand? And unless you consider a feeling of great peace to be an emotional experience, then, in that sense, you could consider it an emotion. Yes.

As a follow-up to the matrimony question, it seems that as we do progress spiritually, we give things up, like we fast. It's my understanding that many people on a spiritual path have done this. And we give up things of the senses, so that we take as little as possible of creation into our lives. So in this respect, pursuing the question that I asked formerly, it sort of seems to me as if a higher path, or a closer path to that which is spiritual, would be relinquishing the form. Moses did this, I believe. Do those of us on our spiritual path eventually relinquish the idea of matrimony on this side or the other side?

Thank you very much. It does seem to be very important here to the students: matrimony. However, in reference to giving up the certain things of what we call the senses, it has been my experience, over many years, that more married people have given up many things of the senses than single people. Now, I haven't yet really understood how this really takes place. But it does seem to me, over these many years of counseling, that it's more of the married, family people that have given up so much more of the pleasure ground of the senses than the single people.

Now we're back to our question of matrimony. My friends, we're constantly giving up because we're constantly gaining. You see, you never give up anything that you don't gain something else. Now, for example, if you decide to go on to do some spiritual studies, well, you will find, as you're spending a little time with the spiritual studies, you're not spending as much time with the things that you were spending so much time with before. So in that sense, we all are constantly giving as we are gaining. In fact, my friends, it's impossible—it is absolutely contrary to natural law—to gain without giving. Talk to any good, intelligent, sensible businessman: he'll tell you it's not possible to gain a thing unless you're willing to give.

You see, my friends, the mind seeks to gain like a sponge. But it does not want to give. So it is a house divided and it cannot stand. We must think and say, "I want to gain this and I want to gain that and I want to gain that." Fine, we have reached our decision. Now we must say, "Let me see what I find is no longer of any benefit to me, so that I may choose wisely what I desire to give up." Because, you see, friends, you cannot gain without giving. It is impossible. And this is why the statement was given so long ago: The joy of living is the Law of Giving.

You cannot gain, my friends, you cannot gain one iota more unless you are giving in some area, some place. A person says, "Well, I don't believe in that." Well, your presence here is a living demonstration that on some level of consciousness that you do. You gave up over an hour of your time to be here and you have received in the process. Perhaps, what you have received you have liked or not liked. That is immaterial. It is a demonstration of the law.

If you decide that you want to sit down at the table and eat something, then you are giving up something else in that process. It is a constant thing: the Law of Giving. Man does not exist without it. You are giving of this breath of life constantly and you are also taking it in, and so you are gaining. And so isn't it sensible that we come to some understanding of balance? And we say, "All right, I want to be more spiritual. Now in the process I'm going to have to give up something, but I will only have to give up what *I* decide to give up and I will only gain according to what I am willing to give up."

But, you see, friends, there is no one here or hereafter that can tell you what to give up to gain spiritually. Because they do not know your soul merit system. Now it might well be that some individual might have to give up golf. The reason they might have to give it up is because it has become such an attachment and such a desire in their life that it has become an obstruction and, therefore, nothing more can fit into their life.

And so it is that each one, being very individual in their merit system, if they are honest with themselves, they will know what they have to give up. And I'll tell you, friends, it's usually quite a surprise when we find out what it is that we have to give up in life to gain what it is we really want. It's usually the thing that's furthest from our mind. Because, you see, there's one thing about attachments: they're very subtle. You know, we walk around life and say, "Well, I'm not attached to that. Doesn't matter whether I have it or I don't have it." Wait till it's taken from you, then you'll know how attached you've been to it.

Thank you, friends. Let us go have refreshments. Thank you very much.

JANUARY 24, 1974

CONSCIOUSNESS CLASS 37 ✀

Good evening, class. Before getting to your questions and answers this evening, I would like to have a short discussion, perhaps, on the discourse that you have just read, Discourse 44. We find a statement in that discourse that is a very important part of the teachings of the Living Light. And it states in that discourse that God is a divine, neutral power that neutralizes anything and everything that comes in contact with it.

We understand by the word *neutrality,* a perfect balance. And so it is that when we find ourselves disturbed and ill at ease, it is a revelation to us that we are out of balance. So what we're saying in this particular discourse is that when you find yourself out of balance, in any level of consciousness, the way to bring balance into your life is to find this Divinity, this God, this Infinite Intelligence.

Now, some students—in fact, many—have stated over the years that they have great difficulty in finding God or this Divine Neutral Power. Difficulties in anything that we are seeking do one of two things to us: either they discourage us, because we are weak and we no longer seek what we were seeking, or they inspire us to make a greater effort to attain what we're striving to attain. This is not something where a person can say, "Well, I have tried for years to find this Divinity, this Neutral Power, and I haven't found it yet." If a person is having difficulty finding anything in life, the difficulty is not the responsibility or the cause of anything outside of our own thinking and our own efforts.

I realize, of course, that many people in life, not finding what they're seeking in one place, will go to another. Surely, in time, someday, somehow, some way, we will find it. But when we find it, friends, when we really find it, we will realize that we had it with us all of the time, but we did not have the patience and the continuity of effort to find it earlier than we did.

You see, so many times the mind dictates to us that we feel peace when we're in a certain circumstance or a certain locality. If that is what we accept, of course, then that is where we're going to find peace. But that's not a very practical way of finding what we're seeking, because we may not always be able to get to that particular place when we need to the most. So isn't it a more practical, sensible, and logical way, to sit down wherever you are and find that that you're seeking.

Now remember, he who chases the rainbow is only chasing himself, because that rainbow, that promise, you already have. All you have to do, friends, is to have the simplicity of a little child and accept it. Then, you will know you always had it.

Now you're free to ask whatever questions that you have, if you'll just raise your hands.

In order to have a degree of balance or harmony within us, we think of saying affirmations to the Divine Intelligence or God daily and we do experience some of God's natural laws. We are in a partial state of balance. I don't know how complete it can be at that particular time, when, say, our life may not be so completely harmonious. Is there such a thing as complete balance and complete harmony? And does this refer to the eighty-one levels of awareness?

Yes, indeed, it does. And I do not know of any form on Earth that is maintaining and sustaining a perfect balance at all times. Because if we did manage to sustain a perfect balance, while in form, for any extended period of time, we would not long be in form. Because it is these opposites that do keep us in the form and keep the divine spark in all forms.

However, what we are teaching is the value and the benefit of attaining this peace, this great peace, this perfect balance, periodically, during the course of our acts and activities of our days. Does that help with your question? Yes. And if you can, if you can even get a glimmer of this peace that passeth all understanding, just a glimmer for a fraction of a second, then you have truly made great effort. Yes.

I would like you to explain, "Many are called, but few are chosen."

Thank you very much. Yes, I have been asked that question before and it's a very important one. It's stated in the Christian Bible and it states that, "Many are called, but few are chosen." And what a very truthful statement that is. Multitudes of people are called to the Light of eternity, to the eternal Light of Truth, which is known, we understand, to be God. But very few people choose to remain. It is not God, the Divine, that selects them: man selects himself. And so this is our understanding of the biblical statement that, "Many are called, but few are chosen."

Sir, could you please elaborate a little bit on soul faculties and sense functions and give some very sound, basic examples?

I'll be more than happy to give what examples I can. Of course, I'm sure we all accept and realize the soundness of any statement is dependent upon the recipient and our own levels of consciousness. But I will be more than happy to share with you my understanding of the soul faculties and the sense functions.

Now we have spoken before on—we'll take, for example, the most important soul faculty, most important in the sense that it is the first soul faculty. And that one, you all know, is duty, gratitude, and tolerance. Now when our energy, our conscious-ness is expressing through a soul faculty, there is no thought of concern. There is no interest in the effect of our efforts. That is one very important difference between a sense function and a soul faculty.

Now many people—as we're all in this sense world—are con-cerned with what is commonly referred to as material substance. We have stated before that gratitude opens the door to eternal supply. Now it appears that many people do not understand what that really means. So let us put it in as sound, as down-to-earth, and as practical an example as perhaps we can. We're all in a material world. We're all in a spiritual world. We're in those worlds here and now. They are not something that we are moving to. Most people think that they are going to a spiritual world. The spiritual world, friends, that you may experience ten years from today is the spiritual world that you're already in.

Now this is very important, that we get this understanding. Death, so-called, or passing from this dimension, is not some-thing to look forward to, unless you look forward to your pres-ent moment. We are not going to have a transformation when we leave the physical body at so-called death and arrive in a heaven where the light never fades. Let us not delude ourselves with this type of thinking. Our soul faculties, which have no concern for the effects of our efforts, are the very things that are building our spiritual body that we may function in a spiritual world right here and now.

Now, I don't want to be misunderstood. I'm not saying that people who are psychic already have a spiritual body or that people who are mediums already have a spiritual body. Because that is no demonstration of truth. They may or they may not. I want to clarify that we do not seek the gifts of the Spirit: we seek the Spirit itself.

Now what does this have to do with soul faculties and sense functions? It has a great deal to do with both. We stated that gratitude is the principle through which the door of supply, of eternal abundance, flows into our life. Now, if we are honest with ourselves and we say, during the course of our days and our thoughts, "Am I grateful for what I have? Or am I not grateful for what I have?" Now there's a little, simple exercise you can do and find out very quickly whether or not you're really grateful—all of us—and that is to visualize that you have absolutely no material supply. It has all disintegrated before your very eyes. You have nothing. You don't have a car. You don't have a house. You don't have a bank account. You have nothing which is known as material substance. Now, after you have accepted that visualization, you write down the five most important things that you will do in your life, now that you have no material substance. After you have done that, then you visualize that you have whatever material substance that you desire: cars, houses, bank accounts, etc. Be honest with yourself, friends, and you'll find out where you are and you'll learn about the soul faculties and the sense functions. Now write down the five most important things in your life: the five things that you really want to do.

If there is any difference between the five things that you wanted to do that were most important to you when you had nothing of a material nature and they are not the same as the five things that are most important to you now that you have all the material substance that you want, then you may be rest assured, my friends, that the soul faculty and the principle of gratitude is blocked and you're in very deep water. It means, my friends, that you are out of balance between the sense function and the soul faculty.

Now, why are you out of balance? Well, it's very simple. Because the things that were important to you in one area are not important in the other. And you are not in principle, but you are in personality. You are controlled by form.

Now, if you will do that little exercise, you will find the soundness of the soul faculties and the sense functions. You will not only find their soundness and their practicality, but you will find the wisdom of learning who you are and what you are, so that you may know at any given moment where you are.

Now if I sat here and I listed for you the states of consciousness and went through all of the gymnastics of the letter of the law, that would certainly feed information into your brain, but it would not, my friends, help you to grow. I'm happy to answer your questions, whenever I am able to, but you must do your part. And your part, as students, is to think.

Our educational system puts a great deal of statistics and facts into our brains. But let us be honest and ask ourselves the question, "What does it do for my own soul? What does it really do for me in helping me to use the faculties that the Divine Intelligence has given to me?" I hope that's helped with your question.

In my daily activities, I hear so much about selfless service. If people want you to do something, they say, "Now, do this selfless service. Bring this. Take that." Would you give us a true meaning of selfless service and if it's where we are, when we are there, or do we have to do something special to give selfless service?

Thank you very much. You brought up a most important point. If we feel that someone is requesting us to do selfless service and we feel that they are using what is commonly referred to as a device—this is what you brought up.

Yes.

Then, wisdom dictates that we stop and think. We're not concerned about the person that is using what we call selfless service as a device. But we must be most concerned that it's coming to us. Now this is important, students, if you want to help yourselves. Right here and now we stop. And we must ask ourselves the question, "Why does this experience come to me? And why does it come to me now? Why doesn't it come tomorrow? Or why didn't it come yesterday?" Because the experience is a revelation of the level of consciousness that we, as individuals, are expressing.

So, you see, everyone we meet and every situation that we encounter is, in truth, the best friend we ever had. Because what it is doing for us, friends, if we will have a little bit of self-control and reasonable control and just a little bit of common sense, is to say to us, "Look, that's where you are and you didn't even know it." Now isn't it a blessing, truly—perhaps, in seeming disguise—to know where we are at any given moment? Because if we know where we really are, then we will know what to do.

Now, we'll speak on selfless service, the principle of selfless service. But you did bring up an important point which is commonly referred to as device. You do understand, don't you?

Yes, I do.

And I hope that has helped all of the students.

What is selfless service? Well, selfless service, my friends, is really quite simple. It is a service for the sake of service, without the thought, need, or concern for recognition or attention. Now, if we are truly doing a self*less* service, then we are doing a service for the principle of service itself.

We have stated before, and state again, that God, the Divine Intelligence, is the greatest servant of all. After all, it is this Divine God that keeps all things in space; that sustains all things everywhere. Well, if that isn't service, I don't know what service is.

So when you're doing a selfless service, what you are is an instrument, unobstructed, for the divine flow and expression of God. However, if you have a need to state what selfless service you are doing, or contemplating doing, then, my friends, you have just gotten your reward: it is not selfless at all. I hope that's helped all of our students.

Could you elaborate a little bit on sense functions?

Thank you very much. Yes, I will be happy to share a little more on sense functions. It is a sense function to eat, which sustains the physical body. It is a sense function to desire things of the flesh. It is a sense function, such as greed, envy, jealousy—these, my friends, are sense functions. Now let's take a sense function known as greed. What is greed? Does anyone know what that word means? Anyone care to venture? What is greed?

Well, a synonym would be covetousness.

And what is covetousness?

Wanting something that doesn't belong to you. Or it could be wanting something that or—desiring is a better word—desiring something that someone else has. You already have it, but you want what they have; so that's a double thing.

Thank you very much. Anyone else have an explanation of the word *greed?*

Is it a reaction of the self-preservation?

Does anyone else have an explanation of the word *greed?*

Selfishness?

Selfishness. Thank you very much. Anyone else have an understanding of that word?

Uneducated desire?

Uneducated desire. Thank you.

Lack of control?

Lack of control. Thank you. Do you have an expression of the word *greed?*

Rejection of the true source.

Thank you very much. Now, we're discussing one of the sense functions that's known as greed. Now remember, friends, there's absolutely nothing wrong with a sense function if it's brought into some kind of balance. Now, "What is greed?" has been the question. Let us consider that greed is desire without the balance and counterbalance of the soul faculty of reason. A student explained this quite nicely in one way: she felt it was uneducated desire. It is desire without the balance and counter-balance of the soul faculty of reason.

Now, again we state, Keep faith with reason: she will trans-figure thee. Say that a person sees, perhaps, a suit. They like that suit. Well, the desire for the suit, there's nothing wrong with the desire for the suit. What becomes wrong, in the sense that it's out of balance, is when the desire demands ten suits or twenty or fifty or two hundred or five hundred, which is beyond the reason and the logic of use.

Now we have another statement, which is, More than you use is more than you need. On the other hand, The lack of use is abuse. Now if we are greedy and we have to have five hundred suits, well, it doesn't matter to the suits: they're a piece of mate-rial. But it certainly matters to the individual who is unable to use the soul faculty of reason and bring some degree of balance into their life.

Now, let us not go around and say, "Well, you have too many of these. You have too many of those." Because each individ-ual has their own balance and counterbalance, and some peo-ple's needs are greater than others. But let us face the sense functions, not with fear, because you'll only go further out of balance, but let us face them openly and let us face them objectively. Because they are a part of the form and we're not going to get rid of them. Don't try suppressing them. Because if you do that, you're going to be in real trouble, because they're going to come out in some other way. But bring them up to the fore and recognize them and accept them for what they are. They're our own children. They belong to us. We're the creators of them. So let's treat them kindly, sensibly, and logically. And let's not hide and fear that we have so many frailties to grow through. Well, friends, if we didn't have these frailties, well, what would be the sense of growing? What would you grow to?

Life is a variety of experience. And it's going to constantly come and it's going to constantly go. It's a movie that keeps passing on by. So what is so important in life, what is really so important that we should be disturbed over this or over that? Because it's coming and going constantly. And there are experiences that everyone has, when everything fails but the Divine itself. Now I hope that's helped with some understanding on the functions and the faculties.

While we're on the functions, I wonder if you would discuss continuity. This is a very important faculty that seems to kind of permeate so many things that we do in life. Why is it that it takes so long to develop a pattern, and yet once that pattern is broken, it's so easy to break it again and again? What triggers this?

Thank you very much. In reference to patterns, all of us here, everywhere, have patterns that have been established for many, many, many, many years, depending on how old we are, depending on the type of form that our soul merited on its evolutionary process.

Now, it seems for some people, of course, that it's easier for them to change patterns than for others. But if you look deeper, you find that the longer a pattern is expressed by anyone, the more difficult it is to change the pattern. So it is that a person desires to go on to a new pattern in life, a new way of thinking.

Perhaps they spend a year, two years, or ten years in their effort. Well, say that they're fifty years old. They have forty years of all the other patterns that are working. So what happens if they are not consistent in their efforts and they do not demonstrate the Law of Continuity? It's very easy and it's a very natural process that they would go back to the pattern that is the strongest, the most established. See, water reaches its own level by its own weight. And so it is with the patterns of mind, the attitudes of mind, that we have entertained for a lifetime. This is why it is difficult—but not impossible, as life itself demonstrates—for a person to make changes in their life.

Now, a person might say, "Well, I had a pattern for a lifetime, and it really didn't take a great deal of effort and I changed that pattern." Well, that's what the conscious mind sees. It doesn't see all of the years of effort and desire to change the pattern thirty years ago or twenty years ago. But that was going on all the time. But the conscious mind that was so satisfied with its patterns, you understand, kept blocking out that inner voice, that inner impression, that says, "It's time to make a change." It kept trying. So what we really did, we finally arrived, but we spent years in the process. Do you understand? But that's gone on beneath the conscious level.

Now we're talking about this continuity and the importance thereof. A person makes a decision. If they're wise, they sit down in some type of meditation or peace with their own vibration, hopefully, and they decide that they're going to do this or they're going to do that. Now they've gone through as many levels as they're capable of being consciously aware of, hopefully, in reaching their decision. Once they reach their decision, you see, that's the most important step, because the mind, its very nature, has a tendency to look back, backward in regret. If only it had done this, instead of that. You can't do anything—no one can—with what has passed. That that has passed, has passed. This moment—that's known as the eternal moment—is the only moment that we really have, in truth. So this is the moment, moment by moment by moment, that we demonstrate this Law of Continuity.

Now where people fail is this, usually: perhaps they've been going on for six months or maybe even a year or two, and their conscious mind cannot see any improvement. The reason their conscious mind cannot see any improvement is because their conscious mind has never been trained to see the inner depths where the process is really taking place first, you see. So it is important that an individual, in any endeavor of changing a pattern, receive some encouragement from somewhere, because that is necessary for the conscious mind that has not been trained to look at the inner depths and the inner levels, where this change is really taking place. Then, as the years pass, it becomes obvious to the conscious mind. I hope that's helped with your question.

I'm interested in illness in small children. I understand that illness is a reflection of being out of balance within oneself.

That is correct.

And therefore, I wonder what an adult can do to help a child who has become ill to regain his or her balance?

By the adult responsible for the child making an effort to bring himself into balance, because the child is reflecting the parent's vibration. You see, the soul merited that type of a parent, you understand, in its evolutionary process and its education. Say that you have a child that's born and there is what you call an imbalance or an illness or a defect. This is the direct reflection or effect of the parent's own imbalance. So if you want to help the child—of course, we do have healing prayers—but if it's the parents that want to help the child, the parents must work on themselves. Yes.

What if the parents are not together?

Well, whatever parent is with the child, that has the responsibility of the child, the spiritual responsibility, you see. The child has to be living with someone. Is that not correct?

The child I have in mind lives with both people about equally.

Then both should share the responsibility. Because if you have a child and they're six months with the father and the father is making an effort to bring himself into balance for the benefit of his own child, and then they go six months with the mother, who doesn't care about making the effort to come into balance, then the father's efforts, of course, are being wasted. You understand? That's not very sensible or practical. Yes.

I ask this in all reverence, after reading The Living Light, *and coming into the understanding that God is neutral and all in all: Why do we thank God? I mean, does God have to be thanked? Or do we thank God in our affirmations, in our thoughts, to bring us into harmony? Would you explain this? I've been thinking about this all week.*

What soul faculty is expressed through the word *thank?*

Gratitude.

Gratitude. And what does that soul faculty do?

It brings us into balance.

It opens the door of continuous supply. Yes. Now isn't it beneficial, wouldn't you think it would be beneficial, friends, if you had received some good in your life, to express the very faculty that guarantees its continuity? So, you see, friends, we don't have some God up there that needs to be thanked. But the "thank you" is a reminder to this thing of the true source of our supply. And that reminder is opening up our soul faculty known as gratitude. Does that help?

Yes.

You see, when I thank a person, I don't thank the person. I am thanking the principle through which the flow is flowing. Perhaps that will help you.

It does help me. Thank you.

Yes. When we see the God, you see, we experience the godhood. You see the good in everything, then that's all that you can attract out of them. Because that's all your eyes will view.

Just like a man and his wife. Well, they can have problems every day, if they want them. But if one of them is smart—it only takes one, really—and if they're smart enough, they can only see the good in the individual. And sooner or later, that's all that that individual can possibly express, because their partner refuses to see anything else.

Now, I'm not concerned about what the neighbors say or the so-called friends of the family. But I'm talking about the two individuals. You see the good, if you demonstrate the Law of Continuity and you're the strongest, then that's all that can come back to you, you see. Yes. You know, there's a saying that, "Well, he's a great family man, but a terrible so-and-so in business." That's understandable.

In reference to the parents and the children, I heard you mention before about the sins are passed—I'm sorry, I'm not quoting it correctly.

Yes, the sins are the errors of the parents and the grandparents. Third generation.

Could you explain that further, please? And why it's the third generation?

Yes, because what happens—and it's in the Bible also, by the way, for you people who are interested in the Bible and care to study it. The third generation: the three is the principle of manifestation. Now, for example, a person, today is the effect of their parents and their grandparents. You understand? They are the effects of those vibrations. Now a person may say, "Well, I have my own individuality." That is not true. They have certain characteristics, very strong ones, that are an effect of their parents and their grandparents. Now whether or not we can see them is something else. We'll have to make the effort to try to find them, you see, and make that study. But that is the manifestation. That is the Law of Manifestation. The three. The trinity. And so it is that it says in the Bible, the errors of the parents shall be invested unto the third generation. It is a very accurate statement.

I have a lot of struggle with reason and thinking versus stilling the mind and being at peace.

When the mind is still and we are at peace, reason reigns supreme. It's when man decides that he must do all the thinking that we have all the problems.

Then, I don't think I know what reason is.

Perhaps you have it confused with analyzing. The statement, Keep faith with reason: she will transfigure thee, means that the soul faculty of reason, once expressed, will transform and renew the mind. It will bring it into balance. You don't have to think and have concern and use the function of concern, you hear, about how is this going to be.

Now, what happens is this: say that a person is in some venture, business or otherwise, or even a family relationship, and they're trying to find the answer to a serious problem that they have. Now the first thing, usually, that they do is they start to think about it. And as they think about it, all of the blame is over there. You understand? That's the number one step. And, of course, that's the emotional level. Then, gradually, if they keep on thinking, they will entertain the possibility that some of the error is in themselves. That's the next step. Then, they go to the third step of trying to find a way to get the other individual to change, because they're willing to change themselves only that much and there's a need for the situation to change *that* much. So, you see, they go right back to the first principle that they started off with, in truth.

Well, after you go through all of that with the mind and with the thinking process, if you will sit back and let go of this, all this thinking process, and you will be at peace, truly at peace—no thought, no concern—you will get an impression. You will get a feeling from within your being. And that is the voice of reason that whispers in many ways. And that will be the balanced way. It will be the right way, for all concerned. That helps you, I'm sure, distinguish between the thinking process and the soul faculty of reason.

You see, remember this, friends: You do not have to feed into the computer your problem for reason, because reason already knows. See? Reason knows the whole situation before it took place. That's why anyone with any sense keeps faith with reason: She knows all. Yes.

We are taught that what we entertain in thought, we experience in life.

That is correct.

Is this always true? Or if one person has a thought and, perhaps, another person has an opposing thought that is stronger, would that stronger thought overrule that particular experience?

Well, that would depend on how much power the individual had given the other individual over their life. Does that help? Yes. That would depend, don't you see? You see, you're talking about two people, like two people together. Yes. Now each one has a thought. They're entertaining thoughts. And so the law says, What you entertain in thought, you will experience in life. However, they are associated with another individual and they are entertaining other types of thoughts. What kind of experiences will come back to the two of them?

Right.

As I say, that depends entirely upon how much this individual, A, gave power to B, this individual over here. Yes.

Now how do we give power to people? It's very simple. Every time an individual makes you angry, disturbs your emotions, causes you joy or sadness or disaster, that reveals how much power you gave to them. No more, no less. And it's the same way with our material things, and with our cars and TV sets. If it breaks down and you have an emotional explosion, that shows you how attached you were; that shows you how much power you gave to the object, you see. Yes. Thank you.

In the Law of Merit, it says that whoever enters our life has been attracted to us by some divine law. Does this, also, have something to do with other Eastern religions that say it's karma or karmic ties in some particular way to an incarnation on another universe? And if we have sought the kingdom of God or serenity or anything of a spiritual nature, can we continue to grow and evolve? And what are some of the pitfalls? Do we fall back and falter and leave spirituality later on?

Well, thank you very much for a combination of several questions there. A person on the spiritual path is distracted by many things. Many, many things. Now, the truth of the matter is, we're constantly distracted, but when we're on the spiritual path we start to become aware of those distractions, you understand? And anyone, of course, they can leave the path that they have chosen. That, of course, is their free choice at any given moment.

Now in reference to the law of karma, which in our understanding is simply the Law of Cause and Effect, our entering this earth realm is an effect of the cause that we set into motion. And we enter another dimension: that's an effect of the causes that we're setting into motion right here and now. This is the importance, friends: you see, be prepared. Be prepared each moment. Because you don't know the moment you're going to leave the clay, the physical body.

See, we're not preparing for over there. We are preparing for this moment. You know, we can go out there and walk across the street, and that's the end of the old physical body. You know, just because we're X number of years old, that's no guarantee, in any sense of the word, if you're using any degree of reason, that you're going to stay in this physical world. So what we're trying to do is to prepare you for the here and the now. And the here and the now is the physical world, the mental world, the astral world, the vital world, the spiritual world, and all those other worlds right here and now.

Now, if we are honest with ourselves, we'll say, "OK, I've got five minutes left and I've got to go over there. Am I really prepared?" Well, the question arises in the mind, "Prepared for what?" You see. Well, what are we facing inside of ourselves? Look inside and see what kind of—do we have angels tucked in the depths of the deep? Or do we have demons tucked back here? Now which ones do we have and how many of them do we have? That's what we should prepare ourselves for, because that, friends, is what we have to live with, because it's what we're living with right here, this instant.

But because we don't see them—you see, most people here on Earth do not see the projections of their own thoughts. I've often wished that it may be in divine order that this whole world could just wave their hand and see, for only a minute, what a thought looks like and see what an attitude looks like, see what an emotion looks like, and then see what the soul faculties look like. Now that, my friends, is what we're living with right now. We don't see them, but we're controlled by them. One minute, we feel good; the next minute, we're furious at somebody or something. That's what we're living with here and now. And when you leave the physical body, you will see those thoughts, those emotions, and they take on very strange forms, because they do it right here and now. So let's prepare and prepare this minute.

Thank you, friends, very much. I see our time is up. Let us have refreshments.

JANUARY 31, 1974

CONSCIOUSNESS CLASS 38 ✲

Good evening, class.

Let us all turn to Seminar 1, toward the back of *The Living Light*.

[A student reads Seminar 1 aloud, after which the class meditates.]

Before beginning our question-and-answer part of our class, I'll discuss a few things concerning the seminar that was just read. At times, along the path of study and application in this type of class work—which is, in truth, of course, a self-aware-ness process—there is a tendency, with some people, to become critical of the levels through which they are trying to rise above. Now, I'm sure we will all agree that criticism, of course, is an expression of a level known as intolerance. And intolerance is not a soul faculty. And the thing not tolerated, of course, will befall us in order that we may be granted the understanding of it. So we find from that teaching and application that it is not beneficial to oneself to criticize, which is being intoler-ant of the levels that we're having difficulty in trying to grow through. Now that applies to one individual personally. It cer-tainly applies to all individuals collectively. If we find the need to repeatedly or constantly criticize anything outside of ourselves, then what we are, in truth, doing is expressing an intolerance of the level inside of ourselves, which, in time, will guarantee that level of consciousness to be attached to our life expression and experience.

So we find from that understanding that the students on the path of light make greater, constant application to be at peace and to accept themselves the way they are at any given moment. Now that doesn't mean that we accept the way we are at any given moment and do not make any effort to change from that level of consciousness. But we do face ourselves objectively. We know that we are on such a level of consciousness, that we have evolved to that particular point in time, and we make the effort, the way that we feel is the effort for us, to grow even more.

Now any time you have a class or a course of awareness, it is not going to be pleasing to certain levels of consciousness, because we have to face ourselves, if we truly want to grow and to be free and to fulfill the purpose of our soul entering this earth realm. Now there are many ways, and we have discussed before the multitude of ways that our mind will use in order to gain the attention or the energy, which, of course, is the love that we are seeking. But a path is shown through this course whereby you may receive all of the energy or love that you need. And the path is the simplest path of all: it's known as selfless service.

Now many people, seemingly, do not understand, or at least they state they do not understand, what selfless service really means. When you do anything in life that is not motivated by a desire for self-gain, then you are expressing a degree of selfless service. A person might say, "Well, there isn't anything I do, not even going to the grocery store, that is not for myself." Well, if you're on that level of consciousness and you wish to make a change from it—that you are not pleased or satisfied with your life experiences at this particular point in time—then there are many different things that you can do to be freed from the self-orientation or the prison house which your soul is locked in.

And a fine exercise that was given some time ago—and I'll be happy to share it again—is, in the course of each waking hour, to make a little note of how many of your thoughts and your motivations were truly self-oriented and how many of them were not. You see, my friends, this will help you to become aware of yourselves. And this is the purpose of this class: to help you, as individuals, to find out who you really are, by your own personal efforts and your own personal demonstration to yourself. I am sure that many will be amazed, if they'll make that effort each hour of a day, to find out just what it is that is truly motivating their thoughts and their acts.

Now you're free to ask any questions that you may have.

If a person truly tries to live by the Golden Rule, will that, in itself, be enough to be in a greater awareness of spirituality?

Well, that would depend, of course, upon the individual. Because we must realize, class, that the Golden Rule has a different meaning to different levels of consciousness. Now by the Golden Rule, I'm sure that you mean to "do unto others as you would others do unto you." It also means, on other levels of consciousness, to do others before they get a chance to do you. So, you see, my good friends, it would mean knowing the level of consciousness that one has accepted the Golden Rule upon.

In your statement—which is a very fine thing, to do unto others as you would others do unto you, for everyone—well, what happens is, you see, the mind accepts that. But in application, it would depend. Because the mind also may slip to another level of consciousness and it may be in the midst of some kind of a transaction or a business arrangement or something, and before you're consciously even aware of it, the other type of Golden Rule is the one that is motivating the entire situation. So it is very important that we stop and we think, you see. Because one moment we're in a level of selflessness and light and the next moment we're in a level of self and self-orientation and the Law of Self-Preservation. And when our soul consciousness is expressing through that Law of Self-Preservation, which is known as the animal level, when it is expressing through that level, then Golden Rule number two is the one that does the motivating. Does that help with your question?

Yes. Thank you.

You're more than welcome. Yes.

Could you talk a little bit on organization and how it affects the way we think and how it affects us in our everyday activities?

Thank you very much. The student has asked, perhaps, for some discussion on organization and how it affects our lives in our day-to-day activities. And first, I think it might be beneficial to the class, perhaps, to become aware of organization. How does one become aware, personally aware, whether or not they're organized or they're disorganized? And actually, really it's very clear, because Life herself is telling us every moment of every hour how organized we really are. Now, we have stated repeatedly that the people that are attracted into our lives are the mirrors reflecting the level of consciousness that we are expressing.

All right. Now, our abodes, where we live, whether or not our things are cluttered all over our homes, whether each thing has a place and a place for all things, reveals to us in an instant how organized our mind is. Because, you see, those things represent our level of consciousness. Now, if you take a situation where you can hardly get through the door of a person's house because of the clutter and because of the upset, then you can tell the person—you don't have to meet the person—you can tell from the mirror of clutter how organized their mind really is.

Now, we must realize that we have different levels of consciousness and we may be organized on some levels of consciousness, but not organized on other levels of consciousness. Now, living in a clutter does not mean that the person is disorganized on all levels of consciousness. But it does mean that they are disorganized on the personal level of consciousness. Because, you see, the room, the house, the apartment, or whatever we live in, is our personal vibration. It is not our work vibration. It is not our basic business vibration. It is our personal life vibration. And clutter in our personal life, such as a home, reveals the turmoil and the upset of our personal emotions, you see. And I hope that's helped the class with an understanding of organization on that level. Yes.

Sir, regarding selfless service, you want us to do selfless service without any thought of reward. What is the sense of doing selfless service? You see, selfless service has a reward of peace, peace of mind and contentment, a tranquility that is supposed to permeate the soul. And if one is not seeking that—selfless service must have some reward. I wish you'd clarify the reward of selfless service.

Thank you very much. Do you accept that the Divine Intelligence, commonly known as God, is the greatest servant of all?

Yes.

Does it serve all form and sustain it?

Yes, sir.

Yes. If it is the purpose of the student seeking the light of understanding, which, of course, we also understand is godliness—we want to find the God within us—isn't this our basic purpose?

Yes, sir.

If that is the true, basic purpose for the student's efforts and study and endeavors, then the student does not seek any reward, because the student is seeking the godliness within himself. And the godliness within us *is* the great servant of all the universes. Now if we seek that—"I'm going to study and I'm going to apply these teachings, because by applying them, I will have a greater peace. I will have a greater life. I will have and, perhaps, find the fulfillment of my soul's purpose here on this earth realm." Now that is a motivation, but that is not a motivation of a higher level of consciousness. But it is a motivation and it does serve a good purpose. It can serve a good purpose. But if that is the only motivation that we grow to in consciousness, then we're going to be in very deep water when the mind computes in this little computer that it doesn't have this peace and it doesn't have this prosperity and it doesn't have this awareness and this fulfillment that it was seeking. Because the mind has become the judge of what this peace really is. Do you understand?

Not really, sir.

You don't. What is it that you don't understand? That in seeking something you must accept that there is a reward waiting for your endeavors. Is that what you don't understand?

Well, I think everyone does something for a reward.

Well, we all do something on that level of consciousness for what we call effort and reward. What I'm trying to share with you and the class is that there is a level of consciousness beyond that one of duality or creation that is the one that is worth seeking. You see, if we're on the level of consciousness that "I'm going to do this because this is my reward"—you understand?—and that reward does not come, because we're the ones that have made the decision, then we've got real problems, haven't we?

Well, sir, I don't think the rewards need to be tangible.

We're not talking about whether the reward is tangible or not. We are talking about the attachment of the mind to the fruits of action. That's where all our problems are. We are motivated to do things in the temptation that we shall be rewarded. That's where man's problems are; but it is a level of consciousness. Now the dog will sit down and shake his paw, if you have a little candy or a bone for him. That is a level of consciousness that exists in the two-legged animals, as well as the four-legged. But what I'm trying to share with you is, there's a level of consciousness that is of a higher caliber that will not bring you this joy and sadness. Because as long as you have the temptation for the fruits of action, for the rewards that your mind has accepted are waiting out there if you do this or that, you will guarantee the day and you will guarantee the moment of disappointment.

So isn't it better for one's soul to express through a higher level of consciousness and to do the work that they have to do because it is right to do? It is right for them to do. They are not concerned with the effect. They are not concerned with the harvest. When the joy comes in the effort, when man finds his joy in the job, in the effort that he has to do and to express, then man is going to be free. And he's not going to be under this reward and punishment and this so-called effort-and-reward syndrome. Joy must be in the sowing, not in the reaping. That's where the joy really is, if you want to be free. If you find your joy in the harvesting and in the reaping, then you are not going to be free—and neither is any other soul.

I'm not clear on that. I'm afraid I didn't get it. It went by me.

Well, perhaps we could explain it another way. If you are motivated to attend a class and to attend a church simply because the mind has accepted that you are going to reap a certain harvest, then you're going to have problems.

I've got problems.

Well, then, perhaps that will help you in that understanding.

In your explanation, just now, you said that to do the work that you have to do because it is right for the particular individual.

That is correct.

How does a person tell what work is right for him?

Their conscience tells them. Their conscience. Our conscience is a spiritual sensibility with a dual capacity. It knows right from wrong: no one has to tell it. And, you see, our conscience speaks to us, usually, in the very wee hours of the morning, when we first awaken in the morning. Sometimes, as we're going off to sleep at night, even in the course of a day, our conscience will speak. Either you will get a feeling from within your being or you *know* that you should be doing this or you *know* that you should be doing that. And it is an all-consuming inner feeling and you know that. That's our conscience that speaks to us. Our conscience knows what is right or wrong for us. But remember, each person's own conscience speaks to them personally. No one outside has to tell them whether or not they're doing what is right. However, if you solicit advice concerning what is right for you, then, of course, the door has been opened by you, by the individual. But our conscience knows what's right or wrong, yes.

May I go back to selfless service because—

Yes.

This, to me, is something I have done and I have heard others say, "I'm going to do this bit of selfless service." In my thinking, I understand that sometimes we don't even know when we're doing selfless service. We shouldn't be conscious of it. We just do the thing because it has to be done. If we are motivated by the thought—I mean, I'm asking a question really—if we are motivated by the thought of doing selfless service, are we? If we are motivated by the thought of building a spiritual body, is that our motivation for a reward? I mean, we attend class; we become spiritually aware. But if we have a motive to say, "I'm going to class because I want to build a spiritual body. I want peace. I want." If the want is in there, I mean, is this spiritual? Is this, is this—

Well, of course, the moment we say we "want," we have denied what we already have. The moment the mind says that it "wants" this or it "wants" that, it denies its own divinity.

Well, if it has a motive—anything that you do has a motive.

Everything is motivated from a motive within our being, yes.

Well, if it has a motive for reward—even as much as spirituality, even if it's being spiritual, it's still a motive, is it not?

Well, that depends on what the individual means by *spiritual*. Now you must realize, students, that everyone has their own understanding of what spiritual or spirituality is. To some people, it means getting along with their husbands or their wives. To other people, it means having a successful business and justly so, because that could be a very spiritual motivation. It really could be. They could be motivated to have their business work out well in order that they may help more people. That's very true. They could be motivated that they want to get along with their husbands for the sake of their children and it could be a good motive, you understand?

Now, I want to go back to your first question, because it came in two different parts and your first question was on selfless service. Now, the lady has asked in regard to a person saying, "Well, do this because it is selfless service." It is most understandable, to myself, that there is a need to express the words *selfless service* in any organization that is a selfless organization, because so many people are not familiar with the word, let alone understand what it really means. You go out into the world and I have found, in lifetimes, so many people are not familiar with the word *selfless*, let alone with the word *service*.

I don't find in any teachings or religions that I've found so far, outside of what has been brought through in this little book here [*The Living Light*], that God is a servant. Every religious book that I have ever read and any studies I have done of a religious nature, from any source, have taught that God is the master and that you must bow to this great master. So we've first got to get to a point that we have a different understanding of what the masses have accepted concerning God and the Divine. Number one: The teaching is that the Divine is a neutral, impartial, great servant; that it serves all things. The rain falls on everyone; the sun shines on everyone. When it shines, it shines, and when it rains, it rains.

Now, if a student has merited the exposure to a person or group of people who insist upon expressing the need for selfless service to them, we must take this as a personal message, because there's something inside of us that is repeatedly attracting this expression to us. Now, of course, we are never left without choice. We can choose that, "I don't want to associate with those people anymore, because every time I see them, all they talk to me about is selfless service." Well, now, that's one way of getting out of the situation.

But there's a better way. And the better way for all of us is to face the situation inside. I would say to myself, "Every time I talk to someone or someone talks to me, all they talk about is selfless service. Now what does this mean to me? What is it inside of me that insists upon attracting that type of a conversation to me? What is it that I am emanating out of me that calls that forth out of the atmosphere like a great magnet?" Because, you see, my friends, unless we accept the principle of the teaching, we're not going to find the way for ourselves. And the basic principle of the teaching is, my friends, all of your experience you have willed into action: it is a subtle law. So every experience that we encounter, we must go inside of ourselves, if we want to follow the principle of the teaching. We must go inside of ourselves and say, "Now what level of consciousness do I insist upon expressing to constantly attract people coming to me telling me I should be doing selfless service?" It is something inside, students, inside of all of us.

All right, now, if a person sees another individual and they're talking about selfless service and the individual who has some degree of intolerance from hearing about it all the time—otherwise, it would not be expressed—then we must say to ourselves, "Does that individual have a right to their growth and expression? If they have that divine right to express their understanding concerning selfless service and if I respect their divine right to that expression, then my divine right for my understanding will also be respected." Now, if we do not think that way, then we're going to guarantee constant emotional turmoil for ourselves.

We must say to ourselves, "What is it inside of me that insists upon putting everyone into a mold, a mold of my understanding?" Don't you see, students? What is it inside of us that insists that we go out and tell everybody that we know, our so-called friends and associates, "You're not growing right. That is not the way that it is." Now there has to be something inside of us that does that. Is it a basic mother instinct? Is it that we want to mother all of God's children? And with the men, is it a basic father instinct that we know what's right for everyone? And therefore, when they do not express according to *our* mold, then we've got problems. Remember, friends, we're all in a mold. We're trying to expand that mold, which is what we have accepted inside of ourselves, and it's not the easiest thing for any of us to do. But unless we do it—and the expansion of that mold is a broadening of our horizons—then the intolerance that we express through criticism, or however we express it, is destroying us. It poisons our very blood.

This is why the biggest business in the Western world—the Western world, mind you—the biggest business in the Western world is the medical profession. There is one thing, my friends, no matter whether you have a depression or you don't, there's one thing about the medical profession: they'll always have a job. Now the reason they'll always have a job is because people insist upon killing themselves off, you see. That's where all our diseases and things come from. They come from the attitudes of our own being, of our own mind.

You see, we insist upon poisoning our bloodstream and destroying ourselves. We insist upon doing it. And why do we insist upon doing it? Now that's a wonderful question. Is it because man has a basic suicide syndrome? I don't believe so. I believe that man insists upon killing himself off in his efforts to try to find himself. I believe that's why man keeps poisoning his body, because he's truly trying to find God, the true Self within himself. And he has this great struggle because he's deluded by looking outside for all causes and hasn't yet gone home to the cause that lies inside himself. Now I hope that's helped with your question.

In one of our classes, a student asked, "Do the soul faculties and functions continue after death?" And the teacher asked the student, "Does the individuality of the soul continue after death?" And the student answered yes. Then, the teacher said, "Then, the soul faculties and the functions continue." Now is it possible that the individuality need not continue after death? And is it advisable to try to reach for the individuality not to continue after death? And what is, exactly, individuality in relationship to personality?

Thank you very much for your several questions. And we'll start with the last one. What is the relationship between individuality and personality? Personality is merely the outer expression of the individuality of the soul itself. It comes out, however, very distorted at many different times.

Now, the lady has asked several questions, and one of them is, Do the soul faculties and the sense functions continue after this particular earth experience? My friends, as long as you are in form, any form, in any dimension, you have functions and faculties. Now, they are more refined as we evolve, yes.

The lady has, also, asked the question, Is it desirable to seek this freedom from this created form? Is that, basically, your question?

Individuality.

To seek a freedom from this individuality. Freedom from this so-called individuality only comes when we have grown through the individuality. A statement was made some time ago, "He who thinks in a universal way shall express accordingly [Discourse 51]." As we become more universal in our thinking, we start to expand what is known as our individuality. The soul, which is the form or the covering over the spirit, it starts to get larger and larger and larger. The more it encompasses, the less individual it becomes. And so that's known as becoming more godlike.

There is no way that I know of that the so-called individuality can be annihilated. What happens is, there is an expansion of the principle known as individuality, of the individualized soul, and that expansion starts to encompass others. Now, usually, what happens here in this earth realm, they say a person falls in love. Well, they become in rapport with another individual. Now when that happens, they start to expand their understanding, their individuality, to encompass another person and they call that conjugal love. Now, sometimes it continues to expand and it is lasting and enduring, but those are rare cases. Usually what happens, the expansion has been almost explosive. It just happened on impulse, and two people are now mingled in their individuality and there is this expansion taking place. From lack of understanding of what the process really is, usually they start to pull back, back inside of their own personality. This one goes this way and that one goes that way. Those are the beginnings of the expansion process.

Now, however, you can have expansion—in fact, it's happening to all of us in many different ways. Each time that you express a soul faculty, you are expanding what is known as the individualized soul. You see, each time a soul faculty is expressed, like duty, gratitude, tolerance, faith, poise, humility, compassion, understanding—all of these soul faculties—when they are expressed, you, as an individual, begin to expand. The most difficult one, of course, would be the first one. And that one, of course, we know is duty, gratitude, and tolerance.

My friends, when you have gratitude, when you are truly expressing gratitude, you have no thoughts about this individual or that individual, whether they're doing this or they're doing that. You're feeling gratitude. You're grateful and all is well with the world in that moment. Wise is the man who has that moment repeat itself in the course of his day. And when you have tolerance—you truly are expressing tolerance from the level of tolerance within yourself—well, nothing bothers you, my friends. And when you have duty, duty to that spirit within you, when you're feeling that real duty, there's nothing else: nothing disturbs you. You just ask a person, now, when they have worked very hard at something and they're standing at the doorstep, will the door open or will it stay closed? In the moment they see the door start to open, everything is beautiful and they love everyone. The ones that disturbed them before, they don't even think about that, because they're grateful, you understand? And so isn't it wise to make some effort to express through our soul faculties? Now, someone else is waiting. Yes.

In the past, you mentioned something about expressing through principle, rather than through personality.

Yes.

And that is something that I don't feel that I completely understand. Could you expand on that?

Thank you very much. When man is expressing through personality, then, of course, he is expressing partiality. If you have something to do for someone and you are truly willing, ready, and able to fulfill the need of an individual that you know, and you are truly ready, willing, and able to fulfill the same need in another individual under similar circumstances, or twenty individuals, then you're on the path of principle.

For example, now in this world of creation we say, "Well, I'm willing to do this, of course, because that is my job." Well, look at it in another way. Are you willing to help a person that comes to you in need of help or are you willing to only help those that you decide it would be advisable to help? One will put you into personality and the other will guide you on through principle. Now each individual has their own life to live and so they have established for themselves certain rules and regulations in order to continue to express in this world, and that is known as expressing from the level of self-preservation. After all, if a person is in counseling, they don't counsel twenty-four hours a day, because there are other demands upon their time. Is that not correct? However, if they decide, "I like this person. I'm willing to counsel them. But I don't like that person, so I'm not willing to counsel them," then they are in personality.

Does that mean, then, that you are assuming that one person has the power or the capability of helping all people? For example, in some teachings and in some graduate schools and—

Absolutely and positively. If they are working from the level known as the Divine within them, then it is not the individual that's helping them anyway. It is the God within them that's flowing through the counselor to the recipient: that's what's doing the work. Do you understand what I mean? In other words, the Divine is lifting up the other individual's soul to that level of consciousness where they may help themselves. Now remember, in truth, we never help anyone. All we are, are the channels or the instruments for the Divine Intelligence that flows through us to help another to help themselves. It is not the individual that is doing the work.

If you compute, in your computer, in the brain, that you are the one doing the work, you understand, and that without you the work would not be done, then you're into personality, yes. You see, even when we move our hand, it is not this so-called I within that is doing it. It is a Divine Intelligence that's actually doing it and it is our receptivity to that Divine Intelligence that actually does the work. Do you understand? It is the Infinite Intelligence that flows through the form that is the true cause.

And from this evening's discourse, which is very important to all of us, whenever the mind insists upon entertaining any lack or limitation in its life, it is insisting upon denying its own Divinity. We are denying our God. Now, a person may say, "Well, now, just a moment. Prices keep going up, up, up. Even gasoline goes up. The groceries go up. There's so much money, etc." This is not the level of consciousness that I'm talking about. It is not a matter of totally annihilating thrift or prudence, but it is a matter of recognizing the truth. Our God cannot be a small god, because if our God is a small god, then we are going to remain small people. Do you understand? So the purpose is, let us expand our consciousness. Let our God be the greatest god of all or let's annihilate him. Why have a small one that only works part-time? I would not choose that type of god. If the God I believe in is not working twenty-four hours a day around the clock, then why bother to have him? Maybe sometimes my god would decide it was going to take a vacation: then where would I be? Do you understand? So let's encompass a much greater understanding of the Divine Intelligence.

And then, you see, whenever this little brain thinks it needs something, then let's demonstrate the way through what is known as faith. Now remember, faith and patience run hand in hand. And if you say you have faith and you are not demonstrating patience, what you are really saying is, "I don't even know what faith is." Now that's what we're really saying, you see. My friends, we have lived in eternity and we will live many more eternities. So what is the great rush? Out of all these eternities that we've already expressed through, to expect of ourselves, and the Divine that's flowing through us, to illumine us in a matter of twelve weeks or even twelve years? We are talking about eons of time. We are talking about untold centuries of expression. Now let's not look back there and say, "My God, there's eighty centuries passed already for me. Look where I am." That's not going to help you at all.

Getting back to selfless service, since attending Serenity, I have become, say, more aware—or, at least, my understanding— of selfless service, and by reading The Living Light. *I guess most of us have done some selfless service. We have done it sort of unconsciously, without even thinking about it. But now, as a result of attending the awareness classes, I think that my awareness has increased to a point where I am more aware of some acts that I have done—I wouldn't say selfless service—in the spirit of spontaneity or something like that. And yet, I hadn't thought about any reward. But yet, after I've done it, the old ego comes back and says, "Atta boy!" or "Good show!" or whatever. Now, doesn't this take away from that selfless service?*

It serves two purposes; it serves more than one purpose. Number one: If a part of us says to ourselves, "Now you did a very good job there. That was very nice." That, of course, is an encouragement. However, if that part of us that says that is not satisfied and it needs to go out and tell all the world what it did, then we've got real problems. We really have problems.

Now, you know, friends, it's like, sometimes, we're prompted to do something. Maybe we're prompted to buy someone a pair of socks or handkerchiefs or something. And we have a good feeling about that, because it's something we want to do. That's fine and that's very good and that's a good motivation. It's our own motivation. We want to do it, so that's what we do. And then, we take the object and we hand it to the person. As we're handing it to them, "Hopefully," we say, "I hope there's a good audience, so, you know . . ." And we tell twenty people, if there's twenty people there. We just got our reward for any good that we did. Do you understand? Now that is a need, of course: it is a level of consciousness. And what is it that we need? You know, it's like taking someone who's starving a package of rice. And when we take it to them we say, "Now, you know, that's very good rice." And we go and we tell everyone that we meet what we did. What is it that we need? We need a recognition for doing that type of thing. And why is it that we need the recognition? Because it is not something that we have done often in our life, and this is why we need to tell everybody what we did. Now we might say, "Well, now, I've always done that." Well, if we've always done that, we still haven't satisfied that level of consciousness, you see.

God knows. The Divine Intelligence knows every motive, every thought, every act, and every deed. And the Divine computer is just beautiful. I once accused it of making a mistake, for me personally, that I got down here somehow. But I do know that there are no mistakes in the Divine computer. It knows every motivation you have: you don't have to tell anyone. It is all recorded in that great computer.

And, you see, friends, that's what we stand before. We leave this old piece of clay and there we stand before that computer. And it goes through the *whole* process, you see. And it says, "Well, sure, you did that good deed, but look at the reason why you did it." Look at your true motivation, you see. Now, when we seek the gratitude and the recognition of man, then the recognition in the Divine is not waiting for us, obviously, because we've already received it. We've already been told how good we are.

We've already been told how kind we are and the good things that we did in this life. We've got all of that here and now. So if you're speaking on those levels of consciousness, isn't it wiser—you go ahead and do it. So you do it and, you see, you feel good in the doing. Do you understand? This is where the joy must be. The joy must be in the sowing. Because when the joy is in the sowing, you will not look for that recognition: you will not need it. If it comes, accept it. It comes from the Divine. It is motivated from the level of gratitude of the recipient. But you don't have to tell a person what you're doing for them. It's very difficult, you know, for the ego to take, to have people running around saying how much they did for a person. It's most difficult for the recipient, you see. But, then, of course, we must realize the recipient had to have merited it and they have a choice to do something about it.

I would like to continue with that. If you catch yourself, if you become aware that your motive really isn't the motive you should have, maybe for recognition or something, can you stop and say, "Hey, now!" Is that where you pause to think? Can you reverse it then, and say, "No, let this be." Can you stop that yourself?

You can—that is correct. You can become aware, right in the process of the motive. Now, you see, here's another thing, students. There are so many pitfalls along in creation. Now remember, as you become more aware and you start to check your true motives, don't get discouraged. And don't think you're the only person in the universe that has those kinds of motivations. Do you understand? Because we must all face the fact of the law in creation that dictates self-preservation, you see. But self-preservation must be kept under the light of reason. For more than we use of anything is more than we need. And lack of use is abuse. So as we gain in life, the law dictates we must equally give. Otherwise, what happens, my friends, you, as individuals, all of us, we create a blockage to that continuous divine flow, you see. We become the obstruction. No more can come in. So it is not beneficial to hold to anything.

After all, so many people get the flu and colds and things and then they want to get rid of them. But because they haven't demonstrated this Law of Giving, they hold right onto those colds, instead of saying, "That's it! In an hour or a day, it goes away." Sometimes they have them for weeks, because they don't know how to give. In this life many times things come into our life through this attraction and it's not always conscious, you understand. And we say, "My God, I have to get rid of this. I have to get rid of this!" And we keep saying it and we can't get rid of it, because we do not yet fully understand the principle of giving, which is the divine flow.

Most people think, "Well, giving: they want me to give up my income. They want me to give up this; they want me to give up that." We don't want you to give up anything. Nothing at all. The church does not ask of any student or member that they give up anything. It tries to show them a principle of continuous, guaranteed flow, which works through the principle of givingness. Do you understand? Because when you're in the principle of the divine flow of givingness, you are giving from your heart, not your head. And when you give from your heart, you're not concerned whether or not it's going to come back. It's just an automatic flow, like a stream: that's what life really is.

In our everyday activities when we have an experience or when we are in a level that we really don't like, what's the best way to call upon the teachings at that time?

To help you out of the level of consciousness that you're not pleased with?

Yes.

Yes. Well, number one: Of course, the sooner we recognize that the level we are entertaining, our attitude, our feelings, the sooner we recognize and decide that it's not beneficial to us, the better off we are. Number one. Because the longer we entertain it, the more difficult it is to get out of it. So we make an effort to recognize that, "This is not what I want to experience, having experienced it before." You see, if we haven't experienced the level yet, then, of course, we're going to slide on down with it, because we don't really know what it's like. So we make an effort to recognize the level and make the decision that it is distasteful to us and we don't want to go there: we've been there before. Then, we redirect the energy, through what is known as the vehicle of thought and we choose something that is pleasing to us.

Now, there are a million different things that are pleasing to our minds. And we have the ability and the power within us to direct the energy to that that is pleasing. The reason that we direct it to something that is pleasing—and this comes through the talent of imagination. You want to develop the talent of imagination so that, say that you're having what you call a bummer level and you're starting to slip down, you can instantaneously, through the power of imagining, see yourself in Hawaii on the beach, if that is something extremely pleasing to you. It must be pleasing to your senses, because of the principle and the Law of the Magnetic Field. Because when you're slipping down into the level of consciousness, you're coming under the power of the magnet, of the emotions. Do you understand? So you must use the magnetic principle to pull yourself out. And, therefore, you must choose something that is pleasing to your functions, to your senses; then you'll come out of it. Do you see what I mean?

Yes.

You're welcome. Yes.

On those so-called bummer levels, can we call upon our guides to help us?

Yes, we most certainly can. We can call upon those who have been attracted to us to help us. Now, that will work for those who have faith directed in that direction and it will work, of course, to the degree of faith that we are expressing. You understand? It won't work any greater or any lesser than our own faith, because our faith is what opens up the door, you understand. Yes.

I wonder if you would discuss, in terms of the electromagnetic field, why one part of the body might be affected and not the other? For example, one might have the right shoulder ache, but not the left, and maybe the left foot, but not the right.

Yes. Because one is what they have been emanating and the other is what they have been receptive to, the left being their receptivity and the right being their emanation.

Would you discuss that a little bit further?

Well, in what way?

In terms of the using understanding or suppressed desire, as an example, or courage.

Well, let's use courage, considering that you brought up that point. Now, it is our understanding, and it is demonstrable, that each part of our anatomy is represented by an attitude of mind. And it just happens that the shoulders are courage. Now, if a person is having some problem—let us say that they're having a problem with their right shoulder, which would be representative of the courage that they are emanating, instead of the courage that they need within themselves or that they are receiving from within. Now, this would be indicative, you understand, that the particular individual faced with situations that they were experiencing was having problems with their courage in order to do what their conscience was dictating was right for them. Because it would take courage on their part to make certain necessary changes—do you understand?—which would affect other people. So the battle goes on inside, in the emotions, in the subconscious. The battle goes on whether or not this will be the wisest thing to do based upon prior experiences, when courage was called on before. Do you understand? Now that's very, very important that we understand how that principle works.

Now, we want to use that in comparison to a condition of the left shoulder, which is the magnetic, which is the receptive. In comparison, a person has a discussion with us concerning—directly or indirectly—the need of expressing courage. And we, in our own thinking and understanding, are unable, you understand, to express the necessary courage to share our true belief and understanding. One is going out from us; the other is something that is coming into us. Does that help with your question?

May I ask another?

Yes.

Yes, that's very helpful. One shoulder emanates a red vibration and the other, blue.

That is correct.

Is there some relationship, then, with understanding?

There most certainly is, yes. It takes understanding to express courage. Would you not agree?

Yes.

It takes understanding something inside of us to have the courage of our convictions. And without understanding, we do not, in truth, have the courage of our convictions and we guarantee to face the day and the situation when they will be tested inside of ourselves. So the first thing we get, as the prophets have said for centuries: In all your getting, get understanding. That is the basis, that is your foundation for life here and hereafter. The thing to get, my friends—you know, we're all in the "getting" vibration. We either get food and put it into our stomach or we get this or we get that. So, you see, we're all, all of us, all of the two-legged animals are very familiar with the principle of getting. And so let us get the thing that is more important than all the passing panorama of forms: let us get understanding. And how do we get understanding? By working on the first soul faculty: duty, gratitude, and tolerance. Without that triune faculty, my friends, there is no getting understanding.

Could you tell us, please, how to recognize when we get into the intellect in carrying on discussions of spiritual matters with another individual?

Thank you very much. A most important, most important question. And the lady, the student, has asked, How do we become aware that we are in the level of intellect when we are discussing things of a spiritual nature? Was that your basic question?

Yes.

Well, of course, that depends on many, many factors. But the number one factor, I would say, when two people are discussing—supposedly discussing—things of a spiritual nature, if they find themselves entering a state, mentally, of fascination, and one question and statement after another does not seem to be fulfilling, but constantly generates a type of whirling or fascination, then their inner being, in the level of their heart, it will try to give them an inner feeling in that area of the anatomy—it really will—and tell them to stop. You'll have an inner feeling that you know you've got to stop or you've got to move or you've got to change, because, you see, our spirit knows. It knows when it is intellectualizing and it knows when it is expressing. Now I am sure the student that has asked the question has had some experience with that inner feeling, where they just had to move. And this is why I bring up that point, because that is one's own spirit that is talking to them. But it comes as an inner feeling and you don't feel just right. Isn't that right?

Yes, that's right.

Well, when you get that feeling that you don't feel just right, that's the time to stop.

Thank you.

You know, I can tell you that from experience, in the sense that, you see, I don't guarantee, and never have, any particular length of time for counseling. Only a fool would guarantee a length of time, because there are sometimes, in counseling, when the counseling lasts five minutes, although a full hour has been allotted. But you see, when I get that feeling, I move. And I do what my inner being tells me is right, because that's what will save you. Does that help with your question?

It does. Thank you.

Yes. We're running way over time. Just go ahead, please.

I'm very grateful for the last question because I find, at times, all of a sudden, I'm not there. I mean, a person is talking and I don't know what happens to me, but I'm just not there listening. I'm there, but I'm not hearing. I wanted to ask you a question. We are inspired many times—we have been by mothers and sisters and certainly by our spirit guides—to do what we might call a good deed or a piece of selfless service. I only know this: sometimes my heart expands and I want to do something so much, you know, for something. And then I draw back and I don't do it. I want to give: I would like to take my whole bank account and give it away. But I pull back within a little bit. And I'm wondering, what do I do to these guides, when I have been inspired to give and I don't?

Well, the thing is, sometimes when we have an inner feeling and we know that we really should do something, whatever it is or wherever it is—you're talking about that feeling that you have—and the reason why we don't do it, when we have an inner feeling and we know that we should, the reason that we don't— we pull back—is from fear. And the battle goes on inside of us. Do you understand? Because, you see, we feel that we should have done this or that. Now I'm not just dealing with materiality. It deals with all levels of consciousness. And we have this inner feeling and we really, really want to do this or we want to do that. Because this is what you're talking about.

Yes.

Then, all of a sudden, we pull back and we don't do it, because that's the fear that wells up from our own subconscious.

Now, every time a human being does anything, there is a battle of the senses that takes place within us, in this dual creation. One level of consciousness says, "Well, have faith! Do it!" The other level of consciousness says, "Don't do it! Don't do it! You remember what happened before." Now this battle, my friends, goes on inside of us right around the clock. Constantly. Constantly. But, you see, it's been going on so long that we are no longer aware of it. Now many times a person will start to do something and they'll get halfway, and that other side will come up and say, "Look what a fool you are. You'd better get out of this." You understand? This goes on when you go to the grocery store. It goes on when you go to work. It goes on when you make a telephone call. It goes on all the time, friends. That is a part of the duality of creation.

You see, fear, which is faith in the negative—and that's all it is. The negative is constantly at battle with the positive. The form is always at battle with the formless. And so this battle goes on within us all the time, constantly. But if we will recognize that this is a part of the Law of Creation and the duality of form, if we will recognize that and say, "Well, that's a part of form and this too shall pass. And I will just go on with what my inner being feels is right for me." Now, why is it that we repeatedly ask, when you have something important to do, to hold it for seventy-two hours, not to discuss it with anyone? My good friends, it's enough for you to go through the battle inside of your own feelings, without triggering the battle and the influences of twenty other people.

Thank you all very much. Let us all go have refreshments.

FEBRUARY 7, 1974

CONSCIOUSNESS CLASS 39

We will begin our class with the reading of the discourse here. If the class will turn to Discourse 31.

[A student reads Discourse 31 aloud. After this, the class meditates.]

This evening, in keeping with the discourse that has been read, I'd like to speak for perhaps a few moments on this so-called divine merit system and the soul's evolutionary incarnation into form and forms unlimited. But before speaking on that, I'm sure that most of you, if not all of you, have found that the Living Light philosophy does not offer to you a rock upon which you can rest your understanding, because a rested understanding is no longer understanding.

You see, my friends, the moment we *think* that we have anything in life, in that moment, it begins to leave us. So we find the moment we think that we have found God, the God that we have found is in the process of changing. For our God, of course, we understand, is ever in harmony and an expression of our awareness or our understanding. And so you'll find in this philosophy that there is nothing stagnant upon which you may rest, because all of Life herself is the spirit of action and of activity. And so you move in this activity in an ever-expanding consciousness. And if you rest yourself upon a level of consciousness, that is not the final destiny. There is not a final destiny in consciousness, because it is so designed, this Infinite Intelligence, to truly be infinite.

Now, going along with that understanding, if you think that you are working and striving and studying to put yourself in a position where, "I now have it. Therefore, there is no need for me to go any further," then you have rested your understanding and are demonstrating that you have not yet found one. Because Life herself teaches an eternal, a constant progression.

Now at times we do think that we need to rest. And when we think that we need that, of course, then, for us, that is what we need. So if you have studied the book [*The Living Light*] and the teachings that are offered, you will, at times, reach a level of consciousness which the mind computes as bewilderment.

When you reach that level of consciousness, it's a very good sign: it is very indicative that you are beginning to think in new ways.

You see, we've all been thinking according to the way that we've been taught to think. We have been thinking by feeding into our brain, into our mind, certain information and assimilating this information according to what already exists there. Society and our educational system have taught us that that is thinking. I assure you, my friends, that is not the thinking that we are discussing in the Living Light.

You see, when you reach that level of consciousness where you feel that you're a bit confused and you feel that you're a bit bewildered, and the pieces don't seem to fit, then one of two things happens. You make a greater effort to understand what you have absorbed and you begin to think for yourself—which is the true purpose of awareness—and you start to change the way you've been trained to think. In other words, students, you begin to think for yourselves. Now when that happens, there is also a danger, when that first happens with us. And the danger is that we become so enthusiastic at this new way of thinking and of living that we want to share that freedom of thinking with the rest of the world and especially with our friends, co-workers, and other students. You see, without a little bit of guidance and a little harnessing from the faculty of reason, we find that we get into serious problems because other students taking the same courses are not thinking the way that we are thinking and that causes problems for some people.

So you see, friends, we're beginning to think for ourselves. The teachings are a guideline to show you a way to use your faculty of reason, your divine birthright. There is nothing in them that states that you must accept them or reject them. The acceptance, by the student, is dependent upon his own efforts in applying the knowledge and the understanding that he or she is receiving, no more and no less.

Now in speaking of the soul's incarnation into the various forms, if we will look at this life—because this is what we have a view of. We have a view of this moment; we have a view of the moments of yesterday and of our early childhood. I spoke before on this planet being the fifth planet in this solar system and five being the number of faith. The souls that enter this planet have entered this planet to use what is known as the soul faculty of faith in the lessons that they have merited.

Now, we well ask, "What are the lessons that we, as individualized souls, have come to the earth realm to learn?" Life herself is revealing what your lesson is. And for each person it varies, for each person is different and has had different lessons in their prior incarnations. But you can tell what your lesson is, or combination, by looking at life and finding what are the most difficult things that you have to do or to face; because the things that are difficult for you are the lessons that you have flunked in your prior expression. You know, it's always more difficult the second time around when we try to do something. So you can imagine what it's like when it's the third or the fortieth time around. And, you see, we have had this expression throughout eternity and we have merited flunking in certain lessons and passing in others.

I have spoken to some of my students on what is commonly referred to as a natural soul talent. Now our soul talents are the lessons that we passed, and passed very well in prior expression. However, in this life, as we look around and about us, ofttimes we do not use our natural soul talents. We usually think that, "Well, I really can't make a living off of that talent" or "It would take me so many years to learn it," little realizing that we're like a duck to water with it, because it is a very natural, what we call talent, because we were so proficient with it in prior expression.

Now, my friends, our most difficult lessons: that is where we face things. Now for some people, it's tolerance. For some people, it's consistency. For all of us, it is faith. You see, this planet offers faith for use in the lessons you have to learn. Each planet offers something different. This planet offers the lesson of faith. So in the things that you find difficult, use what the planet offers. Use that faith. Because, I assure you, if we keep backing away from those so-called difficulties, they will become more difficult as life goes on; not only hereafter, but, of course, in the here and now. And I know that everyone knows what their difficulties are.

Now, usually what happens, when we face something that's a difficulty for us—for some people it's speaking. For some people it's even such a thing as driving a car. And for others it is patience and, of course, for all of us it is faith. What the mind usually does—and the mind is an instrument that always qualifies itself: it always finds an excuse for anything that happens to it. That's one of the most interesting and fascinating things about the human mind. It can always qualify any condition, any circumstance, any experience that it has. And it can always find what is commonly referred to as a scapegoat. Now, if it can't find one, it will instantaneously manufacture one.

What do we mean by *scapegoats?* When we use people or things as scapegoats because of our unwillingness to face the struggle that is going on within us, then, my friends, the lesson will become more and more difficult. And, like the great boomerang, it will keep returning to us.

There is a part of us—we call it the spirit that flows through us, we call it the Divine Intelligence, we call it many names—but there is a part of us that knows what our difficulties and struggles are. You don't have to go to anyone to have them tell you. There's something within you that knows. And it keeps whispering to you to have faith and to have patience and to make greater effort. That's the thing to listen to, friends. Because, you see, if you get discouraged, it means you've been discouraged before and you'll just keep on that vicious cycle over and over and over again.

I know that much time has been spent in these classes and in these different courses on the importance of our attitude, the importance of our feelings, the importance of a thought. Now, I know that we have all accepted, at least to some extent, that nothing happens to us that isn't caused by us. But we consistently and repeatedly slip into the level of consciousness to cast the blame outside of us, out into circumstances. The reason we do that is because we have done it already for a lifetime. I know that the process of change is taking place, for nothing in the universe stands still. Now if nothing stands still, we would be most foolish to think that God is still and we can meet him face-to-face and we don't have to go any further, because there is nothing that isn't in a constant process of movement.

So, you see, what happens to us when we don't get into this process of movement, when we don't get into the spirit of activity with our thinking, then we cannot be in the spirit of activity, of course, with our acts and our activities.

When we think harmoniously, when we feel that harmony that is flowing, that is *trying* to flow through us—we are the obstruction, of course, to that divine flow of harmony in the universe—then we have what is known as a breakdown with the natural function of our own body, the vehicle through which our soul is expressing.

Now you're free to raise your hands with any questions that you may have.

I have a great interest in the particular chapter about a soul, upon the return to the Allsoul, who had a choice of returning for the upliftment or the good of mankind. My question is, Who would determine that factor? I also have one other, short question. What is it that teeth represent?

What do teeth represent?

Yes.

Determination. In reference to your first question—What would determine the decision that is made whether or not the particular soul may return to a certain expression?—that is dependent upon the level of consciousness that they have reached, known as total awareness, you see. And that's as it is stated in that particular discourse.

Now, don't misunderstand, friends. When you leave this dimension, and when we all leave this particular dimension, that does not imply or indicate that we're going to arrive at a state of consciousness known as total awareness and, therefore, we can make a decision whether or not we're going to go into the next level of expression. You see, our form and our level of expression are determined by the laws that we have set into motion as our soul continues to express. You see, the soul set these laws into motion—man is a law unto himself—and the soul set the laws into motion. Now once the law is set into motion, the soul must travel that path. But as the soul travels the path, it is constantly making choices within the framework that it, as an individualized soul, has established. Do you understand?

For example, if you set a law into motion that you are going to Detroit, well, you would definitely go to Detroit. That is your destiny that you have established. However, there are also many variables on your journey to Detroit. Do you understand? You might stop over here or you might stop over there, if that is what you have established, when you first established the law of going to Detroit.

Well, I don't wish to dwell on this, but to further understand this, may I use this example? To my understanding, Jesus was a very good person on this earth realm of his existence. But what is in question is, upon his passing and on his evolutionary path, reaching the qualifications that this soul expressed on Earth, after his passing, say, for example, he might feel, "Well, maybe I could be of more benefit back there again." I'm not speaking for myself. Lord knows, I would not merit it. But I'm speaking of Jesus or someone of that nature, you see. I don't understand who is going to call the shots, other than themselves. And I would think it would be an ego trip if they did.

No. Because, you see, if it were an ego trip, then they would not yet have arrived at total awareness, where the decision could be made and the law could be fulfilled.

You see, friends, let us try to realize that there is a Divine Infinite Intelligence that is constantly operating through all universes at all times. Man, the individual, is working within the framework, not only of the divine, intelligent laws of the universes, but within the framework of the 10 percent free will that he has a choice in. This is the law that man establishes for himself. So if an individual who still was grounded in what is known as the ego or self, you understand, chose to return or go to a certain planet, they would not be on a plane of consciousness where that law could be fulfilled. Do you understand?

I'll let it rest. Thank you.

I'm sure if you will give it some thought and consideration, you will understand it.

This isn't a question. I guess I just want an opinion on a thought that I've had. When the other student brought up Jesus—a person who has interested me for a long time. But it's almost like conditions were set up, when you look at it. From the time of Jesus' birth, he was told that he was special. And he believed it and became special. So I think there's other things, rather than just self, that you have to put into it. And Wise men came and told Jesus' parents about the star. And I don't know—something about Jesus' own belief in that. He was born just a child. But it was the way he was conditioned.

Yes, because that is what the soul had merited. If the soul had not merited that experience, it could not have had it. It would not be possible. It would not be possible to have an experience that we have not merited. That law is applying to us this moment. You see, my friends, that's why we stress to study this moment. Study these effects of the here and now, because, you see, if a law is a law that is a universal, divine law, then it is a law that is universally applicable. And it works in the here and the now, and it works everywhere at all times. Because it is an immutable law. It is a law known as a divine law of the Infinite Intelligence. So it works whether you're driving your car down the street or you're baking a cake or you're teaching philosophy. The same divine laws apply. Yes.

This needs to go a little further for me. When you said that the soul has merited that—that Jesus' soul merited what had happened in this earth life—how can you—I can't connect—or where did it start? That all the other people merited their roles within his life, such as Pontius Pilate, and just everything that happens seems so—

Certainly. Absolutely. Because these are laws that are established. For example—

Where?

We all merit—where? You cannot find—

How do you establish all that?

Yes. Thank you. I'll be happy to share with you my understanding. You cannot find the beginning of anything, unless you choose to discuss it on a limited level of consciousness. You see, the beginning of a thing is the ending of a thing. So if you want to discuss it in form, if you want to put it down into this dimension of form, then you're going to have to limit your understanding in order to comprehend it, don't you see?

You see, a person could say, "All right. Well, what did I start from?" The teaching is that we come out of what is known as this Allsoul and we are impulsed into being as an individualized soul. But the individualized soul that we are this moment expressing is not eternal, because it is a covering of the formless spirit. It returns to that Allsoul substance. But, you see, friends, you have nothing to fear, because you are not going to return to the formless and the free until *you* have merited returning to it. You're certainly not going to lose who you are, your identity, until you are ready to expand your identity. This is why we teach to think in a universal way. Because if you will think in a more universal way, through the Law of Consideration, and you will consider all of the other expressions of the one Divine Intelligence and you will consider that you are an inseparable, united part of that one whole, then you are expanding your consciousness. And as you expand your consciousness, you are closer to the formless and to the free. It is our limited thinking, through the Law of Identity, that is, in truth, our own obstruction. I hope that has helped with the question.

I have two questions. May I ask them both?

Yes.

One of them has to do with the talk that you gave before the question-and-answer period. I'm interested in what kind of a lesson a person has merited if they enter this earth plane retarded.

Yes?

The other question is, it seems to me that I sometimes experience a time lag between setting a law into motion, noticing that I set that law into motion and trying to change it, and working my way out of the effects of the law that I have set into motion. I would like to know what your understanding of that process is. Is it possible for one to end the effects of a law? Is it possible for me to end the effects of a law I've set into motion right now? Does it take a period of time? If so, how long? What affects it? That sort of thing.

A very important question. In reference to that question about setting a law into motion—and the lady has expressed a certain time lapse before she experiences the effects—one of the easiest ways to become aware of your growth and the levels of consciousness that you are attaining is when you set a law into motion and the effect comes back almost instantaneously. Now the reason for this is because you are reaching a more refined, higher level of consciousness. And so what goes out comes back within, sometimes, a matter of hours, days, weeks, or even minutes.

Now, the lady is asking the question, Can she change—can a person change—a law that they have set into motion? Yes. That is possible at a certain point. Now, I'll try to explain that. Each level of consciousness is governed by the particular magnetic field of that level, the electromagnetic field of the level of consciousness. The higher the consciousness rises to those higher levels, it is more refined and it works much faster and much more quickly, at a much higher speed. The more gross we are, the slower is the effect coming back to us. So it depends on what level of consciousness that the law is established on and how quick you are to establish a counterbalance to that law. And that would depend on your level of consciousness. But it can be done.

Well, let me, perhaps, explain that a little more clearly. If you are on a level of consciousness where it takes ten seconds for the law that you have established to leave your magnetic field—you see, it goes like a circle: it leaves your own magnetic field. Now, once it has left your magnetic field, then you have much greater difficulty in changing it. Because once it leaves your own magnetic field, it gathers up from the atmosphere all of the like vibrations. And you have to use, sometimes, a hundred times more energy, you understand, to reverse what you've set into motion. However, if you can get it while it is still within your own magnetic field, your chances of changing what you have set into motion are certainly much, much greater.

Now, your first question was?

About retardation.

Yes. And that's a very important question. First of all, to intelligently answer the question on what lessons a soul has to learn through what is referred to as retardation of the form, number one: The person would have to know which part of the body is being affected and which part of the brain, or the intelligence, is being affected. Because each and every part of the anatomy is the effect—the direct effect—of a certain attitude of mind or state of consciousness, and they are all represented. So that, my friends, is a very deep study. You would have to study the full anatomy and also know what part of the body is affected.

May I ask, well, if I am retarded, how do I work to fill out my laws?

You're working on other levels of consciousness. There is a level of consciousness that knows you're retarded. We're using that word because that is the word that you chose.

Right.

There is a level of consciousness that knows that you're different and it looks at you and it learns its lesson in the process. Now it is limited from the expression in that particular dimension. That is not where the lesson is being perceived, my friends.

Thank you.

That that goes with the soul onward, that level of consciousness, it knows and it has all of the experiences. Whether it is humility or whatever it has to learn, it is learning those lessons.

But our conscious mind, it looks and just sees the covering. It doesn't see the other levels of consciousness. You see, there's a part within us—and we have spoken on it many, many times—it watches and it sees what we're doing, what we are about to do. Some people call that the higher self. We call it the Divine Spirit that's within us. It knows that we're going to step into a pit and the battle goes on. Now remember, because of what is termed as free choice, the Divine Intelligence within us, though it impresses us through what is known as our conscience to do what is right and in our best interest, we still have the ability within us to go ahead and make the mistakes. Yes, we certainly do.

Now this lady, here, was waiting. Right here. Please.

I would like to ask about welfare and when we give something like that. It seems to me, like, sometimes that does more harm than good. And I know that there are people who need help that way, but I also know that when you give people things like that, it stops their growth.

Very, very true. Very true. You see, unless a person is helped to help themselves—if it is education that is necessary, then education it must be. What we, in truth, are doing—what anyone is doing—is helping them to stay where they are, to make them a cripple on the level to which they have become attached. Now that does not mean that we are implying that we should not have some type of a self-assistance program in the world. Absolutely. And it does not mean that we deny the wisdom of charity.

But, you see, if you just hand a person something and you repeatedly do that without their own spirit activated to improve their own conditions, that isn't charity, my friends. That's not being charitable to the level of consciousness that is crying out to express itself as an individualized soul. That is not very charitable at all. So if we're going to be charitable, friends, let us be charitable to all levels of consciousness and let us not limit our charity to just the physical dimension.

You know, it's just like—I remember reading years ago—when Gandhi said that he did not care to have the rice missionaries in his country. And what a wise man he was. Because, you see, he was wise enough to see that that wasn't charity, as he knew charity. They brought the rice to gain the converts to support themselves. Now what's charitable about that? And so many of the programs in society are, in truth, designed to keep the weak, weak, so the strong can get stronger. Yes. Now I hope that's helped with your questions.

Can you elaborate on what they're doing on the Patty Hearst kidnapping case?

I think that you will find that that would not be in the best interest of the class that we have present, in the sense that everyone, on different levels of consciousness, has their own feelings. By putting it into person, or a personal case, then you're going to have your students in personality and principle will not flow freely. Yes. But I'm sure you have your own understanding, which is very right for you.

I should like to go back to another student's question regarding law set into motion and counterbalance. It's my understanding that we are on a level of consciousness for such a short time. How can we be sure that the counterbalance law that we are setting into motion is on the same level? And what happens if it is not?

Only by self-awareness. And what happens is, if it is not, if we're on another level of consciousness when we set a counter-law into motion, the counterlaw goes to work on that level of consciousness. You see, friends, a person says, "Well, I had this experience and I didn't do anything, nothing, absolutely nothing to merit that experience." Well, what the person is saying is true in a sense: they did nothing on the level of consciousness at which they are expressing that they did nothing. But if they'll be honest with themselves, they can go to the level of consciousness on which they set the law into motion and say, "Oh, that's what you were talking about! Now, I see." Yes.

But so often, you know, we say, "Well, I didn't do anything to have this experience and this struggle that I'm having." Well, that's true: we didn't do anything on that level of consciousness. But we must become aware of the different levels of consciousness on which our soul expresses and then, we will feel so much better and so much freer. Yes.

I have two questions. The first one is on when you were speaking on choice, and particularly on Buddha or the illumined ones. When we rise in consciousness to final illumination—I just have a feeling about this and would you tell me if I'm right, so I can register it in my own thinking—we become aware of universal

needs and then, would be able, ourselves, to choose, through this
awareness, where we wish to go. No one says, "You go here. You
go there." I mean, God doesn't tell us where to go, not even here.
So do we just become universally conscious of wanting to go to a
place to help?

Thank you very much. We'll be happy to share our understanding. You know, clarification is always important in sharing
understanding, that you may build some type of foundation.

Number one: We do not, to my understanding, in a level of
total awareness become aware of the needs of the universes. We
become aware of the errors of the universes. Now, you see, most
of us say that we need this or we need that. What we understand as a need is an error. It is an error in our thinking. Now,
the reason that it is an error in our thinking is very simple, my
friends. You've heard for a lifetime, I know, that God is the one
and only source of my supply, of all our supply. All right. If God,
a divine intelligence, infinitely expressing through all forms, all
planets, all universes everywhere, is taking care of the *seeming*
needs—the seeming needs—of the smallest, minutest insect that
crawls the ground, then it is an error in our thinking to accept
that there is need in the universes. There is no need in people or
in the universes. There is error in people and in the universes.
Now, what do we mean by this error? The error is a refusal to
accept the limitless, divine, abundant supply that is available to
all of God's creatures.

Now, you take the wildest of animals. They never starved to
death until man, the two-legged animal, began to interfere with
the places where they lived and expressed themselves. When
man, the part of him that says, "I have to do this and I have to
do that," when that part of man takes a break—just a little coffee break—for a minute or two, that Divine Infinite Intelligence
will be able to flow through an unobstructed vehicle and there will
be no such thing as accepting the error in the thought known as
so-called need.

Man has created what we call need. God didn't. God sustains all things and so the Divine sustains. Man wants need, so the Divine Intelligence sustains what man wants. What a kind God that is. So man wants supply, the Divine sustains that. Man is the one that set that law into motion.

Now we all fall prey to this error, this error of thinking, you see. Because—how do we fall prey to this error? We fall prey to it through what is known as the creative principle and that part that's known as belief. If we believe in need, we will experience need. If we believe in supply and abundance, we will experience it. My friends, it's worthwhile to believe in abundance. Not just for food, but for our health and our peace of mind. Don't you see?

So, you see, it goes right to the core and to the nucleus of the lesson to be learned on this planet. We must use faith. This is what the planet offers. If we say that, "Well, there's a shortage here and there's a shortage there," then that's how much faith we are demonstrating. We are demonstrating faith in the error of our own thinking. Then, man gets into a level of consciousness and he says, "Well, if I don't work for a living, then I don't have any supply." Well, everything works for a living. The little bugs crawl on the ground. Don't you think that movement isn't work? Did you ever hear a cricket rub his legs together? Well, he works like a little troubadour. Everything works in the universe. No matter how big the creature and no matter how small the creature. Everything works or it is not flowing in the divine plan of abundant, limitless, complete, and whole supply.

Now, we all have a choice to work in the way that we have chosen, according to what we have merited. So it isn't up to somebody else to say, "Well, you're not working." We know whether we're working or we're resting. We know that. So I do hope that has helped the class in reference to the error that is known as need.

Yes, you had another question with that.

I was just going to bring up that we hear people say, "I need reason. I need humility. I need these things for a special life." Now, how does need—

Then, we keep chasing it. Because, you see, what that means, when we say we have a need for reason, it simply means that we are not experiencing what we decide reason is. Now, first of all, friends, if you say you need something, you must first decide what that is that you need. Now you understand? So you're coming under the law of man's creations, when man is a law unto himself.

Man says that he needs illumination. Well, of course, he says that, because he has created the darkness. The Divine didn't. You see? Man has created the need, what he calls need, by an error in his thinking. Man has put his faith in the things he can feel and touch and see with one level of consciousness. That's what man has done. If he doesn't see the supply with his physical sight or hear it with his physical ears or touch it with his physical hands, then to that level of consciousness, it doesn't exist. And that's where the error is. Don't you see?

Now it takes faith, it takes the absolute belief and conviction within oneself that it is there. And when man truly believes that and he truly demonstrates that great law known as faith, then he will physically experience it. Does that help with that question?

A lot.

Now, the danger, of course, as the lady has said, Well, you feel that you have a need. You have a need for reason. Well, now, if we start entertaining on this lower level of consciousness, here, that we already have reason, we have to be very careful, because it will go right to the brain. And that isn't where reason expresses itself. Reason doesn't express itself through the brain, friends. You know where reason expresses itself? It's a soul faculty. Without consideration, there's no reason. What is it within us that has true consideration, that can express consideration? Well, it's our heart. That's where reason truly expresses. It's from our heart. Because our heart feels, and it feels and it knows through consideration, you see.

Thank you very much.

You're more than welcome.

Well, sir, this question might come out a little strangely, but I'll just try to say it as best as I can. I have found, repeatedly, with the teachings of Serenity that a certain feeling keeps coming up. It seems to me right now that I have the understanding that we are never to rest on anything or be too sure of anything, because everything is in movement and in the process of change. Well, movement and change compute to my mind as energy, and I can relate that to a physicalness, where I suddenly get fatigued because of perpetual motion. So even when I hit on a truth or something, and I say, "Well, reason dictates this is true, but don't sit on it, because truth is liable to change." And this has come up several times. And in the book [The Living Light] the Wise One says, "Think and think, and when you think you have thought enough, that is the first indication that you have not begun to think." So is there anything at all that we can hold tight to? Is there any fixity ever? And this perpetual change in the universe and our evolution, of course, understood in a physical sense, has a wearying effect. Is there any rest? Is there any peace? When can we hold still? When have we found something where we needn't go on? Could you kindly give me your understanding?

Yes, thank you very much for bringing up that point. And I'd like to first clarify, according to the teachings, truth does not change. That's why it's truth. But man's receptivity to truth does change. So, you see, as it states here, truth is individually perceived. And so it is our own receptivity to the Divine Light, known as Truth, that is in a constant process of change.

Now, as long as the Divine Spirit is expressing in form, the form is ever in a constant process of change. It is the nature, the law, the inescapable Law of Form, because form is a dual principle. Now anytime you have a dual principle, you have the principle of change, whether it's in physics, mathematics, or anything else, as long as you have what is known as a dual principle. However, the Divine Intelligence that expresses through that dual principle does not change. It is beyond change, for it is the sustaining power of all of the duality.

It is advisable, and it is taught in the teachings, to have a daily meditation, and a daily meditation for a short period of time. This is where, in time, according to our own efforts and our own evolution, we will find this peace that passeth understanding. Now, why is it a peace that goes beyond understanding? Why? Because it is a peace that does not have the dual principle and, therefore, cannot be expressed by a dual vehicle. And that is the peace that passeth all understanding. It is beyond duality to express: it is not possible to be expressed.

Now, what happens to the form through which the Divine Intelligence is expressing? If a person, having found that peace, decides to stay in it most of the day and night, then this vehicle, you understand, that the soul has merited according to laws that it has set into motion, starts to disintegrate and does not, seemingly, fulfill the purpose of creation on this planet.

Now, the lady has asked, Is there anything that we can hold onto? My friends, the desire, or whatever you care to call the thought or feeling that seeks to hold on, is an inseparable part of the principle of duality, known as form. And that duality and that principle of the "two-ness" of the duality of the form is eternally destined to rise and to fall. It is eternally destined, by its own nature and character, to go through a repeated and continuous eternal cycle, known as change. The teachings of the Living Light are, be ever ready and willing to change. Because, my friends, if we are not ready, willing, and able to change, we're not going to free ourselves.

It's most interesting, because in today's paper—I read the *San Francisco Examiner*—I was attracted to read a certain article. They've run some tests on a number of people and they have found, these doctors and scientists, that, in reference to longevity, people who have serious pressures—not the everyday, basic pressures, but serious pressures in their life that they do not change (like, with some, it's divorce; like, with others, it's a change of business)—their lives are shortened considerably. They're talking about businessmen. It was in today's paper and it's most interesting. Well, what does it mean to these teachings? And what does it mean to the question that the lady has just asked? Well, it means a great deal. It means that if we are seeking security—and to hold on is indicative of one who seeks security, no matter who we are—then it means that we have seen as much as we feel that we want to see of the constant flux and flow, of the constant sun rising in the morning and of darkness descending in the evening. Because this is what life in form really is.

Now, through a proper type of meditation and attaining these moments of the peace that passeth all understanding, then we can look at the vehicle. We are not discouraged, because we are beyond those feelings, which are a part of creation. We're beyond those parts of creation. And we can look and we can see the form moving constantly back and forth.

Now, why is, we may ask the question, form designed with these cycles of constant duality and constant repetition? Think of the repetition that we have already gone through in our lives, a constant repeating of events and thoughts and etc. If we are seeking rest, we will find it, but we will find it when we are ready to leave the duality known as creation.

Regarding belief and faith and God's ability to supply anything that a man has faith in, such as a man who becomes, say, not necessarily a millionaire, but who rises to the top and is very successful businesswise, but yet, on the other hand, he's, maybe, not very spiritual. Now, is his soul faculty from a previous incarnation? Or has he merited this? Is he spiritual in a particular sense?

Well, I would like to clarify one thing, so that we won't have a misunderstanding. A man that is successful in business, such as one that you are describing—that does not necessarily mean that businessmen are not very spiritual, because, you see, many very successful businessmen are extremely spiritual. But, you see, where, perhaps, we might have a misunderstanding is that the discussions of many businessmen who are successful do not appear to us to be spiritual, because they may not use the language with which we have become familiar and, therefore, we have decided that that isn't spirituality. So we must clarify that understanding and we must also look beneath and beyond the seeming appearances. Number one: If they are successful—you know, we're all successful at something. In varying degrees, everyone is successful and, also, everyone is a failure, you see. You can't have gain without loss. So we might as well face it: on some level, we've lost. As we're gaining on other levels, we're losing on some others. And so we want to move proportionately, as the slow growth is the only healthy growth.

Now a person can be extremely wealthy and extremely spiritual. Poverty does not, in any sense of the word, to my understanding, guarantee spirituality. In fact, my friends, to be perfectly honest with you, poverty implies a lack of use of God's divine, natural laws. And by not using the divine, natural laws and experiencing what we call poverty, we are abusing those laws for ourselves, you see. So I did want to clarify that point with you and the class.

Say, organization and continuity and the help that, possibly, employment of other individuals who benefit by him, apparently this must—

I would say that, certainly, because the individual has obviously been put into a position where they can employ many people and generate work. And, of course, work is a very spiritual duty, you know. It is the duty of all souls, just like the beetles, to work, you see. This old body isn't meant here to lay around on a stone, like a toad, and bask in the sun. Of course, the toad, he works too, but much less than some of the other creatures on the planet. But, you see, it is our duty, it is our duty to ourselves to produce. Otherwise, we would not be given this body. Our souls wouldn't merit this type of body. We'd merit, perhaps, a tree or a stone and be more limited in our expression. But our soul's evolution, you see, is in this type of a form where we can produce more and we can be a true benefit in the world of creation. It is my understanding, my friends, that the workers win. And if you stick with it long enough and you have a little bit of patience and a lot of faith, you will be victorious in anything that you set out to accomplish.

But, you see, it's the old brain that doesn't want to wait. You know, it wants it right now. It still thinks it's a kid, you see. We can be sixty and still act like we're ten, with that impatience. They say, "Well, youth is so impatient." Well, if youth is so impatient, then we have eternal youth. Because I find impatience all over, in every age bracket. It's not restricted to just the teenagers. It is so easy to say that youth is so impatient. They're impatient in areas that are obvious to the world. Well, as we get older, you see, we get a little bit more clever and our impatience doesn't show so much to other people.

Now, friends, we've gone way over time. Thank you very much. Let us have refreshments.

FEBRUARY 14, 1974

CONSCIOUSNESS CLASS 40 ✖

Good evening, class.

[A student reads Discourse 17 aloud. After this, the class meditates.]

Before going into our question-and-answer period this evening, I'd like to discuss, for a few moments, the influences in this atmosphere, and in the universe, that we are constantly exposed to and bombarded by and what it is, in truth, that builds up, so to speak, our protective shield, which is known as our aura. Now I know that many of you are aware that there is a level of consciousness to which we are all exposed, where thoughts expressed in the atmosphere, verbally or silently— we're exposed to these multitudes of thoughts and feelings and influences on a certain level of consciousness.

Now that was brought to my attention, just the other day, in a particular program on the television by this mentalist who's known as Kreskin. The demonstration was indeed most interesting, but more than the entertainment was the principle by which the suggestions work. So I'll briefly discuss, for those who have not seen the particular phenomenon, what took place.

First off, several people were exposed to certain tests to get the most susceptible subject. Having selected the couple that are the most sensitive (or susceptible) to suggestion, they placed this couple at a table where they had a board with certain playing cards face down. Now the mentalist had placed four particular playing cards in a sealed envelope. The people simply touched this glass on the board; it was more or less on the principle of a Ouija board. Beyond their conscious control, the glass moved across the board and it selected the four cards that he had placed in the sealed envelope.

Now what is the principle by which this works? And I'm bringing it up to you because this is what's happening to all of us, all of the time, to some degree. It is evident that the mentalist concentrated upon the cards. Had he not known which cards were in the envelope, then he would not have been able to mentally suggest to the people who were playing this particular game where to move the glass on the board. So first off, we realize that it takes a sender, a transmitter, to transmit the message.

Now what is happening and what does this have to do with our spiritual awareness? All students in this Association are taught to concentrate upon peace. We have not chosen that word, and its meaning, arbitrarily. The reason for concentrating upon peace is that it places that level of consciousness, which is highly susceptible to thought, into a perfect stillness, where outside thoughts and influences and inside thoughts and influences have no effect. So the value of our exercising and using this principle of peace is, of course, for our own protection.

Now, I know that sometimes when a person begins to feel a certain way that it is most difficult to say an affirmation which, through the Law of Association within the human mind, will place the soul in the level of consciousness where peace and protection reign supreme. But it cannot be overemphasized, the value of practice, so that at any given moment in your time of need, when your mind feels the need to protect yourself from influences that you do not consciously see and that you do not consciously hear—it's known as staying in your own vibration.

Now, we don't stay in our own vibration, which means our own sphere of action, our own plane of consciousness, without some type of conscious effort. We look out into a world and we see many things that are tolerable and we see many things that, to us, are intolerable. Now we have the choice to either stay in our level of consciousness that we are enjoying or to be influenced by what our eyes view and our ears hear. Now that's a hard enough step to make. But think of the step to make where you are not aware of the influences that you are exposing yourself to. They are just as effective as this little story on television, as this demonstration of this mentalist revealed. They are just as effective, if not more so, than the influences that you are consciously aware of.

So a person makes the effort, consciously and constantly, to keep themselves at peace. After all, peace is that that brings us prosperity. It brings us harmony. It brings us health and it brings us the good things in our life. And we have the right to do that. Now a person can say, "Well, perhaps I haven't merited that." My friends, opportunity does not knock at any door that hasn't merited the knocking. And so, opportunity is presenting itself to you. It is up to you what you do with it.

Now you're free to ask any questions that you have concerning this spiritual understanding.

[After a long pause, the Teacher continues.]

It's amazing how the vibration of peace works. But it doesn't mean for us to be resting, you know. There's a difference. Peace does not mean to sleep and it does not mean to rest.

In the discourse read tonight, it mentions that the first soul faculty is duty, gratitude, and tolerance, corresponding with self, pity, and friendship.

Yes.

We've had quite a bit of discussion on the grounding in self and so on. We've also had discussion on friendship. I wonder if you would discuss a bit on the function of pity.

Thank you very much. In discussing the function of pity, we first realize that it is not possible for us to pity anything, inside or outside, unless we have given it considerable negative attention. And so we find that pity is the effect of the directed negative energy to whatever the mind is entertaining.

Now, a person can say, "Well, someone has just had an accident and they're very ill. And you mean you have no pity for them?" Well, of what benefit would it be to the individual, who is in need of harmony for health, who is in need of peace, to direct to the soul a negative projection of pity? You see, the only thing that pity does is to help us deny the Divine Intelligence and its infinite wisdom.

Now, if a dog gets run over and we feel pity and we express pity, we are not helping the dog that was run over. And we certainly are not helping ourselves. However, that is a human emotion and it serves a purpose. The purpose that it serves is that if we express enough pity long enough, we will soon find out that life is not worth living that way. If we truly believe in a divine justice, in a perfect, infinite balance in all of creation, if we truly believe in that type of a God, then we cannot possibly express pity to anything because we are denying the divine justice itself. Does that help with your question? It is nothing more than a negative projection of energy and it has no benefit whatsoever, except to awaken us sooner or later.

Can you clarify the difference between pity and compassion?

I'll be more than happy to. First of all, a man does not express compassion without understanding. Pity has no understanding. It is strictly an emotional function. Compassion has some degree of understanding. When a person feels compassion for anything, for another person or another creature, when they feel and express compassion, they do not have the emotional feeling of how sad or unfortunate this individual or this creature is. Compassion sees, at least to some extent. It must be kept in hand, however, with the soul faculty of reason.

Now whenever we have compassion, there is some degree of understanding. However, when that compassion leaves the guiding hand of reason, it opens the door to be imposed upon. Now, if you want to help an individual to help themselves, you must first have demonstrated help in that level of consciousness. Because, you see, we cannot help another to help themselves, unless that particular level that they are in, we have had some experience and understanding with, you see. So it takes an expression of compassion, believe me, to serve what we call the Divine or the Spirit. But it must, also, have with it the soul faculty of reason.

When we see a little child, and the little child, perhaps, has some physical defect, and if you express pity, you're certainly not helping the child. The only thing you're helping them to do is to go deeper into a negative projection and helping yourself along the way to go there. However, if you have compassion, you'll have a little understanding. You will recognize and realize that that particular soul has the divine right to have merited that particular body. And because your eyes only see what the mind computes as a retardation or a defect, it does not see clearly that the soul is learning an invaluable lesson, a lesson that it has the divine right to learn.

I think that sometimes we get indifference and compassion mixed up. I never could feel indifferent. If I worked with physically handicapped children, I couldn't feel indifferent. But I know many people do. Could you explain the difference between indifference and disassociation?

You see, each of us has our own understanding of the word *indifference.* Now would you care to share your understanding of that word with the class? What does *indifference* mean to you?

I feel that indifference *is when a person has—I know you said it in your last class, and I've taken it to heart: that there is no such thing as need. But we do see a need for spiritual studies. We do see a need for hospitals to help people. You go to people and ask them, as sometimes we do for this organization, for help with the building fund and they're indifferent to it. They'll say, "It's not my business" or "I'll do it some other time." This is a type of indifference. A hospital needs a lung to help somebody that has polio, perhaps, and people are indifferent to this appeal. Now how do we handle this? Because you can't be open to every appeal that comes along.*

You just answered your question. You can't be open to every suggestion and everything that comes along. You must be indifferent. Now, so there we have found the understanding of the student of the word *indifferent.*

Is indifference a necessary function for the human being's own survival? That's the question. Is it? Well, of course, it is. If we were not indifferent to the problems overseas in certain areas, if we were not indifferent to certain political involvements, if we were not indifferent to many things in this world, we would not be able to fulfill the purpose of our incarnation into this form. I know of no human soul that is not indifferent to something. It is not within the realms of probability for man's own balance and sanity not to be indifferent to something.

Now, let us analyze that a little deeper. Let us take a man who decides that he doesn't want to be indifferent to anything. So along his path comes the cloud of ignorance. And he says, "Well, I'm practicing the principle of not being indifferent to anything. Therefore, I will accept this cloud of ignorance that is coming my way, and in accepting it, I will become it." Does that benefit our soul? So we must realize, friends, all things in balance. Each function and each faculty serves a purpose. What we are seeking to find out here is, what is the purpose that that function or that soul faculty has been designed by this Infinite Wisdom to serve? So let each faculty and each function serve its purpose.

Now, the question arises, "When I ask for something for a good purpose, the individual is indifferent." Now we must go to the principle of the law so that we can find it, no matter who we are. Now, if we talk to an individual and the individual is not receptive, or indifferent, to our projection, then we must ask ourselves the question, "Why?" We must ask that honestly of ourselves. "Why is it, when I try to do some good in this world, that I am attracted to people who are indifferent to the work that I am trying to do? I am not trying to do it for myself, to my conscious awareness. I am trying to do it for what I understand to be God or Good." All right, we ask ourselves that question. And we say that this is the law and it's demonstrable for all of us. We say, "Like attracts like and becomes the Law of Attachment. I am attracting people who are indifferent to my efforts to help in a spiritual work. What am I, in truth, indifferent to inside of myself which is associated with my spiritual efforts?"

Now, if we do not ask ourselves those questions, we're not going to find the cause and we're not going to find the way. All right, a person can say, "Well, I've asked myself the question and there is nothing that I'm doing that I am indifferent to inside of myself in my spiritual efforts." But if we truly believe the living demonstration of the law, then that is not true. We've got to knock harder. We've got to keep knocking, until we find inside of ourselves what it is that is bringing us into a rapport with and into attraction of people who are indifferent to our efforts.

Now the question is asked and there are many answers for it: it depends on the individual. It is quite possible that we could be indifferent to the projections and suggestions of other people who are trying to serve God in their way. That is quite possible. And so we must ask those questions. Does that help with your question?

And I know any student here that truly puts in that effort, they're going to find the cause. And the moment they find it, they will demonstrate the cure.

Yes, sir. I wonder why the faculty of gratitude is compared with the function of pity. Why are they paired together? We've talked about the other two faculties and functions in this triad.

Duty, gratitude, and tolerance.

Yes. Well, why is gratitude paired with pity?

Is that the only question that you have?

Well, that's the question I have at this time, sir.

All right. Would you ask, "Why is duty paired with its function?" Read off all three. You see, all functions and all faculties are triune and inseparable. So, you see, you take one, you take it out of context. Let's take all three.

All right. Duty, gratitude, and tolerance.

Yes?

With self, pity, and friendship.

Right.

Why are they all three compared with each other?

Fine. Now the one that you're particularly interested in is gratitude and pity. Is that correct?

Yes, sir.

Yes. May I ask you a question? Do you have any feeling of gratitude at the moment that you are expressing pity?

I never thought of that. Do I have pity, I mean, gratitude that I'm not—

No, I didn't ask that. Only one question. Do you have any feeling or expression of gratitude at the moment that you are feeling and expressing pity?

You want to say you're glad you're not there or glad you're not experiencing that particular form of pity that you're expressing pity to.

Well, you know, pity can be expressed to ourselves, as well as to another. And usually it's to ourselves that we express pity. Usually.

I'm not sure that I know how to answer that, sir. Yes or no: you want an answer. But I'm sorry, I can't give you a yes or no answer.

Well, perhaps we could ask it this way: If a man finds himself short of funds and he begins to feel emotional and he feels pity—you understand?—is he at the same time expressing the feeling of gratitude?

He's not expressing the feeling of gratitude, if he isn't glad for what he has.

Thank you very much. In other words, your understanding means that at the time we are expressing pity, we're not expressing gratitude. Is that correct?

Yes. That would be right.

Yes. All right. Now, we have discussed before the soul faculties and the sense functions: that it is the one Divine energy;

that it flows through the soul faculties and it flows through the
sense functions. And our understanding is to bring some degree
of balance between the faculty and the function. And so we find
with the soul faculty, you see, of duty, gratitude, and tolerance—
we have what sense functions? Self . . .

Pity and friendship.

Self, pity, and friendship. Now, I know that if you will apply
the one that you have asked, pity and gratitude, you will find
that when we are in pity, if we will express the soul faculty of
gratitude, we will begin to bring about a balance in our lives. And
that is the purpose of the balance between your soul faculties
and your sense functions. Does that help with your question?

Thank you, sir. Yes.

Yes. Now, for example, a person can easily find out at any
given moment whether their energy is imbalanced in any particular soul faculty or sense function. All you have to do, if you
find yourself short of the divine flow—you know, I think they
call the word *broke*—if you find that and that bothers you emotionally and you're spending some of your thought and energy
on it, you may be rest assured, my friends, the more you entertain that thought, the more you express that feeling, the more
will the door of gratitude close, because there's no more energy
going into gratitude.

Now, the teaching is quite simple. It states that ingratitude
closes the door to divine supply. Well, of course, it does. If all of
your energy is going into pity, that door of that soul faculty of
gratitude is closed. There's no energy going in it to keep it open.
And so, you see, my friends, what is it that happens when we experience gratitude? Gratitude is not something that we say, "Oh,
God, I'm grateful." Many people say they're grateful and they
don't demonstrate it. And so that's not gratitude at all. Gratitude
is a living demonstration in which we flow with the Divine.

There is great benefit in counting one's blessings. The
teaching is very simple. It says whatever you put your attention

upon—your thought—you have a tendency to become. So if man entertains thoughts, you understand, of pity and he entertains thoughts of being broke, he cannot demonstrate anything else. He'll just go on the cycle and the merry-go-round of delusion and be broke for all eternity. You know, there are many people in the lower realms of the next dimension who are still broke, because they took it with them. I happen to know a lady that's worth millions of dollars. Yet she's broke, because she's broke in the head. That's where we're broke, friends. We are broke in our mind. And I'm very grateful you brought that up. Because, you see, once we start entertaining that thought, we go deeper and deeper and deeper into pity. And the further we go down into pity, the smaller our universe gets, and it just keeps right on shrinking. So the only thing that we can attract, around and about us, is like kind. So everything we attract, of course, is going to be broke.

My gosh, let's expand our understanding, that we can have a bigger god. Let's think big, because if we don't think big, we're not going to be big. We're going to stay small. And we're going to stay limited, because *we* have limited ourselves.

Now remember, God doesn't limit us: we limit God. Because God is equal to our understanding. If we want a bigger god and we want a god that's closer to us and we want a more abundant god and we want a god of great health for us and prosperity and peace, then we must demonstrate our receptivity to that type of a god.

It isn't a matter of you saying, "Oh, well, I believe in that kind of a god," and go demonstrate something else. My goodness, let us take some lessons in this dimension from some very wise men that have walked our paths. Look at that wonderful man, Rockefeller. He didn't have very much, but he got some brand new shiny dimes at the bank and he stood on the street corners of New York and he gave them out. It isn't the matter that he gave out shiny, brand new dimes: it is the matter that

VOLUME 2

he believed what he was doing. He so believed in it that he *became* it.

We have so believed in our lack and our limitation, my friends, we have become it. Don't feel alone. After all, we're all working to get out of it, including myself. So let us expand our consciousness and stop entertaining this limitation, this narrowness, this smallness of consciousness. You can't be free if you don't think "free". You can't be loved if you don't give love. You can't be prosperous if you don't think "prosperity". You can't be healthy if you don't believe in health. And you can't weigh the number of pounds you want to weigh unless you learn to believe in it. That's the only way I know that it works.

Now you're free to ask any other questions. Yes.

A question came up a few weeks ago about meditation. In the affirmation, "Thank you, God. I am at peace," is it wise to go into the silence with that if you're in a group? I mean, you see things are happening around you and they become disturbing. We're still human. Is it wise to go inward at a time when we're with a group of people who are arguing and fighting and carrying on?

The affirmation, "Thank you, God. I am at peace," can be used at any time, day or night. The more that it is used—it's like playing the piano: the more you play it, the more proficient you become. That's the same thing with affirmations. This is a little child's affirmation to reach the child within us. As the Bible says, it is the children that will inherit the kingdom of God. And, of course, it is. So it is that little child within us that we're trying to reach. The more you use the affirmation, "Thank you, God. I am at peace," the more you will be at peace. And in being at peace, you will thank God, because that's the power that helped you get there. Yes, it can be used at any time.

There's another biblical statement, "Suffer the little children to come unto me." I never quite understood exactly what that meant.

Thank you very much. Now what does that mean to us today? Does it mean that the little children are to suffer to go unto God? Is that what it means? Suffer the little child to come unto me. It means the suffering that the so-called adult experiences in life frees the child within us to go back to God, back to our true source. The suffering, my friends, is this thing upstairs that we call the intellect, the house of the senses. And it's commonly referred to as the ego. That is the suffering that takes place when the little child, in pure humility, returns to its Divine source, which is known as God. And so I understand, of course, the statement has finally come down to us through many translations and changes: "Suffer the little children to come unto me." Yes. To our understanding, it means to suffer— the old ego—and suffer the pride of the senses, that the child and the soul within may return to its source.

Would you explain the difference between self and ego?

Well, thank you very much. The student asked a very fine question: perhaps to share an understanding on self and ego. Well, if our level of consciousness is habitually expressing through the house of our senses and, in its habitual expression it accepts the delusion that it is the source, then self and ego become one and the same.

Now, if our level of consciousness, while expressing through the house of the senses, recognizes its true divine Source—that this house of the senses is a vehicle; that it is not the lasting, eternal spirit; that it is temporary—then the self and the ego come into balance.

Now, what is it that puts the house of the senses out of balance? It is the acceptance by the house of the senses that it, and it alone, is the real self. It denies its divinity. Do you understand? The house of the senses, which is created form, rises, only to fall. But when it gets a thought into its form that it is the source, instead of recognizing and accepting that it is only the vehicle through which the divine self is expressing, then you have the problems. Does that help with your question?

You see, it's a matter of acceptance, a matter—first, we have to recognize; then, accept. Yes. You see, my friends, a wise man once said we've become overeducated. We've become overeducated into what we call self. We have forgotten that we are not the eternal. This form that moves and speaks and breathes is very, very temporary. And we never know the day or the hour when it is going. So let us put a little reliance on something that's a bit more stable, because this is so very temporary.

Can you give your understanding or explain why people should not participate in promiscuous sittings?

Thank you very much. If you mean by the term "promiscuous sittings," sittings that are not organized and established in certain ways that the highest possible levels of consciousness may be reached, then I'll be happy to share with you my understanding.

Now we discussed, earlier, the importance of becoming aware of invisible influences that are affecting our lives around the clock, so to speak. When a person goes into a spiritual sitting or meditation, what they are, in truth, doing is opening up themselves as a receiving set. Now they are going to receive on the level of consciousness that they are on at that moment. If they are sitting with groups of people, they are not only going to receive on their own levels of consciousness, but they are going to receive on all harmonious levels of consciousness that are around and about them. Do you understand? All right.

Now, if a person feels that they are able to attain a certain level of consciousness and remain on that level of consciousness and not be pulled by other emanations around and about them, then, of course, that is their own protection: their ability to stay in a level of consciousness that is known as peace. If, however, they are highly susceptible to thought projections and suggestions and other influences, and they know within themselves that they are not able to sustain a level of peace for themselves, which is their protection, then it is not advisable to expose themselves.

Now, a person may say, "Well, now, I'm going to have a sitting. It's for peace and it's all for good and to help everyone here." Well, remember that hell itself is paved with good intentions and broken promises. Now ofttimes we have a good intent, you understand, but because we are not fully aware and able to demonstrate certain laws that govern these influences does not exempt us from those influences affecting us.

Now each student, of course, of this understanding has been instructed and is being instructed to have a daily sitting at a certain time, every day, seven days a week. That's not much to ask of yourself. You have twenty-four hours in the day and night. What's twenty minutes? If it means enough to you, of course, you'll get out of bed in the morning at whatever time you have decided, preferably before the noon hour. And you'll do that every day and you'll do it seven days a week and you'll bring about a little bit of self-discipline and a little bit of control. Because it's our lack of control that's causing us so many problems in this life.

So each student is aware of that teaching and that understanding. But there is no one that stands over them and says, "You didn't sit today." Because that's their divine right, to keep on stumbling, if that's what they want to do. If it doesn't mean that much to them, well, that's their right. There's no one there that's going to constantly take them by the hand. That's what you do with the little children. If you're a father and you've got two or three little children, you say, "Now it's time for our prayers and our meditation." And you take them in, because you establish that pattern for them. But, you know, when you get to be thirty, forty, and fifty and up, then it's about time we did some things for ourselves: giving up twenty minutes out of twenty-four hours to the eternal part of ourselves. Now I hope that's helped you in reference to promiscuous sittings.

You see, my friends, ask yourself the question, do you open the door of your home and invite everyone in that passes by? If you do, you're a very unusual person. Well, when you go to meditate, you open up the door of your universe. And you open it up to you-don't-know-what, unless you have perceived on those levels of consciousness. So these things are entering your universe.

Now I'm a little bit particular, I will admit, about opening up the door of my house. I don't walk into my bathroom and have everybody run in and out whenever they feel like it. That's known as a little privacy. And I value my privacy in this life and all lives. And so it is I value the privacy of my communion with my God. And it is hoped that all of my students will see the wisdom of that. Thank you very much.

In reference to this question on meditation, when one has to go to the hospital or something like an emergency comes up.

Yes?

And they give you a drug and you sleep through it. Or something happens that the time you've established is not met. Can one, then, go a little bit later and, maybe, apologize to the powers that be and say, "I'm here." Can I meditate at another hour?

Yes. Yes, if you're in the hospital and that happens. However, you know, you could set the law into motion before they give you the shot. And no matter how strong the shot is, if you have set the law into motion, you're going to wake up and do your meditation. Because, you see, there's a power greater than the chemical.

You see, my friends, the physical body is nothing more—it's a chemical combination. What changes those chemicals? All right, eat certain foods and etc.: that has an effect upon the chemistry of our body. But I will tell you this: there is a power greater than all the food you eat, greater than all your physical experiences that change the chemistry of your body. And that power is the power that flows through your attitude of mind. Our attitude of mind literally poisons or heals our body. And that is an absolute, demonstrable truth.

Now, I don't mean that a person says, "Well, Lord, I'm healthy and therefore I'm healthy." It's our attitude, my friends. It is our attitude in all things and in all ways. Because, you see, our attitude keeps us in harmony, mentally and spiritually and physically, or it keeps us in discord. It is our attitude that reveals our good health. That's what it is. And it reveals the state of mind that we habitually entertain.

Now, it is a scientific, known fact that when we get angry, we release certain poisons in our system. Where do the poisons come from? They don't come out of the air. They are already in here. They already exist in our body. What happens is the poisons are increased. There's a chemical change that takes place in our body according to our emotions and our attitude of mind.

Now, every part of our physical anatomy has been revealed in these teachings. They have not all, yet, been revealed to this particular class or to certain students. Be patient: we get it as we earn it. That's how we all get everything in life. However, if we will be objective and honest with ourselves, no matter what the experience may be, we can find out why we have this condition or we have that condition.

Now, one of the first indications that we're getting close to the truth is our absolute refusal to accept it. You see, if we have a certain condition—and we understand that certain parts of the anatomy have certain meanings—when it happens to us personally and we absolutely refuse to accept that truth, you can be rest assured we're getting very close. We haven't yet opened the door, but we are getting close, you see. And the old self-protective thing, known as the brain or ego, is not going to face it. But the sooner we face it, the better off we're going to be, you see.

Now, for example, I walked out of the car over here this evening. And obviously, or evidently, I stepped into a hole and twisted my ankle. I said to myself, "Why blame the hole? You could have walked around it." Now the next step is, "Well, it's dark and I couldn't see it." "Well, why did you merit walking out at that time in that direction in the darkness with a hole in front of you?" But it's very simple, my friends: I could either entertain how painful my ankle was or I could work on another level of consciousness. And by the time I walked into this church, I no longer had a pain in my ankle, because I did not accept it. I am simply sharing it with you, because the mind can accept or reject anything in this life. And that's what happens with all of us. We are constantly accepting or rejecting.

Now, in any kind of spiritual teachings, you know, it's very easy to accept certain teachings and say, "Yes, I can see the truth of that! I can see exactly what she's doing and this is why she has that condition." However, the greatest step of all is to say, "You know, here I'm having this experience. It's the same law. Yes, I accept that for myself." When we accept it for ourselves, we'll start to free ourselves, you see.

You know, it's interesting to me that here, in this church, that, of course, many people coming to the church are not aware of the different representations of the human anatomy. And it is so fascinating, sometimes, when we get to hear this one or that one couldn't show up because they had a sore throat. Well, anyone in my classes is aware that the throat represents resentment. But, you see, it's so beautiful how nicely it's repeatedly demonstrated, don't you see?

So, my friends, why don't we just give a little bit more thought to it. I mean, what is it, when we have an illness in a certain part of our body, what is it that doesn't want to accept that this certain attitude of mind in this level of consciousness is the cause of it? Why are we embarrassed? If we're embarrassed, then we should be very secretive and not let anybody know that we've gotten sick, you see. Then, we won't have to be embarrassed. But if we don't let anybody know that we're sick, then we're going to have to live with the experience ourselves: we can't share it. And it is the nature, it is the very nature of the being to share, you see.

Now what we try to do is get them to share all the good. You know, there's no problem at all getting a person to share the problems, you see. That's not ever been a problem in life, you see. You'll always have plenty of that. I tell you, there's one level of consciousness that does not accept a shortage, and that's the level that accepts problems. Now I've never known of a human being that says they're short of problems, you see. So we're all givers. What we're trying to do is to get that principle of giving onto other levels of consciousness, because, I can assure you, friends, in thirty-three years in this work, there's been plenty of giving of what man calls problems. All we want to do now is to get them into a givingness of that level where they can be free. Don't you see?

So there is no such thing as a human being that is totally grounded and doesn't give in some level of consciousness, you see. Because we have to give to survive. We can't survive without giving. You *give* the breath of life. You *give* of your thoughts. You *give* of your emotions. You *give* of your feelings. You *give* of your problems.

Now, if you don't bring balance into that givingness, when you have some problems, you won't be able to give them away, you see? Because you stopped the flow. Everything is coming in and you stopped giving. I tell you, there's great wisdom to giving, because there's a lot of stuff we want to give up. You don't have to believe me: just stick with your levels of consciousness and your problems and someday you'll see what I mean. You'll be so grateful to give that you'll wonder why you didn't do it all the time.

Why do you think—and it was printed some time ago—that we stated, "The Law of Giving is the joy of living." Now just think of your life experiences and think how joyful you felt when you were able to give them up. I mean, after all, not all experiences we accept are the ones we want to keep. Let's ask ourselves this moment, "Now, all of the experiences that I have, all of the feelings and the emotions, which ones do I want to keep for eternity? Which ones do I want to be the yoke around my neck?"

You know, it's interesting to me. It's just like two people when they get married. Well, that's fine and dandy. But do they truly accept that they're married for eternity? I know that they have some days that that thought, they give it right up. Immediately!

So the joy of living is the Law of Giving. And if you want to have more experience of the good, then give more of the good from yourself. You see, my friends, whatever it is that you want, you must give that, because in that giving, you will receive. If you feel that you are short of something, what you really mean to say is, "I have an inability of giving in this level of consciousness." Don't you see?

You see, now a person may say, "Well, when I have it, I give it. But I don't always have it. You know?" Well, that's understandable. But we've got to go beneath that and we've got to find out why we don't always have it. If we don't always have it, there is a level of consciousness that is not giving in harmony with this divine flow. The balance is not there. The perspective is not there. So what we want to set into motion is, "I always give, because I always get." Isn't that a better way to live?

I mean, you don't even have to worry about if you're going to pay your bills tomorrow, because tomorrow has a flow of whatever you think you need. Don't you understand? So, you see, you get into that law of that flow, of that givingness and that gain, and it's a constant process. But you accept that for each moment of your life. And you don't permit yourself to think or to listen to other levels of consciousness. Then, my friends, you're going to be free. You're going to flow with the Divine. It will come to you and it will go. And in the moment it goes, it's guaranteed to return.

What do you think that man did with his shiny dimes? He gave, knowing that was going out into the universe to multiply and to return unto himself, because that was the law of the Divine. He knew, as the leaves fall from the tree, they go into the ground and they fertilize the soil and the roots absorb the energy and they return back to the leaf again. You see, whatever goes out, returns. So if you are not satisfied with what you are receiving, become aware with what you are giving. And when you become aware of what you are giving, you will become satisfied with what you are receiving.

Now, I know that a great many people say, "Well, look at all this I am receiving! This is not what I am sending out." My friends, we're deluding ourselves with that kind of thinking. Because whatever we are receiving is ever in accord and in harmony with what we are sending. That law cannot be changed, my friends. It is an immutable law of the Divine. It is a divine law. No man, however great or small, can change that law. All things we receive are in proportion and reveal to us what, in truth, we are giving.

Thank you all very much. Let us have refreshments.

FEBRUARY 21, 1974

CONSCIOUSNESS CLASS 41 ✖

Good evening, students. We will begin our class this evening, if you will turn to Discourse 36.

[A student reads Discourse 36 aloud. After this, the class meditates.]

This evening, before we go into our regular questions and answers, I'd like to speak for a few moments on one of our teachings that is known as reflections from within. Now, these teachings have been given to many students now for some time, and it does appear that there are few who really understand what that sentence, that statement, means.

So often in our daily experiences we insist upon entertaining the thoughts that the causes for the experiences exist outside of ourselves. Often we find that we are experiencing feelings and thoughts of rejection. Perhaps, we feel that we're not wanted in the jobs we have in life. And we don't seem, yet, able to awaken our minds. We don't seem, yet, able to accept the truth that these feelings of rejection and a lack of acceptance are really reflections inside of ourselves. What we are doing, in truth, is rejecting certain levels of consciousness that our soul is striving to attain.

Now, if we will go, seriously go inside of ourselves, we will find that our soul aspiration is not yet as strong as our sense desire to remain in the patterns of mind that we have become addicted to. Therefore, along life's ways, again and again and again, we experience these emotional feelings of sensitivity and rejection and feelings of not being wanted. However, you may take the good from those feelings, if you will sit down each day and each time you have those types of thoughts and have a little talk with yourself, with your own soul. Then, you will make a greater effort in demonstrating the law that there is no experience in the universe that is not taking place inside of our own mind. It is our view of these things that causes the delusion and the illusion that its cause is outside of ourselves.

Now, my friends, one of the main purposes of these classes, and this Association, is to help you to help yourself to free your soul from these many disturbing levels of consciousness. Now, it's fine to say, "Well, all is well in my world and I don't have any of these disturbing feelings or thoughts." Well, if you feel that way, it's best to take a second look. Perhaps it's coming out—these experiences—while you're asleep, while you're dreaming, while you're not consciously aware. We all have these multitude of experiences of blaming the causes of things outside of ourselves. We will never be free, my friends, until we accept the freedom which comes from truth. And the truth is demonstrable: It does not exist outside of our own cranium. It does not exist outside of our own feelings and thoughts. We can—and I once again stress the importance of it—we can change our view: we cannot change the world. We can only change our own world, our own universe, and its relationship and view of another universe.

Now you're free to ask any questions that you have.

Yes, there are many ways of understanding dreams that are available to us—of studying them. I wonder if you could offer some of your understanding of how those of us who are studying might become better acquainted with or understand our own dreams better.

When man makes a conscious effort to understand the dream that he is dreaming in his conscious state, when that effort is made, then it is time for man to make the effort to understand the dreams he dreams while in a subconscious state of mind. And so it is, my friends, when you make that constant, conscious effort to understand the experiences that we are experiencing while we are consciously aware—remember that the soul faculty of reason flows through the conscious mind. And so we have that tool to work with, if we will make the daily effort to understand the conscious dreams. Because, you see, we call this—this moment—a reality. It is a reality only because we have a conscious realization of these passing events. That is what makes it a reality to us. And so I do hope that has helped with your question. Let us first make the effort, apply the law, and demonstrate the truth to understand the dream moments of which we are conscious. Yes, someone else had a question?

This has come up in my life and I'd like to be able to get an answer, with your help. Can one go to the spirit world prematurely? They say we have a life span, say, seventy-five years. And we leave that through accident or by our own hand at the age of thirty-five. Does one go immediately, if one has built a spirit body, does one go there? Or does one have to fulfill this life span in the spirit world an extra thirty-five years? Or does one go into the astral body? I'm confused as to what body they go into. But does one have to wait for that time to be ripened to go into this other sphere of existence?

In reference to your question about accidents, there are no accidents in the universe. It is only an effect of a law that we do not understand or, for some reason or other, are unable to perceive.

If a person is destined by the laws of their own merit system, their own efforts, through the evolutionary process, to come to the earth realm and to take their life and to go into another dimension, then, of course, that is what happens to them. As far as it being premature—no. I do not know of any law that says that man will come to Earth and spend twenty years and another will spend ninety. Each individual has established a law. There is a basic time span for the soul's incarnation on the earth, but I don't know of anyone that is fulfilling the full span. Each one has set these laws into motion. They come to the earth; some are here for two years and some are here for a hundred. But these are only the effects of the laws that we have established. Yes.

Now, I'm sure that some of you are aware there are people who live 150, 180, and the Bible mentions those who lived for 700 years. Well, there is in the overall divine plan—the planet has a certain life span. No one is fulfilling it, from errors of their own thinking. Thank you.

I would enjoy enlightenment on the difference between judgment and choice. For example, I may like a person. To me, this seems like it could be a judgment and also it seems it could be a choice. Also, one other small question: As light gray is reason, I'm concerned about what soul faculty that is. Is it in the consciousness or in the conscious state? Thank you.

In reference to your last question, the soul faculty of reason, you see, is a soul faculty which flows through our conscious mind. Yes, its color is light gray.

In reference to your question concerning what is the difference, if any, between judgment and choice, choice—the ability to choose—is dependent upon our ability to judge what we consider is right for us at any given moment. That is something that takes place within our own mind. Now, in order for us to choose wisely, to be able to judge what is best for us, to bring a balance into our life, we have to express total consideration. Now without total consideration, the soul faculty of reason is not flowing unobstructed. Consequently, we see that all choice is dependent upon our ability to judge inside of ourselves what is best for us through the soul faculty of consideration. Does that help with your question?

Thank you.

You're welcome.

Well, I had trouble knowing what was really right and wrong. And it's pertinent to a situation that I'm now in, but I think I could share the situation and I think it's applicable to everyone. I'm trying to help someone who's quite ill. And I've spread myself, I think, a little too thin doing things. I've let him call me for meditation and I thought, "Well, whose need is greater?" And I find that I've been in this state of confusion, but my motive— I've tried to keep a good motive and to really and truly throw myself headlong into this job. Now, I had the effects of a cold and I thought, "Well, OK, my consideration is off." Right?

That depends on which part of the anatomy is affected.

OK. But anyway, I'm just confused as to the fine understandings of the law. It seems like I go into something, which I feel is backed by an honesty, but somehow I miss the fine understanding of truth and what is right. And I sometimes see two sides of the coin. Presently, I would like, perhaps, to get out of the situation,

but I feel I just can't leave this person, because there might be a
decline in his present condition. So, selfishly, I would like more
time to do my writing and my spiritual work, but I also recognize
the fact that what's happening to me is caused by me. But I don't
understand the fine details of what's happening. And this situ-
ation has repeated itself in my life. I don't know when I'm being
selfish or when I'm being giving. There's not a clarity there. Do
you understand?

Yes, thank you very much. I think, perhaps, we could go to
the point which is most important, as an example, of course, for
all the students and, in the process, help those who are receptive to the help. And the lady has stated that she does not know
whether or not it is being selfish to leave a certain individual in a
condition, perhaps, that is critical, because something may happen to the individual. Now this is where the entire conversation
can be based. And what is the question that we must consider?
Are we interfering with the divine law? If we are concerned that
our leaving or staying with any individual, if by that very act,
we will be filled with what is known as a guilt complex—if we
entertain that type of thinking, then we are interfering with
the divine right of each human soul to express itself, to pass on
when it is to pass on or to stay in this particular life.

So what is it that is necessary for us to be freed from those
types of feelings and those guilt complexes? It takes one word:
Faith in the divine wisdom of the Infinite Intelligence. You see,
my friends, what is it? What part of our anatomy opens up the
doors? Does anyone know? Is there any student who knows
what part of our anatomy opens the doors in this life?

The heel?

That deals with another level of consciousness. Thank
you very much. It does, yes. There's another question I want,
however.

The heart?

Dealing with this particular situation. What part of the anatomy?

The anatomy? The nose.

Nostrils.

Anyone else?

Reproductive organs?

Anyone else?

Emotions.

Feet.

My friends, it's the mouth. That's what puts us into a multitude of things. This. It opens up the doors. And after we've opened the doors, it is so difficult to get them closed. Now remember, the spoken word is life-giving energy. We have heard it a hundred thousand million times. The mouth opens—when we open our mouth, remember, friends, we have opened a door. But because we do not think on three levels of consciousness before we open that part of our anatomy, we find ourselves in a multitude of problems.

They say that silence is golden. And golden is divine wisdom. Why is silence golden and why is it divine wisdom? It keeps the door closed, so that we can go and find our true self inside of our own being.

Now, it is not within the purpose of this class to go into private communication for any student, but I do want to point out, in the situation brought to the class, that it will take the soul faculty of faith to close the door that has been opened, if that is what the student chooses to do. Thank you very, very much.

And let's choose wisely. You see, it isn't a matter of speaking. It's a matter of not thinking before we open the mouth. Yes.

In the stage that I am in and the knowledge that I have, do you have guidelines for how you help children, so they will be, perhaps, a little more advanced in spiritual thinking when they come to my age?

Thank you very much. And I'll be more than happy—there's one thing, one thing that is number one in the growth of a child. When a child is taught the truth, that whatever, in all of life, happens to us has been caused by us, that will send the child's thoughts inward. And as the child grows, they will find their God. And they will not go into this panorama of experiences and blaming the world and everything in it for their feelings and their emotions. Once a child has accepted that great truth that all things are caused by our attitude of mind, by our own thoughts and feelings—every experience we encounter—that type of an upbringing will bring freedom to any soul.

With regard to reflections of the subconscious, it's been stated in one of our classes, if I recall correctly, that as we pass from this dimension, that is one of the first things we encounter, if I'm speaking about the same thing. It's also been given that we stand before this divine computer and many religions have taught on this so-called judgment. And I wonder if you could speak a bit on that and how it might relate to these particular teachings. And what is it, really, that we're putting ourselves through?

Of course, you're speaking of when the soul leaves the form and it faces all of the experiences that it has encountered, all of the reflections of the experiences of the soul's incarnation. Is that what you're referring to?

Yes, sir.

Yes. What actually takes place, when we face that—and what is so beneficial is to make the effort to face it daily. Then, there isn't such a heavy cross for us when we face the totality of it all. What actually takes place? All of the experiences that we have encountered in this life and our reactions to them are balanced within our own being. Now when the mind has an experience, it has a choice. It has a choice to use the balancing power of the soul faculty or to be out of balance in its corresponding sense function. Now, if we ourselves make this effort to direct this divine energy in any experience that's taking place within us, balanced through the corresponding soul faculty—that is where the judgment is, because that is where the choice is. And this happens every instant with all of our experiences. So man, using total consideration in any experience, permits this divine energy to flow through the soul faculty of understanding.

And this is why the teachings of the ages have always been, In all of your getting, get understanding. But we cannot get understanding unless we express the soul faculty of tolerance. And we cannot express the soul faculty of tolerance unless we express the soul faculty of consideration. And so we see the inseparableness of the soul faculties in all of our experiences.

The balancing that takes place is done by the conscience, as we review our life's experiences. Now the conscience, as we have stated before, is a spiritual sensibility with a dual capacity, knowing right from wrong, not having to be told. So this is what this review, before this divine, so to speak, or so-called computer really is. It reveals to us, in the experience, whether or not there was a balance of the divine energy flowing through the soul faculty and the corresponding sense function. And according to those laws that we have set into motion is our soul destined to its continued experiences. And I hope that's helped with your question.

Very much.

You're welcome.

Would you please tell us how we might best learn to express the spirit of spontaneity?

The lady has asked, How may we best *learn* to express the spirit of spontaneity? The number one problem is the word *learn*. If it is a spontaneous expression of spirit, the learning process is an obstruction, created by the intellect or the mind. Now, we must choose wisely what we consider to be spiritual spontaneity and impulsive desire expression, because there is a great similarity in the feeling that one experiences. Now a person may say that they had a spirit of spontaneity and so they did that, when the truth of the matter is, they had a compulsive-impulsive desire and chose to call it the spirit of spontaneity.

Now how does one tell the difference between the spirit of spontaneity and the compulsive drive of one's own desire? Well, first, we must become aware of our own desires. So often, my friends, the expression of our desires are not even in our conscious thought. And they happen. So when we are truly expressing the spirit of spontaneity, there is total consideration, there is the flow of divine reason, and only harmony is made manifest. That is the effect of the spirit of spontaneity. Now the effects of compulsive desire are a war of the emotions and a continuous turmoil and discord. Perhaps that will help with your question.

With all the prejudice we see in the world today, is that a form of judgment? And if it is a form of judgment, is it through understanding that will break that down? I just lost the words. Do you know what I mean?

Yes. Thank you very much. Now, we must remember that if we are viewing life a certain way, then we are interested, of course, in the way that we are viewing it. For example, if we see a world that is filled with prejudice, then we must realize that prejudice is something that concerns us, and that which concerns us is certainly in need of understanding. Now the reason that we are in need of understanding is because we have accepted concern. Man cannot be concerned about anything that he understands. For if you have understanding, you have total consideration and, therefore, you no longer have any concern. Therefore, we can make a change for ourselves, but we cannot directly change the world. But if each individual considers changing their own private world, then this whole world will be totally transformed. I hope that has helped with your question concerning your view and understanding of the word *prejudice*.

Yes, sir. I would like a little help with a word and that word being consideration. *It seems the word has been used both in the sense, as it was used just now, of consideration of things—simply considering a situation; and then it's been used in the sense of showing some consideration for. Is there a difference in the faculty-function relationship? I would appreciate some clarification.*

When the inward acceptance becomes the outward drive, then you have consideration for things outside. But you cannot consider things outside of your universe until they have been considered inside.

We have a teaching here, and an affirmation of total consideration. Now we must ask ourselves the question—total consideration, we've also had a discussion on consideration, the divine will. Is it possible for the mind to consider anything that it has not accepted? I ask the question, Is it possible? Can the human mind consider anything that it does not accept? No. I'm sure we will all agree that we cannot consider what we do not first accept.

Now, a person says, "Well, I don't accept that." What are they really saying? What are we really saying when we say, "I don't accept that. I don't accept that. I don't accept that" or "I don't accept that"? What is the mind really saying? It is saying, "I am not going to spend the time to consider it."

Now, perhaps the mind has considered it before and, having considered it, has made the choice, and the judgment, that it is not in its best interest. However, we must go beyond that point and ask ourselves why it is not in our best interest. What sane man would reach a decision and say that something was not in his best interest if he had not given it thorough investigation? That's the mark, of course, of a very ignorant person. So I think we will all agree, as students, that that is some type of mark of some type of ignorance someplace inside of ourselves. So we find that it behooves us to consider all things.

Now the teaching states very clearly, "Love all life and know the Light." Now I think that's a very simple, definite statement: to love all life and know the Light. Well, my friends, can you love that that you haven't accepted? Can you accept that that you

haven't considered? Can you consider that that you don't understand? And so we go right back to a very ancient teaching that
we mentioned earlier: In all of your getting, get understanding.

Now, we are all seeking the Light. And by the Light, we understand that to be God, to be Freedom, to be Truth. So if we
are all seeking God, we are all seeking Truth, we are all seeking Freedom. What are these constant rejections that we insist
upon expressing? Now if the teaching is demonstrable—and
demonstrable it is, to those who care to make the effort—then,
my friends, we're not going to find Truth, Light, or God if we
do not follow the principles by which it is to be found. Now why
is the teaching, "Love all life and know the Light" so important
to all of us? Because, my friends, everything is sustained by the
one Divine Light, known as Truth, Freedom, and God. And so
if we don't consider all of God's manifestations, we are not considering all of God. And if we don't consider all of God, we're
certainly not going to find God, the Light, in its fullness.

*Would you enlighten me on "and sees the tides of creation, as
a captain sees his ship"?*

What would you like to understand?

I just don't understand that.

Would you repeat the affirmation once more, please? *[For
the complete affirmation, see the appendix.]*

*OK. Without beginning or ending, eternity is my thought and
sees the tides of creation—*

"Eternity is my true awareness and sees the tides of creation, as a captain sees his ship." Is that the part you wanted
explained?

Yes.

How does a captain see his ship?

That's what I'm not clear on.

Would you not agree that a captain sees his ship as a vehicle
of transport to take him where he wants to go, to the port that
he chooses, under his own direction? Would you not agree that

a captain knows that the ship is only a vehicle, that it is at his command and it will do what he directs it to do? Now, would you like to repeat those lines again? I think, perhaps, you will have your answer.

"And sees the tides of creation . . ."

"As a captain sees his ship."

Thank you.

So we look and see creation as the vehicle through which the Divine may express itself and direct the ship itself. Does that help with your question?

It does.

Yes.

Sir, I'd like to ask a question about karma. Since there is no time in eternity, cause and effect, could we in our earth minds see, when something happens to us, the cause happen to us before the effect? I mean, could the cause happen to us before the effect? Could we in our earth minds see it that way? And also, a lot of times what an average or not too learned spiritually aware person would consider as a bad happening, somebody who is on the path of light would consider as a good happening, meaning disaster. The same disaster could occur to two people and it could be a great disaster in the average mind and it would cause the average man suffering, and it might also cause the enlightened man suffering, but he would look upon the disaster, so-called, as a benefit. So actually, whether you're enlightened or not, the disaster is going to happen. And if you're enlightened, it's easier to accept. Am I making myself clear?

Yes. And we'll first go to your first question, which is dealing with the law, what you call the Law of Cause and Effect, commonly referred to by many people as karma. And the lady has asked the question, Does the effect come before the cause, since, in truth, we're in a timeless dimension? Well, first of all, students, we would have to be in the level of consciousness known as timelessness. And I can't find anyone present here that's in that level of consciousness. However, in the level of time, which we are all in, in that dream and in that illusion, each cause is an effect and each effect is a cause.

Now, in reference to two people, one seemingly illumined and the other not illumined, both receiving a so-called disaster, one sees it objectively, as the effect of laws that he's set into motion. The one not having as much light, perhaps, sees it emotionally and reacts accordingly. Now which man is the wiser? One uses reason to get through the experience and the other uses emotion to stay in it. I think it's rather self-evident, my friends, that the one who has a little light, using the soul faculty of reason, is indeed the wiser and, of course, the one with the greater benefit.

Thank you. It's relative to something in tonight's discourse. Could you please share with us the significance of the words "heavy cross"? Why a heavy cross? This is mentioned through-out the Bible, for example, and in various other philosophical books, as "It's a heavy cross to bear." Could you share—

Thank you. You would like our understanding of that term "a heavy cross," which means "burden"? Yes. Whenever there is, by the choice of man, an imbalance in the direction of the divine energy going into what is known as the sense functions of expression, man experiences what he calls a burden or a heavy cross. Of course, we all understand that it's all self-created. We open the door, of course, by opening our mouth. And so that is our understanding of what is meant by the phrase "it's a heavy cross". Now, we say, "Well, now, this person, they were born with a heavy cross to bear in this life." Well, that's the effect. The birth is an effect, you see. It's an effect of what the soul has set into motion in its evolutionary journey. Does that help with your question? Go ahead, please.

Somewhat, sir. May I ask more?

Yes. If that answer is not clear to you, you may feel free to carry on with your question.

Well, the Wise One says here, regarding his return to this dimension by choice, "But once having made that choice, the law shall be fulfilled." And then he goes on to say, "But, my children, it bears with it a heavy cross that you have merited, as I have merited."

Of course, it bears with it a heavy cross.

Why does it have to be a heavy cross?

Because, you see, you first must understand the individual and whether or not they desired to return or whether or not that they had set a law into motion and they had to return and fulfill the purpose of their soul's incarnation. Would you not agree? Once having left this physical world and finally gravitating to levels of light and spheres of beauty, to return to it, would you not consider it a bit of a heavy cross for you?

Yes.

I think any human would. And I do think, when he made that statement, right here in this book [*The Living Light*], that he was quite human. Wouldn't you agree?

Oh yes.

Yes. I hope that's helped, now, with your question.

This duty to our soul—we realize this is duty, gratitude, and tolerance, but the way it's put here, "Is my duty a true responsibility or is it a fabrication of the illusions of my mind?" And I have read this many times. And I had beloved parents, whom I felt I had a duty to and still the duty became a burden to me at the last. And I was very confused as to what my duty was. I knew, because of other teachings and because I've been in this a long time, that they had their individual illnesses that they went with. Still, it didn't make me feel any better, within, to know that. Within myself, I didn't know what my duty was. I didn't know whether I was in illusion. I still do not know, at times. The minute you open your mouth and say I'll do something, you're in it.

Yes. What was the question?

How do we know the difference between a duty and a fabrication of the illusions of our mind?

Oh, thank you very much. The lady has asked a question in reference to duty and, How do we know what is a duty to our own spirit, to God within us, and what we are expressing is duty, which is an illusion and a fabrication of our own mind? Well, first off, friends, we have to find God inside of us and find our own spirit, so we will be able to make a wise decision and a choice between what is the Spirit and what is a fabrication of our mind. So the first thing to do is to get understanding, so that we may understand what *is* inside of me that is my spirit and God and what is a fabrication of my mind. So the first thing that man does is to make an effort to know himself, class. And that's how we will be able to know which is duty to our spirit within us, flowing through us, and which is a duty to a fabrication and an illusion of our mind. I hope that's helped with your question.

It's a hard way. Well, there is no way that I know to wave a magic wand and say, "There you are, student, you are now awakened to your own spirit." It doesn't happen like that, my friends. Because, you see, we didn't go to sleep that way. We just didn't close our eyes and go to sleep. It was a gradual process through eons of time. The sleep of satisfaction has not come over us in the blinking of an eye. It is an evolutionary process, my friends. The more energy, the more thought we give to the senses, the more we go to sleep in the realms of satisfaction. You know, our teaching is, Irritation wakes the soul: 'tis satisfaction that lets it sleep. So be cautious and beware, when all things in your universe go well. Which part of you are they going well for? Are you in satisfaction? Well, if you're staying in satisfaction, you're asleep. But it is your divine right to your slumber. But do not expect some special law in the universe to touch your cranium and awaken you so that you may find your true self again, because that is not the way we went to sleep in this great eternity.

Now I am not saying or implying that man should not have some satisfaction in life. After all, we have a sense body and it has its needs. But, you see, my friends, balance in all things is a path to wisdom. So let us balance these soul faculties with these sense functions. Let us use the vehicle that we have merited. Let us use it, not abuse it.

Now, there isn't a book anywhere, that I know of, that says, "All right, you can get to this point before you abuse the automobile that you have merited." No, friends. Inside of you, you know. Nobody has to tell you if you're eating too much or doing anything else too much. Because, don't you see, you know what is too much for you. No one has to tell you that. And isn't it wonderful that no one has to tell us!

Thank you all very much. I see we've gone past the hour. Let us go have refreshments. Thank you.

FEBRUARY 28, 1974

CONSCIOUSNESS CLASS 42 ✷

We will begin our class this evening by turning our books [*The Living Light*] to Discourse 41.

[A student reads Discourse 41 aloud. After this, the class meditates.]

This evening, I want to speak to you as Richard Goodwin, before we get into the regular class. That may seem strange to some of you, but it is rare that I get to give a personal announcement for myself in a class or in our church during its services, without being censored. Hopefully, I won't be, because I have my own feelings on the matter.

Now, it is a most proper time, I feel, to bring this matter up, considering that over 90 percent of the attendance—the students in this class—are members of this church. Now most of you are aware that your church—my church, our church—has been on an active building fund drive since January of 1973. Now, over the years I have had many requests from students with their thoughts and ideas of how you can get your own church building, which we all believe, I'm sure, would be in the best interest of all of us, as students and members of the church, especially those souls who have to carry all of these books and different things back and forth to this church, and all of the truckloads of things and coffee urns and silverware that must be carried every single month to your socials. So I'm sure that we all agree that we all want our own church building.

Well, I'm bringing this up because it's a lesson in life and this is what we're studying: is lessons in life. Now nothing that is healthy grows overnight. Nature demonstrates that to us, as she plants the seed. The small acorn of the mighty oak tree doesn't grow overnight. And so a church of your own, its own building, will not grow overnight, if it's going to be a stable and healthy one.

So we're going to go through the stepping-stone process, which we have been doing. And I want to speak for a few moments on the suggestions that have been given by students and members of our church on a compulsory tithing system. Now in the six years of operating the Serenity Association and in the over two and one-half years of operating the church section of it, I have refrained, as president and pastor, from enforcing a compulsory tithing system, which, let us say, over 90-some percent of all churches have. Now the reason that I have refrained from encouraging that type of system in our church is because I am well aware that the gift without the giver is of no value.

So the question is, How is our building fund really doing? Now, in order to satisfy the interest of our own people, and in the best interest of this church, beginning next month—that's the month of April—in the April issue of your monthly magazine [The Serenity Sentinel], all donors who have donated $100 or more will be listed each month. This will help us all to know where our church really stands. The total amount of the building fund to that date will also be listed.

Now, I spoke to a group of my students who were at the office Tuesday night. Now, how do we, as members of our church, really want our building to come about? The next step toward our church—when you find out how little there is in your present building fund, you will realize that you can't even get a lot and put up a $350,000 church. You can't even talk to the real estate broker. However, we can, with this donation and with your support, we can, at least, move into our own church office. And the dollars you donate will, then, be going into your own property, which, in turn, at the proper time, can be converted into cash and go into your own church building.

Now, I know in all honesty that I have no member in my church that is, at present, a charity case. I know that as an honest fact. Perhaps I know that because I'm a little bit psychic. Now the point I'm really getting to, friends: if I look from a level of real self, I'll be perfectly honest with you, as pastor and president of this church, I could be extremely discouraged. I could be very discouraged to find that my own students, the highest percentage, have not yet subscribed to a building block for their church. However, I know if I entertain that level too long, I won't sit here very long, be rest assured, because I know that I wouldn't. Because looking at that level of consciousness, it is so discouraging that I would just go out and do my work in my own little way and not go through this whole system.

So I'm going to talk to you heart-to-heart. Your church, on its step to moving to its own building, needs to move to its own church office to pay on its own mortgage. I have put one simple stipulation in my donation to our church, and that simple stipulation is that the outstanding debt to paying off the equipment of this church (the printing equipment, etc.)—the outstanding debt of $6,850.72—be first paid off. I'm a very practical person. I know that you cannot go out and buy a house with $15,000 down and pay a mortgage, which would run approximately

$500 a month, plus taxes, at least, and pay an additional $350 a month on machinery to pay off that $6,850.72. So I am not going to donate the $15,000 until the membership of the church are willing to demonstrate what they feel that they can, and get this paid off.

Now I spent the time today to divide the number of members in good standing by the total amount due. And, actually, it didn't turn out very badly at all. It simply means that if each one pulls their own weight, if each member of the church gives $190.92, your existing debt will be paid off. And we can move into our own church office.

Now, I know that some of us, perhaps, and justly so, can say, "Well, I don't have $190.92 at this time." I, personally, am not asking you to donate $190.92 today or tomorrow. However, if you are willing and you feel that you want to pull your own weight in your own church and do your part, I know that the church board can work out a system whereby you can pay it the way that you can. However, that must be your own decision.

Now, if we want to look at numbers, we can say that we have exactly thirty-six members in good standing. Fifty-some members are in bad standing. That means that fifty-some members have not paid their dues. Now your dues were finally increased to $27 a year, which includes your $3.70 per year *Sentinel* subscription. Now, it is true that when the dues were raised from $18.75 to $27 a year, your church lost a few members. But I want to ask you the question, friends, Are those the kind of members you want in your church? That their own soul and their church and the efforts and the work it's trying to do are not worth an $8.25 annual increase?

When we started these classes—and I'm so grateful the Friends are letting me speak from my own feelings and my own viewpoint—when we started these classes, we tried to have it as reasonable as we possibly could. We even went so far as to make a special system for people who didn't have the $45. And so we said, well, that they could pay $5 down and they could pay so much a week for twelve weeks. Well, when we looked at the records, friends, in one course alone your church lost over $600. We had to make a change. We had to insist that the people taking these classes, unless they had proven themselves—that they were capable of paying their bills, the debts that they incur—we would have to ask for a minimum of half of the registration fee and the other half the following week. Because it's just simply bad business. You can't build a church that way.

Now, I went through the records today—don't feel badly, anyone: you're going to have your full hour of class. I believe in giving, because I believe in getting. And I don't ever mind asking for God or to keep this work going. Now, the simple fact is this: that since January 1973, your church has taken in $8,250.63 in its building fund drive. And that's wonderful, except for one fact: your church has had to borrow $7,500 from its building fund in order to operate. So, you see, though we've managed to take in over eight thousand, your church has had to borrow over seven thousand just to pay the rents: the rent of the church office and the rent of the Legion and the payment of its bills.

Now that, in and of itself, can be most discouraging, with one exception: in the past six months there has been a genuine show of increase of our people and their donations. So your church, as it goes on, must pay back to its own building fund over $7,000.

Now, what is it and what is the point we're getting to? What do you, as the members of this church, really want to do? Do you want to enforce a compulsory tithing? If you do and if that is your wish, I will definitely propose it to your board of directors. And if you do, what percent of your total income do you want to put into your church? It is not my wish. I hope that we, as members of this church, surely can find a better way.

Now, some of our people feel that the church, to pay off this debt so they can move into their own church office, should come up with some projects. Well, I want to tell you something, friends: We've got every project going that you can possibly imagine and we've got all of our workers working on them. And that's just to pay your regular expenses.

Now, I'm not crying poverty. God forbid! I know the law.

All right. Now, what is it that we, as members of our church, really want to do? Do we want to subscribe to a building block each month? If so, how much do we want to subscribe?

Now, it is true that whatever effort we do for God, God knows what we're doing. We don't have to tell people. But I do want to tell you this: Every nonprofit organization in the world has found it advisable to list their donors. And they have not only found it advisable to do that, they have found it advisable to list the bracket in which they have donated, for example, $100, $500, $1,000, etc. Well, now I don't know of any nonprofit charitable organization that hasn't found that beneficial, because they all do it. And, therefore, your church is moving into that system.

Now, that doesn't mean—please, don't be hurt—that we're going to list all of our members and put a zero after their name if they haven't donated to their church building fund. Now I'll tell you the truth: if I had my way, I just might do that. I would certainly give ninety days' notice, but, you see, I don't want to have to do that, friends. It's too humiliating. Now then, I thought, "Well, maybe it would be nice if I just listed down every member, don't you see, and how much they actually donated, down to the nickels and dimes." And then, I looked at my own donation from my allowance and I saw that, well, I gave $3. And I said, "Well, I'm just humiliated." But I said, "Now, if that's what the Council and the Spirit want is for all the members to be listed with the exact amount, I'll list my $3." We'll just put everybody's name down alphabetically and we'll list the exact amount. But I don't think that's what you want. You know, not just for myself and my $3, but—don't worry, I'm going to give more—but that's all I've been able to give so far, because I would not let the church board give me a raise. Because, to me, the church comes first. And I'm not going to take more than a $50-a-month salary until this church is solvent. And it's not yet solvent when it has to borrow $7,000 from its own building fund savings. And that broke my heart, too. But however broken it got, I'm still here.

Now, what do the members want to do? What do the members of the church want to do?

Please, don't add any more projects onto your church. We hardly have enough workers to take care of the projects we've already got. When you stop and think, friends—look. We have a building fund committee. We have a men's club committee. We have a ladies' guild committee. We have a bake sale every month. I mean, we sell books. I sell toothpicks. Whatever there is to sell, I try to sell. I give the church every donation that comes into my office from my private counseling and any other donation that I can get. So if you add any more projects on top of us, you're going to submerge me. Because somebody's got to do the work.

So, you know, let us look at it lightheartedly and cheerfully. I mean, after all, you know, when I saw in those books that there were only thirty-six members in good standing, I kind of felt a little sick inside. And then, my mother came in and she said, "Well, Richard, you ought to be grateful: Jesus only had twelve." *[The class laughs loudly.]* Now that's pretty good, considering just a short time, you know. And he's got a lot more today. A lot more. So let me have just a few and let them be strong spirits.

Now, I'm very happy because this has come about today, this final decision, and, you know, not even a few hours went by when a student of mine and a member said, "I'm going to donate that!" And that's exactly what she has done. Well, that's fine.

Now, what do we really want to do to get our church built, see? What is it we really want to do? If you tell me to cut expenses, I'm going to cut your head off! Because I can't see where I can cut them any more than I've already cut them. After all, you know, at your church office—any of you who have ever visited— if they leave the lights on, they have to pay a level expenditure. I finally got them brainwashed to the fact that the church, you see—that money didn't grow on trees. And if they were going to cost the church money and leave the lights on, they had to pay for it out of their own pocket. And if they were going to break something, they had to pay for it. And so please don't suggest for me to cut expenses.

Does anyone have a suggestion of they'd like to, you know— well, let's see the hands that want a compulsory tithing system, even though I'm against it. All right.

What do you mean by "compulsory"?

Well, no, a compulsory tithing system is where a church just simply takes 10 percent off the top of your salary. And I'll tell you the truth, I'm enough of a psychic talent to know that if we did that, your church would be built in less than two years. I mean, our church is not filled with poverty, be rest assured. But that's what "compulsory" means. It simply means that, as a member, you've got so much—X percent of your total income goes to your church automatically, you see. You wouldn't want that, would you?

Well, that might be one way to get it.

Well, it's a very good way to get it, because it works for all those other churches. I mean it really works, but—

But what about your tithing?

Well, I think that's wonderful. That's our building block system. You know, I think that's just wonderful and that's how it's going to be built. You see, if you will just subscribe and sign up and do what you feel is right for you—do you see what I mean?—then your conscience and your spirit can work, instead of us forcing a percentage on you. Wouldn't that be better?

What I'm asking is—yes, I agree—do you have a system now where you could tithe and you set—

Yes, we most certainly do.

—where you say a certain percentage is to go to the building fund.

You certainly can, yes.

But do you have people go out and call on new members?

No, we don't do that yet. Would you like us to do that?

That always helps me.

Well, you see what works! And you see why all these churches have all that gold. Well, I'll tell you what we can do. We can remind you every month.

Oh, well, once I've done it, I stick to it.

All right.

Once I've committed myself.

Sure. Would you like to do that?

Commit? Oh yes, I'll tithe.

Would you? All right. Now, thank you very much.

Time is, I think, sort of, of the essence now. I think that you should get some pledges from individual members. We have just become members. But I think we have never signed up for a building block program. But I think I will pledge a certain amount of money to you.

Certainly.

And I think there are others here who could pledge a certain amount, whether it comes in now or it comes in later.

That's right. Remember, when we make a pledge, friends, who are we really making it to? We're making it to our own soul and our own spirit. And while you brought up the mention of pledge, how many people present would like to have a pledge system? Just raise your hands. All right. My goodness' sakes, that's almost a majority—it's almost a totality.

Now, how many would like to have a compulsory tithing system? Good. I'm not in favor of it, either.

Now, will each person that raised their hand, that wants to give a monthly pledge to their church, please see the Building

Fund Committee, because that committee will take not only your name, but the amount of your pledge. And then, we can pay off that $6,850.72. Then, you can get what I've got left, get into a little piece of property, and we can meet the monthly mortgage. And if you have great faith, there's a lot more coming. I can assure you of that. And the years are not going to be long. Then, you can have your own place.

Now, I know that all thirty-six of our members in good standing are not here present. So it's up to the ones who are present to talk to the ones who aren't present, you see, and help them to pledge what they would like to pledge. Now that way, friends, your church is going to be built, believe me. And that's the only way it's really going to be built. And it will be built.

You know what's wonderful? It's very important to me, because I want to tell you something: it's personally important. I'm speaking for myself. I thought Wednesday, I said to myself, "Well, what am I doing anyway?" I look at the building fund drive and it's just heartrending. Then, I said, "Well, what am I doing all this for anyway?" I mean, after all, I can tell you, friends, I know that I can make at least a thousand dollars a month, if I want to go into the commercial rat race in my particular profession. That is not what I feel like I want to do, you see.

Now, I'm not saying that you have to give up your vacation this year. I'm simply telling you I'm giving up mine for the eleventh year. Because, you see, if I'm your teacher and I can't demonstrate what I'm preaching, then you'd best get yourself a new teacher, because you're on the wrong track. And you're not going to find freedom that way. So let's become the living demonstration.

We don't need a cathedral that has gold altars. God forbid. I wouldn't want to serve in one. And we don't need some palace someplace. But wouldn't it be really nice not to have to cart all this stuff every Thursday? Every Sunday? Every Saturday you have a social? The first of the month at every brunch? And not to cart all this stuff back and forth, back and forth, back and forth. It really would be nice.

And it would be nice to have a building of your own where you have your counseling rooms, you have your healing rooms, you have a nice social hall with a nice fireplace, you have rooms for your printing, and all of those different things. I'm sure that's what you all want for your church. I'm just trying to be receptive to your suggestions of just how it's going to come about, you see.

You see, we're going to have to say, "OK, this is my church. Now what am I doing to get the thing built? See, what am *I* doing?" Not, "What's Mary Jane doing over there?" Because that's a total waste of energy and effort. See? We've got to say, "Now what am I doing?" Because, I assure you, I have joined the Building Fund Committee. I have joined it as the co-chairman. And if I join something, friends, it's going to move. I can tell you that. It is going to move.

You're going to have the total amount in your *Sentinel* every month. And I'm going to keep a very close eye on it. But it's going to move one way: up. In and up.

Because this is all a part of your class. Because, you see, this is going to help us face ourselves. See? Not what we think we are, but what we really are. How much does it mean to us?

You know, a thought crossed my mind today, you know, perhaps the message is a little strong. We've got new members, etc. Well, that's good, because, then, we know who our new members are. Isn't that right? Sure. It either means something or it doesn't. Now, if it knocks us out because we're going to face a personal pledge that we're making or something, we shouldn't be in, isn't that right? See, it isn't like I'm saying, "Now you've got to donate at least $25 a month." It's not like that, is it? And besides, I assure you, any nickel you give to Spirit, Spirit makes sure that you'll be saved in other areas.

Every Monday I go through the same process. Every Monday there's X hundreds of dollars to pay out on bills and every Monday it's there.

Now the other Monday—and I told my Tuesday night group there, I said, "You know, we had $6.37 left in your church account, in your checking account." Well, I add up the bills. I know what has to be paid. The following Monday, which was seven days later, we had to pay out over $650. Well, I can look at that $6.37 and really get sick, but I know better. I have a little faith, directed faith. And I said, "Well, Lord, it's already on its way in." Every Monday I sign the checks and every single Monday, with every check I sign, I say the same thing: "Thank you, God. I'm moving in your divine flow with this church. It's going out so that it can come back in again." Well, the following Monday we had over $650 in the bank!

Now, this is the thing. Believe me, friends, it doesn't come from your church collection. I will not discuss how much that is, because I don't want anybody to get sick before class. But anyway, let's say it's improving. It is improving. We're working at it.

So the question is, Where does it come from? Well, I'll tell you where it comes from. It comes from God. But it comes through many channels. There's cakes and the bake sale. There are a few dollars that come in from your advertising. There are a few dollars that come in from your men's club. There are a few dollars that come in for the level expenditures from the workers at the office, because whenever they cost your church, they have to put the money in the box. After all, it isn't up to the rest of the members to pay for somebody else's unawareness. And it comes in from counseling. And it comes in from all of these different things that we have open. Don't you see? And that's what really takes place.

Now I am happy to see that 100 percent of the students of this church have decided that they want to make a pledge to build their church. Now I think that's a record. I really do. Thank you all very much.

As a person who hasn't been involved in the church very long, I'm sitting here thinking . . .

Yes.

Why is it that I have not heretofore made a pledge? I've certainly had the thought to do so. And it seems to me that what gets in my way or part of what slows—I allow to slow me down—is that I have not had a clear idea of what I could do. What I am trying to say is the system is not clear enough. For example, I've come to counseling. Now, I know that I charge people for the counseling that I do. And, of course, it crossed my mind that I would like to pay. However, part of me says, "Well, maybe I'll offend him if I try to pay."

Yes, this is necessary for our own members to pass the word that a donation is acceptable for all counseling, because, you see, every one of our counselors and every one of our healers—every penny that comes from counseling, not one of our counselors or healers takes that for themselves. That all goes directly to your church. Yes.

If some kind of a system or some periodically printed material or something is available to people to help put the idea into their minds, I—

Well, we have a pamphlet. We have "Nine Points to Remember in Consulting a Spiritualist Medium" and it says very clearly in the last part of that pamphlet that every servant is worthy of their hire. Although a set fee is not charged for counseling, the Serenity Spiritualist Association recognizes that every servant is worthy of their hire and accepts donations for its Association. It does say that in that green pamphlet. Yes. I put that in there when we first had it printed.

Would it be against any philosophy in the church to make such an announcement on Sundays, along with the announcement that counselors and healers are available?

Well, the thing is, it would be in the best interest for that to be handled as a private matter. Now, we could consider, in fact, we *will* consider someone stationed at the door, when counseling is requested of our counselors, and give them this green pamphlet that we have and state in a nice way that although set fees are not charged by our counselors, donations to our church are definitely acceptable, you see. Yes.

Now, as a counselor for thirty-three years now, be rest assured I'm so grateful things have improved. Now they really have, you see. It's rare that we get left a dollar anymore. It's an average of, usually, at least ten. You know, bread isn't 5¢ a loaf anymore, you know. And so I'm very grateful that in that area things have improved and I will certainly ask that we consider some type of a system whereby, when people are waiting for counseling, that they may be educated in the procedure. Yes. Without being offensive to the person seeking the counseling and without being offensive, of course, to our own church. That's a very good thought. Thank you very much.

First of all, I want to thank you for sharing the human side of yourself. You share the spiritual side so readily. But—

Oh, I don't mind asking for a dollar at all. I don't mind at all. You know, I have one philosophy and it's a very definite one: I never saw poverty lead to spirituality. It never guaranteed spirituality. That's my personal philosophy. Yes.

And secondly, I want to apologize for being one of the members—I don't mean this as any inspiration for any other member, but personally I understand about those cornerstones and I definitely want to be included in that. Because I don't know what I was thinking, I mean, the teaching is so spiritual, so we've always had the church, as far as I'm concerned. You've kind of brought me down to earth.

Yes. Thank you very much. Wonderful. Now isn't that beautiful? You see, if we get 100 percent here. Now, I think we only have one person that isn't, yet, a member. Thank you. You see, we have 99 percent membership attendance in this class. Were you considering membership, is that it? You were? I mean, we don't want to leave anyone out, you know. After all, I was told when I was a kid I'd make a good salesman. But, you see, you've got to sell something in this life: that's what life's all about. Who could sell anything better than a way for a person to help themselves?

You know, friends, when you give your dollars, think of it this way. Just talk to yourself and say, "Thank you, God, for this opportunity to let that circulate, like fertilizer, you know. So it can spread all around and come back."

On the building fund, there are two questions I have on the pledge. I'm willing to pledge. Of course, you know that. I'm a Spiritualist from way back when and I know the law. This $190.92, is this supposed to be pledged?

No, no, no, no, no. No, that's not what is to be pledged. I'm just stating the facts: with thirty-six members divided into $6,850.72. That's what it figures out to. That's just to take care of the existing printing machinery and all that stuff.

Well, this pledge is a continuous pledge off the top of the salary. I mean, you know, whatever amount you want.

That's up to the individual.

But if we already are taking a building block, we can increase the amount of that building block in this—

Certainly.

But the pledge is really for a building block.

Absolutely. That goes to build your church. Yes.

Now I was wondering. You know, to give means to get. Why couldn't we have an event or a charitable outlet? We have Indian guides. I've brought this up so many times, but it was turned down by another group. But there's a conviction of mine. We talk about our Indian guides, but we do nothing for the Indians that are here—or some other groups. But we could have some sort of a charitable event: put ourselves in Marin County's view and

make ourselves known a little bit, that we're doing something for
something outside of our own little group. I—

May I speak just a moment in reference to this?

Yes.

Thank you very much. Number one, this church has for a long, long time donated all of the clothing that it receives, including my own, to the American Indian Relief Fund in San Francisco. Now, because, in the present financial state of your church (that your church has had to borrow over $7,000 from its own building fund) we did not feel that it was in the best interest, when we have to borrow to pay the bills to pay the rent, to make a cash donation to the American Indian Relief Fund. However, we have a letter in our files of their gratitude for the things that we were able to donate to them.

Now, I would like to see the day when this Association is in a position when it can give a scholarship, a Serenity scholarship, to a worthy American Indian for an education. So that hopefully, through that, the individual, or combination thereof, can do some good for their particular race. However, there is a law that states, "Physician, heal thyself". We must, first, work and bring our own organization into a solvent state. So let us first get Serenity in a position, spiritually, mentally, and materially, so that we can do these things. Then, I think it's just a bit premature at this time. This Association repeatedly does donate what it can, as far as clothing, to the American Indian Relief Fund. And when the members of the church demonstrate that divine supply for its church, then we certainly will consider doing something financially toward some type of a scholarship.

Now, I think, friends, that we're all in the flow now. I see so many dollar bills, I don't know how I'm going to see anything else, but I will try. And so you're free to ask any questions you have.

Now, I would like to pass this on to you. A lovely lady, who was the founder and the pastor of the Golden Gate Church in

San Francisco for fifty-five years, built them a beautiful church. So that they don't have to worry, now that she's gone these past three years. Well, all her students in class—you know, it's so interesting—because she would kind of give you a little healing when the lights were out. And she always said one thing. She always said, "As freely as I receive, do I give." Well, you know, thousands of students heard that statement, but they never knew what that meant. They never knew. She was a smart woman. Do you know what she did? She declared the truth: she declared the law of the universe. She was telling them in no uncertain terms, "My dear student, what you give to me, I give to you. As freely as you give what you can give to me, that's as freely as I give what I've got to you." Now that's what she said. And she did it to every single student and she did it every week for her full course. No wonder they've got a beautiful church! No wonder they're solvent and they've got money in the bank! Because she touched everyone's head every single week that they were in class, and she made the same truthful statement. Now isn't that a beautiful demonstration of divine balance and justice?

Now I understand why I was allowed to go to every class, to her home, to socials, to her beautiful open house—

Well, as freely as you give, that's as freely as you get. I mean, there's nothing wrong with that. That's good business, wouldn't you agree? That's only sensible. You know, there's nothing in spirituality and awakening that says, "Get rid of all of that gold down there. It's terrible." Well, if it is so terrible, then why do we have it in this earth realm?

The thing is that you put God first. But let's not deny being practical. I mean, the Friends that have been with us since the opening of this church, they know, they know how many people have come in and through which doors. And they know how many people have felt that they shouldn't be contaminated with money. My, I've had clients that tell me they don't know contamination with money. Well, you don't think they left any, do you? Not with that kind of thinking. Absolutely not. They didn't want to be contaminated with it, so they kept it all in the bank! Don't you see, they didn't want any in their pockets, you know. It's kind of a funny thing, you know, but life is truly beautiful. It really is.

Now, friends, you know it's getting late. Although you've had my personal class work tonight, you may feel free to ask your questions.

May I make a suggestion? Mr. Goodwin is working awfully hard. Why don't we waive the rest of the questioning in this class and pick it up maybe next week?

Well, thank you very much. But I want to tell you something. Because I see all that is coming, I want to give in equal proportion. Believe me. And I'm going to stand at the door, considering I've nominated myself the assistant co-chairman to the Building Fund Committee and I'm going to be there, friends. So I want to give as much as I possibly can, because I don't want to block the flow of receiving all that I see coming for your church and mine. Now you go ahead with your questions. And I'll try to get to the other side for a minute here and give an intelligent answer.

I would like to know, sometimes when I give, I give feeling that I don't really care whether I get anything back or not. Now, I know that we always receive something in return. Should we give with that attitude or should we give feeling that as things go out, it will come back? I mean, should we have a conscious awareness that something is coming back?

Thank you very much. Now in reference to giving, and the lady is discussing, When a person gives, should they have thought of it returning or should they just give and not care about it? My friends, there is a very definite law involved. Whenever you give, you see, anything, and you demonstrate that law inside of yourself, you are giving out into the universe, knowing that it returns.

Now, there is a difference between giving and knowing that it returns and giving and being concerned how much you're going to get back. Do you understand? Now it's a different level of consciousness. So whenever you give anything, it's a wonderful feeling, if you give it knowing that it goes out on the great circle and is returning. You are not concerned that it comes tomorrow. You're not concerned that it comes twenty years later. You just know that that is the law of the universe. Do you understand? Then, what you are doing is you are directing your faith along with your gift, you see? There's a big difference.

Now, people who do that from the level of absolute knowing— they know it in their soul. They know it in their being. In fact, they can even feel it. It goes out with that energy and it returns. But they are not mentally or emotionally concerned when or how it returns. Does that help with your question?

Yes. Thank you.

Because the law is totally impartial. That's just the way that it works. But, you see, if you give and you say, "Well, I don't care if it returns," you're putting it onto a mental level. This is why the Bible says, The gift without the giver is of no value. You see, you give your soul, you give your spirit, with your gift. And when you do that, you, your spirit knows that it's only going out to multiply, increase, and return. And then, my friends, that is exactly what takes place. It really does. Thank you for bringing that up.

Anyone else with a question now?

Discourse 41, which we read tonight, says that the number nine, any number added to that, comes back to that number that was added to it. And it says that number nine is service. And, as we know, that other numbers represent different things.

I believe it says that it is the number of service.

The number of service. Well, would that mean that if we use service, plus whatever the other numbers represent, and combine those two, that we will have that number, what represents that number?

That is correct. You want faith?

Yes. I would like—

What number is it?

Five.

All right. Then, you serve faith and you will have faith. But you must serve it. You must serve that that you desire to become. And when you do that, you will become it. You see? Now we have just gotten through discussing that, you see, for a whole hour on your church, you see. You want your church to become? Then, you serve it and then it becomes. Anything becomes that you serve. That is the number of service and that is how it works, yes. Thank you for bringing that up.

Yes, in the discourse tonight, it was discussed on the Law of Harmony and also in our affirmation we have, "The Law of Harmony is my thought." I wonder if you might discuss a bit on the Law of Harmony as it pertains to thought.

Yes, thank you very much. Now it says—we were discussing in the discourse concerning the Law of Harmony. And the student has asked concerning "the Law of Harmony is my thought," which is a part of our ["Total Consideration"] affirmation. *[See the appendix for the text of the affirmation.]* Now in our affirmation, we must carry on with that sentence, and it says, "The Law of Harmony is my thought and guarantees Unity in all my acts and activities." Now what does that really mean? All right. "The Law of Harmony is my thought and guarantees Unity." Can anything be united that is not in rapport or accord? Can it? It cannot be united. If it is discordant, then it is not united. "The Law of Harmony is my thought." Now what that means is that all of our thoughts must be brought into harmony within ourselves, which guarantees unity in our acts and our activities.

How does man bring about harmony with all of his thoughts, when they're so contradictory? Now, for example, a person's on one level at one moment and then ten minutes later he or she is on another level. And they're certainly not in harmony: they're totally in contradiction with each other. What is it that brings harmony between the levels of consciousness?

Faith, poise, and humility.

Faith, poise, and humility. What brings faith, poise, and humility?

I don't know, but I feel that it means a bringing together in unity of your thinking and your speaking, not speaking one thing and thinking something else. Uniting your whole being into a united whole and, therefore, you have peace. And when you have peace, you have poise. And when you have poise, you're in the faculty of humility.

But what is the one thing, the indispensable thing, that is necessary to bring contradictory levels of consciousness inside of ourselves into harmony? There is something. There's one thing that will bring all of the levels of consciousness into a harmony and a united whole, which will make us complete and fulfilled. Yes.

One word that comes to my mind is peace.

Peace.

[Various students respond.]

Faith.

Balance.

Understanding.

Understanding. You asked the question, so you have the answer, right? Yes. That's the demonstration of the law. That's why we were waiting. Understanding. If you understand a level of consciousness, what that really means is, you know what's causing the effect or the expression. And when you understand each level of consciousness, you will have harmony in your thought, in your thinking process, and you will demonstrate unity in all your acts and activities. And you will not experience all of this disturbance in life. And so it is, again and again, that in all the getting, let us get understanding.

Now, look at all of the wonderful things that grow from understanding. From understanding, you have tolerance. From understanding, you have duty. From understanding, you have gratitude. From understanding, you have faith. From understanding, you have poise, power, and all the soul faculties. The foundation stone of the soul faculties is understanding.

Now anytime we express intolerance, that simply says we don't have understanding, no matter what we think. There is no understanding. When we, as individuals, express intolerance to anything, it simply means that we, at that moment of expressing the intolerance, do not have understanding.

If you understand that a person is ill, then you do not have intolerance toward them, because you understand the illness. You understand the cause and you're so grateful that you are not personally experiencing it. So the foundation of all soul faculties is understanding.

Now, how often can we express understanding? We can't express it unless we give conscious, moment-to-moment thought about it. We must learn to think, friends. Not reaction-thinking. Our brains are computed to think according to a computer. We see something and it reminds us of something and we think accordingly. We meet a person and they remind us of a person that we didn't like and we react accordingly. Don't you see, my friends? So is that thinking? Honestly, now, is that thinking? What kind of thinking is that? It's computerized thinking.

This is what these classes are all about: to help you to grow out of computer thinking. Because computer thinking is not thinking. It's a computer bank of records. And something happens and you think accordingly. But you're not thinking at all. We are not thinking. We are reacting to what that particular computer bank has listed in that computer. Yes. And I'm sure you will all agree we no longer want to be slaves to a lifetime of patterns that have not proven beneficial to us.

So isn't it time that we started to start thinking? You see? And you can't start thinking, friends—you see, when a thought strikes a blow to the mind, before the body reacts, think! Say, "Now why am I thinking this way?" Stop and ask yourself the question, "Why am I thinking this way?" You will be *amazed* as the answer starts coming up from your computer. And it says, "You're thinking that way because you had a similar condition and circumstance twenty years ago. You're thinking that way because this individual reminds you of another individual that you had an unpleasant condition and experience with." Well, my Lord, friends, is that thinking? That's not thinking at all!

And on that note, friends, let us go have refreshments.

MARCH 7, 1974

CONSCIOUSNESS CLASS 43 ✧

Good evening, students. Remember, now, that this is your eleventh class of this particular course—I believe my memory's correct—so that means that we will have one class next Thursday, which will be the final one for this particular course.

Now this evening, if you will kindly turn your book [*The Living Light*] to Discourse 45.

[*A student reads Discourse 45 aloud.*]

We will go into our meditation. And I'm sure, here in this level of class, that you all know your affirmation, your "Total Consideration" affirmation, by heart. So let us unite in that prior to our meditation.

[*The class speaks the "Total Consideration" affirmation aloud and then meditates.*]

Now remember, students, that whatever you have received at this time, as we're working through these various soul faculties, that does not necessarily mean that we're going to be in that particular faculty for the rest of this life. Hopefully, it won't take us that long. After all, there are so many faculties to grow through. We wouldn't want to spend twenty years or so in just one. But that is given to you to help you. And if you will give it some thought and consideration, then you will understand the experiences that you are presently having.

So this evening you may feel free to go ahead and ask whatever questions that you have.

On page 106 [Discourse 38] in The Living Light, *it says, "It is life, light, and love. The solar plexus or father aspect of your universe will be revealed to you at another time." I wonder if the time is right to reveal what the passage deals with.*

I might, perhaps, shed a little light upon that particular page. If you will all recall, we have discussed before that man is the microcosm of the macrocosm: he is the small universe of this whole universe. And the parts of anatomy are affected and represented by certain planets that are in this particular solar system. And the solar plexus in the human anatomy is the location in our microscopic universe—we are this universe within our being, within ourselves—of the sun or the father aspect or the positive aspect of the universe.

Now, we've also discussed, I'm sure, with many of you students, that the moon affects the emotions of all forms on this planet because it is a magnetic influence and it affects the liquids or the waters of the planet, whether it's in the human brain or it's in the animal brain or it's in the plant.

Now, remember that we've also discussed that the electrical vibration becomes the magnetic and the magnetic becomes the electrical. And so it is that Nature teaches us all of these things: she reveals to us that the moon, the magnetic principle, in and of itself, has no light, but that it acts as a reflector of the sun, of the positive or electrical aspect. And so we find in our own personal life, as we study the universe, that our emotions are magnetic: they attract to us and they are reflections from within our own being. Therefore, when a person is trying to awaken themselves, they do not place their attention upon their emotions, but they direct their attention to what we call the soul faculty of reason. Now, we have also discussed that reason is an electrical, positive vibration and that is within the human form. And, of course, it is. We've also discussed that if we keep faith with reason, that it is reason that will transfigure us. It is the electrical, positive vibration within the form that does the transformation. It is not the emotions. They, in and of themselves, have no light. They simply reflect the light of the positive aspect within us.

Now, what is it, we ask ourselves, that blocks us from this natural soul faculty known as reason? Well, the obstruction, of course, is our own emotions, which are the effect of our own addiction to our own habit patterns. This is what blocks the light of reason and is the only obstruction that stands in the way of the renewing of our mind, which is necessary for the transformation of our lives.

Now we have to stop and we have to think, "What kind of patterns do I really have? What am I really like? Not the way that I *think* I am, because that is not the real self." Man is constantly presenting a certain image of himself under certain conditions and circumstances with certain people. A businessman, usually—and I would say 99 percent of the time—acts quite differently at home than he does on his job or in his business. And so it is that we have many faces that we present under different circumstances and conditions.

Now, one of the main purposes of these classes, which are entitled "awareness classes," and the basic purpose of your church, is to help you to face the other faces of the self. Now, we have opportunities here in this Association—we are able to present you with these opportunities, so you can see objectively how you react under certain circumstances and conditions. Now how we react to things, my friends, reveals to us how strongly we are addicted to any particular pattern of mind. Now when that is revealed to us—you see, truth is simple and unconcealed: it is falsehood that is complex and deeply hidden—so when these things are revealed to us, that gives us the opportunity to talk with ourselves and find the patterns of mind that control our emotions, that are the obstruction to our own freedom. Because when you express through the soul faculty of reason, you no longer, you understand, will remain in darkness. So we must be honest with ourselves if we want to be free. But we must first see how we react under certain circumstances and conditions.

You see, a man that does not go out into the world cannot grow. The easiest thing to do is to go up on a mountaintop and just be by yourself; maybe have one or two animals or something. Well, that's fine and dandy, but, you see, you're not being given the opportunity to see what your mind is really like, not the way that we *think* it is. Now, every day offers a multitude of golden opportunities for us to see what we're really like.

Every time we get upset, stop, pause, and think. It's not the person that upset us. That's not where you will find the answer. Where we will find the answer is, number one: "What level of consciousness was I on to attract this individual into my life?" Number two: "What are they revealing to me, according to my own merit system, that I can see a level of consciousness that I have refused to face inside of myself?" Now if you look at life that way, you will start on the path to freeing yourself. Because you will look at it objectively and with reason.

Everything that exists in the universe exists inside of us on some level of consciousness. But we have educated ourselves out of ourselves, so we can no longer be objective. I hope that helps with your question.

In this Discourse 45, he brings up, "If man is born without feet to walk or hands to write" and the rest of it. I won't go into it all. Is this symbolic of if a man is born without understanding, action, perception, or reason, or am I reading this correctly?

That is an explanation. That is correct.

The only thing I'm puzzled about is the tongue, taste.

What does the tongue represent?

Aspiration?

I didn't say it represented aspiration.

No, no. I didn't say you said—I'm sorry. I don't know.

You know most of the parts of the anatomy that are listed there, though, don't you?

Yes.

Yes. And so, therefore, if a person will give it some thought, then, of course, they will be able to help themselves. The tongue has not yet been given.

This discourse seems very appropriate, at least for me, to-night. I don't know about the rest of the class, but is it given spiritually for the entire class?

The discourses that are selected?

Yes.

They are selected at the moment, here at the class. That is, it's dependent upon the receptivity of the highest percentage of the students present, yes. Also, to fit in with their evolutionary process of spiritual understanding.

Then, we should really just go right back, like, I know for myself, just going back to the triune faculties of faith . . .

Poise and humility.

Poise and humility. Or—what are the others? Understanding?

Duty, gratitude, and tolerance has been given.

You were saying, what level we are on. We want to ask our-selves—I'm trying to do this—"What level am I on that attracted this person into my universe, that I merit this or I merit that?" Now many times in my work with counseling, I've had to—not had to, but I have—protected someone. And I wondered, in truth, is there such a thing as righteous anger, indignation? If you see someone burst out with something and it's so unfair to the person that they're doing this to at the time—it appears this way, anyway. Is there any time, is it right at any time to have a righteous anger?

Thank you very much. Now students, we all must realize, and I'm sure that we do, that what is justifiable on one level of consciousness is not guaranteed to be justifiable, of course, on another level of consciousness. So what we must first look at objectively is, number one: What level of consciousness were the individuals concerned with in the discussion, and therefore, was—for that level of consciousness—anger justifiable? Now that's basically the question, because, you see, my friends, you can't say that something is justifiable on level thirty-nine, you understand, and then it must also be justifiable on level two. Because you're dealing, of course, with different states of consciousness.

Now, there is a very simple thing, class, that would behoove one to keep their eyes upon. And that is, What fruit does the tree bear? For example, if one has a feeling or an impression to express themselves, and according to their understanding to them it is known as righteous anger, and the harvest bears good fruit from the expression, then, of course, to that individual, it is justifiable. All right, now we must go beyond that point, because we say, "Well, if it's justifiable for a certain level of consciousness to have what the individual calls justifiable anger, well, what about the victim?" Well, of course, my friends, the victim would have had to have opened the door because, you see, whatever happens to us is caused by us. So not only the individual that expressed or is expressing what they feel is justifiable anger, but the victim who is receiving the wrath, you see, they, too, have merited the experience. Because if they hadn't merited the experience, whoever we are, then we never would have it. Do you understand?

Yes.

Now, you see, it is not the position or the purpose of these classes to condemn or condone any personal experiences which are personal to an individual. However, we do try to share our understanding that if an individual feels, you understand, on their level of consciousness that they are doing what is right because it is right for them to do right, and they wish to term that justifiable righteous anger, then, of course, that is up to the individual. However, the individual who expresses it must, also, be prepared for the payment. Because, you see, my friends, there is, in this life of creation, there's always attainment and payment. So if one attains to the level of consciousness where they are expressing what they consider is justifiable righteous anger, then they must be willing to pay for it. And what is the payment? Well, the payment is, of course, whatever the circumstances offer to the individual whenever he or she is finished with their expression. Does that help with your question?

It does very much.

Thank you kindly.

Would you give your understanding of the faculty of understanding? What obstructs us from truly understanding and what is the relationship between acceptance and understanding?

Thank you. The lady has asked a question, "What is the relationship between acceptance and understanding?" and also our understanding of that soul faculty. Well, let us begin with number one: Understanding is the foundation; it is the foundation of all soul faculties. And this is why we teach, In all your getting, get understanding. Because if you don't get understanding, you don't get any of the other soul faculties.

You see, my friends, you cannot really, in truth, get what you don't understand. Now, therefore, unless man is willing to accept a thought, he can never understand what he does not accept. So, you see, this is why we teach that acceptance is the divine will. Because it is in the divine will that man get understanding.

Therefore, if man does not accept, he cannot understand. So that would be contrary to the divine will itself.

Now, we have—and we have discussed this before—what we call selective—or we have choice. We may select at any given time what we care to accept, you see.

Now, we say, then, this must be contrary to the divine will, if you believe in the teaching that acceptance is the divine will. Well, now you stop and think, my friends. If you don't like what someone is doing and, therefore, you decide that you will not accept that experience—do you understand?—then what you are doing is closing the door to the possibility of understanding what they are doing. Therefore, I'm sure we will all agree, that acceptance, indeed, is the divine will.

Now that does not mean if we find something in life distasteful, that in accepting it, we have to experience it. We accept it objectively, in order that we may see clearly the causes for the particular experience. But we cannot see the causes and cannot gain understanding unless we first accept it. Does that help with your question?

Yes. Thank you.

Now what stands in the way of our getting understanding, besides that? Well, what stands in the way is our own emotions. That's what stands in the way, because it's our emotions that say no or yes to anything in the universe.

Now what are our emotions? We discussed that just a few minutes earlier. They are the effect—the *effect*—of our addicted thought patterns, the thought patterns to which we are addicted. Does that help with your question?

Yes. Thank you very much.

Yes.

I'm trying to feed back in my mind what you said earlier. Were you offering, for each person, when you went around the room, a soul faculty on which they are working at this point?

That is correct. Now that doesn't mean you're only working through one soul faculty. But that means that that one is predominant in your universe at this time. Yes, that is correct.

You mentioned several that I have not encountered in—

That is correct. All soul faculties have not been given.

That's what I'm after. Is it possible for you to give any of those this evening?

When the students reach a level of consciousness, through the Law of Application, more will be given concerning the soul faculties. Yes. Thank you. Because it's ever in balance with the students' ability, you understand, to receive it. And that ability of receptivity is always dependent upon what we're doing with what we already have, you see.

Yes.

You see, if the cup runneth over, only a fool pours more in. Do you understand?

Yes.

Yes. And so let us try to fill our cups, but let us not waste the life-giving powers of the divine water itself. I hope you won't be disappointed with me in that statement, but it is a most demonstrable one. You know, friends, no one ever has to tell us where we are. We all know where we are. Don't need anybody to tell us where we are. Each and every one of us knows exactly where we are on the evolutionary path of spiritual freedom to the Light itself. We all know. We know when we stop and we say, "All right. Here I am. Now how am I really thinking? Not the way I'm *trying* to be, but the way I *am* is truth to me." Remember that, friends. Not the way I *try* to be, but the way I *am* is truth to me. And it's the truth that we're seeking in life, you see. We may put an E on the blackboard for effort, but let us keep an A up there for application. That's where the transformation is.

You see, this is why we teach that hell itself, the lower depths of the astral hell—you know what it's paved with? I can tell you what it's paved with, my good friends: good intentions and broken promises. That's what hell is paved with. And that's where those souls all trod, trying to get to the level of application that may free them from that living hell they've placed themselves in.

Now a person may say, "Well, I'm not there yet, so I'll worry about it when I leave the clay." My friends, that's when it's too late. We're already treading those paths of broken promises and good intentions. We're already going through it here and now. Here and now is where we ought to make the application to do something about it, you see, to do something about it because it's the only sensible, logical thing to do.

Now, when we stop and we think and we say, "Well, I promise this or promise that," let's use reason when we make promises. Let's not make promises as a cop-out, because we want to get out of the experience that we're encountering. That's not the way to get out of a certain experience, by making a promise and then breaking it two minutes later, you see. That's not the way to free our soul.

When we make a promise, let's be very careful about it. Let's stop and say, "Well, now, let's see, if I make this promise, then what am I going to have to give up?" Because if we ever promise to do something, we're always going to find that we're going to encounter an experience where we've got to give up something. So let's try to look at all of our levels and all of our patterns to make sure that we want to make this promise, whatever it is. See, I'm not a person that's in favor of New Year's resolutions, because, to me, every minute is a new year. It's a new year when you stop to think of what you really, really are and what you have to go through. So if you make a promise, give it very good thought. Try to reach all your levels of consciousness to the best that you can. Otherwise, my friends, it's going to hit you back like a boomerang and you're going to be very, very sorry.

Now, who or what do we make promises to? Well, if we have any sense, we make them to our own soul. Because the other kind of promises always end in disaster. Take a look at the world to see how filled it is with promises and good intentions. Just take a look around at your life and see what you've had to go through already in this short physical lifetime. Stop and say, "Let's see, have I made any promises in the past ten years?" Well, I can't see anybody within the view of my eyes that hasn't made promises in the past ten years. I can't see anyone at all. Everyone's promised themselves or somebody else something. Now we must be honest with ourselves and we must say, "How many of those promises did I fulfill?"

My friends, a promise is a commitment. You're committing your soul when you make a promise. That's a commitment to your own soul. Well, you might say, "Well, I promised this or promised that just to get rid of them." Well, don't you worry, you'll have the experience back and it will come in ways that you really aren't prepared for. Because that's the way the law works. It's so nice and impartial.

Well, recently I've been sort of nit-picking over some spiritual points, like I'll look at something one way and I'll say, "Yes, now that's reasonable." And I'll turn the corner and say, "But that's reasonable, too." Then, I'll try to go into it, like, is it the ego levels? Or suppose you don't want to do something, but you start to do it and, then, you clearly see why you didn't want to do it. And you've overcome that factor, but you don't, really, have the heart to continue doing it—is that clear?

Very clear to me.

And then, another question, which is a part of that, is that I find that thought can take me so far. It puts me in balance and puts the part of me, or the part of God that is in me, in balance. But if God is something more than just us, what starts when thought stops and thinking and reason stop? What goes beyond that? Because I cannot understand how we, in our greatest understanding, can ever really know beyond the God within us, if there is that beyond.

Thank you very much. First of all, let's get to the first part of the question and that is, that a student has had, or is having, the experience of what they term nit-picking with spiritual principles. Well, my friends, that's a total waste of your energy, time, and effort. Number one: What you call in your world nit-picking is nothing more than a dissatisfaction of our own ego or cranium. Now, if we are looking at spiritual principles through the so-called shadow of our ego, then it is not spiritual principles that we're going to see. So the first step is to work on ourselves to get ourselves out of the way so that we can view spiritual principles from a spiritual level of consciousness within ourselves. That's the number one step.

Now the brain, the ego, it serves its purpose. It serves its purpose here in many, many ways. It is not a matter, as we have often said, of annihilating it, but it certainly is a matter of educating it. Now, therefore, we see that nit-picking at spiritual principles is not reaching spiritual principles in any sense of the word, because nit-picking is not a spiritual level and, therefore, would have no effect upon a spiritual principle.

Now the other part of the question concerns, of course, as the lady has spoken, Is there a place beyond thought, a place beyond reason? Well, my friends, number one: We're teaching a Divine Infinite Intelligence. Now if this Divine Infinite is intelligent, then it is reason and it is thought. Otherwise, it could not be an intelligent, divine, infinite expression.

Now, it has been stated many times, of course, that God is equal to our understanding. If our understanding is a big understanding, then our God is very big. If our understanding is a small understanding, then, of course, our God is a very small god. And so it is, friends, that it behooves us to direct our thought, which is the vehicle through which our divine energy expresses itself, to gaining greater understanding so that our God may be bigger in our consciousness.

Now, the question arises—and it seems this whole class has been on one thing: understanding and how to get the obstructions out of the way. Well, now here we are. A person, a student, seeks spiritual awakening. Now, it doesn't matter who we are when we seek spiritual awakening, but it does matter that we take a close look at ourselves because we must see ourselves as we really are, if we truly want spiritual awakening. Now, if we decide in our thinking that what we are receiving does not fit into our computer, into the patterns that are in here, and we are unwilling to let more come in and the possibility of new thoughts and ideas, then the truth for us, of course, is that we are not seeking spiritual awakening, because we are not yet ready, willing, or able to permit new thoughts and ideas to enter our universe, go through our computer and our system, and be put into application.

Now there is one beautiful lesson in life: there are millions of them, but one is so beautiful. When we, in this life, think that we are the ones who, without any help from any dimension anywhere, can transform and change our life the way we want it to be, when we are in that type of thinking, life becomes so beautiful because it becomes so miserable. And we suffer sufficiently that the day comes in our lives that we pray to whatever God we care to call it, God or something, for a change, a transformation. When that day comes, according to our own merit system, opportunity knocks at our door—maybe it knocks several times before the door is opened—and we start to face ourselves.

Now, the student also brought up the point that sometimes one starts into something and they will go along with the new thought and changes to a certain point. And then, they don't want to go any further. This is a very natural process for all people in self-realization, in an awakening to the truth of the way we really are. This is a natural and a normal process. This is why in this Association, and this is why in any association that is helping man to face himself, the Bible prophets are 100 percent correct: Many are called, but few are chosen. God doesn't choose them. Man chooses between his soul awakening, facing himself as he really is, or going back out into the illusion, back out there, where he was before.

So, you see, my friends, though it is a struggle up the Mountain of Aspiration to find the eternal light and freedom, it is one that every soul has to make someday. Now, doesn't it only stand to reason—hopefully, we're partway there. Why do we want to go back down to the valley again and make the same process all over? God only knows we have done that a multitude of times already. So we're partway up the mountain, you see. And we have like-minded people around and about us that are partway up the mountain. Do you want to slide back down and start over next year? Or maybe ten years later? Or a hundred or a thousand? You see, I'm sure that none of us want that. We have done it so many times already that we just don't want to go through that all over again.

Well, they say one thing: When victory is at hand, the night is the darkest and the hissing hounds of hell will scream the loudest. So if you are struggling and if you are suffering and if life is difficult in trying to get through certain emotions that you are finally becoming aware of, be grateful, my friends: you're on the way up. But if you are drifting on the sea and everything is just beautiful, not too much effort in any direction, wake up in the morning very slowly, because you don't want any abrupt starts in your life. Then, open your eyes: you're sleeping in the realm of the dreamland and you will in time, being the dreamer, you will become the dream itself. Yes. Thank you.

I have two questions. One: I'd like to have some help with the fountain exercise. In the concentration in the morning, The Living Light *tells of certain colors, but I don't think those colors are meant for the entire group. Were they? I try to visualize the fountain. It's a little difficult for me to do. I'm trying to work on visualization. It's white. And I see the water and then I have to drag that brain back again to see the water. And then, it changes to another hue. But were the colors that are in the book the colors to follow: the red, green, and blue? Can I use my own colors as I start out?*

Thank you. If a student is adverse to anything that is offered in their study class, it is their divine right, as an individualized soul, you understand, to change it to fit their own particular computed needs of the time. The colors, in respect to the fountain exercise, that were given, were given, my good friends, for a very valid reason. They were not chosen haphazardly out of the spectrum of color in the universe. However, if a student feels, on a certain level of consciousness, that they prefer a different color, then, by all means, the student should do what they choose. But I do say this, my friends, and I will repeat it: What is given—colors, numbers, and etc.—in this book [*The Living Light*] has been given to serve a specific purpose. Now remember, because we are not aware of many things, it does not mean that we are not affected by many things, because, indeed, we are. However, we do not intend, nor is it our purpose, to interfere with the divine rights and choices of any soul. And I hope that has answered your question.

No, I didn't choose those. I didn't know that we were to use these colors. I thought it had been given to another group.

No, it's truly for that purpose.

Yes, that's what I really meant.

You're welcome.

Now can I ask something—

Certainly.

We're talking about broken promises. And I have done it for so many years and years and years, and here I am, almost at the end of the path, learning something about spiritual awareness and not breaking promises. How much of this, actually, do we—I can't use the word erase—*but how much of this do we not have*

to face? I mean, all this stuff behind us—are we making up for it
by our aspiration of trying to follow the spiritual path? I mean,
when I finally go over, how much of this will I have to face? All
the things that I did that I was not conscious of?

Now that's a very important question. The lady has asked,
Will we have to face the things we've done that we weren't consciously aware of? My friends, there is nothing that any soul
does that they're not aware of on some level of consciousness.
You see? Nothing. Absolutely nothing. Therefore, when we
reach the level of consciousness, you understand, where we are
aware, then, of course, we're going to have all those experiences
waiting to be paid for. Because, you see, with all of our levels of
consciousness, there's no experience that man encounters that
he is not aware of on some level of consciousness.

Now, because man has chosen to put his thought, which is
his energy, which is his attention, onto a limited number of levels
of consciousness, that does not, in any way, exempt him from his
own transgressions. No, it doesn't exempt him at all. He had the
choice to limit his—like the radio, you can tune in two or three
bands on the radio or you can tune in eighty-one, you see. Well,
God doesn't say, "Now, let's see, for this incarnation you may
tune in four bands. And that's all you're going to be responsible
for." No, it doesn't work that way. No. Man is responsible for all
his thoughts, acts, and activities throughout eternity. And we
might as well face it, grow up, and be gentlemen and ladies and
say, "All right, fine. I'm responsible. Then, I'm going to have to
pay the price. Let me pay the price graciously. Let me not gripe
and complain because of the merit system that I have." If we
don't like our merit system, let us talk to ourselves and say, "All
right, I don't like my merit system. Well, let's start working to
change it." See? But let's remember, the changing takes place
inside of *us:* it doesn't belong to somebody else. See?

If we find ourselves with someone that we can't tolerate,
well, be grateful we merited it: they could be a lot worse. After

all, it's our merit system. It's not hers or his. It's ours. And they are the person that we have guaranteed to come into our lives so that we could learn and so that we could grow. Be grateful, you know, for the lesson itself, you see. Certainly. I mean, after all, you know, self-pity doesn't free any soul.

Does that also have to do with mass consciousness, like Hitler and Nero and all these people that suffered so terribly? Did their merit system bring them under this?

Absolutely, definitely, and positively. There's no one that pushes a button and says, "These people, I will care for. The others, I will not." No. Our soul merits its experiences. And when we face that truth, we will stop griping about everybody else and all the other merit systems in the universe. We'll say, "All right. Now, this is my merit system. Let me find out what I am doing inside to merit this, because I don't like it." Then, my friends, we'll start getting free. But first, let's face that truth inside of ourselves.

See, we can't be free until we face the truth. And we can't face the truth until we make an effort to know ourselves. And we can't know ourselves until we take some time during the course of a day and we pause to think. We can't know ourselves while we're running around with all this emotionalism. Of course, we can't. That's all darkness, friends. Yes.

I've been doing some reading about Wilhelm Reich's orgone theory and—

I'm not familiar with it.

Well, I wondered if there were, in your understanding, something you could offer about orgone. The writing that he does seems to fit with what is taught in this understanding a great deal. That is, he finds the orgone is a streaming, pulsating energy force that is, like—it made me think of what's in The Living Light *about visualizing a cloud that's put out in the form of our own brainwaves. And he conducted experiments where he took bionous material, boiled it, froze the water—nonliving material—and claims that he has developed life from nonliving materials.*

Let me share one thing, if I may. I'm not familiar with the individual, nor his writings, of course. And, of course, it would not be fair to the class if they had not studied this particular book that you are referring to. And we have had these questions brought up before in other classes, because there are many books on the market today. And, of course, we all know that truth is one: that truth reveals itself in many garments or through many books. And therefore, it would not be in the best interest of the class, of the students, or the purpose of the classes to discuss other writers' books in this particular type of awareness class. It would not be fair to the rest of our students.

However, I would like to say one thing. Something cannot, by the very laws of creation, come out of nothing. Therefore, no man nowhere at any time, past, present, or future, creates life. He may be instrumental in bringing together the poles of opposites in ways that man does not fully understand, but man, in and of himself, cannot create the Divine Intelligence, which is necessary to give the form, what we call life. I hope that helps with your question.

It did. Thank you.

Yes, you're more than welcome. Now, we're running overtime, but perhaps we can get to one or two more questions. Yes.

When something happens to us and we think it happens to us most of the time and we say, therefore, that it is the effect. But in a sense we could be causing, instead of effecting. Could you just—I just can't seem to say what I really want to say.

I'm sure you will find that—and we have also discussed this before, my friends. It does seem like a review class this evening. Every cause is an effect, as every effect is a cause. The electrical is the magnetic and the magnetic is the electrical. Now what we try to teach our students is to try to find that perfect balance point: that balance point between where they may have a neutral, an objective view, of Life and the experiences that she offers to us, according to, of course, our own thoughts, acts, and deeds.

Well, now, when we take this type of teaching and we say, "Well, these effects are terrible," and we start becoming very downhearted in our thinking, remember that energy follows attention. So if you look down, friends, you keep going down further. That's why we teach that he who sees the obstruction shall never find the way. If your mind can only view the obstructions in your life, you will never, ever find the way. So naturally, a person does not entertain their mind with concern, because if they do, that's all they're going to experience. They're going to guarantee its continuity. If we're in a fret and a tizzy about this and that, if we insist on saying, "Well, I don't understand," well, the more we feed energy to the thought, to that level of consciousness that doesn't understand, then we will guarantee to stay right down there, where we can't understand.

Now it's one thing, my friends, to question. It is something else to give the answer and intend it to be a question. That causes a state of confusion, don't you see, within our mind. So first, we want to formulate in our thinking; we want to pause and say, "All right, I've given this some thought. Here, I have a question and I lay it out right here in my mind. And then, I open the door." Because, remember, friends, if it is true—and life continually demonstrates it to us—that what goes out, comes back in, where is man's freedom and what is it dependent upon? What goes out there: that's what it's dependent upon. Because this is the thing that keeps opening the doors. So if we say, "Well, all I get into my life is confusion," then that's all that we're opening the door to. So let us be peaceful and let us say, "All right, let me open the door to some light and some understanding. Let me open the door to simplicity."

What a beautiful thing, simplicity. Because simplicity, my friends, is the direct effect of unadulterated truth. That is simplicity.

Thank you very much, friends. Let us go have refreshments.

CONSCIOUSNESS CLASS 44 ✣

Good evening, class. This evening, of course, as we all know, is our final class for this particular course. And before we get to our regular question-and-answer time, I should like to take a few moments in review and in discussion of a subject that is, of course, of great import to all students of this understanding.

Now, for those of you who have been with us for a while, I'm sure that you have heard much about sense functions and soul faculties. And I'm also sure that many of us do not have a clear perspective of what we mean by a sense function or a soul faculty. Now, we have discussed that all faculties and all functions are triune in expression and we have also stated a few of these functions and faculties.

A soul faculty *is* a divine principle. Now a divine principle *is* a spiritual law. And this is how, as we have discussed, your spiritual body is being built here and now as you, your soul, expresses through the soul faculties. Now, the very first soul faculty on the foundation of understanding, upon which all soul faculties stand, is duty, gratitude, and tolerance.

You have been given an affirmation entitled the "Divine Flow." *[See the appendix for the text of the affirmation.]* Now through which soul faculty does limitless supply of anything— through which soul faculty does it flow? So often when we speak of divine abundance, it seems that many think we're talking about material supply. Well, there's divine abundance, my friends, on three levels of consciousness. There is a seeking of divine abundance in the material dimension, there is a seeking of the divine abundance in a mental dimension, and there is the seeking of the divine abundance in a spiritual dimension. So when we are discussing divine flow and limitless abundance and supply, let us not limit that supply to one dimension. Are there any students present who know through which soul faculty divine abundance flows?

I believe it's gratitude.

Thank you. Anyone else?

The faculty of faith, poise, and humility.

Thank you. Anyone else?

Now the truth of the spiritual Law of Flow or what we call supply or abundance is the first soul faculty. Now a person may have gratitude and not have the abundance that they're seeking simply because their expression of gratitude is not in balance with the triune faculty of duty and tolerance. We are all seeking a supply or an abundance of something. If we are on a mental dimension, then we are seeking an increasing supply of knowledge. If we are on this material dimension, then we are seeking a supply or an increase in material substance. If we are on a spiritual expression, then we are seeking an increasingly abundant supply of what?

I think it was wisdom.

No. Understanding, my friends. Your spiritual body is composed of spiritual elements. Those spiritual elements are garnered up whenever the Divine energy flowing through the body is directed through the soul faculties. If you do not have understanding, if you do not seek understanding and garner it up as a substance, you will not be able to move in a spiritual dimension. This is the reason that the feet are representative of understanding. They are what all the soul faculties rest upon. There is no motion without understanding.

So when we're speaking of soul faculties, we're speaking of their use, not just in the here and now—that is extremely important, if you want to rise to a state of consciousness known as a realm of illumination—but we're speaking of the here and the hereafter. So we see that we seek to gain understanding and to gain that understanding we must move through the soul faculties, the first one, those spiritual laws being duty, gratitude, and tolerance.

Now we have been asked for more of the soul faculties, but what does it behoove a man to garner up in the intellect? You see, my friends, so many of us have spent our lifetime unfolding intellectually and sensually. Don't you all agree that it is time that we spent a little effort to unfold spiritually? Because we are out of balance on the triune manifestation of the Divine itself. So we try to bring into balance our thought and our energy, to direct it through the soul faculties, which are divine principles and spiritual laws.

Now, if we find ourselves in short supply in any dimension, it simply means that we are transgressing the spiritual law of duty, gratitude, and tolerance and that is the only reason that we find ourselves in short supply. Now, we can find ourselves, of course, as I said before, in short supply in any one of those three dimensions. But you now know the way and, of course, it's up to you, as an individualized soul, to demonstrate through the Law of Application and bring your life into balance. That is your decision and that, of course, is your choice.

Now there are no shortcuts through the eighty-one levels of consciousness, the eighty-one states of mind, that I have ever found. If you find a shortcut, I will be most grateful to listen, because, my friends, only a fool closes his ears to the possibility of something better or something greater.

Now you're free to ask any questions that you have.

Recently I saw a drawing of a brain in a magazine that had to do with the formation of the brain. It showed certain centers and certain cells and had to do with functions. And if this brain had in some way been impaired by whatever we do or before birth—I realize that this is a merit system. But how can we get understanding, if we cannot—if that part of the brain is injured in any way? Can we through listening or if we—suppose you had part of the brain where the hearing is no good, how can we get understanding in this life? How can we even know what we're doing? Is there a divine law that heals us of this? Is it all our merit system or, I mean, are we just going to wait until we get over to the other side to be able to have clear hearing?

Thank you. Yes. And it is my understanding from your conversation that you are speaking in reference to gaining understanding in the physical dimension, as you mentioned an impairment of the physical healing. Is that correct?

No, I mean—

That is my understanding from what you were discussing.

I put it poorly. I'm sorry. No, I mean, to hear spiritual truths, if we do not hear or if we cannot see, if the brain is impaired, if the cells in the brain are impaired—

That's just what I was answering to your question. If the physical cells of the brain and the ear cannot hear, we're speaking of hearing in a physical dimension. Is that correct?

Yes.

And the lady has asked the question, If a person has a physical impairment to their hearing, then how can that soul gain understanding? My good friends, understanding is not limited to the physical ears. Many people with a so-called hearing problem and even those who are so-called deaf since birth have great spiritual understanding. So, you see, my friends, if we have a physical so-called defect, that in no way is an excuse for us that we do not gain understanding. I do hope that's helped with your question.

On the cover of The Living Light *and on the title page of* The Living Light *is a diagram of two intertwined triangles and a pyramid in the center, surrounded by a snake eating its tail. I wondered, sir, if we could have a discussion of that diagram this evening to understand what it means.*

Thank you very much. Is that an interest to most students of the class, that particular question? Raise your hands. Then, it is evidently of an interest to speak on the particular symbol that's been used on the cover of this book.

And we'll begin with the outside of it, which is the snake, representative of wisdom consuming itself. Now why does the symbol of wisdom consume itself? Does anyone know? Does anyone know why wisdom is self-consuming? Because, my friends, if it's wisdom, then it can gain nothing from outside of itself: it already *is* wisdom. So all that wisdom is—you understand, you don't gain wisdom and neither do you give wisdom. Wisdom is self-sustaining. When you rise to a level of consciousness where wisdom expresses itself, then you will become it and it is self-sufficient unto itself. So the snake consuming itself is representative of wisdom, in comparison to what one might call knowledge. Now, knowledge is something that you gain. It's something that you put into your brain and you feed back at your discretion—but not wisdom.

[The image below is on the cover of the deluxe edition of The Living Light.*]*

The next step is the interlaced double triangle, which is a very, very ancient symbol. It is the meeting of the spirit with matter. It is the power above that meets the forces below. And at that junction, when those two triangles meet, that's the negative and the positive poles come together in creation and the divine spark, the rays of light, life is so-called born into matter.

Now you all know that all poles are triune. The negative pole is triune and the positive pole is triune. In fact, my friends, as we've stated before, all things that are manifest are triune and that is why three is the number of manifestation.

Inside of the interlaced triangles you'll notice on the top of the pyramid in the rays of light is the all-seeing eye. Now the all-seeing eye is that that is not distracted, because it sees everything and so nothing gains its attention. And that is why it is the all-seeing eye. The triangle itself, the pyramid upon which all knowledge, the all-seeing eye, all wisdom, and all life rest, is the pyramid of manifestation. All things in all universes (physical, mental, or spiritual) are triune. There are three parts to all things: that is an absolute fact of physics and it is a truth of the universe. I hope that that's helped with your understanding of that particular symbol.

I would like to draw a little back together with what you offered at the beginning of the class that's been a puzzle to me. For example, the faculty which includes duty, gratitude, duty, and tolerance—I'm not remembering it exactly.

Yes, duty, gratitude, and tolerance.

OK. Every once in a while I have glimmer that duty is triune, gratitude is triune, and tolerance is triune. And I get confused sometimes. For example, last week when you offered people what you said was a soul faculty that they were working on. They did not appear or seem to be triune. That may be just my lack of understanding. But sometimes I hear you speak of things as faculty that do not sound triune and I get confused about that.

Yes. Have you asked yourself the question why, in the mentioning of a soul faculty, that some appear to you as triune and some do not? Have you asked yourself that question?

Yes.

And what is your answer?

Well—

Let's take an example. Which soul faculty doesn't feel triune to you?

Well, by going through The Living Light, *I feel that I only come up with two or three that really showed themselves or, you know, where it had been offered exactly what the three parts are.*

And which ones didn't seem triune to you?

I'm not remembering them exactly at this point.

You see, what I'm trying to do is—perhaps you could share how you arrived at that understanding. Then, perhaps we could find which level of consciousness is partial. Do you understand?

Yes.

For example, my friends, I could say to you this evening, and it has been said before, that cooperation is a triune soul faculty, because, indeed, it is. I can also say to you that patience is a triune soul faculty. Indeed, it is. I can also say to you that duty or tolerance or hope or many of the other things are triune soul faculties. But the question arises that a student will receive some of them as a soul faculty, as a triune soul faculty, which is a spiritual law, and some will receive it that it is not a triune soul faculty. So the question is presented to the class for discussion: What level of consciousness inside of ourselves will accept one statement and reject another? Upon which foundation are we basing our understanding?

Well, let's use duty, then.

Yes.

You just named that as a triune soul faculty.

That is correct.

And yet duty is a part of another triune soul faculty. That's where I get confused. Did you not list it off as the first soul faculty is duty, gratitude, and tolerance?

That is correct.

Just now I heard you say that duty is—you could say, as I understand what you said, that duty is itself a triune soul faculty.

All of them are a triune soul faculty. But what I'm trying to do is to get the student to see. For example, if I give you the other two points of the triangle of cooperation, which is a spiritual law and a soul faculty, then if everything is handed to us, will we make the study and the effort and the application to find the others?

Then, you are offering that—only infrequently do I have the idea all of a sudden that you have the first soul faculty, then we have duty, gratitude, and tolerance, which means that each of those is triune, which means that each of the things under them is triune. And that's where I start, you know, beginning to get my head—

Because you go off into infinity.

Don't you?

Yes, you do. But, my friends, if we don't make an effort to understand the finite, surely we will not be prepared to understand the infinite. And so it is, you see, that the teachings are in bits and pieces. Now, why are these teachings designed to be given to you in bits and pieces? I would much prefer to give you the entire course, volume upon volume upon volume, in all of its minute detail, but then, you would not grow. The reason that you receive understanding in bits and pieces is because man— the students' application is in bits and pieces. It isn't under the direction of the Law of Continuity, consistent day after day after day. That is a very rare case. It is a rare student that I can find, out of twenty-four full hours in a course of a day and night, that spends, dedicated and organized, every day at the same time, one full hour to the study of what he or she is receiving. And so until that day comes, my friends, we will continue to share with you this understanding in bits and pieces, because that is the divine law that as we give, we gain.

You see, we must give a part of our effort and our time and we must put it into application. Of what benefit is it to mankind for him to know all of the triune soul faculties if he is not consistently applying one? By consistently, I mean daily. Then, of what benefit is it? It is of no benefit. It's fine for the intellectual, for the theory, but, you see, friends, we can take in many things intellectually and mentally, but it takes some concerted effort to put it into application. Truth is taught, again and again we say, through indirection, demonstration, and example. Until we apply what we receive, it is not going to benefit us. These teachings are designed to benefit you, not just in the spiritual dimension, but to benefit you here and now in the mental and the physical dimension.

Now, whenever we want to receive more, there is a guarantee of how to do it. And what is that guarantee? Do you know?

No.

If man desires to receive more understanding, then he uses the first soul faculty of duty, gratitude, and tolerance. And in using that soul faculty, more understanding shall he receive. So we must work on what we have, my friends. Now you may ask any other question.

I understand from the teachings—I hope I understand from the teachings—that our duty is to our soul and gratitude for its manifestation and tolerance. I wish you'd explain the tolerance.

Tolerance for the levels of consciousness inside of ourselves that are difficult to grow through. Because when we understand that everything expressed in the universe is a part, an inseparable part of ourselves, when we not only understand it, but we accept it as the divine truth, then we will express that point of the first soul faculty. *Tolerance* doesn't mean "to tolerate." Tolerance deals with understanding, my friends. You can't have tolerance, you can't express tolerance, until you gain some understanding. And how do we gain understanding? We can't understand something we don't know. So how can we have understanding if we're not making the effort to know ourselves? And how can we know ourselves if we're not willing to face ourselves? That's what this course is all about. We are here to face ourselves, not the way we want to present ourselves to others necessarily, but the way we really are. My friends, we cannot gain understanding until we're willing to face ourselves, to know ourselves. Then, we will move to understanding ourselves. And when we understand ourselves, we will express duty, gratitude, and tolerance. But we cannot—we cannot gain understanding until we put these laws into application, until we apply them consistently.

Well, I was thinking about the way I grow. I seem to work on something for a while. Sometimes I'm not aware of it on a conscious level—what I'm working on—and then find that things come together. And when they come together, usually my conscious mind goes into a tailspin. It's very hard for me to face it. And then, I'm tired and I want to rest for awhile.

It's most understandable. Whenever we're grounded, we get tired, yes.

I don't understand.

Whenever we're grounded—whenever we're grounded in self-thoughts and in contradiction of those thoughts within our own cranium, we experience what is known as being tired. Yes, it's most understandable.

Well, then, that adds even more to my problem. How does one consistently look within and apply without becoming grounded—without allowing oneself to become confused or tired—and without giving up?

By going through the electrical field, not the magnetic field. The magnetic field is the emotions and functions. And the electrical field is the principles of the spiritual laws.

Well, those two functions must be in balance.

That is correct. They're obviously out of balance or the problem would not exist.

Therefore, what you're saying, as I understand it, is that my emotions are more in the situation than my intellect or reason, and that what I—

Any student that has that problem, yes. It is the magnetic field that is out of balance with the electrical.

Well, then, suppose I am in the middle of being out of balance with my magnetic field.

Yes.

What is the best way that I can help myself come back into balance so that I can begin to apply the electrical field?

Through a daily process of meditation upon peace. Immediately following the meditation, to make the effort to bring yourself into balance. Immediately following a daily meditation, to spend an hour making the effort, you see, because you will be in more of an objective vibration or electrical vibration than the magnetic or emotional, you see.

Does that mean thinking about what's going on? Or isn't that being grounded in self? When you say, "spend an hour" to do it, does that mean thinking about what's going on?

That means becoming objective, mentally objective, and looking at the individual—in this case, yourself—without any feeling or emotion.

That's an interesting exercise. Thank you.

You're more than welcome. It is a most worthwhile one if the student is sincere. There is also an exercise given in *The Living Light* for you to come into rapport with another individual that you may gain understanding. Well, it's the very same law that's involved. But in your case, you're applying it to yourself, but it is the same principle law.

Thank you.

Yes. Remember, friends, we must get out of the brainwashing that we're one person, because we're more than one person. We're conscious, we're subconscious, we're superconscious. We're physical, we're mental, and we're spiritual. So let us be objective and let us become aware which person is expressing at any given moment. You know, many times students have received this understanding, and intellectually they know the way and intellectually they can discuss it, but time and time and time again, experience reveals that we're not yet applying it. And this is what we discussed earlier. Then what benefit is it if we're not applying it? What good is a physician if he can't heal himself? Why bother to take the time and the effort and the energy? If we cannot awaken ourselves, then we are not qualified to help another to awaken. Do you understand? Yes.

Could you give your understanding on energy: its use and abuse, and zappers and the person being zapped and how it all comes about?

Thank you very much. That, in fact, was discussed a little bit here in tonight's discourse on energy and that is, of course, an important question to all of us, considering that many seem to experience a seeming need to rest, to sleep X number of hours in the course of a day or a week. Many articles have been written about what the student has spoken about zappers and energy producers. Now, the question arises, Just how does this really work? We all know—and I'm sure we've all had the experience of carrying on a conversation with an individual and being totally exhausted afterward. I'm sure we've all had some type of experience of just sitting quietly in the corner and not saying anything at all and being totally exhausted afterward. So the question arises, What is really, really taking place? Well, the answer was given in the discourse that was read this evening. Now the student that has asked the question will kindly read the last paragraph of tonight's discourse [Discourse 36] and I'll show you that your answer was already given.

"There is no limit to the divine flow of eternal energy. We find a lack of energy when our thoughts are in contradiction with each other; and therefore garner up your thoughts and channel them to the Divine and you will find all the energy and, yea, even more than you could possibly use."

Thank you very much. Now, so what really happens? We go somewhere and we don't carry on a conversation, but our ears are exposed and our aura is exposed and whatever is going on triggers the level of contradiction of our thoughts within our own being. Now because we are not necessarily aware of these contradictory thoughts that are taking place within our cranium does not in any way relieve us of the effect. And so we find that sometimes we're in conversation with an individual, and we feel fine and we go home and we have to sleep three or four hours. We're totally exhausted. Sometimes we're just out somewhere, we've hardly even said a word, and we go home and we're totally exhausted. What it means, my friends, is that we have exposed ourselves and are not controlling our thoughts. Now, if we say that "I have no control"—do you have a problem?

Excuse me.

Now if we say that we are not aware of our thoughts, that doesn't mean that they're not swimming in our own subconscious and are in contradiction, because they are. And this is where we experience this great depletion.

Now let us be honest with ourselves, friends, and let us face life. Let us remember that all experience takes place inside of our own being. The world is filled with blaming everyone else. This is why we're here: Blaming everyone else has not worked for us. And so we're seeking to find a better way. We're seeking, our souls, to be free. So it's up to each of us to become aware—more aware of ourselves, more aware of our own thoughts—so we won't find ourselves so lacking in energy and, of course, initiative. Because, my friends, if you don't experience energy, you can't have any initiative.

Is this more or less a phrase—for example, say a person in the desire realm, one could say that they have more of an animal vibration.

If they choose to label it, yes, certainly.

This has nothing to do with an animal, but you do have the incarnation of animals on this planet. So it's just, more or less, a phrase of speaking.

Well, usually, when man refers to a person being in an animal vibration, of course, ofttimes it's reflections from within. But usually they are referring to an over so-called unfoldment in the sensual dimension. Yes, that's usually what they mean.

Well, but it's not really.

See, we're trying to unfold spiritually.

No, I understand that.

The whole world's unfolded intellectually and sensually. That doesn't need a teaching, my friends, you see. I've spent a long, long—many centuries trying to get that understanding into my students' heads.

No. I understand that very well.

Yes.

It was just, more or less, a conversation piece.

Well, of course, the spoken word is life-giving energy. And I'd rather have you speak something spiritual, hopefully, to help your level of consciousness, as a student, yes, yes. See, all things in balance and in proportion.

That's true.

You see. And, of course, it is more difficult to unfold spiritually, because we've spent so much time unfolding the other way, you see. So it takes a little effort. You know, it's kind of like learning a new hobby. You know, it takes time and it takes effort and it takes a change of our patterns, you see. We spoke before about the addiction that we get into, you know, in our lives, addicted to our patterns and different things. You know, there's one thing we try to share here with our students: You all are given what we have to give. You all have the divine right to understand it, to accept it, or to reject it. But let us not forget in life that acceptance *is* the divine will. But acceptance does not mean expression. There is a vast difference.

The point I'm trying to make here, is that's, more or less, a phrase of speaking. And you could possibly say that person's in the mental realm instead of the animal realm. It makes no difference to me one way or the other, personally.

Well, to clarify it, as I mentioned earlier, perhaps it would be better simply to say that the individual soul is now expressing through the sensual dimension or the intellectual dimension or the spiritual dimension, yes. Does that help with your question?

Thank you kindly.

You're more than welcome.

You mentioned in your opening remarks that a soul faculty is a divine principle, a spiritual law. Would it be possible to get some deeper understanding of what spiritual law is?

That's a wonderful question. And the student has asked, perhaps, that a deeper understanding of a spiritual law be given. Therefore, I shall ask the student the question, What is meant by gratitude? What does it really mean? What is gratitude?

Well, to me, it means an appreciation without any emotional— being a mirror of ourselves.

Thank you. Now we're discussing a spiritual principle—a divine principle and a spiritual law. And we're discussing, at this point, gratitude. Let us give some consideration to this word. After all, we all seek supply in something. So let us give more thought to that faculty. Gratitude is a recognition of and an acceptance of and an expression of and respect to something

greater than the self. Now without that, there is no true gratitude. I think if you will give that some consideration, class, you
will find the true meaning of the soul faculties, which are spiritual laws. Does that help with your question?

Yes. Thank you very much.

You're welcome.

*Yes, it says here that imagination is the vehicle of expression
of the life force, the prana that holds all things in space. Can
you define imagination, say with daydreaming? And it says here,
"Image constructively and you shall serve the Light and it shall
be good."*

Thank you.

*Does that mean that you can picture yourself doing some-
thing well or picture someone else as an individual in a good
image or a sick person being healed or being well or being allevi-
ated of their sickness or illness?*

Thank you very much. I think we'll get to the first part of
your question. The student, I believe, had asked, Well, what is
the difference between daydreaming and imagining? I believe
that was the first question asked in discussion. A person who is
daydreaming is not in control of the dreams that he is experiencing, but he is the victim of his own subconscious computer,
in contradistinction to a person who is imaging.

Now a person who is imagining is in control. I image a beautiful white elephant here in front of me. And therefore, I have
created it and that is the truth to me. It is also the truth to any
soul that is expressing on that level of consciousness at that
moment, because they cannot help but experience the same
thing. Do you understand? That is imaging. Now imaging—
imagination—is the doorway to the world of spirit, to the spiritual substance, but it is not the spiritual substance itself. It is
only the doorway to it. Imaging can be most beneficial and most
constructive, not only for oneself, but for another, if they know
the laws involved, the laws of solicitation. For example, man is

in a constant process—and when I say "constant," I mean split second by split second—of imaging. He's imaging many things, but his conscious mind is not alert to all of his imagining. All we have to do to know what our mind is imaging is to look at our surroundings. And when we look at our surroundings, we can see the effect of the process of imaging and imagination.

Now, this is how our minds work, one of its many ways. We look around our home and we have a desire, perhaps, to have a new chair. The image pops up from the depths of our mind. The next step is, according to man's patterned computer, he says, "I don't have the money. Going to take about six months, maybe a year and a half." Man is a law unto himself. So for that limited man, that level of consciousness, it takes six months or a year and a half. Because man is a law unto himself, he establishes that law. And no matter what happens, he cannot get that chair for the length of time that he has specified. Now, I ask you, which is the best way? To image what it is that you're seeking—because you're imaging anyway, all the time—and to know, through the soul faculties, those spiritual laws, that it is already there, then move in time of consciousness to that point where you meet. That's known as opportunity. Not telling God, the Divine Infinite Intelligence, how it's to come about.

You know, my friends, when we're honest with ourselves, doesn't it take a fantastic, undeveloped ego to think that we know better than God how to run our life? I mean, when we really stop and think about it. Tell me, when does man pray? When disaster strikes. Well, sure. How often do we pray? How often do we really think about God and the Divine? Well, now, doesn't that tell our ego something? Doesn't it tell us we've made a terrible mess of our life and hadn't we better let go and let God move in? Surely, at our age, it surely has told us that by now. But now that takes a little bit of faith, that takes a little bit of faith. It takes a little bit of faith to get out of God's way and let things be peaceful and good in this life. Now, we're still speaking on imaging. But this is what we're doing all of the time, you see.

See, it's like this little church. It's already in process, because when you image, you believe; and when you believe, you become. That is the power of faith, my friends, directed faith, see? We all have faith, but we're directing it to the way *we* have made life. Do you understand?

So every day you image. And you know why man likes to image disasters in this life. Don't you know why? Because it excites the senses. You see, my friends, you look at a serene sunset, that doesn't excite your senses, but it excites your soul. It brings great joy to your soul, but it doesn't do a thing for your senses. And so it is that man has to have disaster upon disaster upon disaster, because he's in a constant state of excitement.

You know, it's like a little child. It'll burn the house down if it needs attention and that's the only way that it can find of getting it. It'll even burn itself in it if that's the way. It'll break your furniture or it'll do anything, a child will, if you are not giving it what it thinks is the attention that it needs. Now we're all children, so we do all kinds of things to get this attention, which is this Divine Love. Think about that. That's what's happening all the time. Man says, "That's all I have." God says, "If you're so smart, that's all you'll get." Is that the way we want to live? Is that the way we want to live?

God does not shut the doors to his divine abundance, and by that I mean the positive divine energy of the universe, intelligently expressing itself. Man is the one that opens the door and man is the one, he alone, that closes the door. Now, if we can gain more love, more affection, more attention by being broke, then we're going to go through this whole incarnation being broke. If we can gain more attention by having a little supply or even an overabundance, then we're going to go through life that way. My gosh, friends, just take a look around the world, you see. Just look around the world. We enjoy, that is, our senses,

being in constant disaster. The psychologists say that it's a syndrome. Well, they can call it many names, but man isn't going
to get off the treadmill until he recognizes what he's doing to
himself. Thank you.

*On this imagining and meditation, you said earlier that we
should or that the students should give an hour to meditation
on peace.*

No, we said that they didn't give an hour a day, not an hour
of meditation. That is not the teachings.

No, no. I'm glad you corrected me.

Thank you.

*Well, should imagination or imagining, in other words, be
separate from the meditation?*

Yes, it should be separate from the concentration and
meditation.

*I mean, should it be a sitting? We would take that same type
of time and sit quietly and image.*

Yes. You see, my friends, we're imaging constantly. We are
doing this like an automatic computer and we're not even consciously aware that we're doing it, because we've done it for a
lifetime. So if this is the nature of the mind—and, I assure you,
that is the nature of the mind—then doesn't it behoove us to
take some time—actually, it's preferable to consciously image
all throughout your conscious awareness, to become aware of
what you are imaging and then to control it, you see. All of life
is an effect of our belief. All of life is an effect of our imagination. We've said it here many ways: "Dreamer, dream a life of
beauty before your dream starts dreaming you." Well, what do
you think, my friends, that that statement meant? You are the
dreamer. You are the one that is imaging your life, do you understand? But because you have lost awareness of that process, you
have become the dream. And what is the dream? Our circumstances, our conditions, and our experiences: that's the dream.
But we can change that—that quick—*[The Teacher snaps his*

fingers.] by dreaming a life of beauty at all times and in all ways. We can only experience what we image. That's the only thing that we can experience: what we and we alone image. So you image disturbance, you experience disturbance. You image lack, you experience lack.

Now what does that have to do with the spiritual laws, the divine principles that gratitude is the soul faculty through which abundance and limitless supply flows? Well, now, you just stop and think. Many people, they say a spiritual affirmation of the divine abundance and things get shorter. Well, of course, they get shorter, because they don't believe it. What is belief? It's imaging, my friends. It's imagination. That's what the world is all about. And until you become aware of that and you start doing something about it, then you will continue to be the victims of your own dreams that you have lost control of.

Thank you all very much. We're way past time. Let us go have refreshments. Thank you.

MARCH 21, 1974

SAYINGS

Creation denies God, and that is when suffering begins.

Creation is a price tag; choose wisely what you buy.

Man in God is pleasure while man in self is pain.

Man's God is equal to his understanding.

When the crown denies the king, all is lost.

Why give the key to wisdom's door when fools hope and nothing more.

All things in God are good.

Though your light
May be my night

Because I am
Not you,
Someday to you
It will be true
When all shall know
Their right to grow.

The key to wisdom is a quiet mind.

Presumption is the Law of Descent.

Bad news is only good news misunderstood.

Husbands, like babies, require a lot of nursing.

Fondness is desire hidden from view.

There is a power greater than I
Expressed through all the earth and sky,
Its many forms we see without
And wonder why so many doubt

This God of love the humble know,
For they have found the greater goal
Which all may have if they but seek
To help the lost, the sad, and weak.
Thy will I find expressed divine
When all of life is seen as mine
And I am ready and willing to share
The part of me that's known as care.

The lamp of heaven is the heart of man.

When the dream of life becomes the nightmare of life, man changes.

What the mind calls balance is dependent upon the preservation of its own dreams, for only reason knows balance and reason is total consideration.

He who loves God more than he loves creation does not deny creation, but uses it wisely.

When our fear of man is greater than our love of God, personality becomes our king and principle, our slave.

❧

It's not what you have to put into the mind that frees it; it's what you must take out of the mind to free it.

❧

An open heart fears no man.

❧

A sane man finds joy in a home of reason.

❧

O God, help me to consider and accept a greater authority in my life than the limited importance of my so-called ego.

❧

There's no tomorrow when tonight the eyes see but the self, for the prison you are building binds beyond the chains of night.

❧

That that we like loves us, and that that loves us frees us.

❧

God lives in laughter and dies in despair.

❧

Gratitude is applied appreciation.

The degree of retaliation is equal to the degree of rejection.

Today I am an apple,
Tomorrow I'll be a tree,
And when I am an apple tree
I'll no longer be just me.

Man's needs are his hopes for the times.

He who thinks his gain is much and forgets the source, guarantees the loss.

Remember that he who loves himself more than he loves me shall lose himself to find me. But he who loves me more than he loves himself has found the truth, eternity.

Direct your energies through the vehicle of thought ever upward, and I will let you view my paradise.

Truth is the fountain of eternal youth.

❧

Freedom without wisdom is the path to license.

❧

Saneness is the awareness that life is a dream. Madness is the illusion that it is a reality. And so, survival is the miracle of life.

❧

The will is the law of our universe.

❧

What thought limits, it attracts and guarantees the loss thereof.

❧

Awareness is dependent upon the education of desire, not its need.

❧

When a foolish student cannot tolerate his teacher, a wise teacher tolerates his student.

❧

He who sees the loss never finds the gain.

❧

Men without thought are like tadpoles; they don't know what's happening.

When of pride
Power comes,
The feeling fingers
Become all thumbs.

Progress is the inevitable path of all life.

Man's freedom is equal to his thought, his bondage, his desire.

Man's limitation is God's denial.

Friendship ends when desire begins.

Self-pity, like a cesspool, has an obnoxious odor.

Divine will is the ceaseless flow or essence of all experiences or dreams and knows that reality is only the shadow of truth, to which a wise man does not attach.

❧

Wise is the traveler who knows where he's going.

❧

It is better to have no shoes and have understanding, than to have shoes and return with them to the elements.

❧

I sail serene on the sea of time, with God at the helm peace is mine.

❧

The things of which we speak the most are in truth our hidden host.

❧

The degree of resentment to the Law of Change is equal to the attachment to self.

❧

Wise are those who question well
And leave the critics to their hell.

❧

It is the lion that saves the soul, the snake that steals the heart.

The spoken word is the principle of the law—life-giving energy.

Heaven waits only the adventurous and courageous of heart. You little man, how sad you make your life.

The floods replenish the lands while the droughts destroy them.

Man opens the gates to hell with the key of self.

Man cannot understand what he cannot demonstrate.

The greatest cancer of the soul is guilt. Guilt comes from rejected desire, and desire is rejected by the educated brain.

What today I criticize, tomorrow I shall idolize.

Truth is simple that it may confound the seeming wise.

❧

When all our efforts fail, we are ready to give it to God.

❧

The fullness of suffering is ever equal to the glory of man's ego.

❧

He who attaches to the gain guarantees the loss, for he has denied his divinity.

❧

When the need for expression exceeds the need for reason, man is lost.

❧

Limitation of God's love is the ship which sails our soul to hell.

❧

To capture is to control
To control is to concentrate
To concentrate is to free
To free is to be.

❧

Man lives with kindness and survives without it.

❧

Only a fool tries to teach what he cannot demonstrate.

❧

Kindness is a dog's love, for humble is his soul.

❧

God grows in gratitude.

❧

A student who tells his teacher what to do has forgotten the first lesson in learning, the wisdom to listen.

❧

When choice is made with the full acceptance of change, man is freed.

❧

The reflection of knowledge is ego.

❧

The hand of greed
Shall know its need
When Love-Supreme
Sees life her dream.

✺

If the light of your world is the love you express, why do you stumble in the dark?

✺

Discouragement is the path to hell; encouragement, the path to heaven.

✺

If you aspire to function in a universal body, you must think in a universal way.

✺

Duty becomes direction when you use wisdom.

✺

If God is like a flea and man is like a dog, who but a fool would disturb the flea while it is expressing.

✺

The ship has greater value than the oars, for the oars are ever subject to change.

✺

Our actions, not our words, reveal our true effort.

✤

God's sadness is nature's joy.

✤

Failure is fear's existence; faith, her firm denial.

✤

Laughter is a brook without rocks and sadness, a cliff without a tree.

✤

When man becomes aware of his true intent, he is freed from the victimization of past experiences.

✤

When our cry for God is as great as our cry for money, we will have the true gold of life, wisdom.

✤

He who loves the tree
The same as he loves me,
Knows that I am I
That thou art thee,
That all is one,
And one is me.

✻

A conscious rejection reveals a subconscious acceptance until such time as desire brings her balance.

✻

He who sees the Light knows the Light and, knowing the Light, becomes the Light and has no need for direction.

✻

When of my God I seek to know
The purpose of my life,
The answer comes,
The pain to grow
And willingness to strife.

✻

Determination is given birth in experience.

✻

Truth wears many garments that she may free man from his dreams.

✻

He who has the inspiration merits the perspiration.

✻

Those who seek the crown must be willing to carry the cross.

For what of ourself freely gives, in God's love forever lives.

He who questions God refuses God, and he who accepts God reveals God.

Man never changes a principle; he only expands its use, and expansion of its use is known by man as change.

Knowledge knows much, but wisdom knows better.

A death wish is an intense desire of the educated conscience to eliminate guilt in order that the soul may be free.

If man has need, it's for greater understanding, not things.

He who loses God anywhere loses God everywhere.

The mothers of men are the character of life.

✖

The pull of the Divine is greater than the pull of creation.

✖

Lack of consideration is transgression of principle, the divine law, and man suffers or pays the price, which is called an eye for an eye, a tooth for a tooth.

✖

Man loses respect when he thinks he's got it all.

✖

Beauty is the perfect balance of the soul's expression, which is known as harmony.

✖

When the student awakens, the teacher has nothing to offer.

✖

Fascination, the Law of Temptation, is man's true bondage.

✖

Man does not want for another what he has denied for himself.

Reason is the acceptance and application of principle regardless of form.

Self-will knows its own face and will find its own place.

The reason man is freed in hell is because the experience thereof guarantees his seeking freedom from it, which is know as heaven.

Self-will knows its own face and will find its own place.

Be at peace, my child, and I will work my wonders.

Man is united in God and divided in hell.

Make friends with the undeveloped good within you.

That that we take shall be taken from us, and that that we give shall be given to us.

Promptness respects and considers the rights of another and is the true mark of one's character.

Only a fool acts without thought.

He who sees the good in all things frees his love from the bondage of desire.

Man's freedom is dependent upon his willingness to educate his ego.

We do not see in others what we are not willing to admit in ourselves.

He who leaves the Light and the way is free to choose and go his way.

Man is freed by hell and saved by heaven.

Through desire and decision action doth reveal the merit of our being, the spirit of our zeal.

What we entertain in thought, we experience in life.

When the day becomes the night and the night becomes the day, man goes beyond creation, sees the light and finds the way.

He who has faith is greater than he who sees and has not.

Man's godliness is his usefulness.

The body cannot illumine for in the absence of attention no sensation is possible.

License tempts us through pride.

Truth is for the honest seekers, not for those of idle curiosity.

It is the way of the child
And not the wild
That leads to heaven's bliss.
The gentle kiss of a heavenly mist
Is more than the mind can know
Though talk is well and thought is good
The fire is naught without the wood.
So open your hearts in a heavenly way
To all life's children who will lead the way.
By this I mean
Though the mind is keen
It is the soul that knows the goal
Be ever a worm, so low in the dust
And watch the world go by,
Doing ever your share in a humble way
For God is love and truth the way.

When the light of the student exceeds the light of the teacher,
the student grows in humility or goes in pride.

Man decides not to grow after he has desired to do so.

Every dog has his day in court.

Man lives in freedom and dies in denial.

Man's limitations are revelations of his ignorance.

It is better to be a mat at the door of understanding, than a weather vane on the roof of the ego.

That that sustains us fulfills us.

Loyalty is a crown. It was never meant to be a cross.

The key of wisdom to the door of freedom is the ability, the willingness, and the joy of change.

Love will never bind. It is desire that's so unkind.

Man cannot teach a student to be free if the student is not free to be taught.

⚜

He who controls that which is within controls that which is without.

⚜

The miracle of life is survival.

⚜

That that we have no value for we guarantee to lose.

⚜

Man's attitude toward that with which he is involved is a direct reflection of his level of growth.

⚜

Self-will is the constant effort of the mind to preserve the accepted experiences or dreams of the past, which man calls reality, and in so doing, establishes man's law.

⚜

All creation cries its tears of limitation.

⚜

Truth is taught through indirection, demonstration, and example.

Functions and faculties are balanced by protection and expression.

He who fulfills the law shall manifest it and in so doing be
fulfilled.

Compassion is the key which locks the door of pride and frees
our soul that it may soar to heaven's heights.

He who fulfills the law shall manifest it and in so doing be
fulfilled.

Man denies God when he forgets how weak he is without him.

Self-awareness is limited acceptance, commonly known as
personality.

Hope is eternal and truth is inevitable.

When of thy mind thou seekest to know the truth, on the wheel
of delusion thou shalt traverse.

✤

The soul awakens when self is forgotten.

✤

The guest will never quest.

✤

The payment is ever worth the price to a man who seeks the fullness of God.

✤

O artist, paint your scene in part knowing I am all of art.

✤

Goal is a lifeline. Choose it wisely.

✤

He who knows where he's not going has an indication of where he is going.

✤

A titanic ego is an atom of rejection.

✤

Freedom feels the truth while will rejects it.

Variety is the balance of creation.

Man insists on questioning God, yet God in humility never questions man.

When students become dependent upon crutches to walk, teachers have failed in act or talk.

That that humiliates us has enslaved us, because the degree of humiliation reveals the power that we have given to our false god of pride.

God's pill is man's will, sickness.

The demands of creation are balanced by the call of the Divine.

Man's loss of God is dependent upon his purity of motive.

❦

Suggestions, like the notes of a symphony, are blessings when the composer is aware of his responsibility.

❦

The tree of life is the roots of God hidden from the passers-by.

❦

Worry is like a rocking chair; it keeps moving and gets nowhere.

❦

A petrified opinion never freed a human soul.

❦

The desire to be liked is stronger than the desire for reason.

❦

Pride reveals a man in self; humbleness, a man in God.

❦

Truth expands the self, fear contracts it. So broaden your horizons and ever be the pea and not the pod, the seed and not the sod, the joy and not the bliss, the light and not the mist.

That that we accept we experience. That that we reject enslaves us.

Presence is the Law of Solicitation.

Time is the temptress of impatience.

God, help me, in a spirit of humility, to do your work no matter what it takes or how weary I get.

God declares the truth in simple thoughts and acts, while man supports his theories and calls confusion facts.

Students become teachers when they remember to respect the teachers of which they are students.

Justice, the lady, is blindfolded that she may not be deceived by form, for being that which conceived form she knows her own deception.

✳

A man who does not see beauty is better blind that he may know God's fullness and wisdom of being kind.

✳

Man's values are dependent upon the availability of what he desires.

✳

I'd rather be a worm in the dust than a bird in the sky, for 'tis better to be a soul that crawls than a brain that soars to fall and die.

✳

When the heart rules, the head bows, and when the head rules, the heart bows.

✳

Knowledge is the reflection of understanding, the form of principle, the deceiver of the soul.

✳

God, help me to release this desire to you knowing in truth that which I desire in principle desires me.

✳

Men without love are like bread without yeast—all flat.

❦

The turtle is greater than the hare, for wisdom lives in patience.

❦

God is like a flea because you never know where you might find him.

❦

Wishes are the fantasies of the mind; realities, the truth of the Light.

❦

A stupid man sees weakness where strength lies supreme.

❦

Growth is revelation, not change, in truth.

❦

Security is maturity to a man of common sense.

❦

Fools are the fathers of fear, and courage, the mothers of freedom.

❦

Curiosity is the father of frustration.

✣

When disrespect manifests, wisdom demands change and reason shows the way.

✣

Drop your anchor in principle and you will have greater service to God.

✣

Be free in thought and ye shall be eternally free in life.

✣

License is bondage because it is the child of desire.

✣

When we find God inside, we will know Him outside.

✣

That that we hold destroys us. That that we free unfolds us.

✣

That that has the greater meaning has the greater fulfillment.

Man's suffering is a direct revelation of his rejection of God's divine right of expression, which guarantees his destiny of bondage.

O man, you little god, what wisdom hath you found
O man, you little god, what power can you keep
O man, you little god, know that I am humble but never sound
asleep.

When the motive
Is pure
The manifestation
Is pleasant.
However,
When the motive
Is right
The manifestation
Is inevitable
For it
Is the law.

Freedom of the soul is pride's payment.

Man's needs are Divinity's denials.

❧

Man's individualization or self-preservation is dependent upon his identification with the dream of life, which is, in truth, a constant review of his own acceptance, granting a false security in the bondage of creation which keeps him from experiencing the joy of living, eternal truth and freedom.

❧

On the wings of genius the soul is lost.

❧

Shut off the B.B.S. (Brain Broadcasting Station). Turn on the SOUL.

❧

When man views form, he finds personality, which is bondage, and loses principle, which is freedom.

❧

Gratitude is the law of supply.

❧

God's invitation is man's opportunity.

❧

Freedom in creation ever seeks to find the part of self that loves, the joy with which to bind.

He who limits another in truth has limited himself.

Attachment is the weakness of familiarity and the strength of license.

O God, help me to accept the divine right of all your expression. Let me not judge its worth but strive to understand its true cause.

When the struggle is the greatest, victory is at hand.

God waits upon the ones in need, with justice as the balance, to weigh grief's pain with greed.

O sleeper, doth thou wake serene knowing life is but a scene.

A man who cannot see is like a gopher, never satisfied with the hole that he digs.

�֍

Only a fool tempts temptation.

✖

Awake my soul and ever be a joyful servant God to thee.

✖

True friendship respects the right of difference and will weather any storm.

✖

If God is the king and creation the queen, who shall reign and yet be free?

✖

In God everything is good.

✖

Man's godliness is revealed in his consideration for others.

✖

Never expect what you are not ready to give.

✖

Irritation wakes the soul and satisfaction lets it sleep.

Silence is God's revelation of truth.

Man's ability to entertain a thought or level of awareness without enslavement is equal to and dependent upon his desire to be with God.

Punishment is a lack of accepting something greater.

When the lips are sealed in silence
And the ears are closed secure
Peace within has found its glory
The soul will play the perfect score.

Reason is the unobstructed flow of the Divine Intelligence known as Spirit expressing itself.

That that is mine knows my face and is already on its way to my heart.

Creation is God's crown till man dethrones Him.

꘠

The power of God is greater than the thought of man for the power of God sustains the thought of man, and that which sustains a thing is greater than the thing, so the power of God is ever and forever supreme.

Amen   Amen   Amen

꘠

When man's need for expression is greater than his need for reason, stupidity reigns supreme.

꘠

A soul in creation is like a bird out of flight, good for viewing its beauty and plight.

꘠

The sense to pause is the lion's strength.

꘠

He who chooses God finds God and in finding God, paradise is revealed.

꘠

No one can define and pinpoint our realms. When you understand yourself, then you'll understand all life's seeming mysteries, not before.

Direction is freedom's expression; desire, the bondage of love.

He who has the strength to suffer has the right to free a soul.

A wise man looks straight ahead; a fool looks up and down.

Man only values that which fulfills his needs.

When it means enough, the transformation is the effect.

Fear protects, but faith sustains.

Blessings are shared, not sheltered.

Aspiration becomes perspiration when man decides what's best.

꧁

A teacher's demonstration is a student's eternal quest.

꧁

Principle is the essence of truth.

꧁

The bondage of review becomes the freedom of preview when man accepts promise, the path of peace. Principle is established and reason flows freely.

꧁

In the river of my mind there's a thought of peace for you.

꧁

The streets of hell are paved with good intentions and broken promises.

꧁

When we say that we do not understand, the mind directs the attention to the obstruction and the student cannot find the way.

꧁

The degree of suffering reveals the degree of attachment.

Truth is the awareness of the divinity within that we express at any given moment.

Consideration is the light which guides God's love. Without it, man is blind—bringing pleasure to one and pain to another, guaranteeing the loss for himself.

When you stop considering yourself, God will start considering you.

He who hath no patience hath no wisdom.

The joy of marriage is the willingness to give.

He who knows the weakness of another and lays temptation at his feet is as guilty as the one who is tempted.

He who is rejected shall reject and in so doing bind his soul to creation.

✥

O God, I am grateful for all life's experiences, especially the difficult ones, for I know that they are in truth my greatest blessings.

✥

The bridge to understanding is the unexpected.

✥

Freedom is the direct effect of self-control.

✥

Patience is the sadness of hope.

✥

He who sees dimly finds responsibility a great burden, but he who has vision knows God's eternal joy.

✥

A free man sees bondage as direction for a time, but a fool sees it for a lifetime.

✥

The chains of bondage are suppression; the wings of freedom, expression.

Man's desires are his denials.

A man in need is like a croaking frog—all mouth.

Emotions are the servants of pride.

Love is the reflection in another of the goodness in oneself.

Embarrassment is a revelation of attachment to a level of consciousness that we are unwilling to change.

We always get what we really want.

Be patient to see what grows from the seed before digging it up.

Like a leap frog, desire is difficult to hold.

꙰

Creation is God's playpen and only children should play therein.

꙰

The foot is bigger than its children of toes; therefore, understanding is greater than decision.

꙰

What comes out of the mouth reveals man's character, not what goes in.

꙰

Freedom, like truth, is divinity and divinity is total consideration.

꙰

It is well, oh man, to know thyself, not as we would like to know ourselves, but know ourselves as we are.

꙰

When man smiles the angels sing.

꙰

To count your blessings is selfish. To share your blessings is selfless.

Reality is simply your entertainment of a dream.

The act reveals the thought.

The wisdom of teaching is for the teacher to be a student, and the student will be a teacher to the teacher.

Whatever you are seeking is also seeking you, and like the hands of the clock, opportunity meets every so often.

Pity, like snow, melts in the light of reason.

A wise teacher suffers well the pain of his students' growth.

Flirtation is the ego's need of challenge to tempt another.

❧

Like a leaf
Upon the water
You are tossed
From shore to shore
Ever seeking
Something different
When but a leaf
You'll be
Evermore.

❧

Man is greater than creation for he is the creator of creation, and the father is greater than the son.

❧

Man's responsibilities are equal to his desires.

❧

A wise teacher uses whatever methods legal to teach the student.

❧

Constant repetition is the law of change.

❧

The weight of responsibility must never exceed the love of God.

✖

The essence of dreaming is the law of life, and the law of life is Divine Will or God's expression.

✖

Desires are like shadows: they disappear in the light of reason.

✖

Ofttimes NO is God's direction.

✖

The pull of gravity is greater than the thought of man, therefore, only a fool chases a ball downhill.

✖

A cross is a crown to a patient man.

✖

He who loses what he values and suffers is a fool. He who loses what he values and is free is a wise man.

✖

When man accepts from God, he is freed from paying creation.

※

A whole is better than many parts because it is complete and yet many parts make the whole.

※

I helped a soul to heaven's heights that it may see a brighter light and know that I am not unkind but only lost in troubled mind.

※

Silence is the savior of the soul and peace, the expression of its love.

※

Temptation leads us to God when all else fails.

※

The mountain is only an obstruction to the viewer.

※

Man in God becomes God.

※

Fear not, my child, for I am never far away.

Faith is the path that leads to God; fear, the trap to hell.

If man is total, then confusion is only rejection of himself.

He who questions bears the direct responsibility of the child he has created.

That that we free frees us. That that we bind binds us.

A healthy mind is a student who disagrees with his teacher. A spiritual mind is a student who knows when to speak.

He who acts in self becomes the slave of hell's emotions, but he who acts in reason becomes a light in the world.

The King of Greed keeps man in need.

※

No moment of life is ever wasted for each and every experience was necessary for man to qualify himself and set his soul free.

※

A seeming obstruction is merely a detour to a wise man.

※

That which you give thought to you give power over you.

※

Man's only suffering is his denial of God.

※

Truth may only be demanded of oneself.

※

The destiny of desire is the denial of God.

※

The hand of God is the poet's pen.

※

When the tools no longer serve the worker, the worker begins to serve the tools.

Feeling good is a necessity, not a luxury.

Put God in it or forget it.

Humility is the key which opens the door of consideration that man may enter God's paradise of peace.

Poise is the humble expression of will in the perfect harmony of reason.

Service is the path to freedom when selfless is the goal.

Humor is the salvation of the soul.

A child is one whose heart is pure and, being pure, has no denials.

Please tire yourself for yourself.

❧

Promise is the right of God, not the will of man.

❧

Whatever happens to us is caused by us.

❧

Love is the language of the soul but not the love of which you know.

❧

The principle of happiness is the willingness to change.

❧

Heaven is not a place we go to; it is a state of consciousness that we grow to here and now.

❧

Reward tempts the ego, while the soul waits to serve.

❧

Imagination is the essence of art.

❧

When man knocks at the gates of heaven he wonders why he waited so long.

Fear not, for I am first, and that that is first shall not be last. I am not first by choice for I came before choice and no one can dethrone me.

Hell awaits the form, ah but heaven awaits the soul.

Self-control is a conscious choice of all experience.

When you love your losses as you love your gains, you will have self-control.

When desire becomes the servant, man is freed from being the slave.

The light of God shines best in a soul freed from self.

Regrets are the errors of the past; worries, the conscience of the present.

❧

Self-will is like a snake, it steals the lesser light. Free will is like a lion, king of the jungle within.

❧

Self-concern is the epitome of the ego brain mechanism declaring and insisting upon its superiority of reign to dictate to God how things shall be.

❧

Pearls of wisdom are the tears of conscience.

❧

That that troubles us controls us.

❧

When we stop wanting what another has, we will soon find what we already have.

❧

He who hurts another
Shall live to see the day
When all his selfish motives
Pain shall take away.

❧

Never feel the gain and you will not experience the loss.

Know within and unto thee all shall be
Thy will shall be done,
O God
Not my will, but thy will
This will is within thee
It is known not by the mind
But it is known within thee.

Emotions sink our soul to hell while reason lifts it to heaven's
heights.

God, I know your laws never faileth for I am this instant the
living demonstration of that. I accept in consciousness your
divine right of expression and I fear not to become the blade of
grass for you are in it and, being in it, I am free.

The Law of Solicitation is the Law of Application.

A little boy knocked at my door and asked me just to be so kind
to help him find his God inside of me.

LITTLE BOY'S DREAM

One night while I was sleeping sound
I dreamed I was a rock unfound
And in my dream I could not see
A living thing outside of me
Oh how I wanted just to be
A part of something outside of me
If I could only try and make
Another rock like me awake
I thought and thought
And then one day
I split in two
And rolled away.

Rhythm, harmony
Balance, peace
Hold, release
Hold, release
Thank you, God
I am at peace.

When the brain is still, God's work is done.

The fullness of understanding is the freedom of the soul.

Acceptance—something good is happening.

I am spirit formless and free. Whatever I think that will I be.

Indecision is dual decision.

Man's desires are controlled by his dreams of the past.

Man's denials are his destinies.

Nothing in life is ever wrong outside unless there is something wrong inside.

Stand guardian at the portal of your thought that you may experience the freedom and joy of your eternal soul.

A friend doesn't have to tell a friend that they are a friend.

❦

Challenge is desire because it stimulates the ego.

❦

God inspires while man perspires.

❦

Man has no concern for reference when he finds principle because reference is security. Security is personality or form. Form is bondage, the opposite of freedom. Therefore, what man rejects he binds.

❦

Man's self-will is like an Alka-Seltzer; it fizzles for a time.

❦

Outward manifestations are revelations of inner attitudes of mind.

❦

Repetition is the law through which change is made possible.

❦

The conscience of wisdom is the love of understanding.

✻

The intensity of density is measured by acceptance.

✻

Applied principle is expression without bondage.

✻

Man is controlled by the patterns of his desires and knowing them not calls their fulfillment freedom.

✻

Hell gave me strength that God may give me heaven.

✻

Our adversities become our attachments. It is a subtle law.

✻

The rear of the donkey is greater than the head to a man on the go, for that that moves a thing is greater than the thing. And so the donkey's value is his go.

✻

When you start to change and grow
Then truth becomes the thing you know
For teachers merely show the way
Students earn their night or day.

✣

True love is expressed and does not have to have a reaction. Conjugal love has to have a reaction. Divine love is the soul expressing itself.

✣

In all your getting, get understanding. In all your giving, give wisdom.

✣

God's temple, the body, is hallowed ground and only peace should reign therein.

✣

He who serves the servant is greater than the servant, but he who serves the servant's servant is wisest of them all.

✣

I have come to free the soul, not to bind it.

✣

Love conquers all for love is harmony perfectly expressed.

✣

Man says, "That's all I got." God says, "If you're so smart, that's all you'll get."

✼

Sanity or mental balance is maintained by freeing the soul, through selfless service, from the personality (brain) consciousness level of awareness.

✼

The God of gods in pure humility granted man the right to deny him.

✼

When teachers remember that they are students, students will remember that they are teachers.

✼

Awareness is the soul of action.

✼

Fear is the fulfillment of desire.

✼

The freedom of strength is the direction of will.

✼

The heaven that awaits you may be a hell to another.

Reason is greater than logic because it has total consideration.

When motherhood becomes brotherhood, the children will grow up.

When our desire to possess is greater than our reason to be free, life is miserable.

In man's search for God, his greatest cross is his need for attention, for knowing what he wants and finding it not, in truth, the burden weighs heavy.

A dog in court is a friend of God.

A full head is a broken wallet.

A half a soul with God is better than no soul at all.

A man without feelings is like a tree without leaves, a body lacking soul.

A stranger to the world is a friend to God.

A tree is better than a forest for it is easier to view God.

A wise man places his attention upon the object of his choice and has the wisdom of patience to remain with it long enough to bear a fruitful harvest.

A wise man sees goal as a lifeline.

A big ear is better than a long tongue, for it is better to receive wisdom than to give false direction.

A foolish student disrespects his teacher in the name of friendship and suffers the consequences.

✆

A humble soul is never lost for God is the greatest servant of all and does not deny his children.

✆

A man of common sense sees the slave of satisfaction and finds freedom in God.

✆

An apology is a recognition and acceptance that the vehicle known as mind is not infallible or perfect.

✆

A problem is nothing more than a lack of faith in the power of God.

✆

The expression of the faculties is equal to the protection of the functions.

✆

I accept that my body, mind and soul is in the hands of God; therefore, I am freed from all self-concern.

✆

If man is a law unto himself, what are you doing with the law that you are?

✻

Greater is he who believes and sees not than the one who sees and believes not.

✻

Be grateful when you ask and receive not, for then you are truly receiving.

✻

Accuser, you are the accused. Forgiver, you are the forgiven.

✻

Unto you is given what you have earned.

✻

Loneliness is self-pity in poor disguise.

✻

Criticism is like a cart without wheels: it's good for storing rubbish.

✻

Truth is like a river for it continually flows from the Mountain of Aspiration.

✿

If all I give is what you gave,
And what you gave is what they save,
Then those who save will learn to give
Before they know the way to live.

✿

Be ever ready and willing to give
That which you hold most dear;
Then, my child,
You shall know not of fear.

✿

The uneducated ego hears only the echoes of its own unfulfilled desires.

✿

When you harbor a thought, you are feeding a form.

✿

The world needs you or you would not be here.

✿

What we cannot tolerate in another, we have not educated in ourselves.

When you have given all, what then shall be left?

Let not your deed be your creed.

Emotions, like ceaseless waves, eternally wash the thirsty shore.

What we entertain in thought, we create in form.

Idle thought, like idle talk, is the greatest enemy in your camp.

O compassion of my soul, gratitude has shown life's goal.

As we give, unto us is given.

Pride is punishment. Humility is harmony.

※

You are making the world and the world is making you.

※

All your experiences you have willed into action: it is a subtle law.

※

When of naught desire is,
In vain does sorrow speak.

※

To be master is the desire of the senses. To be a servant is the wise counsel of the soul.

※

Ask nothing. Want nothing in return. Give what you have to give.

※

Seekers of truth can think only of all life.

※

Today I reap the harvest of yesterday and plant the seeds of my tomorrow.

By their deeds, not their creeds, ye shall know them.

O love divine, a servant be
Till selfishness imprisons me
And warps the reason of my mind
Into the madness of the blind,
When truth cries out, "Not mine, but Thine"
And frees my soul with love divine.

Wise ones live to serve. Fools serve to live.

Our problems are companions as long as we love them.

What of thy heart freely gives,
In God's love forever lives.

When of thyself thou thinkest most,
Thine heart is closed to angel host.

⚜

As I came upon the mountain
And felt the glory of my God,
I looked about in wonder
At the many paths I'd trod.

⚜

O man, think humble yet well of thyself, for in thy thinking is
created the vehicle of the soul.

⚜

We sit to meditate.
We stand to agitate.

⚜

With the blessings, which come from on high, come also its
balance, responsibility.

⚜

Our world is ever as we are within.

⚜

Servants come to teach.
Masters come to preach.

❧

Indecision is the inevitable path to confusion,
Which in time places us
On the wheel of delusion.
Upon the wheel we continue to revolve
Until such time as the power of will is made manifest.

❧

O seeker, doth thou seek in vain
Knowing not of patience's pain?

❧

Man can only be affected by that with which he is in rapport.

❧

Life is eternal and wise ones act accordingly.

❧

Babies are blessings with two eyes, two hands, and two feet.
They become burdens when the parents overshadow the
spiritual with the material.

❧

Thoughts without acts are like seeds without soil: good to see
but waiting to grow.

⚘

The climb is never higher than the fall.

⚘

O, senses, know thou not of me,
For I am I and thou art thee.

⚘

Patience is the only path to Truth.

⚘

Be ever ready and willing to share
The part of you that's known as care
For the world is filled with many a creed,
Thinking first of name and seldom of need.

⚘

It is the heart that conquers, not the brain.

⚘

No one can carry your burden,
No one can lift your load;
But Angels of Light wait patiently
To tell you their stories of old.

Dreamer, dream a life of beauty before your dream starts dreaming you.

Slow steps are sure steps when they are under the guidance of selflessness.

Your creeds, like your shoes, wear out in time.

It is a wise one indeed who knows when his duty is done, so he may go on to another and another and another.

Love all life and know the Light.

I'm only a witness of time passing on,
A witness of things that have come and gone.
Never the jury or judge will I be,
For I am the witness, the life, and the tree.

※

It's the wise who walk their humble way
And let the fools talk and talk
And have their way.

※

What is the motive of one desiring to be a Master? On the strength of the soul we aspire; and in humility we lose desire. Then in truth shall we become Master.

※

Be ever ready and willing to change.

※

'Tis not the help which may seem small
But the motive that answers the call.

※

Self-conscious is the ego clothed in the garment of pride and crowned with the crown of self-pity.

※

When man is chained to dogma and creed,
The soul of reason is ever in need.

He who seeks the praise of man
Loses sight of God's true plan.

As the frog croaked
And the wolf howled,
The ears of ego heard not
For the door was locked
By the key of fear.

As the bird flew
And as the snake crawled,
The lion said,
"Of what good are those?"

Once I was an apple
And then I was a tree
And when I am an apple tree,
I'll no longer be just me.

O God, we love the roses,
The weeds and thistles too;
O God, we love the butterflies,
The snakes that crawl are you.

O God, we love the ones who hate,
The ones who live in fear;
We love them more each day we live
For all to Thee are dear.
O God, we love the ones who see
But even more the blind;
For in our love we hope and pray
Their sight may be Divine.
O God, we love all paths to Thee,
For in them we can see
A light that shines to all mankind
In varying degree.
O God, we love the sunshine,
The darkness and the night;
O God, we love the weak and strong,
For in them is Thy might.
O God, we love all things in life,
For in them we find Thee,
A shining light that's dim or bright
For all mankind to see.

Thank you, God, I'm moving in your divine flow.

APPENDIX

The Divine Healing Prayer

I accept that the Divine Healing Power
Is removing all obstructions
From my mind and body
And is restoring me
To perfect health, wealth, and happiness.
My heart is filled with gratitude
For the Divine Law of Acceptance
That is healing both present and absent ones
Who are in need of help.
Peace, the power that healeth,
Is guiding my thoughts, acts, and deeds
As God and I go hand in hand
Living a life of joyful abundance.

The Total Consideration Affirmation

I am the manifestation of Divine Intelligence. Formless and free. Whole and complete. Peace, Poise, and Power are my birthright.

The Law of Harmony is my thought and guarantees Unity in all my acts and activities, expressing perfect Rhythm and limitless flow throughout my entire being.

Without beginning or ending, eternity is my true awareness and sees the tides of creation, as a captain sees his ship.

As the Light of Truth is sustained by the faculty of Reason, I pause to think and claim my Divine right.

Right Thought. Right Action. Total Consideration.

Amen.   Amen.   Amen.

Divine Abundance

Thank
(Gratitude)

You
(Principle)

God
(Divine Intelligence)

I'm
(Individualizing)

Moving
(Rhythm)

In
(Unity)

Your
(Realization)

Divine
(Total)

Flow
(Consideration)

INDEX